Transforming Economies Through Microfinance in Developing Nations

Yahaya Alhassan
University of Sunderland in London, UK

Uzoechi Nwagbara
University of Sunderland in London, UK

A volume in the Advances in Finance, Accounting, and Economics (AFAE) Book Series

IGI Global
PUBLISHER of TIMELY KNOWLEDGE

Published in the United States of America by
IGI Global
Business Science Reference (an imprint of IGI Global)
701 E. Chocolate Avenue
Hershey PA, USA 17033
Tel: 717-533-8845
Fax: 717-533-8661
E-mail: cust@igi-global.com
Web site: http://www.igi-global.com

Library of Congress Cataloging-in-Publication Data

Names: Alhassan, Yahaya, 1971- editor. | Nwagbara, Uzoechi, editor.
Title: Transforming economies through microfinance in developing nations / Yahaya Alhassan, and Uzoechi Nwagbara, editors.
Description: Hershey, PA : Business Science Reference, [2023] | Includes bibliographical references and index. | Summary: "With microfinance including the provision of small loans to individuals and groups who have no access to credit from traditional banks the focus of this book on the nexus between microfinance and economic development, offering a broadening of ideas on how the provision of microfinance can aid the transformation of the economies of developing and emerging countries"-- Provided by publisher.
Identifiers: LCCN 2022035940 (print) | LCCN 2022035941 (ebook) | ISBN 9781668456477 (hardcover) | ISBN 9781668456484 (paperback) | ISBN 9781668456491 (ebook)
Subjects: LCSH: Sustainable development--Developing countries. | Microfinance--Developing countries. | Banks and banking--Developing countries. | Poverty--Developing countries.
Classification: LCC HC59.72.E5 T73 2023 (print) | LCC HC59.72.E5 (ebook) | DDC 338.927091724--dc23/eng/20220811
LC record available at https://lccn.loc.gov/2022035940
LC ebook record available at https://lccn.loc.gov/2022035941

This book is published in the IGI Global book series Advances in Finance, Accounting, and Economics (AFAE) (ISSN: 2327-5677; eISSN: 2327-5685)

British Cataloguing in Publication Data
A Cataloguing in Publication record for this book is available from the British Library.

Advances in Finance, Accounting, and Economics (AFAE) Book Series

ISSN:2327-5677
EISSN:2327-5685

Editor-in-Chief: Ahmed Driouchi, Al Akhawayn University, Morocco

MISSION

In our changing economic and business environment, it is important to consider the financial changes occurring internationally as well as within individual organizations and business environments. Understanding these changes as well as the factors that influence them is crucial in preparing for our financial future and ensuring economic sustainability and growth.

The **Advances in Finance, Accounting, and Economics (AFAE)** book series aims to publish comprehensive and informative titles in all areas of economics and economic theory, finance, and accounting to assist in advancing the available knowledge and providing for further research development in these dynamic fields.

COVERAGE

- Statistical Analysis
- Comparative Accounting Systems
- Banking
- Economics of Agriculture and Biotechnology
- Corporate Finance
- E-finance
- Internet Banking
- Accounting information systems
- Health Economics
- Applied Finance

IGI Global is currently accepting manuscripts for publication within this series. To submit a proposal for a volume in this series, please contact our Acquisition Editors at Acquisitions@igi-global.com or visit: http://www.igi-global.com/publish/.

The Advances in Finance, Accounting, and Economics (AFAE) Book Series (ISSN 2327-5677) is published by IGI Global, 701 E. Chocolate Avenue, Hershey, PA 17033-1240, USA, www.igi-global.com. This series is composed of titles available for purchase individually; each title is edited to be contextually exclusive from any other title within the series. For pricing and ordering information please visit http://www.igi-global.com/book-series/advances-finance-accounting-economics/73685. Postmaster: Send all address changes to above address.

Titles in this Series

For a list of additional titles in this series, please visit:
https://www.igi-global.com/book-series/advances-finance-accounting-economics/73685

Advanced Machine Learning Algorithms for Complex Financial Applications
Mohammad Irfan (CMR Institute of Technology, India) Mohamed Elhoseny (American University in the Emirates, UAE) Salina Kassim (International Islamic University of Malaysia, Malaysia) and Noura Metawa (University of Sharjah, UAE)
Engineering Science Reference • copyright 2023 • 292pp • H/C (ISBN: 9781668444832) • US $270.00 (our price)

Exploring the Dark Side of FinTech and Implications of Monetary Policy
Sheraz Ahmed (LUT University, Finland) John Agyekum Addae (LUT University, Finland & Ghana Communication Technology University, Ghana) and Kwame Simpe Ofori (International University of Grand-Bassam, Côte d'Ivoire & University of Electronic Science and Technology of China, China)
Business Science Reference • copyright 2023 • 300pp • H/C (ISBN: 9781668463819) • US $250.00 (our price)

Blockchain Applications in Cryptocurrency for Technological Evolution
Atour Taghipour (Normandy University, France)
Business Science Reference • copyright 2023 • 308pp • H/C (ISBN: 9781668462478) • US $250.00 (our price)

The Past, Present, and Future of Accountancy Education and Professions
Nina T. Dorata (St. John's University, USA) Richard C. Jones (Hofstra University, USA) Jennifer Mensche (St. Joseph's College, USA) and Mark M. Ulrich (CUNY Queensborough Community College, USA)
Business Science Reference • copyright 2023 • 300pp • H/C (ISBN: 9781668454831) • US $215.00 (our price)

Handbook of Research on Changing World Economic Order in the Post-Pandemic Period
Sushanta Kumar Mahapatra (IBS Hyderabad, The ICFAI Foundation for Higher Education, India) and Vishal Sarin (Lovely Professional University, India)
Business Science Reference • copyright 2023 • 470pp • H/C (ISBN: 9781799868965) • US $325.00 (our price)

For an entire list of titles in this series, please visit:
https://www.igi-global.com/book-series/advances-finance-accounting-economics/73685

IGI Global
PUBLISHER of TIMELY KNOWLEDGE

701 East Chocolate Avenue, Hershey, PA 17033, USA
Tel: 717-533-8845 x100 • Fax: 717-533-8661
E-Mail: cust@igi-global.com • www.igi-global.com

Table of Contents

Detailed Table of Contents

This chapter examines the role of microfinance in the transformation of rural communities in Ghana. To achieve this aim, a synthesized review of existing literature on microfinance outcomes on employment creation, poverty reduction, female empowerment, and microenterprise development in Ghana was conducted. The review shows that microfinance has contributed significantly to the transformation of rural communities in Ghana by helping to reduce poverty and improving the living standards of the poor. The review also demonstrates that microfinance contributed positively to the socio-economic well-being of women in Ghana. Microfinance has also played a positive role in the transformation of rural communities in Ghana by providing credit to support microenterprise projects. Furthermore, the analysis shows that microfinance contributed positively to the transformation of rural communities in Ghana by providing credit to individuals and microenterprises to create jobs and improve living standards.

This chapter examines the effect of commercialisation of microfinance on the performance measurement practices of MFIs and the implications these measurement practices have on the achievement of the mission objectives of MFIs using as a case, the microfinance industry in Ghana. Mainly qualitative research techniques were employed in the study, relying on the views and perspectives of MFIs, clients, practitioners, and experts. The study results indicate that MFIs have not appropriately met this dual expectation of pursuing both financial and social objectives and cannot therefore possibly improve their understanding of the mission drift phenomenon with their existing measurement practices. The authors therefore propose a conceptual framework, as well as core social and economic performance, and impact indicators for measuring the attainment of the double bottom line or convergence.

This chapter critically examines how microfinance has been used to reduce poverty rates in developing economies. To achieve this goal, a critical review of existing literature on microfinance outcomes on reducing poverty in developing countries was carried out. Based on the review of literature, this chapter concludes that microfinance positively impact poverty levels in developing countries. However, the chapter also shows that access to microfinance may contribute to higher poverty rates as some studies have produced marginal or negative success, while others yielded positive successes, making it very difficult to generalise the outcomes. The growing popularity of microfinance as a financial inclusion strategy and the high number of empirical studies on the subject have produced new evidence that needs further examination with complex research methodologies to determine its impact on poverty reduction, as outcomes of the current studies are mixed.

The development of financial sector lays a positive impact on the economic growth of a country. It serves as a foundation for mobilisation and allocation of finance which is life and blood for the growth and development of an economy. Therefore, the existence of an efficient financial system facilitates economic activity as well as growth. The large part of the population in rural areas is dependent on agricultural activities for earning income. India, being a rural and agrarian economy, needed some special institutions that could focus on the financial needs of rural poor, particularly those who are engaged in the agricultural activities. SBLP has become an effective tool for achieving the goals of financial inclusion focusing primarily on the poor women. This paper aims at exploring the present status of microfinance in India with special reference to self-help group bank linkage programme. It is a qualitative review of the present scenario based on extensive available literature which is supported by secondary data taken from latest reports of NABARD.

Financial inclusion involves the provision of basic formal financial services to members of society. Policy efforts and collaboration with the private sector have helped to increase the level of financial inclusion in many countries. Such efforts give rise to net winners and net losers from financial inclusion efforts. This chapter identifies the net losers from financial inclusion efforts. The lesson from the net losers identified in this study is that being 'banked' is only a necessary condition to enjoy the benefits of financial inclusion. Being 'banked' is not a sufficient condition to enjoy the benefits of financial inclusion. A banked adult can be a net loser from financial inclusion despite being banked. This has wider implications for understanding the challenges to sustained financial inclusion.

Microfinance had a clear mission of serving the least privileged. However, 45 years after Muhammad Yunus introduced the first microloans, the global microfinance market has become increasingly commercialized, with high tendencies toward for-profit organizations, in contrast to how it was originally introduced within the realm of not-for-profits. Microfinance is now a multi-billion-dollar financial industry. Microcredit is adopted as an efficient tool to achieve sustainable development goals. This chapter is analyzing how the current Egyptian microfinance regulations can contribute to the achievement of SDGs. The analysis shows that Egypt has developed and enacted a law that is meeting the international standards of microfinance global best practice; however, there is room for ensuring the microfinance institutions are following their social justice mission by regulating other microcredit services beyond financing income-generating activities. The chapter concludes that more regulations are needed to ensure that MFIs are reaching out to women micro-entrepreneurs and doing them no harm.

Microfinance has been associated with playing a radical role in transforming any economy, especially where the goals are to uplift the disadvantaged sectors. It is also considered to be an important tool for helping poor people in order to fulfil their basic needs. It has got an immense capability to safeguard the vulnerable by its ripple effects from certain financial risks and poverty. Some call it a "poverty vaccine" for people living in rural areas. It also aims at assisting the various communities, economically as well as the socially excluded, focus on asset creation as well as for creating source of income. The holistic metamorphosis of rural lives is possible through the microcredit interventions, and the instances are plenty. In this pandemic, where the economies are facing huge economic crises, the rural vulnerable and the excluded sections have suffered the most. In this phase of transformation, the microfinance intervention with re-oriented objectives can again prove to be an effective tool for reviving the economy as a whole.

The COVID-19 pandemic has interrupted operations throughout the world. It also forced all the industries towards unprecedented changes of their business operations, and in some cases, it pushes the businesses to shut down their operations either partially or fully. The microfinance industry is one of the sectors that was affected badly by the pandemic. As a result, microfinance institutions were forced to do some considerable changes to their domestic processes and make tricky decisions to decrease their loan issue process while the loan is required mostly by the borrowers or dropping employees' salaries. In the same way, microfinance customers were also affected. It forced business units to close their operations, and as a result, it condensed revenue generation. Customers also faced the tortuous brunt from the interrupted business support which were frequently incompatible and inadequate for public support. As a result, few customers have realized better income generation during the pandemic.

The growth of micro, small, and medium-sized enterprises (MSMEs) is important as MSMEs constitute the main drivers of economic growth, particularly in the emerging economies of factor-driven and efficiency-driven economies. MSMEs represent an estimate of 90% of business organisations and more than half of job creation worldwide, and the growing global workforce means that growth of MSMEs are often a high priority for governments. However, despite attempts to support nurture and vitalise the growth of MSMEs, MSMEs located in emerging economies are often subjected to more hostile environments compared to their counterparts in developed economies, such as the lack of access to micro-finance and underdeveloped educational institutions. The lack of micro-finance is especially detrimental as MSMEs without creditworthy history could not apply for finance. This research synthesizes growth factors from literature in order to identify and examine the factors influencing growth of MSMEs in the emerging economies of factor-driven and efficiency-driven economies.

Preface

Central to the conceptualisation of microfinance is to provide financial services, particularly in developing and/or emerging economies, to a population that is under the shadow of limited (and often non-existent) access to the conventional financial market system and/or at risk of financial exclusion (Gueyie, 2013; García-Pérez et al., 2020). The sector focuses on low-money products and services facilitating access to financial instruments, regulated return guarantees and simple opening processes, and related phenomena (García-Pérez et al., 2018; Spiegel, 2012; Van Rooyen et al., 2012). Entrepreneurs and businesses seek microfinance for business expansion, development, sustainability, and/or emergencies (World Bank, 2018). This financing of entrepreneurial effort is on the increase lately and has been instrumental in transforming businesses, socio-economic wellbeing of people and poverty related issues (García-Pérez et al., 2020; Alhassan & Nwagbara, 2021; Marini et al., 2017; Ferdousi, 2015). In 2018 about 916 Microfinance Institutions (MFIs), with an estimated $124 billion gross loan portfolio, where 80% of borrowers are women and 65% rural borrowers resulting in 140 million active borrowers globally (García-Pérez et al., 2010).

Fundamental to the tenets of microfinance is empowering the poorest members of society, facilitating development and enhancing capacity building (Alhassan & Nwagbara, 2021) that dovetail with the principles of Sustainable Development (Ferdousi, 2015; Mazumder, 2015; World Commission of Environment and Development, 1997). Sustainable development is the kind of developmental effort that meets the needs of the present ‘‘without compromising the ability of future generations to meet their own needs” (United Nations Development Programme, 2006). It takes into consideration the principles of societal evolution and overhaul premised on a more equitable society for future generations (Nwagbara, 2014; Kolk et al., 2017) and for the foremost part socio-economic transformation for social change (Cohen, 2018), which is at the core of this book. Economic (as well as socio-economic) transformation entails the continuous process of labour transition as well as other resources from lower- to higher-productivity sectors, which aligns with structural change. It also refers to enhancing within-sector productivity and growth. To this end, economic transformation is premised on the notion of transition from low- to high-productivity activities across sectors. Such transitioning is a fundamental factor that shapes social change and economic development – all resonating with social transformation (Cohen, 2018), which microfinance accelerates (Milgram, 2005).

As argued by Aras and Crowther (2016), from a micro-level prism, sustainable development is fostered through corporate sustainability practices and policies that chime with an equilibrium among the social, financial, governance and environmental performance dimensions both in the short and long haul (Bebbington & Unerman, 2018; Bateman, 2011). Globally, poverty is distributed unevenly (Aras & Crowther, 2008); and microfinance can be a catalyst in transforming this situation for a better and more equal world (James, 2018). As highlighted in prior literature that is supported by the data from the World Bank (2018), 736 million people globally live below the international poverty line, and sadly, about 41% these people are located mostly in developing economies – and specifically in Sub-Saharan Africa.

In view of the preceding argument, microfinance is persuaded to alleviate poverty in developing countries, and grassroots development mediated by microfinance practices and systems that have long been considered as a way of not only empowering small businesses but a method of involving stakeholders to actualise sustainable rural development (Ferdousi, 2015). Rural employment generation is a top priority for developing countries and microfinance emphasises economic liberalisation and macroeconomic stability (Mazumder, 2015). Since its inception, microfinance has spread quite rapidly but how much this helps the poor is a contested. Developing economies have made tremendous effort in this regard; however, there is need to further explore the impact of microfinance on rural development and in achieving the broader agenda of sustainable development as declared by the United Nations (Ferdousi, 2015) for social transformation and change.

Microfinance is being considered as a crucial instrument for social change (Cohen, 2018) and poverty alleviation (Alhassan & Nwagbara, 2021; James, 2018), which is fundamental to realising the ideals of Millennium Development Goals (MDGs) and now Sustainable Development Goals (SDGs) (Kolk et al., 2017; Aras & Crowther, 2016). Nevertheless, evidence on the impacts of microfinance is mixed (García-Pérez et al., 2020). For example, some of the essential findings of Nawaz (2010) was that microfinance resulted in a moderate alleviation in poverty but did not reach many of the poorest potential recipients; however, other works in this regard have concluded the opposite (Bateman, 2011). Likewise, focusing on the Bangladeshi context, Bateman (2011) reported that up to 5% of participants in three key microfinance institutions lifted their families out of poverty; whereas Roodman and Morduch (2009) reported that there was almost no evidence confirming that microfinance has any tangible role in poverty alleviation and contributing to sustainable development.

Sustainable development, which stems from corporate global effort towards sustainability started with the publication of the Brundtland Report in 1987 – *Our Common Future* (Aras & Crowther, 2016; World Commission on Environment and Development, 1987). At the core of sustainable development are multilateralism and interdependence amongst nations in the search for a fairer, equitable and more inclusive arrangement around the globe that would not diminish the prospects of future generations (United Nations, 2017; Elkington, 1997). Although sustainable development (and to add sustainability) originated in natural resource economics, it has gained attention and influence as well as wider currency regarding social equality, justice, fairness, accountability, and development (James, 2018).

Microfinance is touted as having important positive relationship with reducing inequality, reducing socio-economic disequilibrium, addressing injustice, mitigating risks associated with weak institutions, and developing microbusiness, which form the logic of the ideals of sustainable development goals (SDGs) (United Nations, 2017) given the limitations of the Millennium Development Goals (MDGs). These SDGs are a collection of 17 interlinked goals established as a roadmap to realising a better, more sustainable future for all and more just world (James, 2018) by 2030. In the main, the logic of the present is moored to the ideals of SDGs particularly Goal 1 (no poverty), Goal 2 (zero hunger), Goal 10 (reduced inequalities), and Goal 16 (peace, justice, and strong institutions).

1. THE CHALLENGES

Based on the foregoing, the relationship between microfinance and socio-economic (and arguably political) transformation cannot be over-emphasised. And any efforts towards bettering the prospects of humanity through the intervention of microfinance for sustainable development is undeniably crucial for realising the ideals and principles enshrined in the United Nation's SDGs (UNDP, 2006).

The problems that microfinance addresses are more complex in developing countries, as has been highlighted earlier, where there is high incidence of weak institutions (Alhassan & Nwagbara, 2021), poor governance regime (Mazumder, 2015) leadership problems (Nwagbara, 2014), and in some instance what development economists refer to "resource curse" (Karl, 1997) phenomenon, which negatively impact sustainable development (Marini et al., 2017). Accordingly, Nwagbara (2014) avers that unless these development, institutional and governance issues are addressed, developing nations would seemingly lag behind in the comity of nations thus negatively impacting the actualisation and manifestation of sustainable development. Such challenges can be classified into these categories:

- The challenge of transforming and reinventing economies towards poverty eradication, social mobility, and urban/rural development.
- The challenge of establishing effective institutions and financial bodies that world regulate lending and business financing.
- The challenge of institutionalising effective corporate governance frameworks and financial policies and procedures that adequately support the ideals of sustainable development through empowering entrepreneurs and small business.
- The challenge of establishing effective structures and institutions for responsibility, accountability and transparency given the spate of institutional voids (weak institutions) in developing nations.
- The challenge of ensuring that microfinance institutions, systems and governance regimes are fit for purpose as well as advance the principles of poverty alleviation, socio-economic development, and mutual co-existence.

Notwithstanding huge human and natural endowments, developing economies are still plagued by developmental dilemma (Marini et al., 2017) militating against achieving the principles of SDGs. Thus, the present book study maintains that examining the interface between microfinance and sustainable development could be one of the most effective means of not only shedding a new light on developing economies' rise but a way to depend on the realisation of SDGs. In extending the confines of this proposition, on the one hand, prior research on microfinance has considered different areas of performance and effectiveness, but they were essentially done from the prism of economic and socio-economic perspective with results and findings that shy away from reaching a consensus (Aras & Crowther, 2016). Nevertheless, to the authors' best knowledge, the relationship between microfinance and sustainable development is still an area of scholarship that is under-researched and under-theorised from a holistic approach, which is the intention here.

2. SEARCHING FOR A SOLUTION

Solutions to the complex issue of microfinance for societal transformation find resonance in the core ideals of sustainable development, which is the mainstay of this book (WCED, 1987). The concept of sustainable development is drawn from a plethora of issues and aspirations aimed at peace, justice, development, freedom, capacity building as well as socio-economic emancipation, societal transformation, and environmentalism (Mazumder, 2015). It is now taking a centre stage in movements, strategies, policies, practices, and beliefs that advance corporate, institutional, business, national and global goals about development (WCED, 1987). Within the spirit of this volume, sustainable development resonates with searching for solutions through socio-economic development on a global level that cannot be separated from issues bordering on ecological stability, equity and social justice and pursuing a community vision that respects human prosperity for co-existence and conflict-free relationship (Desjardins, 2000). This process parallels what has been identified as 'microfinancing for sustainability' (Marini et al., 2017).

3. ORGANISATION OF THE BOOK

The book is organised into 10 chapters. A brief description of each of the chapters is presented below:

The book starts with the chapter 'Transforming Local Economies Through Microfinance in Rural Ghana: Evidence From a Review of Existing Literature', which is aptly titled and lucidly presented by Yahaya Alhassan, Geoff Paul, Samuel Salia and Uzoechi Nwagbara. The chapter brings to the fore how local economies and society can be transformed through microfinance using the context of rural Ghana, which is an interesting, insightful study on a region in dire straits of microfinance for a reinvented society. Correspondingly, in 'Reducing Poverty Through Microfinance in Developing Economies: Critical Perspectives From Literature', Yahaya Alhassan and Hua Jin demonstrated competently with a critical lens how poverty can be ameliorated leveraging microfinance instrument. This chapter is undergirded by searching logically and coherently existing literature on the phenomenon. This conversation continues in the chapter contributed by Manpreet Arora and Swati Singh in their well-articulated chapter on 'Microfinance and Sustainability: Building Perspective Through Literature and Bibliometrics'. The context of India is used in this exploration, which is timely and spatially sound and helps to delineate the interface between microfinance and sustainability in an emerging economy, which further echoes the wider call in Sustainable Development debate.

In taking the above issues further, in 'The Double Bottom Line in Microfinance: Implications for the Performance Measurement Practices of Microfinance Institutions (MFIs)', Abdul-Razak Alhassan, Mamudu Abunga Akudugu, and Margaret Atosina Akuriba eloquently examine the effect of commercialisation of microfinance on the performance measurement practices of MFIs and the implications these measurement practices have on the achievement of the mission objectives of MFIs leveraging the context of microfinance industry in Ghana. This study is provocative and insightful. Similarly, in another case study, 'Proceed With Caution: Protecting the Economic Well-Being of Women Using Microfinance – Egyptian Microfinance Case Study', Shymaa Bedaiwy uses the context of Egypt to argue that the country has developed and enacted a law that is meeting the international standards of microfinance global best practice, however, there is room for ensuring Microfinance Institutions are following their social justice mission by regulating other microcredit services beyond financing income-generating activities. It further elucidates that more regulations are needed to ensure MFIs are reaching out to women micro-entrepreneurs and enhancing their wellbeing and development.

In tandem with the above contextualized studies, Satheesh Pandian Murugan, Dhanabalan Thangam, Kanchan Rajput, and Chandan Chavadi argue with fervour and logic with their chapter on 'The Impact of COVID-19 on the Indian Microfinance Industry and Its Sustainability'. The authors argued that COVID-19 pandemic has interrupted operations of the entire sector throughout the world. It also forced all the industries towards unprecedented changes of their business operations, and in some cases, has pushed businesses to a halt. Therefore, for a more sustainable operation and for the foremost part social overhaul and change, microfinance is instrumental. The chapter found that given the impacts of COVID-19 pandemic, a smaller number of customers have realized better income generation during pandemic, which microfinance could help to change. Also, using the case of Nepal, Seema Kumari Sah, Niranjan Devkota, Udaya Raj Paudel, and Sahadeb Upretee wrote on 'Local Peoples' Perceptions on Microfinance in Nepal: A Structural Equation Modelling Approach', which is methodologically sound and riveting in scope. The chapter found that microfinance needs to focus more on training assessment, better compensation structure and women-friendly policies within the workforce. However, more needs to be done in this regard for microfinance development.

In a more theoretically couched study titled 'Who Loses in Financial Inclusion?' Peterson K. Ozili persuasively brings new vista to the discourse through financial inclusion, and stressing the challenges to sustained financial inclusion, which is cardinal to the realization of sustainable development and transformed economies. The idea of inclusion is quite widespread and can be a huge contributor to a more humanized, prosperous, and equal society, which is timely and topical. Along similar axis, Manpreet Arora's 'The Holistic Metamorphosis of Rural Lives Through Microfinance: A Perspective' brings to the debate the notion that microfinance has been associated with playing a radical role in transforming any economy especially where the goals are to uplift the disadvantaged sectors as well as advance the ideals of poverty alleviation, safeguarding the vulnerable and has been christened a "poverty vaccine". The chapter further reveals that microfinance is implicated in tackling socially exclusion. In the end, the chapter admonished that microfinance finds expression in the holistic metamorphosis of rural lives through microcredit interventions, with particular focus on the pandemic (and post-pandemic) era, where the economies are facing huge economic crises, social exclusion, and vulnerabilities, which are hampering social transformation.

In consonance with the above, 'Exploring Factors Influencing the Growth of MSMEs in Factor-Driven and Efficiency-Driven Economies' by Mohammad Izzuddin Mohammed brings to the debate a more generalised treatise. The chapter admonished that growth of Micro, Small and Medium-sized Enterprises (MSMEs) is important as MSMEs constitute the main drivers of economic growth, particularly in the emerging economies of factor-driven and efficiency-driven economies. However, irrespective of effort to support, nurture, and vitalise the growth of MSMEs, MSMEs located in emerging economies are often subjected to more hostile environments compared to their counterparts in developed economies such as the lack of access to micro-finance and underdeveloped educational institutions. The lack of micro-finance is especially detrimental as MSMEs without creditworthy history could not apply for finance, which can impede social transformation, social change, and development.

Yahaya Alhassan
University of Sunderland in London, UK

Uzoechi Nwagbara
University of Sunderland in London, UK

REFERENCES

Alhassan, Y., & Nwagbara, U. (2021). *Microfinance and Sustainable Development in Africa*. IGI Publishers.

Alhassan, Y., & Nwagbara, U. (2021). Institutions, Corruption and Microfinance Viability in Developing Countries: The Case of Ghana and Nigeria. *Economic Insights - Trends and Challenges*, *10*(78), 61–70. doi:10.51865/EITC.2021.02.06

Aras, G., & Crowther, D. (2008). Governance and sustainability: An investigation into the relationship between corporate governance and corporate sustainability. *Management Decision*, *46*(3), 433–448. doi:10.1108/00251740810863870

Aras, G., & Crowther, D. (2016). *A Handbook of Corporate Governance and Social Responsibility*. Routledge. doi:10.4324/9781315564791

Bateman, M. (Ed.). (2011). Confronting Microfinance: Undermining Sustainable Development. Kumarian Press.

Bebbington, J., & Unerman, J. (2018). Achieving the United Nations Sustainable Development Goals: An enabling role for accounting research. *Accounting, Auditing & Accountability Journal*, *31*(1), 2–24. doi:10.1108/AAAJ-05-2017-2929

Cohen, S. (2018). *Transforming Social Action into Social Change: Improving Policy and Practice*. Routledge.

Ferdousi, F. (2015). Impact of microfinance on sustainable entrepreneurship development. *Development Studies Research*, *2*(1), 51–63. doi:10.1080/21665095.2015.1058718

García-Pérez, I., Fernández-Izquierdo, M. A., & Muñoz-Torres, M. J. (2020). Microfinance Institutions Fostering Sustainable Development by Region. *Sustainability*, *12*(7), 1–23. doi:10.3390u12072682

García-Pérez, I., Muñoz-Torres, M. J., & Fernández-Izquierdo, M. A. (2018). Microfinance institutions fostering sustainable development. *Sustainable Development*, *26*(6), 606–619. doi:10.1002d.1731

Gueyie, J.-P. (2013). *Microfinance in Developing Countries Issues, Policies and Performance Evaluation*. Springer. doi:10.1057/9781137301925

James, V. (Ed.). (2018). Capacity Building for Sustainable Development. CABI.

Kolk, A., Kourula, A., & Pisani, N. (2017). Multinational enterprises and the sustainable development goals: What do we know and how to proceed? *Transnational Corporations*, *24*(3), 9–32. doi:10.18356/6f5fab5e-en

Marini, L., Andrew, J., & Van der Laan, S. (2017). Tools of accountability: Protecting microfinance clients in South Africa? *Accounting, Auditing & Accountability Journal*, *30*(6), 1344–1369. doi:10.1108/AAAJ-04-2016-2548

Mazumder, M. S. U. (2015). Role of Microfinance in Sustainable Development in Rural Bangladesh. *Sustainable Development*, *23*(6), 396–413. doi:10.1002d.1599

Milgram, B. L. (2005). From Margin to Mainstream: Microfinance, Women's Work and Social Change in the Philippines. *Urban Anthropology and Studies of Cultural Systems and World Economic Development*, *34*(4), 341–383.

Nwagbara, U. (2014). *Leading Sustainability in Nigeria: Problems, Processes and Prospects*. Lambert Academic Press.

Roodman, D., & Morduch, J. (2009). *The Impact of Microcredit on the Poor in Bangladesh: Revisiting the Evidence*. Working Paper Number 174. Centre for Global Development.

Spiegel, S. J. (2012). Microfinance services, poverty and artisanal mineworkers in Africa: In search of measures for empowering vulnerable groups. *Journal of International Development*, *24*(4), 485–517. doi:10.1002/jid.1781

United Nations. (2017). *Sustainable development goals report 2017*. Http.www.un.org ›development › desa › publications › sdg-report-2017

United Nations Development Programme. (2006). *Beyond scarcity: power, poverty and the global water crisis*. United Nations Development Programme.

Van Rooyen, C., Stewart, R., & de Wet, T. (2012). The Impact of Microfinance in Sub-Saharan Africa: A Systematic Review of the Evidence. *World Development*, *40*(11), 2249–2262. doi:10.1016/j.worlddev.2012.03.012

World Bank. (2018). *Poverty and Shared Prosperity 2018: Piecing Together the Poverty Puzzle*. World Bank.

World Commission of Environment and Development. (1997). *Our Common Future*. Oxford University Press.

Acknowledgment

We wish to offer this rider: without the various effort made by all and sundry, this book would not have been possible, although, Yahaya and Uzoechi "fathered" the concept of the volume!

Having said that, we wish to heartily thank and congratulate those who have been instrumental to the writing and production of this book.

First, without God the writing of this book would have been possible. We thank Him for giving us the strength, knowledge and sound mind to execute this book project!

Second, we would also like to thank the members of the editorial and acquisition team of IGI for their professionalism, dedication, prop and hard work during the production of this volume. We want to say a big 'thank-you' to them, for the opportunity to co-edit this book. Particularly, we are indebted to Gianna Walker, Assistant Development Editor (Book Development); Jan Travers, Director of Intellectual Property & Contracts IGI Global; and Maria Rohde, Book Development Coordinator.

Third, we are sincerely grateful to all the contributors – Yahaya Alhassan, Geoff Paul, Samuel Salia, Uzoechi Nwagbara, Abdul-Razak Alhassan, Mamudu Abunga Akudugu, Margaret Atosina Akuriba, Hua Jin, Dr. Manpreet Arora, Swati Singh, Peterson K Ozili, Shymaa Bedaiwy, Seema Kumari Sah, Udaya Raj Paudel, Sahadeb Upretee, Surendra Mahato, Devid Kumar Basyal, Purnima Lawaju, Sabina Bohaju, Krishna Dhakal, Satheesh Pandian Murugan, Dhanabalan Thangam, Kanchan Rajput, Chandan Chavadi, Shivaprasad G, Dhanalakshmi A and Sriram VP – for the kindred spirit and sense of commitment shown.

Finally, our profound gratitude goes to our families for the time granted us to do this book!

Introduction

Following the positive impact of microfinance on poverty reduction, women empowerment and microenterprise development in some countries in Asia and Africa, a huge amount of time has been devoted by researchers to understand how this concept can be used as a catalyst for transforming and sustaining the economies of developing and emerging countries. The concept of microfinance also has significant positive relationship with economic development. Though there are a few books on the role of microfinance in reducing poverty in developing countries across world. There is no specific book that explores the role of microfinance in transforming and sustaining economies of developing countries. Certainly, the use of microfinance for economic development in the developing world is growing. However, this concept needs to be expanded to ensure its application with the view to transform and sustain the economies of developing and emerging countries. Therefore, this book seeks to explore how the provision of microfinance to individuals and groups contributes to the economic transformation of economies of developing countries. In this regard, this book hopes to examine the role of microfinance in transforming and sustaining economies of developing countries.

Microfinance is the provision of small loans to individuals and groups who have no access to credit from traditional banks. The concept therefore refers to provision of small loans, deposits, and insurance to financially disadvantaged individuals and households aimed at reducing poverty. Thus, microfinance is intricately linked to poverty reduction and therefore a viable strategy for reducing poverty in poor communities. Access to microfinance has been shown to have helped low-income earners build their assets and improved their income earning capacity leading to an improvement in their quality of life. Evidence of positive impact of microfinance on women empowerment in developing and emerging economies has also been reported by various authors. Besides, the contribution of microfinance to economic development in developing and emerging countries has also been reported by various studies. Furthermore, microfinance has also been shown to provide opportunities for employment generation in poor communities.

Introduction

Research on the role played by microfinance in transforming economies has been on the rise. However, as argued by various scholars and practitioners there is need to widen the ballpark of scholarship in this field from the developing countries perspective, which is currently understudied and under-theorised. This argument is in consonance with some of the works already undertaken – *Transforming Microfinance Institutions: Providing Full Financial Services to the Poor* (2006), *Cambodia's Economic Transformation* (2011), and *The New Microfinanc*e *Handbook* (2013), amongst others. Against this backdrop, the present book enriches our understanding and knowledge about how microfinance is implicated in realistic, sustainable transformation that will find expression in poverty reduction/amelioration in developing countries, empowerment of the masses, social mobility of beneficiaries of microfinance and socio-economic as well as political transformation. These issues are critically important in realising the ideals of transforming developing and emerging economies for better economic prosperity for humankind; it is also inextricably linked to the rationality of the Sustainable Development Goals.

This book aims to examine and bring on board the various views and perspectives on the role of microfinance in transforming and sustaining economies of developing and emerging countries through industry experts, experienced researchers, and policymakers. The role of the concept of microfinance in transforming and sustaining the economies of developing and emerging countries will be explored by these experts and contributors from different perspectives with the view to forming an opinion on the problems, processes and prospects of microfinance in the developing world. The focus here is Asia, Africa, Eastern Europe and South America which have witnessed growing activities of microfinance institutions. Theoretical and empirical insight to be provided in this book will be a priceless resource to microfinance institutions, policymakers, state institutions, managers and non-governmental organisations working in developing and emerging countries.

This book is envisaged to also benefit financial institutions that are looking to expand their product portfolio and outreach. The book will offer great insight into theoretical, policy-oriented and practical ways to address some of the challenges of using microfinance for transforming and sustaining the economies of developing and emerging countries. Given the focus of this book on the nexus between microfinance and economic development, there will be a broadening of ideas on how the provision of microfinance can aid the transformation and sustainability of the economies of developing and emerging countries.

Yahaya Alhassan
University of Sunderland in London, UK

Uzoechi Nwagbara
University of Sunderland in London, UK

Chapter 1
Transforming Local Economies Through Microfinance in Rural Ghana:
Evidence From a Review of Existing Literature

Yahaya Alhassan
https://orcid.org/0000-0001-6700-635X
University of Sunderland in London, UK

Geoff Paul
University of Sunderland in London, UK

Samuel Salia
De Montfort University, UK

Uzoechi Nwagbara
University of Sunderland in London, UK

DOI: 10.4018/978-1-6684-5647-7.ch001

ABSTRACT

This chapter examines the role of microfinance in the transformation of rural communities in Ghana. To achieve this aim, a synthesized review of existing literature on microfinance outcomes on employment creation, poverty reduction, female empowerment, and microenterprise development in Ghana was conducted. The review shows that microfinance has contributed significantly to the transformation of rural communities in Ghana by helping to reduce poverty and improving the living standards of the poor. The review also demonstrates that microfinance contributed positively to the socio-economic well-being of women in Ghana. Microfinance has also played a positive role in the transformation of rural communities in Ghana by providing credit to support microenterprise projects. Furthermore, the analysis shows that microfinance contributed positively to the transformation of rural communities in Ghana by providing credit to individuals and microenterprises to create jobs and improve living standards.

INTRODUCTION

Evidence from existing literature suggests that microfinance presents benefits to the unbanked in society (Alhassan et al., 2022; Malhotra, 2018; Mushtaq & Bruneau, 2019). In the area of funds mobilisation, microfinance has contributed significantly towards financial sector deepening by including the unbanked (Mia et al., 2019; Njagi & Njoka, 2021; Milana & Ashta, 2020). In driving growth, microfinance has empowered a significant proportion of the workforce in poorer communities to set up their own businesses and contributed to economic development (Zafarullah & Nawaz, 2019; Sahu et al., 2021; Shafique and Siddique, 2020). In the campaign for gender development, microfinance is commonly used as a strategy for women empowerment (Reyes & Fattori, 2019; Akhter & Cheng, 2020; Salia et al., 2018). The implications of these findings from the literature are far reaching. Therefore, the recent efforts to provide microfinance services to the unbanked in Ghana raises a significant puzzle. Developing nations are increasingly looking towards microfinance as a means of transforming local communities and decreasing poverty rates. This chapter contributes to this ongoing search and addresses aspects of the puzzle referred to above. Therefore, the purpose of this chapter is to examine how microfinance has been used to transform rural communities in Ghana and provide an outline for future research. Towards these goals, we provide a synthesized review of existing literature on microfinance outcomes on employment creation, poverty reduction, female empowerment, and microenterprise development in Ghana.

In order to present a coherent and succinct review of microfinance literature, we divide our review into four areas of microfinance outcomes that have been reported by various studies in developing countries. In this regard, we focus our review on outcomes of microfinance experiments on employment creation, poverty reduction, female empowerment and microenterprise development in Ghana and discuss the relevant peer-reviewed articles in each section. Accordingly, the remainder of the chapter proceeds as follows. In the next section, we provide the background to microfinance. This is followed by a review of outcomes of microfinance on employment creation. Outcomes of microfinance experiments on poverty reduction is reviewed next, followed by a review of outcomes on female empowerment. The last section reviews outcomes of microfinance experiments on microenterprise development.

BACKGROUND

Evidence from various studies suggests that low income earners across the world are largely excluded from the formal banking sector (Chitimira & Ncube, 2020; Ozili, 2021; Sanderson et al., 2018). This exclusion from the formal banking system has forced the poor to find alternative ways of meeting their financial needs. This has therefore prompted some business organisations to design financial products/services specially for the poor. The most popular arrangement designed by formal and informal financial institutions to provide financial services to the poor is microfinance. In this regard, Hussaini and Chibuzo (2018) define microfinance as the provision of financial services to individuals who are unable to access such services from banks and other financial institutions. Similarly, Khan et al., (2021) define microfinance as all financial products that are available to the poor and low-income earners. Microfinance is therefore intricately linked to poverty reduction in poor communities particularly in developing countries. However, is microfinance merely designed to reduce poverty as suggested by Tasos et al., (2020) and Kumari (2020)? Surely not, as Akhter and Cheng (2020) have shown that microfinance plays a vital role in women empowerment. Besides, Adusei and Adeleye (2021) discovered a crucial role for microfinance in small business financing. Moreso, Alam and Azad (2021) found that microfinance provides opportunities for employment generation in rural communities.

Undoubtedly microfinance has been shown to be the most visible innovative policy for poverty reduction and financial inclusion in developing countries (Hussaini & Chibuzo, 2018). For example, access to microfinance has been reported have helped low-income earners build their assets and improved their earning capacity leading to an improvement in their quality of life (Alhassan, et al 2022; Roy & Mohanty, 2020; Salgotra et al., 2021). Ullah et al., (2020) provide evidence that the provision of microfinance does not merely reduce the occurrence of poverty but also the intensity and severity of it. This view is consistent with Hermes and Lensink (2021) who also discovered that the provision of microfinance could perhaps help users earn more income, thus helping them out of the cycle of poverty. Furthermore, microfinance has been reported to have alleviated poverty of women, considered marginalised in some societies in developing countries (Kumari, 2020). The question therefore is "is there sufficient evidence in existing literature to suggest that the recent efforts to provide microfinance services to the unbanked in Ghana has reduced poverty in rural communities"?

Microfinance has also been shown to play a pivotal role in women empowerment in developing countries. For instance, Niaz and Iqbal (2019) have shown that microfinance has a significant impact on the economic and social status of women. This is because microfinance creates employment opportunities for unemployed women thus increasing the level of their income and productive capacity. According to Al-Shami et al., (2018) microfinance empower women because access to such services improves their ability to make decisions about domestic issues including household income and expenditure. Besides, Debnath et al., (2019) have shown that women who receive microfinance have been found to be more independent and engaged in social and economic decision making in their communities. With regards to economic empowerment, James and Jane (2018) have shown that the provision of microfinance to women entrepreneurs in Uganda has helped increased their earnings and capital stock. In this regard, is there sufficient evidence in existing literature that support the hypothesis that the provision of microfinance empowers women in rural communities in Ghana?

Often, microfinance strategy is broadly expected to produce positive outcomes in developing countries with potential to improve incomes and reduce poverty in poor areas. However, there other narratives that suggests that microfinance practice in most of the 20th century may also be driven by a need to foster microenterprise growth (Adusei & Adeleye, 2021). For instance, Alhassan et al., (2022) found that the provision of microfinance increased the performance of microenterprises in Sub-Saharan Africa. Similarly, Omondi and Jagongo (2018) has shown that microfinance services have helped businesses in Kenya to grow their turnover from micro to small and from small to medium. A recent study that also provides evidence of positive outcomes of microfinance experiments on microenterprises is Alhassan et al., (2022) who found a positive relationship between microfinance services and the success of microenterprises in Africa. Microfinance has also been reported to have made a positive contribution to the development of microenterprises in Asia. In particular, a study conducted in Malaysia found that microfinance impacted positively on total assets of microenterprises (Al Mamun & Hayat, 2019). This may explain why Meilani et al., (2018) concluded that generally, microfinance increases microbusiness productivity and creates jobs for the poor. Therefore, it may be the case that the recent efforts to provide microfinance services to the unbanked in Ghana will produce similar positive outcomes.

The provision of microfinance services to the unbanked has also been shown to produce positive outcomes on employment creation in developing countries. For example, in a quasi-experiment conducted on the impact of microfinance on rural households in the Philippines, Kondo et al., (2008) concluded that generally, microfinance create jobs for the poor. Similarly, a mixed methods study on the role of microfinance in employment generation in Nepal found that microfinance provides opportunities for employment generation in rural communities (Pathak & Gyawali, 2012). The question therefore is "has the recent efforts to provide microfinance services to the unbanked in Ghana provides opportunities for employment generation in rural communities"? Having discussed the background to microfinance and its contribution to the unbanked in developing countries, we now turn our attention to the review of outcomes of microfinance experiments on poverty reduction, women empowerment, microenterprise development, and employment creation in local communities in Ghana.

THE ROLE OF MICROFINANCE IN THE TRANSFORMATION OF RURAL COMMUNITIES IN GHANA

The provision of microfinance services to the unbanked have been shown to have made significant contribution to the growth and development of poor communities in the developing world, particularly in Asia and Africa (El-Nasharty, 2022; Ezeanyeji et al., 2020). In this regard, this section aims to review existing microfinance literature to aid our understanding of how microfinance has been used to transform rural communities in Ghana. The review is divided into four themes: poverty reduction, women empowerment, microenterprise development, and employment creation.

Microfinance and Poverty Reduction in Ghana

In this section, we discuss the role that microfinance institutions have played in reducing or eradicating poverty in rural communities in Ghana. The term "Poverty reduction" is often used as a shorthand for promoting economic growth that will permanently lift as many people as possible over the poverty line (Barder, 2009). The question therefore is "how can poverty be reduced or eradicated"? Ngong et al., (2021) found a long-run relationship between microfinance and poverty reduction. Similarly, Lacalle-Calderon et al., (2018) have shown that microfinance significantly reduces the incidence and depth of poverty. In this regard, analysis of Boateng et al., (2015) suggests that the provision of microfinance services to poor communities in

Ghana helped to reduce the incidence and depth of poverty amongst clients of two major microfinance institutions. The study was purposely designed to ascertain the impact of microfinance on poverty reduction in Ghana using economic and social variables such as individual income, household growth, access to education, housing and participation in social and religious activities as benchmarks for measuring the impact. Undoubtedly, any positive changes in these variables have the potential to improve the living standards of the study participants. Therefore, the positive relationship between microfinance and incidence of poverty reported by the study is an indication that microfinance contributes positively to the transformation of rural communities in Ghana.

Similarly, a study conducted in the Greater Accra region by Gakpo et al., (2021) found a strong association between microfinance and poverty alleviation. This study was designed to determine the relationship between microfinance and poverty alleviation in some communities in the Greater Accra region of Ghana. Using the Pearson correlation analysis, the outcomes of the inferential statistics showed a strong positive relationship between the two variables at a correlation coefficient of 0.535 at p=.000. P=.000, which implies that the relationship is statistically significant. This result as reported by Gakpo et al., (2021) suggests that microfinance institutions have 53.5% predictability on poverty alleviation in the study area and Ghana in general. Since this investigation was conducted in some rural and poorer parts of the Greater Accra region, the outcome of the investigation is a further indication that microfinance contributes positively to the transformation of rural communities in Ghana.

The poverty reducing effect of access to microfinance across rural communities in Ghana is further confirmed by Annim (2018) who argues that overall, microfinance positively correlates with poverty reduction in Ghana. Indeed, Hagan (2018) also examined the contribution of microfinance to poverty alleviation in the Ga South municipality of the Greater Accra region of Ghana and found "a positive link between the provision of loans by microfinance institutions and the minimization of economic poverty within the study area". Annim (2018) investigated the poverty-reducing effect of access to microfinance and the amount loaned to beneficiaries using the Microfinance Poverty Assessment Tool (MPAT). The variables used to construct the poverty profile of the research participants included housing conditions and characteristics, food security and vulnerability, and ability to meet basic needs. Obviously, any significant improvements in these variables will significantly improve the living standard of the participants. In this regard, the results of the study showed that microfinance beneficiary households recorded a higher mean poverty index across all the 10 administrative regions in Ghana than non-microfinance beneficiary households. Therefore, it is plausible to argue as Addae-Korankye (2020) did that microfinance has contributed significantly to the transformation of rural communities in Ghana by helping to reduce poverty and improving the living standards of the poor.

The are other narratives in existing literature that suggests that the contribution of microfinance to poverty reduction in rural communities in Ghana is insignificant. For instance, using data from 120 respondents, Ntim (2018) found that access to credit from microfinance institutions averagely contributes to poverty reduction in the New Juaben Municipality of Ghana. The effectiveness of microfinance in reducing poverty in rural communities in Ghana has also been questioned by Dzansi and Atiase (2014) as they argue that “microfinance is not fulfilling its original mandate of extricating the poor from poverty. The contribution of microfinance to poverty alleviation in very poor communities in Ghana has further been questioned by Darko (2015) who examined the impact of microfinance on poverty in the Greater Accra region of Ghana and concluded that microfinance did not have a significant effect on poverty reduction. These insignificant outcomes of the effects of microfinance on poverty reduction reported by the above studies could be due to the microfinance institutions outreach. Perhaps, this is why Darko (2015) concludes that microfinance institutions reach more of the less poor households than the very poor households in Ghana. To avoid these mixed outcomes of the impact of microfinance on poverty reduction, various studies suggest that microfinance institutions should focus on the very poor communities in Ghana to achieve the desired results (William, 2011; Boateng, 2015; Odoom, et al, 2019; Salifu, 2020).

Overall, there is sufficient evidence in existing literature that support the view that microfinance contributes significantly to poverty reduction in rural communities in Ghana. In this regard, it is plausible to suggest that microfinance is a viable strategy for transforming rural communities in Ghana. Clearly, a national strategy by the Government of Ghana to help microfinance institutions to increase their outreach and focus on the very poor households is indeed required to achieve this transformation.

Microfinance and Women Empowerment in Ghana

The role that microfinance institutions have played in women empowerment in rural communities in Ghana is the focus of this section. Women empowerment is “an active, multi-dimensional process which enables women to realize their full identity and powers in all spheres of life” (Mandal, 2013). Varghese (2011) defines women empowerment as “a process whereby women become able to organize themselves to increase their own self-reliance, to assert their independent right to make choices and to control resources which will assist in challenging and eliminating their own subordination”. The question therefore is “how can women be empowered”? Various studies (Mudaliar and Mathur, 2015; Asad, et al., 2020; Khursheed et al., 2021) provide evidence of a positive relationship between microfinance and women empowerment.

In the context of Ghana, microfinance is widely promoted as a key strategy for addressing women empowerment (Addai, 2017). Outcomes of Addae-Korankye and Abada (2017) suggests that microfinance has direct correlation with women empowerment in Madina in the Greater Accra Region of Ghana. The study specifically concludes that microfinance contributed positively to the socio-economic well-being of women. The study was conducted to assess the effect of microfinance on socio-economic well-being of women (or women empowerment) in Madina in the Greater Accra region of Ghana. A key question that the study was designed to answer was "whether or not microfinance has positively impacted on the socio-economic wellbeing of women beneficiaries in Madina". In this regard, the women investigated stated among others that "microfinance has expanded their businesses, they are now able to send their children to schools, some have bought land and started building, some have even built houses, they are able to afford quality health care, they are now involved in decision making, and their confidence level has improved leading to their empowerment". These outcomes are a clear indication that microfinance has contributed positively to the transformation of rural communities in Ghana by helping to improve the socio-economic wellbeing of women in the Madina area of the Greater Accra region of Ghana.

Similarly, Cooke and Amuakwa-Mensah (2022) found higher economic empowerment for female clients with a higher frequency of microfinance loans compared to those with a lower frequency of loans. This provides further evidence that microfinance contributes positively to women empowerment in rural communities in Ghana. Perhaps, the deliberate strategy adopted by some of the microfinance institutions to target poor rural women account for this positive results. The positive effect of microfinance on the socio-economic wellbeing of women in Nsawam has also been reported by Anderson (2019).

The work of Salia et al., (2018) also suggests that the provision of microfinance helps women to exit poverty and gain better economic opportunities in rural communities in Ghana. These authors examined the impact of microfinance on the success of enterprises, women empowerment, and family well-being in Ghana. The essential outcomes of the investigation are that microfinance promotes female empowerment in Ghana and female empowerment is generally suggested as a key driver for microfinance institutions reaching out to women clients. Therefore, this study has also confirmed the significant role that microfinance plays in transforming rural communities through supporting female empowerment projects in Ghana. However, other accounts about the contribution of microfinance to women empowerment in Ghana suggests that despite the increase in access to credit, microfinance itself may not be sufficient to eliminate barriers to women empowerment in rural communities (Jenkins & Batinge, 2018). For example, Ganle et al., (2015) found that some rural women in Ghana are empowered as a result of their access to credit; some have little control over the use of loans and are not better off; and some are subjected to harassment and are worse off due to their inability to repay loans in time.

Despite the few studies that have shown that microfinance may not be sufficient to eliminate the barriers to women empowerment, overall, evidence from the literature reviewed suggest that microfinance is a key driver for women empowerment in rural communities in Ghana. There is clear evidence that microfinance contributes positively to the socio-economic well-being of women in rural communities in Ghana. Therefore, this chapter concludes that microfinance plays a pivotal role in the transformation of rural communities in Ghana through economic and social empowerment of women in poorer communities.

Microfinance and Microenterprise Development in Ghana

In this section, we examine the role that microfinance institutions have played in promoting microenterprise projects in rural communities in Ghana. The increasing use of microfinance as a key source of finance for setting up and promoting microenterprise projects has generated several studies that have attempted to determine the role of microfinance in microenterprise development in rural communities in Ghana (Salia, 2015; Alhassan, et al., 2022; Eric et al., 2022). For instance, using a control group experiment, Alhassan et al., (2022) found that microfinance impacted positively on microenterprise projects in Ghana. The findings of the study suggest that the use of microfinance services by entrepreneurs in poor rural communities in Ghana significantly improved the performance of the beneficiary microenterprises. These results are consistent with Salia (2015) who also found a significant relationship between provision of microfinance and positive outcomes of microenterprise projects. In view of the study objective to establish the relationships between microfinance and microenterprise development, the author conducted a regression analysis to establish how the outcome variations in the microenterprises depended on the provision of microfinance. The outcomes of the investigation suggest that microenterprises that benefited from microfinance credit experienced a positive return on their capital stock. Besides, the outcomes show that microfinance have the predicted positive effect on the gross revenue of microenterprises in Ghana. In this regard, the regression technique used in analysing the relationships between microfinance credit and gross revenue variables of microenterprises in Ghana found a perfect confidence level in the relationship. The above evidence from existing literature suggests that microfinance contributes positively to the transformation of rural communities in Ghana by providing credit to support microenterprise projects in Ghana.

Another crucial role that is widely discussed in existing literature is the ability of microfinance institutions to address the financing issues among microenterprises in Ghana. However, it is equally vital to examine the effect that the finance provided by these institutions on the beneficiary microenterprises (Alhassan & Nwagbara, 2021). In this regard, outcomes of Eric et al., (2022) suggests positive and significant effects of micro-financing activities (manufacturing activities, agriculture activities, personal activities, trading activities and service activities) on microenterprise expansion in Ghana. Similarly, Odoom et al., (2019) examined the contribution of microfinance to the local community of Takoradi in Ghana and concluded that the provision of microfinance services to entrepreneurs helped to promote and grow microenterprises in the local community. Specifically, this study found that that microfinance institutions in Takoradi contribute variously to the local economy including provision of financial capital to the people; income generation; employment creation; engaging the non-formal economy and providing support for microenterprises to grow. The outcomes of the studies discussed above provide strong evidence that microfinance plays a major role in the transformation of local communities in Ghana through providing financial support for microenterprise development.

Furthermore, Acheampong (2018) found that microfinance participation has a positive and significant relationship with a family's decision to own an enterprise. this study from the outset sought to establish the baseline relationship between microfinance and entrepreneurial behaviour of families in some communities in Ghana. The author's argument in support of this research aim is that access to microfinance resources removes entry constraints that are imposed by a lack of resources to pursue an entrepreneurial vision. In this regard, the study concluded that there is a strong positive relationship between family microfinance participation and entrepreneurial behaviour in Ghana. It is therefore reasonable to conclude that the financial support widely provided to individuals and groups for business expansion or setting up a new microenterprise contributes significantly to the transformation of rural communities in Ghana.

Microfinance and Employment Creation in Ghana

The role that microfinance institutions have played in helping to create jobs in rural communities in Ghana is the focus of this section. Following the success stories of microfinance institutions' role in fostering employment creation in India and some parts of South East Asia, various studies have attempted to examine the role of microfinance in creating employment opportunities in rural communities in Ghana (Alnaa, 2017; Ussif, 2020; Gakpo, 2021). For instance, using data from selected microfinance managers and customers Ussif (2020) found that microfinance institutions have a strong positive impact on employment creation in poorer communities in Ghana. The study specifically found that microfinance programs in Ghana helps to create employment by providing credit to individuals and groups to set up or expand existing businesses. A further observation made about the outcomes of this investigation is that the income that the beneficiaries of the microfinance programs gained help the poor to increase their living standards and condition. "This in a way help reduce their poverty levels". Therefore, through microfinance and their programs, most of the poor people in rural and poor communities gain employment and are now working as self-employed. The above evidence from existing literature suggests that microfinance contributes positively to the transformation of rural communities in Ghana by providing credit to individuals and microenterprises to create jobs and improve living standards in rural communities.

The positive link between microfinance and employment creation in rural Ghana has also been reported by Alnaa (2017). The author argues that microfinance institutions that increased access to credit in the rural areas created more employment opportunities in Ghana. Specifically, the results indicate that access to microcredit has 46 per cent probability of employment creation. Surprisingly, Gakpo (2021) found no relationships between microfinance and employment rate in the Greater Accra region of Ghana. Perhaps this surprising result could be because most of the beneficiaries borrowed for consumption instead of business or entrepreneurial activities. Overall, evidence from the existing literature reviewed in this chapter suggests that microfinance contributes positively to the transformation of rural communities in Ghana by providing credit to individuals and microenterprises to create jobs and improve living standards.

SOLUTIONS AND RECOMMENDATIONS

Although this chapter found positive relationship between microfinance and poverty reduction, women empowerment, microenterprise development, and employment creation, it is recommended that microfinance providers improve their provision to include training to credit beneficiaries to enhance their capacity to further transform local communities. Besides, a national strategy by the government of Ghana to help microfinance institutions to increase their outreach and focus on the very poor households is required to deepen the transformation of rural communities.

To avoid the mixed outcomes of the impact of microfinance on poverty reduction, it is recommended that microfinance institutions should focus on the very poor communities in Ghana to achieve the desired results of alleviating poverty and improving living standards in rural communities. Besides, microfinance institutions are encouraged to focus on providing credit that are intended to be used for business and entrepreneurial activities instead of consumption.

To maximise the contribution of women to the transformation of rural communities, it is recommended that the government and their development partners including microfinance institutions should pay serious attention to female entrepreneurship development training and providing financial support for targeted development of women to become self-reliant and contribute to national development. Also, female owned microenterprises should be given targeted financial support, as women have been found to be better utilizers of microfinance to achieve entrepreneurial outcomes compared to their male counterparts. Although this recommendation is gender driven, it can further contribute positively to female empowerment.

Furthermore, in view of the other accounts that suggest that despite the increase in access to credit, microfinance itself may not be sufficient to eliminate barriers to women empowerment in rural communities in Ghana, it is recommended that policy makers at both local and national level complement the work of microfinance institutions by creating enabling political and social environment to support women empowerment.

A further recommendation that could enhance the use of microfinance to transform rural communities in Ghana is that the government of Ghana should support microfinance institutions financially because through microfinance and their programs, most of the poor people in rural and poor communities gain employment as an employee or self-employed.

Furthermore, strategic partnerships between microfinance providers and the Municipal and District Assemblies is recommended to design strategies to expand microfinance outreach into more rural communities to help improve and transform poorer local communities.

FUTURE RESEARCH DIRECTIONS

This chapter makes significant contributions to our understanding of the relationship between microfinance and the transformation of rural communities in Ghana. However, it is plausible that other initiatives and policy directions by government and their development partners including microfinance institutions could deepen the transformation of rural communities in Ghana. For example, the role of partnership between government and microfinance institutions in the provision of microfinance services in rural communities, which was not explored in this chapter. Therefore, further studies are required to explore the effect of this (partnership) on the relationship between microfinance and transformation of rural communities in Ghana.

This chapter also provide evidence from existing literature that demonstrates that microfinance contributes significantly to the transformation of rural communities in Ghana by helping to reduce poverty and improving the living standards of the poor. Yet, there are other narratives in the chapter that suggests that the contribution of microfinance to poverty reduction in rural communities in Ghana is negligible. This makes the outcomes of the relationship between microfinance and poverty reduction in Ghana inconclusive. Accordingly, further studies are needed to examine the effect of the provision of microfinance services on poverty alleviation to provide conclusive results about the relationship between poverty and microfinance.

This chapter makes further contributions to our understanding of the relationship between microfinance and employment creation by demonstrating that microfinance contributes positively to the transformation of rural communities by providing credit to individuals and microenterprises to create jobs and improve living standards in Ghana. However, the chapter also shows that borrowing for consumption may have contributed the negative relationships found between microfinance and employment rate. Hence, further studies that focus on microfinance beneficiaries who borrow for entrepreneurial and other economic activities are needed to provide a better understanding of the effect of microfinance on employment creation and its role in the transformation of rural communities in Ghana.

CONCLUSION

The most popular arrangement designed by formal and informal financial institutions to provide financial services to the poor is microfinance. This concept of microfinance and its impact on rural communities in Ghana has been widely reported by various studies. In this regard, this chapter sought to evaluate the reported outcomes of microfinance and its role in transforming rural communities in Ghana. Overall, the literature reviewed shows mixed but generally positive results and conclusions.

The first observation from the literature reviewed in this chapter is that microfinance has contributed significantly to the transformation of rural communities in Ghana by helping to reduce poverty and improving the living standards of the poor. However, there are other narratives that suggests that the contribution of microfinance to poverty reduction in rural communities in Ghana is negligible.

Besides, there is clear evidence from the literature reviewed that microfinance contributes positively to the socio-economic well-being of women in rural communities in Ghana. Therefore, this chapter concludes that microfinance plays a pivotal role in the transformation of rural communities in Ghana through economic and social empowerment of women in poorer communities. However, other accounts about the contribution of microfinance to women empowerment in Ghana suggests that despite the increase in access to credit, microfinance itself may not be sufficient to eliminate barriers to women empowerment in rural communities.

With regards to the possible contribution of microfinance to microenterprise development, the evidence from existing literature reviewed suggest that microfinance contributes positively to the transformation of rural communities in Ghana by providing credit to support microenterprise projects in Ghana. This chapter, therefore, concludes that the financial support widely provided to individuals and groups for business expansion or setting up a new microenterprise contributes significantly to the transformation of rural communities in Ghana.

In addition to the above, evidence from the existing literature reviewed in this chapter suggest that microfinance contributes positively to the transformation of rural communities in Ghana by providing credit to individuals and microenterprises to create jobs and improve living standards.

REFERENCES

Acheampong, G. (2018). Microfinance, gender and entrepreneurial behaviour of families in Ghana. *Journal of Family Business Management*, *8*(1), 38–57. doi:10.1108/JFBM-09-2017-0028

Addae-Korankye, A. (2020). Historical emergence of microfinance and the microfinance sector in Ghana. *Business Management Dynamics*, *10*(2), 1.

Addae-Korankye, A., & Abada, A. (2017). Microfinance and women empowerment in Madina in Accra, Ghana. *Asian Economic and Financial Review*, *7*(3), 222–231. doi:10.18488/journal.aefr/2017.7.3/102.3.222.231

Addai, B., 2017. Women empowerment through microfinance: Empirical evidence from Ghana. *Journal of finance and accounting*, *5*(1), pp.1-11.

Adusei, M., & Adeleye, N. (2021). Start-up microenterprise financing and financial performance of microfinance institutions. *Journal of Small Business and Entrepreneurship*, 1–24. doi:10.1080/08276331.2020.1842047

Akhter, J., & Cheng, K. (2020). Sustainable empowerment initiatives among rural women through microcredit borrowings in Bangladesh. *Sustainability*, *12*(6), 2275. doi:10.3390u12062275

Al Mamun, A., & Hayat, N. (2019). Microcredit and microenterprises performance in Malaysia. [IJABE]. *International Journal of Applied Behavioral Economics*, *8*(2), 1–13. doi:10.4018/IJABE.2019040101

Al-Shami, S. S. A., Razali, R. M., & Rashid, N. (2018). The effect of microcredit on women empowerment in welfare and decisions making in Malaysia. *Social Indicators Research*, *137*(3), 1073–1090. doi:10.100711205-017-1632-2

Alam, P. and Azad, I., 2021. Impact of Microfinance on income and employment of women in Jigjiga, Ethiopia. *Int. J. Econ. Bus. Adm*, pp.373-381.

Alhassan, Y., Kuagbela, F., Nurokina, C. D., & Appiah, B. (2022). *The Role of Microfinance in Africa: A Review of Outcomes From Ghana and Nigeria*. Microfinance and Sustainable Development in Africa.

Alhassan, Y., & Nwagbara, U. (Eds.). (2021). *Microfinance and Sustainable Development in Africa*. IGI Global.

Alhassan, Y., Nwagbara, U., & Salia, S. (2022). Analysis of Factors That Affect the Use of Microfinance for Microbusiness Development in Ghana. In *Microfinance and Sustainable Development in Africa* (pp. 103–126). IGI Global. doi:10.4018/978-1-7998-7499-7.ch005

Alhassan, Y., Salia, S., & Nwagbara, U. 2022. Microfinance Impact on Microbusiness Development in Africa: Evidence from a Control Group Experiment in Ghana. In Microfinance and Sustainable Development in Africa (pp. 1-26). IGI Global.

Alnaa, S. E. (2017). Microcredit to rural women, intra-household power play and employment creation in Northern Ghana. *Journal of Interdisciplinary Economics, 29*(2), 197–213. doi:10.1177/0260107916688388

Anderson, F. 2019. *Assessment of the role of microfinance on women empowerment in Nsawam* [Doctoral dissertation, University of Cape Coast].

Annim, S. K. (2018). Outreach and the poverty-reducing effect of microfinance in Ghana. *Enterprise Development & Microfinance*, *29*(2), 145–171. doi:10.3362/1755-1986.17-00020

Asad, A., Hameed, W. U., Irfan, M., Jiang, J., & Naveed, R. T. (2020). The Contribution of Microfinance Institutes in Women-Empowerment and role of Vulnerability. *Revista Argentina de Clínica Psicológica*, 223–238.

Barder, O. M. 2009. What is poverty reduction? *Center for Global Development Working Paper*, (170).

Boateng, A.A., 2015. An examination of challenges and prospects of microfinance institutions in Ghana. *Journal of economics and sustainable development, 6*(4), pp.52-60.

Boateng, G. O., Boateng, A. A., & Bampoe, H. S. (2015). Microfinance and poverty reduction in Ghana: Evidence from policy beneficiaries. *Review of Business & Finance Studies*, *6*(1), 99–108.

Chitimira, H., & Ncube, M. (2020). Legislative and Other Selected Challenges Affecting Financial Inclusion for the Poor and Low-Income Earners in South Africa. *Journal of African Law*, *64*(3), 337–355. doi:10.1017/S0021855320000182

Cooke, E. F., & Amuakwa-Mensah, F. (2022). Microfinance loans, women's economic empowerment, and poverty: A case study of Baobab Microfinance Company. *Journal of Development Effectiveness, 14*(1), 34–55. doi:10.1080/19439342.2021.1953568

Darko, F. 2015. Microfinance and Poverty Reduction: The Case Study of Selected Institutions in the Greater Accra Region of Ghana. In Microfinance and the Millennium Development Goals: Achievements and Strategies for Post 2015 (p. 1).

Debnath, D., Rahman, M., Acharjee, D. C., Latif, W. U., & Wang, L. (2019). Empowering women through microcredit in Bangladesh: An empirical study. *International Journal of Financial Studies, 7*(3), 37. doi:10.3390/ijfs7030037

Dzansi, D. Y., & Atiase, V. Y. (2014). Reflecting on micro finance in poverty reduction. *Mediterranean Journal of Social Sciences, 5*(21), 345. doi:10.5901/mjss.2014.v5n21p345

El-Nasharty, H. (2022). The Role of Microfinance in Poverty Reduction, Countries Experiences by Regions 2000-2018. *International Journal of Social Sciences and Economic Review, 4*(1), 01–09. doi:10.36923/ijsser.v4i1.101

Eric, A., Stephen, N. Y., Augustine, O. M., & Zakaria, A. (2022). The Role of Rural Banks in Micro Financing in Ghana. *Journal of Finance and Accounting, 13*(8), 32–54.

Ezeanyeji, C.I., Usifoh, K.S., Obi, C.O. and Ejefobihi, U.F. (2020). Microfinancing, poverty alleviation and Nigeria's economic growth: the nexus. *European Journal of Economic and Financial Research.*

Gakpo, M. D. Y., Wujangi, M., Kwakye, M., & Asante, V. G. (2021). The impact of microfinancing on poverty alleviation and small businesses in ghana. *The International Journal of Social Sciences and Humanity Studies, 13*(1), 1–28.

Ganle, J. K., Afriyie, K., & Segbefia, A. Y. (2015). Microcredit: Empowerment and disempowerment of rural women in Ghana. *World Development, 66*, 335–345. doi:10.1016/j.worlddev.2014.08.027

Hagan, L. H. 2018. *The impact of Microfinance Institutions on Poverty reduction among entrepreneurs in Ghana. A case study in the Ga South Municipal Assembly* [Master's thesis, OsloMet–Oslo Metropolitan University].

Hermes, N., & Lensink, R. 2021. Microfinance and development. Contemporary issues in development finance, pp.51-73.

Hussaini, U., & Chibuzo, I. C. (2018). The effects of financial inclusion on poverty reduction: The moderating effects of microfinance. *International Journal of Multidisciplinary Research and Development, 5*(12), 188–198.

James, M. and Jane, N. (2018). Role of Microfinance Institutions on the Promotion of Women Entrepreneurship in Uganda. *Available at SSRN 3176583.*

Jenkins, H. and Batinge, B.K., 2018. Microcredit and the Socio-cultural Obstacles to Women's Empowerment in Northern Territories of Ghana. *Kadin/Woman 2000, 19*(2).

Khan, A. A., Khan, S. U., Fahad, S., Ali, M. A., Khan, A., & Luo, J. (2021). Microfinance and poverty reduction: New evidence from Pakistan. *International Journal of Finance & Economics*, *26*(3), 4723–4733. doi:10.1002/ijfe.2038

Khursheed, A., Khan, A. A., & Mustafa, F. (2021). Women's social empowerment and microfinance: A brief review of literature. *Journal of International Women's Studies*, *22*(5), 249–265.

Kondo, T., Orbeta, A. Jr, Dingcong, C., & Infantado, C. (2008). Impact of microfinance on rural households in the Philippines. *IDS Bulletin*, *39*(1), 51–70. doi:10.1111/j.1759-5436.2008.tb00432.x

Kumari, P. (2020). Theoretical Analysis of Microfinance on Poverty Alleviation. *Journal of Economic Info*, *7*(3), 221–236. doi:10.31580/jei.v7i3.1709

Lacalle-Calderon, M., Perez-Trujillo, M., & Neira, I. (2018). Does microfinance reduce poverty among the poorest? A macro quantile regression approach. *The Developing Economies*, *56*(1), 51–65. doi:10.1111/deve.12159

Malhotra, M. 2018. Role of Microfinance in Financial Inclusion in India. In Microfinance and Its Impact on Entrepreneurial Development, Sustainability, and Inclusive Growth (pp. 322-343). IGI Global. doi:10.4018/978-1-5225-5213-0.ch018

Mandal, K. C. 2013, May. Concept and Types of Women Empowerment. In *International Forum of Teaching & Studies, 9*(2).

Meilani, Y. F., Sihombing, S. O., & Kusuma, B. H. (2018). Roles of Microfinance Institutions for Sustainability of Micro Entrepreneurs in Indonesia. *International Journal of Social Science and Humanities Research*, *6*(1), 576–583.

Mia, M. A., Dalla Pellegrina, L., Van Damme, P., & Wijesiri, M. (2019). Financial inclusion, deepening and efficiency in microfinance programs: Evidence from Bangladesh. *European Journal of Development Research*, *31*(4), 809–835. doi:10.105741287-018-0188-6

Milana, C., & Ashta, A. (2020). Microfinance and financial inclusion: Challenges and opportunities. *Strategic Change*, *29*(3), 257–266. doi:10.1002/jsc.2339

Mudaliar, A. and Mathur, A., 2015. Women empowerment through microfinance. *International journal of Arts, humanities, and management studies, 1*(2), 58-65.

Mushtaq, R., & Bruneau, C. (2019). Microfinance, financial inclusion and ICT: Implications for poverty and inequality. *Technology in Society, 59*, 101154. doi:10.1016/j.techsoc.2019.101154

Niaz, M. U., & Iqbal, M. (2019). Effect of microfinance on women empowerment: A case study of Pakistan. *Paradigms, 13*(1), 52–59.

Njagi, J. N., & Njoka, C. (2021). Microfinance Reforms and Financial Inclusion in Kenya. *International Journal of Current Aspects in Finance. Banking and Accounting, 3*(1), 54–72.

Ntim, D. O. (2018). Microfinance and poverty reduction: Evidence from market women in the New Juaben Municipality, Ghana. *ADRRI Journal of Arts and Social Sciences, 15*(6), 12–29.

Odoom, D., Fosu, K. O., Ankomah, K., & Amofa, M. B. (2019). Exploring the Contributions of Microfinance Institutions to the Ghanaian Economy: A Study at Takoradi. *Journal of Economics and Sustainable Development, 10*(1), 77–90.

Omondi, R.I. and Jagongo, A., 2018. Microfinance services and financial performance of small and medium enterprises of youth SMEs in Kisumu County, Kenya. *International academic journal of economics and finance, 3*(1), 24-43.

Ozili, P. K. (2021). Financial inclusion research around the world: A review. *The Forum for Social Economics, 50*(4), 457–479. doi:10.1080/07360932.2020.1715238

Pathak, H. P., & Gyawali, M. (2012). Role of microfinance in employment generation: A case study of Microfinance Program of Paschimanchal Grameen Bikash Bank. *Journal of Nepalese Business Studies, 7*(1), 31–38. doi:10.3126/jnbs.v7i1.6401

Reyes, L.A.D. and Fattori, G., 2019. Microfinance as a means for women empowerment in the Colombian post conflict scenario: Transformational development or a tool for better managing poverty?. *Peace Human Rights Governance, 3*(1).

Roy, S., & Mohanty, R. P. (2020). Microfinance models in improving'quality of life': Empirical analysis on Indian perspective. *International Journal of Business Innovation and Research, 21*(1), 23–55. doi:10.1504/IJBIR.2020.104031

Sahu, T. N., Agarwala, V., & Maity, S. (2021). Effectiveness of microcredit in employment generation and livelihood transformation of tribal women entrepreneurs: Evidence from PMMY. *Journal of Small Business and Entrepreneurship*, 1–22. do i:10.1080/08276331.2021.1928847

Salgotra, A. K., Kandari, P., & Bahuguna, U. (2021). Does access to finance eradicate poverty? A case study of Mudra beneficiaries. *The Journal of Asian Finance, Economics, and Business*, *8*(1), 637–646.

Salia, S. (2015). *The impact of microfinance on microenterprise development in Ghana* [Doctoral dissertation, Birmingham City University].

Salia, S., Hussain, J., Tingbani, I. and Kolade, O., 2018. Is women empowerment a zero sum game? Unintended consequences of microfinance for women's empowerment in Ghana. *International Journal of Entrepreneurial Behavior & Research.*

Salifu, I. (2020). The Influence of Geographical Coverage on the Microfinance Sustainability and Outreach in Northern Ghana. *International Journal of Economics and Finance*, *12*(2), 1–82.

Sanderson, A., Mutandwa, L., & Le Roux, P. (2018). A review of determinants of financial inclusion. *International Journal of Economics and Financial Issues*, *8*(3), 1–8.

Shafique, O. and Siddique, N. (2020). The impact of microcredit financing on poverty alleviation and women empowerment: an empirical study on akhuwat islamic microfinance. *PalArch's Journal of Archaeology of Egypt/Egyptology, 17*(8), 548-562.

Tasos, S., Amjad, M. I., Awan, M. S., & Waqas, M. (2020). Poverty Alleviation and Microfinance for the Economy of Pakistan: A Case Study of Khushhali Bank in Sargodha. *Economies*, *8*(3), 63. doi:10.3390/economies8030063

Ullah, K., Saboor, A., & Ahmad, I. (2020). Effects of Microfinance on Mountain Poverty and Living Standards: An Empirical Investigation from Central Karakorum National Park Region of Gilgit Baltistan, Pakistan. *NUML International Journal of Business & Management*, *15*(1), 30–49.

Ussif, R. (2020). Microfinance institutions challenges in poverty and unemployment reduction in Ghana. *International Journal of Engineering and Information Systems*, *4*(7), 114–123.

Varghese, T. (2011). Women empowerment in Oman: A study based on Women Empowerment Index. *Far East Journal of Psychology and Business*, *2*(2), 37–53.

William, G. B. I. (2011). Understanding the marketing strategies of microfinance institutions within the Accra metropolis of Ghana: Case of selected institutions. *African Journal of Marketing Management*, *3*(2), 45–55.

Zafarullah, H., & Nawaz, F. (2019). *Pathways to women's empowerment in Bangladesh: Employment and microfinance as interventions.* Asian Education and Development Studies.

Chapter 2
The Double Bottom Line in Microfinance:
Implications for the Performance Measurement Practices of Microfinance Institutions (MFIs)

Abdul-Razak Alhassan
University of Surrey, UK

Mamudu Abunga Akudugu
University for Development Studies, Ghana

Margaret Atosina Akuriba
University for Development Studies, Ghana

ABSTRACT

This chapter examines the effect of commercialisation of microfinance on the performance measurement practices of MFIs and the implications these measurement practices have on the achievement of the mission objectives of MFIs using as a case, the microfinance industry in Ghana. Mainly qualitative research techniques were employed in the study, relying on the views and perspectives of MFIs, clients, practitioners, and experts. The study results indicate that MFIs have not appropriately met this dual expectation of pursuing both financial and social objectives and cannot therefore possibly improve their understanding of the mission drift phenomenon with their existing measurement practices. The authors therefore propose a conceptual framework, as well as core social and economic performance, and impact indicators for measuring the attainment of the double bottom line or convergence.

DOI: 10.4018/978-1-6684-5647-7.ch002

INTRODUCTION

Microfinance has over the years been used as a social intervention for empowerment and a tool for poverty reduction. The focus of microfinance on the social good is however, changing as Microfinance Institutions (MFIs) are under pressure to commercialise in order to remain sustainable (Hermes & Hudon, 2018, Wondirad, 2020). The shift towards commercialisation is expected to yield high level of investment in microfinance resulting in the calls for transparency and accountability in microfinance with an important aspect being the growing use of financial and institutional indicators in the measurement of performance of MFIs. These are said to result in better performance, especially when the designing, reporting and monitoring focus explicitly on key measures of performance (Haider et al., 2017; CGAP, 2006). This view is shared by many in the industry including Hermes and Hudon (2018) and Woller (2005), who have argued that support for microfinance as they commercialise their operations has increasingly turned to the question on return on investment. This has made it imperative for MFIs to develop systems that measure progress towards a double bottom-line (financial and social performance) to be able to creditably account to investors and other external stakeholders.

The argument in furtherance of this debate is that microfinance as with any global industry requires accepted standards to assess more accurately its performance. This is because there is a general consensus that institutions that apply industry standards are regarded more transparent (The SEEP Network, 2005). This is particularly necessary as funding providers of MFIs are also placing significant emphasis on assessments, reviews, comparisons, ratings and standardization of financial ratios (Goodman, 2006; Daher & Le Saout, 2013; Leyer et al., 2015; Alaoui & Tkiouat, 2017; Hermes & Hudon, 2018). This suggests that even those MFIs operating with little capital but exhibit good governance, transparency and full accountability for their performance have the edge in attracting support than MFIs lacking these characteristics or qualities (Goodman, 2006; Sierra et al., 2020). This is because transparency and full disclosure are expected by private investors from MFIs, especially when they are faced with multiple investment options.

For these reasons, standards began to emerge since the early 1990s in support for stronger financial management of MFIs particularly in their delinquency management and reporting (The SEEP Network, 2005) in response to the growing calls for the application of performance measurements. Network organisations, the Consultative Group to Assist the Poorest (CGAP), rating firms to mention but a few, have worked assiduously to promote indicators based on common definitions and calculations with the growth in size, type and complexity of MFIs since 1995, creating an increased emphasis on financial accountability, management and viability (Epstein & Manzoni, 2006). Furthermore, not only are performance measurements prescribed for MFIs to adopt and use, but there is a need for the harmonisation and standardisation of ratios and measures for microfinance because of the apparent lack of consistency in the way financial data, portfolios and ratios are presented (Goodman 2006; Hermes and Hudon, 2018).

It is in lieu of these developments in the application of performance measurement processes in microfinance as a result of the apparent shift to commercialisation that this chapter examines the measurement of performance of microfinance, the effect of commercialisation on the performance measurement practices of MFIs and the implications these measurement practices have on the achievement of the mission objectives of MFIs using as a case, the microfinance industry in Ghana.

EMPIRICAL ISSUES IN PERFORMANCE OF MICROFINANCE INSTITUTIONS (MFIS)

Performance Measurements in Microfinance

MFIs unlike conventional institutions, strive for both financial sustainability and the empowerment of the poor (Nawaz, 2010; Moss et al., 2015; Alaoui and Tkiouat, 2017; Hermes and Hudon, 2018; Haider et al., 2017). As they claim to have a dual mission of being financially sustainable and providing financial services for poor clients (Moss et al., 2015; Wilburn and Wilburn, 2014; Wondirad, 2020), they have to measure their performance along these dimensions (Mersland and Strøm, 2007; Hermes and Hudon, 2018). This is because being able to combine financial sustainability with meeting social goals or in other words, achieving the 'double bottom line' of financial and social performance is a fundamental ideal of microfinance (Sinha, 2006; Allet, 2014).

However, such calls for the application of performance measurements have crept into the debate between the emerging schools of thought (*Welfarist and Institutionalist approaches*) brought about by the apparent shift to commercialised microfinance. As suggested by Olivares-Polanco (2005), the two schools of thought apart from differing on whether the commercial approach leads to 'Mission Drift' (a de-emphasis on the social mission of microfinance), also differ in their view on how performance should be assessed.

The Institutionalist vs. Welfarist Approach to Measurements

The performance of MFIs has traditionally been measured using either the *Welfarist* or *Institutionalist approaches* (Nawaz, 2010). The *Welfarists* in measuring performance of MFIs have advocated that the emphasis of measurements must be placed on assessing impact on the welfare of the poor. For the *Institutionalist,* the performance of MFIs should rather be assessed in terms of the institutions success in attaining self-sustainability and breadth of outreach (Morduch, 2000; Cheston and Reed, 1999; Olivares-Polanco, 2005). The different views expressed by the *welfarists* and *Institutionalists* have led to the emergence of different performance measurement methods, dimensions and key indicators or measures for performance. The *Institutionalists* approach basically employs two measurements of success namely outreach and sustainability (Olivares-Polanco, 2005; Nawaz, 2010). These are assessed with measures or indicators that may vary significantly between authors or organisations as they depend on the methodological approach being adopted, which in turn, depends on the need to give priority either to the supply or demand sides of the financial intermediation (Nawaz, 2010). Outreach for example, is measured in terms of depth (i.e., how poor the clients are and measured with indicators of various measures of loan size) and breadth (i.e., the number of people the program is reaching) (Olivares-Polanco, 2005; Lam et al., 2019). Financial indicators such as the Subsidy Dependency Index (SDI) proposed by Yaron (2001), Explicit Subsidy Dependency Index (ESDI) or the Implicit Subsidy Dependency Index (ISDI) are used in the measurement of the level of subsidy (Olivares-Polanco, 2005).

The *Welfarist* approach on the other hand, measures success by how well MFIs fulfil the needs of the poorest (Schreiner, 2002) and therefore advocate for the use of methods or measures aimed at establishing if the poverty reduction objectives of MFIs are being met (Olivares-Polanco, 2005). The *Welfarists*, make use of methods that seek to evaluate the impact of the microfinance intervention on clients by measuring changes in variables such as income levels, levels of production, sales, assets or the general wellbeing of the client (Alfaro, 1999; Bhatt & Tang, 2001; in Olivares-Polanco, 2005) with the underlying assumption that there may be an existence of a direct causal relationship between the loans and the changes in welfare indicators being observed (Rhyne, 1994; in Olivares-Polanco, 2005). The methodology to evaluate the impact therefore consists of, collecting data before (ex-ante) and after (ex-post), the microfinance intervention through direct interviews and at other times, through comparing the results against a control group (Olivares-Polanco, 2005).

The Double Bottom Line in Microfinance Delivery

The term "social performance" together with "financial performance" constitutes MFIs "double bottom line" and refers to social and economic impacts (Simanowitz, 2003 in Pawlak & Matul, 2004; Tulchin, 2003; Wilburn & Wilburn, 2014; Hermes & Hudon, 2018). Few programs in the field of development or commerce promote both economic and social performance more strongly as microfinance and effectively measuring, monitoring and reporting on the double bottom line (financial and social activities), therefore positions microfinance as a solution (Tulchin, 2003; Moss et al., 2015; Alaoui & Tkiouat, 2017; Leyer et al., 2015; Lam et al., 2019). Research on financial performance and financial efficiency of microfinance institutions has been stimulated by the new paradigm in microfinance that is, the debate between the financial system approach (*Institutionalist)* and poverty lending approach (*Welfarist*) in which the recent microfinance paradigm seems to favour the financial systems approach (Hermes & Lensink, 2007; Hermes & Hudon, 2018).

The Double Bottom Line and Performance Measurements in Microfinance

At the deeper level in the debate around the commercialisation of microfinance is the question that points to the precarious balance between the financial and social performances of MFIs (Sanae, 2008; Hermes & Hudon, 2018). Financial and social performance have for some time been treated separately with the former attracting more attention than the latter (Pawlak and Matul, 2004). According to Woller (2007), hundreds of studies examining the empirical relationship between financial and social performance have been produced by researchers with rather mixed findings across the range of studies. These studies mostly conducted among private firms engaged in corporate social responsibility (CSR), which may not always apply in microfinance, have found the existence of some distinct trends suggesting a significant and positive relationship between financial and social performance (Woller, 2007). At the very least these studies tend to rebut any general argument that may suggest an inappropriate and potentially dangerous diversion from the pursuance of profits when attention is paid to an institution's social performance (Woller, 2007; Hermes & Hudon, 2018; Lam et al., 2019; Adusei, 2021).

In terms of microfinance, the evidence of the relationship between financial and social objectives is rather mixed and inconclusive with the little literature available. It has been further suggested that the combination of social and financial measurements will in the long run, lead to a potential increase in financial returns through a better understanding of target clients and the efficient allocation of scarce resources thereby avoiding the unnecessary costs associated with ineffective actions (Pawlak & Matul, 2004). Social performance indicators as suggested, can be employed in ways that give complement to the achievement of wider organisational goals rather than obscure them and without them, organisations may possibly focus much more on financial indicators in the absence of countervailing social performance indicators (Hermes & Hudon, 2018; Copestake, 2007).

By combining social and financial indicators, managers it is argued, can successfully balance institutional and developmental impact trade-offs whiles at the same time improving overall performance and striving to attain the "double bottom line" (Lam et al., 2019; Pawlak & Matul, 2004; Wilburn & Wilburn, 2014; Hermes & Hudon, 2018). This invariably implies that social performance can be considered a complement to and in the same level with financial performance which can be used for comparing peer groups of MFIs (Zeller et al., 2003; Sierra et al., 2020; Adusei, 2021). This view though not shared by all in the microfinance industry, raises serious concerns of whether financial and social performance are complementary or rather contradictory objectives.

The debate as put forward is that the social impact of microfinance as suggested by Woller (2007), may be best achieved by creating financially sustainable MFIs (in other words, commercialised MFIs) with significant outreach. The logic that such large and sustainable MFIs with wider nets are bound to pick up more poor customers than would some MFIs that exclusively target the poor segment of society. Two arguments arise from this alteration. The first, which is the argument in favour of sustainability (financial performance) is that investing in resources to manage MFIs social performance is at best a gentle distraction from the principles underlying the approach for scale and sustainability and at worst, an expensive distraction that will unsuitably lead to a diversion of organisational resources (Woller, 2007). The second argument, which is against the sustainability approach is from those who argue that risks are abound when the antipoverty agenda of microfinance is discarded and in particular, the pursuit for scale and sustainability (profitability) will invariably create pressures for MFIs to target easier to reach and well-off group of clients, abandoning in the process, their traditional clientele (Woller, 2007; Hermes & Hudon, 2018). The resultant mission drift in his view, mean that the very poor, hard-to-reach persons MFIs were originally set-up to serve will once again be without access to financial services.

In answering in a true and false fashion, the question of whether a trade-off does occur between social and financial performance in microfinance, Woller (2007) has suggested that by conventional wisdom, the answer is true in that extending formal financial services to poor and difficult to reach clientele necessarily involve higher costs and lower per unit returns which makes it subsequently harder to scale up. The trade-off inherent in this relationship invariably creates incentives for MFIs to move up-market and to a better-off segment of the population, a phenomenon most commonly referred to as 'mission drift'. However, as often is the case, conventional wisdom he argues, does not necessarily represent the case in the real world as it is often frequently drawn from personal bias and limited anecdotal experience. The relationship between financial and social performance therefore is actually more complex than imagined as existing evidence suggests it is not always a negative relationship and even in certain cases, the relationship may actually be significantly positive, particularly in ones relating to social performance management (Sierra et al., 2020; Woller, 2007).

The contradicting viewpoints regarding pursuing both financial sustainability and social objectives according to Bédécarrats et al., (2009) remain, with some observers suggesting that they are incompatible, pointing to the problems of mission drift (Christen, 2001). Other experts and researchers however emphasize compatibility or synergy with the argument that social performance improves mutual trust, client participation and satisfaction which results in higher repayment rates and lower transactional costs (Sierra et al., 2020; Lapenu, 2007).

Cull et al. (2009) has suggested that in practice, microfinance entails distinct trade-offs between pursuing social objectives and maximizing financial performance. This is further reiterated by Olivares-Polanco (2005) who argued that though breadth and depth of outreach are desirable to both the *Welfarist* (poverty-lending approach) and the *Institutionalist* (financial system approach), they are still regarded contradictory objectives and therefore represent a trade-off for MFIs.

A strong financial orientation however does not necessarily have to result in a sacrifice of social objectives and vice versa (Hermes & Hudon, 2018; Woller, 2007). Furthermore, whether a trade-off exists between pursuing financial gains and upholding to social goals depends on the situation as examples exist of large sustainable MFIs that serve more poor clients and do so more profitably than MFIs that solely focus on poverty and operating in the same markets and some large MFIs that serve fewer poor clients than poverty-focused MFIs (Woller, 2007; Wondirad, 2020). As he points out "scale and sustainability do not guarantee poverty outreach, but a poverty focus does not rule out scale or sustainability" and "conversely, a poverty focus does not guarantee poverty outreach; but scale and sustainability can promote it".

CONCEPTUAL AND METHODOLOGICAL ISSUES IN MICROFINANCE PERFORMANCE MEASUREMENTS

Conceptual Issues in Microfinance Performance Measurements

The question for which this chapter attempts to answer is how to effectively combine the welfare/social and commercial/economic objectives of microfinance delivery across space and time. Thus, how do we effectively and efficiently measure the performance of social and economic objectives of Microfinance Institutions? So, we conceptualize the implications of double bottom line and how to measure the performance of MFIs in this scenario. We also look at the drivers and barriers of the assessment of performance of MFIs under the double bottom line context. In other words, can undertaking both financial and social performance measurements and reporting on them as Zeller et al. (2003) asserts, offer a better understanding of the phenomenon of mission drift? To help understand the linkages, Figure 1 is conceptualised.

The Microfinance "Schism" gives rise to traditionally two dimensions that we describe in this Chapter as Social and Economic Dimensions. The Social Dimension focuses on the welfare of society targeting poverty reduction whiles the Economic Dimension focuses on commercialisation that can lead to self-sustainability of the MFIs. For the double bottom line, we conceptualise a third approach referred to as the Blended Dimension. Whereas the Social Dimension is largely pursued by Not-for-Profit Microfinance Institutions (MFIs), the Economic Dimension is pursued by For-Profit MFIs. Whiles the Social and Economic Dimensions are distinct at the conceptual level, it is the combination of the two (Blended Dimension) that is felt at the practical or individual beneficiary level, hence our conceptualisation in **Figure 1.**

Methodological Issues in Microfinance Performance Measurements

Different methodological approaches and research designs have been in the past to assess performance of MFIs in relation to the Social and Economic Dimensions. Some of the research designs include experimental, quasi-experimental, longitudinal, and cross-sectional research designs with varying results across space and time. The most commonly used methodological approach by researchers in this field is the quantitative research methodology and design is the cross-sectional research design. The cross-sectional research design is best suited for studies aimed at finding the prevalence of a phenomenon, situation, problem, attitude or issues by taking a cross section of the population (Saunders et al., 2014). The cross-sectional design also helps at describing the pattern of relationship before some attempt is made at finding a causal relationship (Bryman and Bell, 2007; Bryman, 2004).

We are however, of the opinion that there is the need to rely on multiple sources of evidence (primary and secondary) including data from MFIs, views and perspectives from microfinance experts, practitioners as well as from clients of MFIs in order to comprehensively assess the performance of MFIs within the context of the double bottom line. This means that there must be a conscious effort to group MFIs as Commercial or For-Profit MFIs and Non-Commercial of Not-For-Profit MFIs. To be Commercial or For-Profit financial service provider implies that that the MFI operates within a regulated commercial environment that allows them to undertake what regulated activities. This involves, deposit taking and granting of credit for whatever tenor as stipulated by relevant country laws (e.g., in the case of Ghana under the Banking Act, 2004 as amended by the Non-Bank Financial Institution Act). Those MFIs that operate outside these regulations are the Non-Commercial/ Not-for-Profit.

Figure 1. Conceptualisation of the double bottom line in microfinance deliver
Source: Authors' Construct, 2022

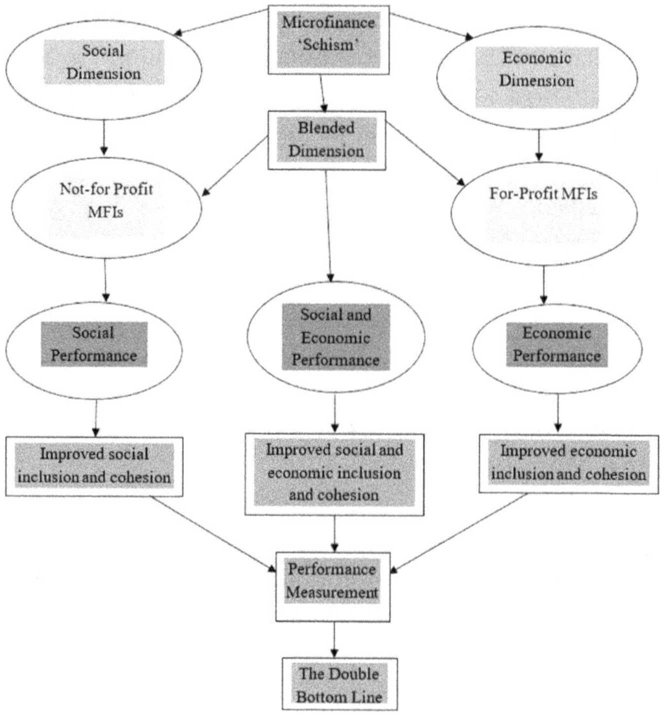

The methodological approaches use so far are based on the existing delineations of MFIs as purely Commercial/For-Profit/Economic or Non-commercial/Not-For-Profit/Social. Whereas these differentiations are conceptually possible and provide convenience to researchers in setting the boundaries of their analyses, it is practically not possible from the point of view of the populations that these MFI services are targeted. In other words, the differentiation or grouping of MFIs into the two broad categories of Commercial/Economic/For-Profit and Non-Commercial/Social/Not-For-Profit makes more sense only from the supply side and not the demand side. And the methodological approaches so far are more aligned to the supply side performance assessment than the demand side performance assessment. It must be recognised that financial services supplied by both categories of MFIs can lead to the same outcomes from the demand side. For instance, financial services supplied by Not-For-Profit MFIs to the poor can lead to increased farm productivity and profits leading to the same target outcome that For-Profit MFIs seek to achieve. Similarly, financial services supplied by For-Profit MFIs to the rich can lead to business expansions that create employment opportunities for the poor, leading to the same target outcomes pursued by Not-For-Profit MFIs. This leads us to what we describe as Convergence or Blended Dimension of MFIs.

Methodological approaches to assessing performance of MFIs irrespective of the conceptual category they belong must take into consideration the Convergence or Blended Dimension at the demand side. We identify two ways of blending or convergence in MFIs services delivery – Institutional and Services Convergence or Blending. Services Blending or Convergence focuses on the supply side where MFIs undertake to provide both social and economic dimensions of services. Here, For-Profit MFIs will in addition to services that target profit making organisations, business and individuals also provide services directly targeting the poor and vulnerable in society. This means that MFIs are required to become blended in their services provisioning and the easiest way to do this is for For-Profit MFIs to have robust Corporate Social Responsibility (CSR) functions for the one hand and Not-For-Profit MFIs to have strong business functions. Institutional Blending or Convergence will require that For-Profit and Not-For-Profit MFIs work hand in hand to enhance their impacts. To easily do this, For-Profit MFIs will implement their social (CSR) functions through the Not-For-Profit MFIs and the Not-for-Profit MFIs will implement their economic (business) functions through the For-Profit MFIs. This will build synergy for transformative microfinance services delivery across space and time.

PERFORMANCE MEASUREMENT PRACTICES OF MFIs

The performance management practices of MFIs have been transformed by the commercialisation of the microfinance industry. MFIs approach to commercialisation has significantly informed how they assess and report on their performance which hitherto they never found the need to do. The realisation for many MFIs across the different categories of microfinance institutions (Commercialised and Non-Commercialised) is that their path to continuous funding, growth and accountability to stakeholders is dependent on having a credible and appropriate performance management practices with which they can communicate their successes. Thus, MFIs notwithstanding their size, have adopted appropriate performance management practices to efficiently communicate their performance, especially to their donors/ investors. Various reasons have been provided as to why there is an overwhelming embrace of appropriate management practices in the face of the commercialisation of the industry. There is a key requirement by donors/investors for robust performance measurements using the appropriate mechanism for reporting key information to regulatory and supervisory authorities (in the case of Ghana for example, the Bank of Ghana). This is critical in determining success areas and areas for improvement and to draw future projections (for in-house auditing and future planning or forecasting) in an ever-competitive industry. These are consistent with the suggestion by Woller (2005; 2007); Moss et al., (2015); Wilburn and Wilburn (2014); Wondirad (2020) and others that, private investors expect transparency and full disclosure from MFIs, especially when faced with multiple investment options as they will only make investments that plausibly offer the highest risk-adjusted blended returns.

Considering the increasing realisation for the need to adopt appropriate performance measurement practices by MFIs and by virtue of the dual nature of microfinance, these institutions are required to strategically assess and report their performance along lines that communicate impact and sustainability. In the words, managers of MFIs must take into consideration what the commercialisation of the microfinance industry has done to the assessment of performance. This is important if they desire to continue to operate and also survive in today's competitive and challenging financial terrain. In other words, the adoption of performance management practices by MFIs in the face of commercialisation of the industry is one of a necessary decision for MFIs to make, especially if they hope not only to operate but also survive and compete in a highly regulated and competitive industry.

Indeed, it must be recognised that it is costly to undertake performance measurements, but the returns are worth the cost because robust performance measurements help MFIs to win the trust of donors and investors because in the absence of these indicators many donors and investors will walk away. So irrespective of the cost in terms of time and other things, performance measurement is a must for MFIs. It has therefore become imperative for MFIs to develop systems that measure progress towards the double bottom line and creditably account to investors and other external stakeholders, a suggestion that seems to be behind the decisions on the performance measurement practices of MFIs across space and time (Woller, 2005; Chikalipah, 2017).

The realisation therefore by institutions of how necessary performance management has become for their survival is driving MFIs to now measure their performance using key measures or indicators most, especially in the area of financial performance as pointed out earlier. It is therefore no surprise that some MFIs have adopted computer generated software such as 'the loan performance software', to help track their performance along some dimensions, as that will enable them to measure and report their performance more efficiently.

Overwhelmingly, across the different types of MFIs, the choice and use of measures or indicators for performance by MFIs are driven or informed by the requirements of donors/investors/partners. Decisions as observed are not based on gathering information to help with necessarily determining areas of strength and weaknesses of MFIs and subsequently improving their performance but rather, in an effort to fulfil the requirements of stakeholders, particularly donors and investors in order to sustain partnerships and ensure continuous funding and investments. Even for institutions not necessarily assessing performance with those key performance measures or indicators with the view of driving or ensuring continuous donor funding, they do so in the hope that, reporting their performance in such areas may attract potential donor or investor funding. This is because such reported measures are those inherently sought by investors to make investment decisions with regards to investing or partnering with an MFI. It is for these reasons that MFIs tend to measure and report on their performance using similar measures or indicators of performance.

As noted by Copestake (2007b) and others, the shift in focus of microfinance to a commercialised one is generating much interest and call for the application of performance measurements. Unfortunately, MFIs in the developing world primarily assess performance in response to external pressures mostly to meet donor/investor requirements. This suggests that the potential of microfinance as a development tool is far from being realised since they are not systematically and routinely undertaking performance measurements in response to internal demand. They rather do to it in response to external pressures. It is only when performance measurement practices are internalised by the MFIs that the potential of microfinance as a development tool could be realised (Chikalipah, 2017; Copestake, 2007b; Sierra et al., 2020).

IMPLICATIONS OF PERFORMANCE MEASUREMENTS FOR THE DOUBLE BOTTOM LINE

Eventually, the issue of mission drift invariably comes down to the fear or concern over a possible trade-off between the financial performance (becoming financially sustainable) and social performance (maintaining one's social commitments), the two common bottom lines expected of MFIs. With this in mind, this chapter is of the view that, an emphasis on financial performance by MFIs over their social performance will not only imply an inability on the part of MFIs to be able to track their progress along their two distinct mission objectives but may further suggest a departure from their social tenets, a position taken in microfinance literature.

The financial and social performance measurement practices of microfinance institutions as discussed above invariably indicate that, MFIs regardless of type and size have a very well structured and laid down practice for their financial performance measurements. These financial performance measurement practices make use of commonly recognised and widely accepted methodological approaches, measures or indicators of financial performance and are reported as such to donors/investors as well as regulatory and supervisory bodies in the industry for regulatory purposes. In addition, the financial performance measurement practices of MFIs make use of indicators or measures of performance that assess or report on all aspects of the financial performance or sustainability of MFIs. It stands therefore to reason and conclude that the financial performance measurement practices regardless of type (Commercial and Non-Commercial) and size, is appropriate and relevant in enabling them and their stakeholders to track the achievement of the MFIs along their financial objectives or mission.

However, in terms of progress towards keeping track of their social mission or achievements with their existing measurement practices, there is no commonality and agreement across the different types of MFIs. Many MFIs do not have any common measure or indicator with which they assess their social performance for the lack of knowledge on the existence of such measures or indicators and even for some MFIs, for the simple reason that it is not a sought-after measure of performance by their financial backers and therefore of no consequence for them to undertake. There appears to be no need for them to therefore spend valuable time and effort to incorporate social performance measurements in their performance measurement practices. Unlike Commercial MFIs that assess their social performance, Non-Commercial MFIs seem not to have industry standard set of social performance measures or indicators to assess their social performance. Most MFIs assess their social performance through one-off or periodic impact assessments carried out by staff, managers, donors and sometimes external contractors.

Commercial MFIs in particular have no way of keeping track with achievements if any at all, of their social mission or objectives with the type of measurement practices they have. Non-Commercial MFIs on the other hand, per their individual impact assessments and strategies or approaches may be able to track to an extent achievements or otherwise, of some aspects of their social objectives but nothing on commercial impacts. Thus, performance measurement practices of MFIs particularly those for Commercial MFIs, place greater emphasis on financial performance and reporting at the expense of social performance assessments. In other words, the performance measurement practices of MFIs most particularly of Commercial MFIs are biased towards financial performance. This indicates that MFIs in the face of commercialisation are expected to not only develop their capabilities for measuring their financial and social performance but also report on it in such a way that it stands the test of external monitoring (Zeller et al., 2003; Sierra et al., 2020). This means that MFIs have only been able to meet such an expectation in respect of their financial performance. MFIs are still very much lacking in meeting a similar level of expectation in respect of their social performance measurements, making it almost impossible for them to assess performance in terms of the double bottom line.

Meeting the dual expectations of economic and social performance should help to improve the understanding of possible trade-offs that may exist between economic returns and social returns on investments (Zeller et al., 2003; Lam et al., 2019; Sierra et al., 2020. However, as MFIs have not appropriately met this expectation, they cannot possibly measure their performance towards attainment of convergence or double bottom line of economic/commercial and social/non-commercial sustainability.

Indicators for Double Bottom Line Performance Measurements by MFIs

To be able to measure the double bottom line otherwise referred to as blended or convergence dimension in this chapter, we propose a set of social and economic indicators. The indicators across the dimensions (i.e., social and economic dimensions) are divided into performance or output indicators and impact or outcome indicators. These indicators must be monitored and measured in order to determine whether the double bottom line or convergence has been achieved or not. For a convergence to be achieved, each of the core areas must be at least equity in the two dimensions. The proceeding subsections provide further details.

Core Social Performance and Impact Indicators

The social performance indicators are as listed below:

- Proportion of target clients who are the poor, vulnerable and excluded (e.g., women, disabled, etc.).
- Extent of adaptation of microfinance services and products to meet the needs of the poor, vulnerable and excluded.
- Enhancement of social capital of target beneficiaries/clients (e.g., safety nets, social networks, etc.).
- Enhancement of political capital of target beneficiaries/clients (e.g., positions held, etc.)
- Enhancement of cultural capital of target beneficiaries/clients (e.g., ability to perform cultural rites, etc.)
- Participation of target beneficiaries/clients in decision at household and community levels (e.g., production decisions, reproduction decisions, etc.)

The social impact indicators are:

- Employment created for the poor, vulnerable and excluded populations (e.g., jobs created for women, disabled people, etc.).
- Position of individuals in their family and communities (e.g., influential member of household or community, etc.).
- Social capital building (e.g., group membership, networks, etc.).

- Health improvement (e.g., access to health care, payment of health bills, etc.).
- Child education (e.g., access to education, payment of school fees, etc.).

Core Economic Performance Indicators

The economic performance indicators are:

- Quality of portfolio (e.g., proportion of loans overdue, etc.).
- Efficacy and productivity (e.g., ability to achieve set goals, etc.).
- Financial management (e.g., liquidity, leverage, activity, etc.).
- Profitability (e.g., profitability rations, etc.)
- Quality and diversity of the financial services offered (e.g., types of services offered, etc.).

The economic impact indicators are:

- Change in income and expenditure of beneficiaries (e.g., income increases, consumption increases, etc.).
- Change in assets and living standard (e.g., increases in assets, improved standards of living, etc.).
- Food security (e.g., food availability, accessibility, affordability, stability, and utilization).
- Employment creation at community level (e.g., job opportunities, etc.).

CONCLUSION

The performance measurement practices of MFIs this Chapter conclude has been influenced by the commercialisation of the industry since it has significantly informed how MFIs assess and report on their performance, which hitherto they never found the need to do. The realisation for many of the MFIs is that their path to continuous funding, growth and accountability to stakeholders is dependent on having a credible and appropriate performance measurement practices, with which they can communicate their successes. Thus, the shift in focus of microfinance to a commercialised one, is generating much interest with calls for the application of performance measurements because of the realisation that it is only when financial institutions systematically and routinely undertake performance measurements in response to internal demand and not from external pressures that the potential of microfinance as a development tool can be realised. The chapter concludes therefore that overall, with the existing performance measurement practices of MFIs, MFIs can only adequately determine their progress or achievements along their financial objectives but are not in a position, especially with Commercial MFIs, to determine their progress and achievement along their social objectives. This makes it difficult to demonstrate the attainment of convergence in their performance measurements. The chapter therefore proposes a conceptual framework as well as core social and economic performance and impact indicators for measuring the attainment of the double bottom line or convergence. This when adopted will help to improve the understanding of MFIs on the possible trade-offs and complementarities that exist between economic returns and social returns on investments. It will help them to appropriately measure the social and economic objectives of microfinance as a poverty reduction tool.

REFERENCES

Adusei, M. (2021). Interest Rate and the Social Performance of Microfinance Institutions. *The Quarterly Review of Economics and Finance*, *80*, 21–30. doi:10.1016/j.qref.2021.01.009

Alaoui, Y. L., & Tkiouat, M. (2017). Assessing the Performance of Microfinance Lending Process Using AHP-Fuzzy Comprehensive Evaluation Method: Moroccan Case Study. *International Journal of Engineering Business Management*, *9*, 1–11. doi:10.1177/1847979017736692

Alfaro, G. L. N. (1999). *Sostenibilidad y Alcance en Instituciones Financieras de Desarrollo Pa ra la Micro y Pequena Empresa: Un Modelo Aplicado a Tres Casos de Estudio (Ademi Inc., Bancosol, S.A. y Génesis Empresarial)*. INCAE, Cento de Políticas Půblicas.

Allet, M. (2014). Why Do Microfinance Institutions Go Green? An Exploratory Study. *Journal of Business Ethics*, *122*(3), 405–424. doi:10.100710551-013-1767-2

Bank of Ghana (2011). Operating Rules and Guidelines for Microfinance Institutions. Notice to Banks, Non-Bank Financial Institutions and the General Public. *Notice No: BG/GOV/SEC/2011/04*

Bédécarrats F., Angora R.W., and Lapenu C., (2009). Is Social Performance Profitable? The Relationship between Social and Financial Performance in Microfinance. *Feature Articles, MicroBanking Bulletin, 19.*

Bhatt, N., & Tang, S. Y. (2001). Delivering Microfinance in Developing Countries: Controversies and Policy Perspective. *Policy Studies Journal: the Journal of the Policy Studies Organization*, *29*(2), 319–333. doi:10.1111/j.1541-0072.2001.tb02095.x

Bryman, A. (2004). Social Research Methods (2nd Ed), Oxford University Press.

Bryman, A., & Bell, E. (2007). *Business Research Methods* (2nd ed.). Oxford University Press.

CGAP. (2006). *Performance Indicators for Microinsurance Practitioners*. Consultative Group to Assist the Poorest (CGAP) Working Group on Microinsurance Workshop Report, Luxembourg.

Cheston, S., & Reed, L. (1999). Measuring Transformation: Assessing and Improving the Impact of Microcredit. *Journal of Microfinance, 1*(1), 20–43.

Chikalipah, S. (2017). Institutional Environment and Microfinance Performance in Sub-Saharan Africa. *African Development Review, 29*(1), 16–27. doi:10.1111/1467-8268.12235

Christen, R. P. (2001). Commercialisation and Mission Drift: The Transformation of Microfinance in Latin America. Consultative Group to Assist the Poor (CGAP), *Occasional Paper No 5*. Washington, D.C.

Copestake, J. (2007). Mainstreaming Microfinance: Social Performance Management or Mission Drift? *World Development, 35*(10), 1721–1738. doi:10.1016/j.worlddev.2007.06.004

Copestake, J. (2007b). Mission Drift-Understand It. Avoid It. Perspectives. *ESR Review, 9*(2), 21–25.

Cull, R., Demirguc-Kunt, A., & Morduch, J. (2009). Microfinance Trade-offs: Regulation, Competition and Financing. *The Handbook of Microfinance, world Scientific Publishing*. https://www.worldscibooks.com/economics/7645.html

Daher, L., & Le Saout, E. (2013). Microfinance and Financial Performance. *Strategic Change, 22*(1-2), 31–45. doi:10.1002/jsc.1920

Epstein, M. J., & Manzoni, J. F. (2006). Performance Measurement and Management Control: Improving Organisations and Society. Studies in Managerial and Financial Accounting, 16. JAI Press (Elsevier).

Goodman, P. (2006). Microfinance Investment Funds: Objectives, Players, Potential. Chapter 2 of Matthaus-Maier, I. and Pischke, J.D., (2006) (1 Ed.). In Microfinance Investment Funds. Leveraging Private Capital for Economic Growth and Poverty Reduction. Springer-Verlag Berlin Heidelberg: KfW.

Haider S.H., Asad M., Fatima M., and Ul Abidin R.Z., (2017). Microfinance and Performance of Micro and Small Enterprises; Does Training Have An Impact. *Journal of Entrepreneurship and Business Innovation, 4*(**1**)

Hermes, N., & Hudon, M. (2018). Determinants of the Performance of Microfinance Institutions: A Systematic Review. *Journal of Economic Surveys*, *32*(5), 1483–1513. doi:10.1111/joes.12290

Lam, S. S., Zhang, W., Ang, A. X., & Jacob, G. H. (2019). Reciprocity Between Financial and Social Performance in Microfinance Institutions. *Public Performance & Management Review*, *43*(1), 206–231. doi:10.1080/15309576.2019.1604386

Lapenu, C. (2007). *Recent Advances on Agricultural Finance: Supply and Strategies. A Review of Literature and Experience*. Paper for the International Conference "What Can Microfinance Contribute to Agriculture in Developing Countries?

Leyer, M., Heckl, D., & Moorman, J. (2015). Process Performance Measurement. In: vom Brocke J., and Rosemann., (2015). Hanbook on Business Process Management. 2nd (Ed). International Handbooks on Information Systems. Berlin, Heidelberg: Springer: 227-241. doi:10.1007/978-3-642-45103-4_9

Mersland, R., & Strøm, R. O. (2007). Performance and Corporate Governance in Microfinance Institutions. Munich Personal RePEc Archive (MPRA), Paper No. 3887, posted 7/11/2007. http: mpra.ub.uni-muenchen.de/3887/

Morduch, J. (2000). The Microfinance Schism. *World Development*, *28*(4), 617–629. doi:10.1016/S0305-750X(99)00151-5

Morduch, J. (2005). Smart Subsidies for Sustainable Microfinance, Finance for the Poor. *ADB Quarterly Newsletter of the Focal Point for Microfinance*, *6*, 1–7.

Moss, T. W., Neubaum, D., & Meyskens, M. (2015). The Effect of Virtuous Entrepreneurial Orientations on Microfinance Lending and Repayment: A Signalling Theory Perspective. *Entrepreneurship Theory and Practice*, *39*(1), 27–52. doi:10.1111/etap.12110

Nawaz, A. (2010). *Performance of Microfinance: The Role of Subsidies. Working Paper No.* Centre Emile Bernheim (CEB), Brussels Solvay Business School of Economics, Business and Management, Université Libre de Bruxelles (ULB), Belgium. doi:10/008.

Olivares-Polanco, F. (2005). Commercialising Microfinance and Deepening Outreach? Empirical Evidence from Latin America. *Journal of Microfinance*, *7*(2), 47–69.

Pawlak, K., & Matul, M. (2004). Realising Mission Objectives.A Promising Approach to Measuring the Social Performance of Microfinance Institutions. *Journal of Microfinance*, *6*(2), 1–25.

Rhyne, E. (1998). The Yin and Yang of Microfinance: Reaching the Poor and Sustainability. *MicroBanking Bulletin*, *2*, 6–9.

Saunders, M., Lewis, P., & Thornhill, A. (2012). *Research Methods for Business Students* (6th ed.). Pearson.

Sierra, J., Muriel-Patino, V., & Rodriguez-Lopez, F. (2020). The Quest for the Evaluation of Microfinance Social Performance. *Revista Iberoamericana de Estudios de Desarrollo*, *9*(2), 54–108. doi:10.26754/ojs_ried/ijds.351

Simanowitz, A. (2003). Microfinance, Poverty and Social Performance: Overview. *IDS Bulletin*, *34*(4), 1–9. doi:10.1111/j.1759-5436.2003.tb00085.x

Sinha, F. (2006). *Social Rating and Social Performance Reporting in Microfinance. Towards a Common Framework. EDA*. Ltd, Argidius Foundation and the SEEP Network.

The SEEP Network. (2005). *Measuring Performance of Microfinance Institutions: A Framework for Reporting, Analysing and Monitoring*. The SEEP Network and Alternative Credit Technologies, LLC.

Tulchin, D. (2003). Microfinance's Double Bottom Line. Measuring Social Return for the Microfinance Industry. Social Enterprise Associates (www.socialenterprise.NET) .

Wilburn, K., & Wilburn, R. (2014). The Double Bottom Line: Profit and Social Benefit. *Business Horizons*, *57*(1), 11–20. doi:10.1016/j.bushor.2013.10.001

Woller, G. (2005). *Proposal for a Social Performance Measurement Framework in Microfinance: The Six Aspects of Outreach. MicroREPORT No. 26*. USAID.

Woller, G. (2007). Trade-Offs between Social and Financial Performance. Perspectives. *ESR Review*, *9*(2), 14–19.

Wondirad H.A., (2020). Competition and Microfinance Institutions Performance: Evidence from India. *International Journal of Corporate Social Responsibility*, *5* (6).

Zeller, M., Lapenu, C., & Greeley, M. (2003). Measuring Social Performance of Micro-finance Institutions: A Proposal. *Social Performance Indicators Initiative (SPI) Final Report,* Submitted to Argidius Foundation and Consultative Group to Assist the Poorest (CGAP).

Chapter 3
Reducing Poverty Through Microfinance in Developing Economies:
Critical Perspectives From Literature

Yahaya Alhassan
https://orcid.org/0000-0001-6700-635X
University of Sunderland in London, UK

Hua Jin
University of Sunderland in London, UK

ABSTRACT

This chapter critically examines how microfinance has been used to reduce poverty rates in developing economies. To achieve this goal, a critical review of existing literature on microfinance outcomes on reducing poverty in developing countries was carried out. Based on the review of literature, this chapter concludes that microfinance positively impact poverty levels in developing countries. However, the chapter also shows that access to microfinance may contribute to higher poverty rates as some studies have produced marginal or negative success, while others yielded positive successes, making it very difficult to generalise the outcomes. The growing popularity of microfinance as a financial inclusion strategy and the high number of empirical studies on the subject have produced new evidence that needs further examination with complex research methodologies to determine its impact on poverty reduction, as outcomes of the current studies are mixed.

DOI: 10.4018/978-1-6684-5647-7.ch003

INTRODUCTION

All over the world, people who are poor are often left out of the formal financial systems. In developing countries where poverty levels are higher, the poor is completed excluded from the formal financial systems. In this regard, to address their financial needs, poor people, particularly in developing countries have created a wide range of informal financial systems. Besides, a number of private and public sector organisations have been purposely set up in recent times to address this financial exclusion gap. The term microfinance has become synonymous to these alternative informal and perhaps quasi-formal arrangements set up to offer financial services to the poor. The basic idea of microfinance is that; if poor people are provided access to financial assistance, including credit, they may be able to start or expand a microenterprise that will allow them to break out of poverty (Bindu and Aanchal, 2013).

Al-Amin and Mamun (2022) define microfinance as the provision of small loans to financially disadvantaged individuals who are unable to access such services from traditional financial institutions. Microfinance has also been defined from the perspective of beneficiaries. For instance, Hasan et al., (2022) described microfinance as a potential source of income to the needy and an effective tool that can assist low-income earners to improve on their living standards. A more comprehensive definition of microfinance is provided by Prathapet al., (2018) who refers to microfinance as the provision of both financial (loans, savings and insurance) and non-financial (financial literacy training, management skills development, group formation and self-confidence building) services to low-income earners and the self-employed.

Evidence from existing literature suggests that microfinance presents benefits to the unbanked in society (Alhassan et al., 2022; Malhotra, 2018; Mushtaq & Bruneau, 2019). For instance, Hussaini and Chibuzo (2018) have shown that microfinance is the most visible innovative policy for poverty reduction and financial inclusion in developing countries (Hussaini & Chibuzo, 2018). Besides, Ullah et al., (2020) provide evidence that the provision of microfinance does not merely reduce the occurrence of poverty but also the intensity and severity of it. Overall, several scholars (Hussain et al., 2019; Cai et al., 2020; Abdullah et al., 2021) regard microfinance, as a significant intervention for reducing poverty and achieving financial inclusion particularly in developing countries. In this regard, developing countries are increasingly looking towards microfinance as a means of decreasing poverty rates. This chapter contributes to this ongoing search by reviewing existing literature to aid our understanding of how microfinance has contributed to reducing poverty rates in developing nations. The purpose of this chapter, therefore, is to critically examine how microfinance has been used to reduce poverty rates in developing economies. Towards this goal, this chapter provides a critical review of existing literature on microfinance outcomes on reducing poverty in developing countries.

In order to present a coherent and concise review of the literature on microfinance outcomes on poverty reduction in developing countries, the review of microfinance literature is divided into three sections which, in the judgement of the author, provide a clear picture of the relationship between microfinance and poverty reduction in developing countries. In each section ranging from methodologies for accessing microfinance impact on poverty to the evidence of actual impact of microfinance on poverty levels, the relevant peer-reviewed articles are discussed. Accordingly, the remainder of the chapter proceeds as follows: In the next section, we provide the background to the chapter. This is followed by a discussion of the main theme of the chapter: reducing poverty through microfinance. A review of methodologies for assessing microfinance impact on poverty rates in developing countries follows next. Existing literature on how the outcomes of microfinance experiments are measured is reviewed next. The third section reviews outcomes of microfinance experiments on poverty rates in developing countries. Solutions, recommendations and future research directions are also provided.

BACKGROUND

From the various definitions of microfinance, it is obvious that microfinance is intricately linked to poverty reduction in developing countries (Bakhtiari, 2011; Imai et al., 2010; Nawaz, 2010; Chowdhury, 2009). For example, Kristof (2009) argue that microfinance is the most visible innovative policy for poverty reduction and financial inclusion in developing countries. The basic idea of microfinance is that; if poor people are provided access to financial assistance, including credit, they may be able to start or expand a microenterprise that will allow them to break out of poverty (Bindu and Aanchal, 2013). In this regard, Bakhtiari, (2011) has shown that access to microfinance can help low-income earners build their assets and improve their income earning capacity leading to an improvement in their quality of life. Likewise, using a cross country data in Bangladesh, Imai et al., (2012) found that the provision of microfinance does not merely reduce the occurrence of poverty but also the intensity and severity of it. This view is consistent with Khandker and Samad (2013) who also discovered that the provision of microfinance could perhaps help users earn more income, thus helping them out of the cycle of poverty. Furthermore, microfinance has been reported to have alleviated poverty of women, considered marginalised in some societies in both developed and developing countries (Islam, 2012).

The poverty reducing effect of access to microfinance in the context of developing economies was further confirmed by Annim (2018) who argues that overall, microfinance positively correlates with poverty rates in Africa, particularly in Ghana. Indeed, Hagan (2018) also examined the contribution of microfinance to poverty alleviation in a developing country and found "a positive link between the provision of loans by microfinance institutions and the minimization of economic poverty within the study area." Besides, Addae-Korankye (2020) has shown that microfinance has contributed significantly to the transformation of local economies in Africa by helping to reduce poverty and improving the living standards of the poor.

However, Ebomuche et al., (2014) suggest that the role of microfinance on poverty reduction is still unclear. In this context, Van Rooyen et al., (2012) have found that microfinance has both positive and negative impact on poverty alleviation as their findings suggest that microfinance increases both capital and loan stocks of beneficiaries. Similarly, Bateman (2012) established that microfinance has rather left several rural communities with more debts, making them more impoverished than before. In fact, he argues that even prominent advocates of microfinance now accept that microfinance has failed to impact poverty positively. The analysis and evaluation of the above studies suggest the role of microfinance on poverty alleviation is inconclusive and therefore requires rigorous evaluation to determine the exact impact of microfinance on poverty reduction in developing countries. Therefore, having discussed the background to microfinance and its relationship with poverty rates in developing countries, the attention of the chapter now is the review of literature on how poverty rates could be reduced through microfinance in developing economies.

REDUCING POVERTY THROUGH MICROFINANCE IN DEVELOPING ECONOMIES

Various scholars (Al-shami et al., 2021; Miled et al., 2022) regard microfinance, as a significant intervention for reducing poverty and achieving financial inclusion particularly in developing countries. Undoubtedly microfinance has been shown to be the most visible innovative policy for poverty reduction and financial inclusion in developing countries (Hussaini & Chibuzo, 2018). The basic idea of microfinance is that; if poor people are provided access to financial assistance, including credit, they may be able to start or expand a microenterprise that will allow them to break out of poverty (Bindu & Aanchal, 2013). In this regard, this section aims to review existing microfinance literature to aid our understanding of how microfinance has been used to reduce poverty rates in developing countries. The review is divided into three themes: Methodologies for assessing microfinance impact on poverty, measurement of outcomes of microfinance experiments and outcomes of microfinance experiments on poverty rates in developing countries.

Methodologies for Assessing Microfinance Impact on Poverty Reduction

In this section, the relevant literature on microfinance impact studies is reviewed with the view to determine gaps in the methodological approaches used in assessing microfinance impact on poverty rates in developing countries. Various studies on microfinance impact have been carried out on different schemes of microfinance particularly, the use of microfinance for poverty alleviation and improving living standards of the poor (Chhorn, 2021; Al-shami et al., 2021; Miled et al., 2022). Indeed, in some cases, studies on the impact of microfinance experiments are conducted to determine outcomes of microfinance projects (Chowdhury et al., 2020). Besides, such studies are also often used as a tool for monitoring the continuity of microfinance projects (Mazumder, 2022).

Analysis of existing literature suggests that various methods (ranging from randomised and non-randomised approaches) have often been used in conducting studies on microfinance experiments on poverty alleviation in developing countries (Awojobi, 2019). For instance, Khan and Bedi (2022), used a randomised test to determine microfinance impact on poverty in Pakistan. Similarly, Banerjee et al. (2015) conducted a randomised assessment of the impact of microfinance on poor households in selected slums in India. Besides Hossain (2012) used a randomised evaluation to determine the social impact of microfinance in Bangladesh.

The outcomes of the above studies provide inconclusive evidence about microfinance impact on poverty reduction. However, Mustapha et al. (2019) argue that in some cases outcomes of microfinance impact studies suggest that the provision of informal credit such as microfinance leads to poverty reduction and improved living standards of beneficiaries. For example, using a randomised analysis, Khan et al. (2021) demonstrated that the provision of microfinance results in poverty reduction Pakistan. Using the financing constraints methodology, Hartarska et al. (2013) found that the presence of microfinance institutions has improved access to financial services for poor people in 15 countries across Central Asia. Similarly, using the triangulation method Kwak and Lee (2014) established that the provision of microfinance has contributed to poverty reduction in 78 countries. Furthermore, using participatory programme evaluation methods Alam and Azad (2021) have shown that microfinance institutions are providing financial resources for the poor to set up businesses, which helped to reduce poverty in Ethiopia. This is consistent with Wondirad (2020) who found that the provision of microfinance services increased the income of individuals living in poor communities in Kenya. Besides, Anglelucci et al., (2015) used a clustered randomised trial to show that the provision of microcredit impacts positively on poverty reduction. These positive outcomes suggest that perhaps microfinance is a viable strategy for poverty alleviation and improving living standards in poor communities in developing countries.

The randomised approach has been frequently used by researchers in examining microfinance impact because of the successful outcomes of the approach (Banerjee et al., 2015; Khan et al., 2021; Khan & Bedi, 2022). According to Muriu (2020) such investigations are often conducted by comparing outcomes of treatment and control groups. The control and treatment groups are usually selected to show the same features except that the treatment group is a receiver of microfinance services (Cai et al., 2020). Similarly, Rui and Nie (2021) argue that samples for the treatment group are often chosen from the target population of individuals or communities who experience the benefits of microfinance whilst samples for the control group are selected from the target population who do not benefit from microfinance intervention. Besides, Shanmugan and Baria (2019) suggest that the units of analysis depend on the scope of the microfinance intervention. For example, individuals are often the unit of analysis if the benefits of microfinance intervention are received on an individual basis. Conversely, if the intervention is received on a group basis, then the group becomes the unit of analysis (Fofana et al., 2015). Prakash (2018) argues that in some cases such as regional studies; countries, towns or regions can also be the unit of analysis for microfinance impact investigations on poverty reduction.

However, some methodological challenges that could adversely affect the outcomes and results of randomised control trials have been reported by some researchers (Hughes et al., 2016). In this context, Osmani (2015) argue that methodological mistakes such as wrong measurement indicators and lack of data sets may negatively affect results and outcomes of microfinance experiments on poverty alleviation. For example, most of the microfinance impact studies conducted on poverty reduction in developing countries were mainly carried out without a baseline (Rajbanshi, 2015). Perhaps the absence of baseline information may have prevented these investigations from examining the circumstances of beneficiaries prior to the receipt of microfinance services. This view is consistent with Duong and Nghiem (2014) who concluded that several microfinance impact investigations in developing countries were conducted without any baseline study to determine the counterfactual conditions of microfinance beneficiaries. The major weaknesses of the such investigations are that the research participants were asked to provide an account of their circumstances prior to the microfinance intervention and at the time of the investigation. Perhaps, this is what prompted Roodman and Morduch (2014) to question the methodological approach used in these studies and argued that evidence of microfinance impact on poverty alleviation is weak in all such investigations. Other potential evidence of weak methodological approaches used to examine microfinance impact on poverty rates are studies that have failed to control for sample selection which often leads to an overestimation of microfinance impact on beneficiaries (Cai et al., 2020).

Recent investigations of microfinance outcomes on poverty using methodologies such as surveys, experimental and pipeline designs have also shown some major weaknesses in research design and high level of bias that makes such approaches very problematic and difficult to replicate using other methods (Duvendack et al., 2014). For instance, a quasi-experimental study on microfinance impact on poverty reduction conducted by Khandker and Samad (2014) suggests that the provision of microfinance to women improves poverty rates. However, using the same survey data Chemin (2008) employed the propensity score matching to examine the impact of microfinance poverty reduction and found no relationship. Perhaps, it is these different outcomes that prompted Duvendack and Palmer-Jones (2012) to further examine the robustness of the propensity score matching approach used by Chamin to investigate microfinance impact on poverty alleviation. Interestingly, they too concluded that microfinance impact on poverty rates varies by borrower's gender. They, therefore, argued that the reported positive relationship between microfinance interventions and poverty rates are not consistent with various research data. Setboonsarng and Parpiev (2010) also used the propensity score matching approach to address selectivity bias in a microfinance impact study on poverty reduction in Pakistan. However, a comparison of the outcome of their study with a number of microfinance impact investigations on poverty rates carried out by Runsinarith, (2014) using the same primary data but employing ordinary least squares analysis (OLS) and logit estimation techniques produced different outcomes. These mixed results and interpretation are contentious and provide evidence of methodological challenges in microfinance impact investigations on poverty reduction in developing countries (Imai & Azam, 2012).

Furthermore, analysis of existing microfinance literature suggests that several studies have examined microfinance impact on poverty reduction, microenterprise development and women empowerment at the same (Banerjee et al., 2015). This combined evaluation of the impact of microfinance is quite common in developing countries (Van Rooyen et al., 2012; Ksoll et al., 2016). For example, Niaz and Iqbal (2019) examined the effect of microfinance on women empowerment, poverty alleviation, and social status of women at the same time in a study in Pakistan. Although, the results showed that exposure to microfinance has a positive impact on poverty but perhaps, a focus on examining the effects of microfinance on only poverty reduction could produce a more robust outcome of the microfinance experiment on poverty rates. Similarly, Gakpo et al., (2021) attempted to investigate microfinance impact on poverty reduction, small and medium enterprises and employment rate at the same time. The results show that there is a strong association between microfinance and poverty alleviation. However, Karlan and Goldberg (2007) have shown that examining the outcomes of microfinance intervention on poverty reduction independently is more appropriate as it offers policymakers the opportunity to develop more targeted strategies. Perhaps, this was what informed Okibo and Makanga (2014) decision to examine the effect of microfinance on poverty reduction in Kenya. The study focused on credit facilities provided by microfinance institutions and their clients perception on income improvement and or reduced poverty levels. The study concluded that microfinance is strategy for poverty reduction and the best vehicle for providing credit to the poor. Conceivably, the best methodological approach for investigating the effect of microfinance on poverty rate is by examining the outcomes of microfinance intervention on poverty reduction independently as shown in Okibo and Makanga (2014) and proposed by Karlan and Goldberg (2007).

Further evidence of the use of different methodologies to assess the impact of microfinance is provided by Al Mamun et al., 2014; Salia and Mbwambo, 2014; Tarozzi et al., 2013. Using a cross-sectional design Al Mamun et al., (2014) found that that use of microfinance increased living standards and reduce poverty rates. Similarly, Crépon et al. (2011) used an experimental design to examine the impact of microfinance on poverty rates in Morocco and found a reduction in the levels of poverty associated with the use of the microfinance. On the other hand, Salia and Mbwambo (2014) used survey data from 217 borrowers and 183 non-borrowers in Tanzania and found that borrowers improved their living standards significantly better than non-borrowers. Furthermore, using a randomized controlled trial, Tarozzi et al. (2013) concluded that the use of microfinance in Tanzania increased income levels and the number of people employed. Besides, a survey on the Zakoura Microcredit Foundation conducted by Isaia, (2005) in Morocco found that the earning capacity of people who received support from microfinance institutions was 58% higher than the individuals who did not receive any credit. Perhaps, the growing popularity of microfinance as a financial inclusion strategy and the high number of empirical studies on the subject have produced new evidence that needs further examination with complex research methodologies to determine its impact on poverty reduction as outcomes of the current studies are mixed.

How Microfinance Influence Poverty Levels

This section provides a review of microfinance literature with the view to determine how microfinance influence poverty levels. Evidence from Boateng et al., (2015) suggests that microfinance institutions have produced some positive outcomes on poverty in deprived communities around the world. The question however is how is the effect of microfinance measured? This section contributes to this debate by reviewing existing literature to aid our understanding of how microfinance contributes to the journey from poverty to reduced poverty or poverty alleviation.

Analysis of Al-shami et al. (2021) suggest that microfinance improves poverty levels through increased borrowers' incomes to total eradication or alleviation of poverty. This is consistent with Chhorn (2021) who argues that access to microfinance is associated with poverty reduction and increased per capita income of households. Similarly, Miled et al., (2022) have shown that microfinance loans have improved the relative income position of the poor in developing countries. However, Elsafi et al. (2020) have shown that the provision of microfinance affects poverty levels through various channels, not only through improved borrower's total income. With regards to the positive impact of microfinance on poverty, evidence from Khan et al. (2021) suggest that access to microfinance credit may enable the borrower employ people, who if poor will cause the poverty level to reduce through the income earned from the employment. Besides, the existence of microfinance institutions in a poor community may provide access to credit and reduced interest rates (Chomen, 2021). Consequently, if people become less poor due to the credit access and low interest rates, this will have a positive effect on poverty rates independent of what may happen to the borrower's income (Santoso et al., 2020).

In addition to the above, new economic or business activities often stimulated by access to microfinance loans have the potential to reduce poverty levels (Zeb, *et al*, 2021). Besides, the new economic activities related to access microfinance loans often raise the purchasing power of poor people, thereby helping to reduce or alleviate poverty levels (Chhorn, 2021). More so, the outcome of Madonda et al., (2020) suggest that access to microfinance enables the beneficiaries to engage in income-generating activities such as small business and agricultural activities. The study further shows that the youth improved their business activities due to the credit provided. Besides the study concluded that access to microfinance has a potential to increase income of the youth, asset ownership, and improve household livelihoods.

However, there are other narratives that suggest that access to microfinance may contribute to higher poverty rates (Tasos et al., 2020; Boussetta, 2022). For instance, Ewusie et al., (2021) provide evidence that suggest that access to microfinance loans may expose borrowers to a higher risk of low level of disposable income, which has the potential to force the borrow to sell off their assets to maintain loan repayments. This undoubtedly will have a negative impact on the borrower's long-term income level and purchasing power. This is consistent with Kaberia and Muathe (2022) who have established that microfinance has rather left several rural communities with more debts, making them more impoverished than before.

Furthermore, most investigations on the impact of microfinance often show that access to microfinance reduce poverty in households. Regrettably, however, most of these investigations repeatedly fail to show the increase in household inequalities as a result of access to microfinance loan. For instance, the account of Miled et al. (2022) suggests that microfinance loans can lead to improved income position of the poor but increase inequalities in developing countries. The next section reviews literature on microfinance outcomes on poverty reduction in developing countries.

Microfinance and Poverty Reduction

Poverty has often been defined based on inequality factors in society. For instance, Lloyds-Jones and Rakodi (2014) described poverty as a situation where an individual's or a household's income is not sufficient to enable them to acquire goods and services required for a decent living. Similarly, Hagenaars (2014) defines poverty as a condition where households' needs are not adequately satisfied. Besides, Elhadary and Samat (2012) found that often the magnitude of poverty in a community is due to the failure of policymakers to address inequality factors in the community over a period of time. Perhaps, this is what prompted Hatta and Ali (2013) to suggest that poverty alleviation strategies are designed to provide resources to disadvantaged communities for the purpose of satisfying their basic needs adequately. Accordingly, Townsend (2014) argues that the IMF, the World Bank and other international organisations are known to have made concerted efforts to reduce poverty in several countries through financial grants and food aid. However, Alvi and Senbeta (2012) found that such handouts provide short term relief with very limited impact on poverty reduction in low-income households, particularly in developing countries.

Omar and Inaba (20120) has shown that achieving greater financial inclusion is perhaps very important if the gap in poverty levels between the rich and poor is to be reduced. This view is supported by Al-Amin and Mamun (2022) as the author argues that providing microfinance credit to the poor could improve their income level and achieve food security. Similarly, Alhassan et al., (2022) have found that increasing access to microcredit by low-income earners engenders greater economic and social benefits (increased income, assets accumulation, and better education) to such borrowers. Likewise, (Zeb, *et al*, 2021) have demonstrated that the provision of microfinance can help create a workable project for poverty reduction. In this regard, Madonda et al., (2020) conclude that microfinance is perhaps the most potent strategy for promoting microbusinesses for low-income earners to move them out of poverty. Indeed, most microfinance schemes designed for microenterprise development are often aimed at reducing poverty (Chhorn, 2021).

According to Sign and Chudasama (2020) outcomes of microfinance projects have often been measured by their contribution to poverty reduction. Similarly, Alhassan et al., (2022) argue that microfinance positive outcomes are frequently determined by assessing the microfinance institution's ability to help low-income households and "unbanked individuals" out of poverty. For instance, the provision of microfinance in Eastern Europe has been found to have helped low-income earners increased their assets, level of income and standard of living (Hartarska et al., 2013).

Equally, other studies have also found that access to microfinance loans has led to increases in savings and per capita income of beneficiaries in both developing countries (Al-shami et al., 2021; Al-Amin and Mamun, 2022; Alhassan et al., 2022). More so, Khanker and Samad (2013) have demonstrated that the provision of microfinance in East Asia is helping financially disadvantaged people out of poverty annually. Perhaps, it is in this context that Khan et al., (2021) concludes that access to microfinance enables low-income earners to acquire goods and services required for a decent living.

Other studies, however, do not support the notion that the provision of microfinance always reduce poverty. For example, analysis of Boussetta (2022) suggest the provision of microfinance alone is unlikely to move people out of poverty. They argue that other factors such as the creation of jobs and good infrastructure are required together with microfinance in order to reduce poverty. Similarly, Van Rooyen et al., (2012) have found that in some cases, access to microfinance can increase poverty due to the high-interest rates charged by microfinance institutions. Besides, Pomi (2019) demonstrates that the expansion of microcredit to rural households in Bangladesh only increased household consumption but no significant impact on poverty alleviation. Furthermore, Crepon et al. (2014) examined microfinance outcomes and found that in the short to medium term, microfinance positively impacted on the capital stock of microentrepreneurs but shown no influence on poverty reduction. Perhaps, the negative outcomes of microfinance on poverty alleviation reported by various studies suggest that the use of microcredit as a poverty reduction strategy is increasingly diminishing. Besides, the implication of the negative experiences of microfinance experiments on poverty alleviation indicates that microfinance institutions are gradually becoming weak. Therefore, should microfinance be remodelled in line with Mersland and Strom (2014) sustainability paradigm to promote growth for microfinance institutions? May be, providing microcredit using the new sustainability model could yield positive results on poverty reduction and achieve greater financial inclusion in disadvantaged communities.

SOLUTIONS AND RECOMMENDATIONS

Although this chapter found that overall a positive relationship exists between microfinance and poverty reduction, there are a number of methodological challenges that need to be addressed.

First, investigations on microfinance effect on poverty levels should first conduct a baseline study to determine the circumstances of beneficiaries prior to the receipt of microfinance services.

Secondly, most studies have examined microfinance impact on poverty reduction, microenterprise development and women empowerment at the same. However, examining the outcomes of microfinance intervention on poverty reduction independently is more appropriate and recommended as it offers policymakers the opportunity to develop more targeted strategies. focus on examining the effects of microfinance on only poverty reduction could produce a more robust outcome of the microfinance experiment on poverty rates.

The growing popularity of microfinance as a financial inclusion strategy and the high number of empirical studies on the subject have produced new evidence that needs further examination with complex research methodologies to determine its impact on poverty reduction as outcomes of the current studies are mixed.

Investigations on microfinance impact on poverty levels should adopt methodologies that control for sample selection to resolve the common issue of overestimation of microfinance impact on beneficiaries.

Providing microfinance using the new sustainability model could yield positive results on poverty reduction and achieve greater financial inclusion in disadvantaged communities.

It is further recommended that investigations designed to determine microfinance impact should be conducted to determine outcomes on beneficiaries as mots studies on the impact of microfinance experiments are conducted to determine microfinance projects.

FUTURE RESEARCH DIRECTIONS

This chapter makes significant contributions to our understanding of the relationship between microfinance and poverty levels in developing countries. However, the evidence suggests that the effect of microfinance on poverty reduction is inconclusive as some studies have produced marginal or negative success, while others yielded positive successes making it very difficult to generalise the outcomes. Further research using more appropriate research methodologies is needed to determine the appropriate impact of microfinance on poverty reduction in developing countries.

Furthermore, the growing popularity of microfinance as a financial inclusion strategy and the high number of empirical studies on the subject have produced new evidence that needs further examination with complex research methodologies to determine its impact on poverty reduction as outcomes of the current studies are mixed.

This chapter also provide evidence from existing literature that demonstrates that most of the microfinance impact studies conducted on poverty reduction in developing countries were mainly carried out without a baseline. Further research with baseline study to determine the counterfactual conditions of microfinance beneficiaries is needed to accurately determine the effect of microfinance on poverty levels.

CONCLUSION

The term microfinance has become synonymous to the informal and perhaps quasi-formal arrangements set up to offer financial services to the poor. The effect of microfinance on poverty rates in developing countries and elsewhere has been widely reported by various studies. In this regard, this chapter sought to review existing literature aimed at reducing poverty levels in developing countries. Overall, the literature reviewed shows mixed but generally positive outcomes and conclusions.

The first conclusion drawn from the literature reviewed is that most of the studies attempted to determine overall microfinance impact rather than measuring the impact of microfinance on only poverty reduction. The best methodological approach for investigating the effect of microfinance on poverty rate is by examining the outcomes of microfinance intervention on poverty reduction independently.

The second observation from the literature reviewed is that some methodological mistakes such as wrong measurement indicators and lack of data sets may have negatively affected the results and outcomes of microfinance experiments on poverty alleviation.

In addition to the above, a conclusion that can be drawn from the literature reviewed is that several microfinance impact investigations in developing countries were conducted without any baseline study to determine the counterfactual conditions of microfinance beneficiaries. Other potential evidence of weak methodological approaches used to examine microfinance impact on poverty rates are studies that have failed to control for sample selection which often leads to an overestimation of microfinance impact on beneficiaries.

The reported positive relationship between microfinance interventions and poverty rates are not consistent with various research data. These mixed results and interpretation are contentious and provide further evidence of methodological challenges in microfinance impact investigations on poverty reduction in developing countries.

This chapter also concludes that microfinance improves poverty levels through increased borrowers' incomes to total eradication or alleviation of poverty. Besides, access to microfinance credit may enable the borrower employ people, who if poor will cause the poverty level to reduce through the income earned from the employment. Furthermore, the new economic or business activities often stimulated by access to microfinance loans have the potential to reduce poverty levels.

Overall, the literature reviewed provide evidence that microfinance positively impact poverty levels. However, there are other narratives that suggest that access to microfinance may contribute to higher poverty rates as some studies have produced marginal or negative success, while others yielded positive successes making it very difficult to generalise the outcomes.

REFERENCES

Abdullah, W. M. Z. B. W., Zainudin, W. N. R. A. B., Ismail, S. B., Haat, M. H. C., & Zia-Ul-Haq, H. M. (2021). The Impact of Microfinance on Households' Socioeconomic Performance: A Proposed Mediation Model. *The Journal of Asian Finance. Economics and Business*, *8*(3), 821–832.

Addae-Korankye, A. (2020). Historical emergence of microfinance and the microfinance sector in Ghana. *Business Management Dynamics*, *10*(2), 1.

Al-Amin, M. and Mamun, H.A.R., 2022. Exploring the impact of microfinance on socio-economic development: Empirical evidence from Balunnaghar Village. *International Journal of Social Science and Human Research ISSN (print)*, 2644-0679.

Al-Mamun, A., Wahab, S. A., Mazumder, M. N. H., & Su, Z. (2014). Empirical investigation on the impact of microcredit on women empowerment in urban Peninsular Malaysia. *Journal of Developing Areas*, *48*(2), 287–306. doi:10.1353/jda.2014.0030

Al-shami, S. A., Al Mamun, A., Rashid, N., & Al-shami, M. (2021). Microcredit Impact on Socio-Economic Development and Women Empowerment in Low-Income Countries: Evidence from Yemen. *Sustainability*, *13*(16), 9326. doi:10.3390u13169326

Alam, P. and Azad, I., 2021. Impact of Microfinance on income and employment of women in Jigjiga, Ethiopia. *Int. J. Econ. Bus. Adm*, 373-381.

Alhassan, Y., Kuagbela, F., Nurokina, C. D., & Appiah, B. (2022). *The Role of Microfinance in Africa: A Review of Outcomes from Ghana and Nigeria*. Microfinance and Sustainable Development in Africa.

Alvi, E., & Senbeta, A. (2012). Does foreign aid reduce poverty? *Journal of International Development*, *24*(8), 955–976. doi:10.1002/jid.1790

Angelucci, M., Karlan, D., & Zinman, J. (2015). Microcredit impacts: Evidence from a randomized microcredit program placement experiment by Compartamos Banco. *American Economic Journal. Applied Economics*, *7*(1), 151–182. doi:10.1257/app.20130537

Annim, S. K. (2018). Outreach and the poverty-reducing effect of microfinance in Ghana. *Enterprise Development & Microfinance*, *29*(2), 145–171. doi:10.3362/1755-1986.17-00020

Awojobi, O. N. (2019). Microcredit as a strategy for poverty reduction in Nigeria: A systematic review of literature. *Global Journal of Social Sciences*, *18*(1), 53–64. doi:10.4314/gjss.v18i1.5

Bakhtiari, S. (2011). Microfinance and poverty reduction: Some international evidence. *International Business and Economics Research Journal (IBER), 5(12.*
Banerjee, A., Duflo, E., Glennerster, R. and Kinnan, C., 2015. The miracle of microfinance? Evidence from a randomized evaluation. *American Economic Journal. Applied Economics*, *7*(1), 22–53.

Bateman, M. (2012). The role of microfinance in contemporary rural development finance policy and practice: Imposing neoliberalism as 'best practice'. *Journal of Agrarian Change*, *12*(4), 587–600. doi:10.1111/j.1471-0366.2012.00376.x

Bindu, A., & Aanchal, S. (2013). A comprehensive literature on impacts of microfinance. *Online International Interdisciplinary Research Journal: An International Multidisciplinary Journal*, *3*(5), 346–358.

Boateng, G. O., Boateng, A. A., & Bampoe, H. S. (2015). Microfinance and poverty reduction in Ghana: Evidence from policy beneficiaries. *Review of Business & Finance Studies*, *6*(1), 99–108.

Boussetta, A. (2022). Microfinance, Poverty and Education. *Comparative Economic Studies*, *64*(1), 86–108. doi:10.105741294-021-00145-4

Cai, S., Park, A., & Wang, S. 2020. Microfinance can raise incomes: evidence from a randomized control trial in China. *HKUST Business School Research Paper*, (2020-006).

Chemin, M. (2008). The benefits and costs of microfinance: Evidence from Bangladesh. *The Journal of Development Studies*, *44*(4), 463–484. doi:10.1080/00220380701846735

Chhorn, D. (2021). Microfinance illusion, poverty and welfare in Cambodia. *Journal of the Asia Pacific Economy*, *26*(4), 694–719. doi:10.1080/13547860.2020.1826074

Chomen, D. A. (2021). The role of microfinance institutions on poverty reduction in Ethiopia: The case of Oromia Credit and Saving Share Company at Welmera district. *Future Business Journal*, *7*(1), 1–10. doi:10.118643093-021-00082-9

Chowdhury, M. S., Ahmmed, F., & Hossain, I. (2020). Methodological dilemma in microfinance research: Applicability of a qualitative case study design. *Qualitative Report*, *25*(2), 271–290. doi:10.46743/2160-3715/2020.3962

Crépon, B., Devoto, F., Duflo, E., & Parienté, W. (2011). *Impact of microcredit in rural areas of Morocco: Evidence from a Randomized Evaluation*. MIT Working Paper.

Crépon, B., Devoto, F., Duflo, E., & Pariente, W. (2014), *Estimating the impact of microcredit on those who take it up: Evidence from a randomized experiment in Morocco*. Working Paper, MIT.

Duong, H. A., & Nghiem, H. S. (2014). Effects of microfinance on poverty reduction in Vietnam: A pseudo-panel data analysis. *Journal of Accounting. Finance and Economics*, *4*(2), 58–67.

Duvendack, M., & Palmer-Jones, R. (2012). High noon for microfinance impact evaluations: Re-investigating the evidence from Bangladesh. *The Journal of Development Studies*, *48*(12), 1864–1880. doi:10.1080/00220388.2011.646989

Duvendack, M., Palmer-Jones, R., & Vaessen, J. (2014). Meta-analysis of the impact of microcredit on women's control over household decisions: Methodological issues and substantive findings. *Journal of Development Effectiveness*, *6*(2), 73–96. doi:10.1080/19439342.2014.903289

Ebomuche, N. C., Ihugba, O. A. & Bankong, B., 2014. The impact of Nigeria microfinance banks on poverty reduction: Imo State experience. *International Letters of Social and Humanistic Sciences, (05),* pp. 92-113.

Elhadary, Y. A. E. and Samat, N., 2012. Political economy and urban poverty in the developing countries: Lessons learned from Sudan and Malaysia. *Journal of geography and Geology, 4*(1), 212.

Elsafi, M. H., Ahmed, E. M., & Ramanathan, S. (2020). The impact of microfinance programs on monetary poverty reduction. *World Journal of Entrepreneurship, Management and Sustainable Development*, *16*(1), 30–43. doi:10.1108/WJEMSD-05-2019-0036

Ewusie, E. A., Annim, S. K., & Brafu-Insaidoo, W. (2021). The density of microfinance institutions and multiple borrowing in Ghana: Are rural borrowers vulnerable? *Journal of International Development*, *33*(8), 1217–1237. doi:10.1002/jid.3551

Fofana, N., Antonides, G., Niehof, A., & van Ophem, J. (2015). How microfinance empowers women in Côte d'Ivoire. *Review of Economics of the Household, 13*(4), 1023–1041. doi:10.100711150-015-9280-2

Gakpo, M. D. Y., Wujangi, M., Kwakye, M., & Asante, V. G. (2021). THE IMPACT OF Microfinancing on poverty alleviation and small businesses in Ghana. *The International Journal of Social Sciences and Humanity Studies, 13*(1), 1–28.

Hagan, L. H. (2018). *The impact of Microfinance Institutions on Poverty reduction among entrepreneurs in Ghana. A case study in the Ga South Municipal Assembly* [Master's thesis, OsloMet–Oslo Metropolitan University].

Hagenaars, A. J. (2014). The perception of poverty, s.l.: Elsevier.

Hartarska, V., Nadolnyak, D., & McAdams, T. (2013). Microfinance and microenterprises' financing constraints in Eastern Europe and Central Asia. In *Microfinance in developing countries* (pp. 22–35). Palgrave Macmillan. doi:10.1057/9781137301925_2

Hasan, N., Singh, A.K., Agarwal, M.K. and Kushwaha, B.P. (2022). Evaluating the role of microfinance institutions in enhancing the livelihood of urban poor. *Journal of Economic and Administrative Sciences.*

Hatta, Z. A., & Ali, I. (2013). Poverty reduction policies in Malaysia: Trends, strategies and challenges. *Asian Culture and History, 5*(2), 48. doi:10.5539/ach.v5n2p48

Hossain, M. K. (2012). Assessment of social impact of Microfinance Operations: A study on BRAC. *Interdisciplinary Journal of Research in Business ISSN, 2046*, 7141.

Hughes, D., Charles, J., Dawoud, D., Edwards, R. T., Holmes, E., Jones, C., Parham, P., Plumpton, C., Ridyard, C., Lloyd-Williams, H., Wood, E., & Yeo, S. T. (2016). Conducting economic evaluations alongside randomised trials: Current methodological issues and novel approaches. *PharmacoEconomics, 34*(5), 447–461. doi:10.100740273-015-0371-y PMID:26753558

Hussain, J., Mahmood, S., & Scott, J. (2019). Gender, microcredit and poverty alleviation in a developing country: The case of women entrepreneurs in Pakistan. *Journal of International Development, 31*(3), 247–270. doi:10.1002/jid.3403

Hussaini, U., & Chibuzo, I. C. (2018). The effects of financial inclusion on poverty reduction: The moderating effects of microfinance. *International Journal of Multidisciplinary Research and Development, 5*(12), 188–198.

Imai, K. S., & Azam, M. S. (2012). Does microfinance reduce poverty in Bangladesh? New evidence from household panel data. *The Journal of Development Studies*, *48*(5), 633–653. doi:10.1080/00220388.2012.661853

Imai, K. S., Gaiha, R., Thapa, G., & Annim, S. K. (2012). Microfinance and poverty—A macro perspective. *World Development*, *40*(8), 1675–1689. doi:10.1016/j.worlddev.2012.04.013

Isaia, E. (2005). *Microcredit in Morocco: The Zakoura Foundation's Experience*. University of Turin.

Islam, T. (2012). *Microcredit and poverty alleviation*. Ashgate Publishing, Ltd.

Kaberia, S. K., & Muathe, S. M. (2022). Economic Empowerment of the Poor: Myths and Facts about Microfinance Institutions in Africa. *International Journal of Social Science and Education Research Studies*, *2*(6), 179–186.

Karlan, D. & Goldberg, N. (2007). Impact evaluation for microfinance: Review of methodological issues. *World Bank, Poverty Reduction and Economic Management, Thematic Group on Poverty Analysis, Monitoring and Impact Evaluation.*

Khan, A. A., Khan, S. U., Fahad, S., Ali, M. A., Khan, A., & Luo, J. (2021). Microfinance and poverty reduction: New evidence from Pakistan. *International Journal of Finance & Economics*, *26*(3), 4723–4733. doi:10.1002/ijfe.2038

Khan, M., & Bedi, A. S. (2022). Returns to Interest-free Microcredit: Evidence from a Randomised Experiment in Pakistan. *Journal of Development Effectiveness*, *14*(2), 93–107. doi:10.1080/19439342.2021.1964578

Khandker, S. R., & Samad, H. A. (2014). Microfinance growth and poverty reduction in Bangladesh: What does the longitudinal data say? *Bangladesh Development Studies*, *37*(1 & 2), 127–157.

Kristof, N. D. (2009). The role of microfinance. *New York Times.*

Ksoll, C., Lilleør, H., Lønborg, J., & Rasmussen, O. (2016). Impact of Village Savings and Loan Associations: Evidence from a cluster randomized trial. *Journal of Development Economics*, *120*, 70–85. doi:10.1016/j.jdeveco.2015.12.003

Kwak, S., & Lee, J. (2014). *Financial Inclusion and Microfinance: On the Cases of ODA and Analysis of the Poverty Reduction Effect.* World Economic Update, 14-13.

Lloyd-Jones, T., & Rakodi, C. (2014). *Urban livelihoods: A people-centred approach to reducing poverty.* s.l.:Routledge. doi:10.4324/9781849773805

Madonda, A.E., Nyangarika, A. and Nombo, N. (2020). Impact of Youth Microfinance Asset's Ownership in Masasi Districts Council Mtwara Region. *IJARIIE-ISSN(O)-2395-4396, 6*(5), 1345-1353.

Malhotra, M. (2018). Role of Microfinance in Financial Inclusion in India. In Microfinance and Its Impact on Entrepreneurial Development, Sustainability, and Inclusive Growth (pp. 322-343). IGI Global. doi:10.4018/978-1-5225-5213-0.ch018

Mazumder, M. S. U. (2022). The effects of microfinance programs on recipients' livelihoods in rural Bangladesh. *European Journal of Development Research, 34*(3), 1383–1418. doi:10.105741287-021-00425-w

Mersland, R., & Strøm, R. Ø. (2014). Measuring microfinance performance. In *Microfinance Institutions* (pp. 12–30). Palgrave Macmillan. doi:10.1057/9781137399663_2

Miled, K. B. H., Younsi, M., & Landolsi, M. (2022). Does microfinance program innovation reduce income inequality? Cross-country and panel data analysis. *Journal of Innovation and Entrepreneurship, 11*(1), 1–15. doi:10.118613731-022-00195-7 PMID:35036286

Muriu, P. W. (2020). The Impact of Microfinance Programs: A Review of Data and Methodological Dilemma. *Journal of Economics and Sustainable Development, 11*(22), 100–109.

Mushtaq, R., & Bruneau, C. (2019). Microfinance, financial inclusion and ICT: Implications for poverty and inequality. *Technology in Society, 59*, 101154. doi:10.1016/j.techsoc.2019.101154

Mustapha, M. B., Yusuf, B. I., & Abdullahi, A. N. (2019). Micro-financing and rural poverty reduction: A case of Rima microfinance bank in Goronyo Local Government Area, Sokoto state, Nigeria. *Journal of Development and Agricultural Economics, 11*(10), 256–264. doi:10.5897/JDAE2018.0974

Nawaz, S. (2010). Microfinance and poverty reduction: Evidence from a village study in Bangladesh. *Journal of Asian and African Studies, 45*(6), 670–683. doi:10.1177/0021909610383812 PMID:21174878

Niaz, M.U. and Iqbal, M., 2019. Effect of microfinance on women empowerment: A case study of Pakistan. *SSRN 3419834*.

Okibo, B. W., & Makanga, N. (2014). Effects of micro finance institutions on poverty reduction in Kenya. *International Journal of Current Research and Academic Review, 2*(2), 76–95.

Omar, M. A., & Inaba, K. (2020). Does financial inclusion reduce poverty and income inequality in developing countries? A panel data analysis. *Journal of Economic Structures*, *9*(1), 1–25. doi:10.118640008-020-00214-4

Osmani, S. (2015). The Impact of Microcredit on Rural Labour Market in Bangladesh. *Institute of Microfinance (InM), 37.*

Pomi, S. S. (2019). Impact of microcredit on rural poverty alleviation in the context of Bangladesh. *International Journal of Economics and Finance*, *11*(6), 1–70. doi:10.5539/ijef.v11n6p70

Prakash, B. B. (2018). Impact Assessment of Microfinance in India: Survey, Issues and Challenges. *Society of Economics and Development, 14*(4), pp.734-742.

Prathap, B. N., Subrahmanya, K. C., & Harisha, B. S. (2018). Microfinance Delivery–Challenges and Remedies. *International Journal of Management Studies*, *3*(9), 138. doi:10.18843/ijms/v5i3(9)/17

Rajbanshi, R. H. M. W. B., Huang, M., & Wydick, B. (2015). Measuring microfinance: Assessing the conflict between practitioners and researchers with evidence from Nepal. *World Development*, *68*, 30–47. doi:10.1016/j.worlddev.2014.11.011

Roodman, D., & Morduch, J. (2014). The impact of microcredit on the poor in Bangladesh: Revisiting the evidence. *The Journal of Development Studies*, *50*(4), 583–604. doi:10.1080/00220388.2013.858122

Rui, G. U., & Nie, F. Y. (2021). Does empowering women benefit poverty reduction? Evidence from a multi-component program in the Inner Mongolia Autonomous Region of China. *Journal of Integrative Agriculture*, *20*(4), 1092–1106. doi:10.1016/S2095-3119(20)63436-0

Runsinarith, P. (2014). The impacts of microcredit on poverty reduction: Evidence from Cambodian rural villages. *The Philippine Review of Economics*, *51*(2), 121–150.

Salia, P. J., & Mbwambo, J. S. (2014). Does microcredit make any difference on borrowers' businesses? Evidences from a survey of women owned microenterprises in Tanzania. *International Journal of Social Sciences and Entrepreneurship*, *1*(9), 431–444.

Santoso, D. B., Gan, C., Revindo, M. D., & Massie, N. W. G. (2020). The impact of microfinance on Indonesian rural households' welfare. *Agricultural Finance Review*, *80*(4), 491–506. doi:10.1108/AFR-11-2018-0098

Setboonsarng, S. and Parpiev, Z. (2010). *Microfinance and the Millennium Development Goals in Pakistan: Impact Assessment Using Propensity Score Matching,* s.l.: eSocialSciences.

Shanmugan, K., & Baria, B. (2019). Major Themes and Concerns of Impact Analysis in the Indian Microfinance sector: Analytical Views. *International Journal of Research in Social Sciences*, *9*(1), 668–682.

Singh, P. K., & Chudasama, H. (2020). Evaluating poverty alleviation strategies in a developing country. *PLoS One*, *15*(1), e0227176. doi:10.1371/journal.pone.0227176 PMID:31929549

Tarozzi, A., Desai, J. and Johnson, K. (2013). On the impact of microcredit: Evidence from a randomized intervention in rural Ethiopia. AEA.

Tasos, S., Amjad, M. I., Awan, M. S., & Waqas, M. (2020). Poverty alleviation and microfinance for the economy of Pakistan: A case study of Khushhali Bank in Sargodha. *Economies*, *8*(3), 63. doi:10.3390/economies8030063

Townsend, P. (2014). *International Analysis Poverty.* s.l.:Routledge. doi:10.4324/9781315835099

Ullah, K., Saboor, A., & Ahmad, I. (2020). Effects of Microfinance on Mountain Poverty and Living Standards: An Empirical Investigation from Central Karakorum National Park Region of Gilgit Baltistan, Pakistan. *NUML International Journal of Business & Management*, *15*(1), 30–49.

Van Rooyen, C., Stewart, R., & de Wet, T. (2012). The impact of microfinance in sub-Saharan Africa: A systematic review of the evidence. *World Development*, *40*(11), 2249–2262. doi:10.1016/j.worlddev.2012.03.012

Wondirad, H. A. (2020). The impacts of mobile insurance and microfinance institutions (MFIs) in Kenya. *Journal of Banking and Financial Technology*, *4*(1), 95–110. doi:10.100742786-020-00021-2

Zeb, N., Jalal, R. N. U. D., Fayyaz, U. E., & Zaheer, M. A. (2021). Micro Finance and Economic Development: The Role of Microfinance Institutions Outreach in Pakistan. *The Journal of Asian Finance. Economics and Business*, *8*(5), 117–126.

Chapter 4
Microfinance and Sustainability:
Building Perspective Through Literature and Bibliometrics

Manpreet Arora
https://orcid.org/0000-0002-4939-1992
School of Commerce and Management Studies, Central University of Himachal Pradesh, Dharamshala, India

Swati Singh
Maharaja Agrasen University, Baddi, India

ABSTRACT

The development of financial sector lays a positive impact on the economic growth of a country. It serves as a foundation for mobilisation and allocation of finance which is life and blood for the growth and development of an economy. Therefore, the existence of an efficient financial system facilitates economic activity as well as growth. The large part of the population in rural areas is dependent on agricultural activities for earning income. India, being a rural and agrarian economy, needed some special institutions that could focus on the financial needs of rural poor, particularly those who are engaged in the agricultural activities. SBLP has become an effective tool for achieving the goals of financial inclusion focusing primarily on the poor women. This paper aims at exploring the present status of microfinance in India with special reference to self-help group bank linkage programme. It is a qualitative review of the present scenario based on extensive available literature which is supported by secondary data taken from latest reports of NABARD.

DOI: 10.4018/978-1-6684-5647-7.ch004

BACKGROUND

Attaining desired level of development is a primary goal of every developing nation. The development of a nation is not limited only to its structural development, but it is the development of everyone residing in the country, both in terms of economic as well as social aspects. Basic facilities like food, water, shelter, education, and employment are some of the parameters. But these facilities are available to them only when they are financially sound or they are able to earn (United Nation, 1995). India, being a developing nation, includes a great portion of population who do not have enough money to avail even these basic facilities. Certain issues like poverty, inequality, unemployment, and regional disparities are faced by developing countries which create hurdles in attaining the developmental goals. Thereby it becomes important that these issues should be addressed at various levels.

The development of financial sector lays a positive impact on the economic growth of a country (Levine, 1997). It serves as a foundation for mobilisation and allocation of finance that is life and blood for the growth and development of an economy. A formal financial system helps in channelizing savings into investments that lead to capital formation and finally contributes to the growth and economic development of the country. Formal financial system is indispensable for an economy as it helps in creating a bridge between demand and supply of financial resources in the market. A well-structured financial system can be divided into different institutions and markets (Pathak, 2003). The informal financial sector is an unorganised, non-institutional and a non-regulated system. Most of the developing nations are characterised by the co-existence of formal and informal financial sectors.

Indian financial system can be divided into two parts i.e. formal and informal financial sector. The formal financial sector comes under the purview of Ministry of Finance, Reserve Bank of India (RBI), Securities Exchange Board of India (SEBI) and other regulatory bodies. It includes various categories of banks and financial institutions. This sector follows the banking regulations and other regulations as prescribed by some apex bodies to function smoothly. On the other hand, the informal institutions are those which are not regulated by government or any other agencies. It constitutes of informal moneylenders, group of persons operating as associations, local brokers etc. They lend finance on mutual trust basis with or without collaterals (Ledgerwood, 1998).

The financial system of a country is based on the four fundamental pillars namely existence of financial institutions, operation of financial markets, existence of financial instruments and providing financial services. The developmental financial institutions are specially engaged in contributing to the upliftment of rural areas by focussing on agricultural sector, small-scale industries and other priority sector areas. The Indian banking sector has an important and crucial role to play in meeting the financial needs of various segments of society (Pathak, 2003). Nationalization of banks in 1969 was a necessary step for the improvement of the banking sector as well as the economy as a whole (Joshi, 2006). Reserve Bank of India has also concentrated by augmenting different measures on priority sectors in different five-year plans. In the era of nineties after the initiation of banking sector reforms, this sector witnessed an overall growth in many aspects including reaching to the rural population by adopting financial inclusion measures.

Undoubtedly, the Government of India initiated many schemes and programmes aiming at including the poor in the formal financial structure, but they were not able to achieve desired results. Formal financial sector faced certain limitations due to which it was not able to serve the rural poor (Fisher, Sriram, & Harper, 2002). A major problem faced by these banks was that they were not able to cater to the needs of weaker sections of society due to the distinct and peculiar credit needs of the rural poor. In rural India, the credit needs of the people are very small, it involves high degree of risk, and high transaction costs for the banks to deal in such transactions. Banks incur huge amount of cost in maintaining the accounts of clients irrespective of the amount saved/involved (Rajasekhar, 1996). This cost involves the cost of assessing potential clients, their repayment capacity, assessing their creditworthiness and administration of the disbursed loans. This high transaction cost problem created hurdles in the smooth flow of mobilisation and allocation of credit to the needy. Further, banks needed collateral or any other security before sanctioning credit to its customers, which is another big issue for the poor households to meet with. Loan disbursement involved a lengthy documentation process which again acted as a hindrance for lending credit to the rural public. Due to such problems involved in the formal banking structure, it forces the poor and the needy to borrow money from informal moneylenders and stuck themselves in vicious cycle of poverty. Hence, the ultimate aim of removing poverty and hunger thereby sustainability is at stake. This shows that all the efforts of the banks were not sufficient and not suitable for fulfilling the expectations and needs of the poor clients.

METHODOLOGY

The chapter is conceptual in nature and it highlights the importance of microfinance in the growth of an economy. The tool has been proven to be effective in dealing with various social issues and economic problems. The literature has been used to contend the viewpoint. Moreover the inherent objective of uplifting the poor starts in rural areas which in a way are related with sustainability. One of the important goal of sustainable development goals is poverty and researchers believe that microfinance has not only answers to solve issues relating with poverty but also related issues like empowerment, hunger, reduction in domestic violence, gender equality etc. So in its purest sense microfinance and sustainability are inseparable. Authors have attempted bibliometric analysis also to analyse the present work done especially in the field of 'sustainability and microfinance' by extracting bibliometric data from SCOPUS database. It gives us idea as well as future direction of research in this area. The paper has been divided into two parts. The first part deals with the concept of microfinance and the applicability of concept in Indian Scenario. The second part shows the bibliometrics of work done in all over the world particularly in the area of sustainability and microfinance to know the emerging areas of research in this field.

MICROFINANCE AND SUSTAINABILITY: BUILDING PERSPECTIVE THROUGH LITERATURE AND BIBLIOMETRIC

Microfinance has been proven to be an effective tool for uplifting of poor and vulnerable sections of society. It has been regarded as effective instrument in dealing with central problems of economies. The inherent concept of microfinance is associated with sustainable development goals. In order to achieve sustainable development goals like eradication of poverty and dealing with hunger including prevention of degradation of environment micro financing can act as a booster dose especially in developing nations. This chapter aims at exploring the present status of microfinance in India with special reference to Self Help Group Bank linkage programme. It is a qualitative review of the present scenario based on extensive available literature in relation to Indian scenario. It also examines work done especially in sustainability and microfinance by using bibliometric analysis.

The Indian Rural Economy and Its Peculiarities

Developing rural financial markets is a complex process especially in developing economies. In the early years of this century, co-operatives were introduced for creating credit structure for agriculture and other rural activities in India. In 1954, the All India Rural Credit Survey Committee (AIRCS) built a formal organization for developing policy guidelines for institutional credit. This committee highlighted that in rural areas of India there was a dearth of delivery of institutional credit which is true for many nations. The committee presented a proposal of restructuring more committees as well as invited suggestions for improvement in this regard. Constant examination and analysis of this system lead to the development of approaches like priority sector lending, lead bank scheme and setting up of NABARD (National Bank for Agriculture and Rural

Development). In 1989, the Agriculture Credit Review Committee (ACRC), explored and investigated the available credit system of rural sector. It showed that the gap between income earned and costs incurred by rural credit institutions was quite high, thereby demanding external support. This committee suggested that a greater autonomy should be given to commercial banks. The widespread weaknesses of RRBs were evident in the system with apparent non-viabilities built into them. A stress on strengthening the co-operatives was highlighted by improving deposit mobilization and reducing political interference. In India, the Narasimham Committee on Financial Sector Reforms 1991, further, recommended a redefinition of priority sector, and deregulation of interest rates with certain other landmark recommendations (Tatikonda & Suresh, 2013).

India, being a rural and agrarian economy, needed some special institutions that could focus on the financial needs of rural poor particularly who are engaged in the agricultural activities, they are vulnerable and needy, they lack support and initiatives. Insufficiency of the financial resources is one of the biggest limitation for the development and improvement of the socio economic status of households and it effects the development of rural areas in India (Vatta, 2003). They do not even have access to financial services through formal financial institutions. According to RFAS 2003 report, 70 percent marginal, small and landless farmers do not have bank accounts, 48 percent of these farmers have borrowed from informal sources of finance at least once in twelve months (Basu, 2005a).

In India, only 27 percent of the households have access to formal credit and 22 percent of the households have borrowed credit from informal sources. The marginal and small farmers have no formal access to credit (RBI, 2006). The average holding of marginal farmers is less than 2 hectares of land (NABARD, 2014-2015, p. 38). 21.92 percent of total population and 25.70 percent of the rural people are living below the poverty line (Planning Commission, 2013). Therefore, the four important pillars of the financial system become indispensable for the smooth functioning of economy and they cannot work in isolation. Therefore, the existence of an efficient financial system facilitates economic activity as well as growth thereby contributing to the sustainable development goals. The financial system in India too directs its savings toward more productive uses and helps to increase the output of the country. In this scenario, it becomes imperative that equal opportunity of savings and investment should be provided to the weaker section of the society and all the four pillars of financial structure play a responsible role towards such sections. Providing credit through microfinance is one such way of giving opportunity to the deprived/ weaker section of the society which can help them to get rid of poverty and become part of mainsstream. How microfinance can act as a bridge between the apex institutions and general public at large can be shown with the help of Figure 1.

Figure 1. Relation between Formal and Informal financial sector
Source: Author's work

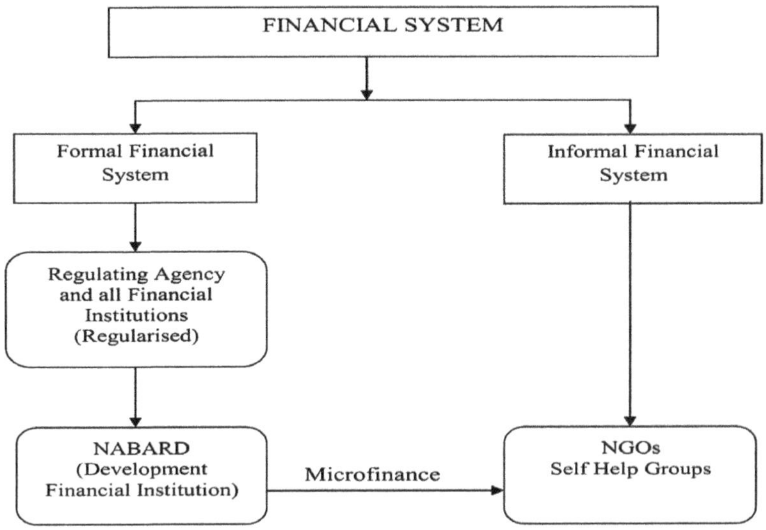

Evolution and Importance of Microfinance in the Growth of an Economy

"Microcredit is based on the principle that the poor have skills which continue to be unutilized or underutilized. It is absolutely not the lack of skills which create poor people poor, charity is not the answer to eradicate poverty. It helps poverty to continue. It makes dependency and takes away the individual's plan to break through the barrier of poverty. Set free of energy and creativity in each human being is the answer to poverty" (Yunus, 2003).

The Microfinance is considered as an important technique of providing small loan or financial assistance to the poor and the needy people who do not have access to the services of a formal banking sector (Khandker, 2005; Littlefield, Morduch, & Hashemi, 2003; Otero, 1999; Young, 2010). The financial services include creation of savings facility and disbursement of the credit, but also providing services of insurance, leasing, money transfer, equity transaction, etc (Dasgupta & Rao, 2003). It has emerged as a significant concept; helping poor to reduce vulnerability and bring regional balances in terms of increase and development. The microfinance programme is modified and adjusted according to the requirements of the deprived section of the society, especially women (Mishra, 2004). These programmes bridge the gap between the demand and supply of savings and credit facility to become socially and economically independent.

Mohammad Yunus introduced Grameen Bank model of microfinance in Bangladesh. Along with his students of Chittagong University in 1976, he initiated a credit programme with a motive of making credit available to the needy clients who did not have enough resources for keeping as collateral (Aghion & Morduch, 2004). The Microfinance model adopted by India is similar to the Grameen Bank Model built and set up in Bangladesh (Sankaran, 2005). The Government of India has given priority to the formation of such environment that promotes the creation of financial system which is suitable for the poor (Basu & Srivastava, 2005b). The concept of Microfinance in India gained momentum through SHG Bank Linkage Programme initiated by NABARD. Various voluntary associations and NGOs took this initiative to help the rural people and deprived sections of the society to understand the concept of microfinance and micro lending.

NABARD as an apex institution for promoting and developing the rural sector has played a crucial role in Indian economy. NABARD helped MYRADA in the process of formulation and nurturing these SHGs and works on various other projects providing financial assistance to other NGOs. It helps people to organise themselves into these groups by providing them proper training and support (Fernandez, 2006; NABARD, 2014). The Asia Pacific Regional Agricultural Credit Association (APRACA) encouraged the agricultural and rural development financial institutions to inculcate the saving behaviour and providing credit to the poor households. NABARD in association with some institutions of APRACA conducted a survey to study the functioning of SHG and promotion of linkage of SHGs with banks (Seibel, 2007).

Microfinance helps to accelerate economic growth of the country in which microcredit services help to improve their status in the society (Maksudova, 2010). It has helped them to increase their borrowing capacity with the help of microcredit available at the financial institutions. Microfinance is a broader concept as compared to microcredit as it includes micro savings, micro credit and micro insurance and other related financial services (Kaladhar, 1997). Microfinance programmes are based on joint liability lending system. The joint liability lending helps to solve problems like adverse selection of borrowers and moral hazards. Adverse selection means bank may lend loan to less creditworthy borrowers which may prove risky to the lenders. Whereas moral hazard means that the borrowers may indulge in risky project and cause loss to the lender (Aghion & Morduch, 2004). These problems arise due to the information asymmetry (Ghatak & Guinnane, 1999). In SHGs, members have more information about each other, which help to solve the adverse selection issue. Monitoring the process of loan utilization by the borrowers is necessary to improve the repayment performance and reducing the moral hazards.

Self Help Group's (SHG's) play a role of intermediaries for the disbursement of microfinance services (Seibel, 2001). SHG is a voluntary group of 10-20 people who are homogenous in character as well as have somewhat similar economic status.

Many studies provide the evidence that the microfinance is a more beneficial concept as compared to the individual approach of lending finance (Ghatak, 1999; Ghatak & Guinnane, 1999). NGOs play an important role for the promotion of SHGs and they perform necessary steps for better management of these SHGs (Husain, Mukerjee, & Dutta, 2014; Pitt, Khandker, & Cartwright, 2006; Shankar & Asher, 2011). NGOs also act as an intermediary between the microfinance service providers and the poor (Kaladhar, 1997). Further SHGs also receive various kind of technical and financial support from NGOs. Government of India and Reserve Bank of India have recognised the importance of microfinance and group lending schemes. There are many financial institutions in the market which are providing the facility to the poor and needy to have an access of financial services in a better way. It is undoubtedly contributing to the growth of rural poor and finally to growth of rural economy.

Empirical Evidences of Microfinance as a Tool for Development

Many authors have examined the role and effect of microfinance in poverty alleviation as well as how financial services can be used in for reducing poverty (Hermes & Lensink, 2007; Hulme & Mosley, 1996; Khandker, 2005). Studies also show that microfinance has laid a profound impact on the social and economic status of the participants positively (Hashemi, Schuler, & Riley, 1996; Khandker, 2005; Young, 2010). There are some of the authors also who are against the view that microfinance helps in economic and social improvement of the status (Adams & Von Pischke, 1992; Buckley, 1997; Montgomery, 1996). Different issues like women empowerment (Hashemi et al., 1996; Kabeer, 2001; Li, Gan, & Hu, 2011) and repayment performance of these SHGs have also been studied in respect of assessing the success rate of these programmes. The success and sustainability of the microfinance programme actually, depends upon the repayment performance of the members. The recovery rate of the loan should be high, and then only the sustainability of a group can be ensured. Therefore, this tool should be used in a phased and strategic manner. Microfinance is disbursed through group lending mechanism. Repayment performance of the group is used as one of the indicator measuring the performance of SHGs (Verhelle & Berlage, 2003; Zeller, 1998). The social cohesion and better information about each other in the group is regarded to be helpful in improving the repayment performance. Studying the pattern and sources of repayment are also important for improving the repayment performance (Mathew, 2006). A blind intervention with no proper planning would not be helpful. The intervention requires proper training and mentoring at various levels of the borrowers to achieve is desired objectives.

The Women Self Help Group (WSHG) members have been proved to be better performers in microfinance programmes as compared to their male partners in various studies (Aghion & Morduch, 2004; Pitt & Khandker, 1998). There is a great probability that the women use the amount of credit for the benefit of their children as well as family. Thus, the credit disbursed not only help the members, but it also improves the living condition of the whole family. In India, most of the borrowers of SBLP are women. This will not only provide an easy access to the credit and other banking services to women but also provide them ample opportunities to get involved in income generating activities and finally uplifting their family status. On the other hand, there are certain studies which show that no doubt women have an access to credit but they have no control over use of credit amount (Goetz & Gupta, 1996; Kabeer, 2001). Control of women over the use of credit amount is also an important issue that needs attention of researchers (Rahman, 1999). Measuring empowerment level of members through microfinance programmes is also an important issue to be considered without which the impact study of microfinance programme is incomplete.

Microfinance has helped women to gain freedom, to earn independently and support their family in various aspects. Different authors have studied the concept of empowerment associated with microfinance. Decision-making is used as one of the important variable for the measurement of empowerment level through microfinance (Hashemi et al., 1996; Kabeer, 2001). Microfinance with the help of SBLP has helped a number of women to gain empowerment in India (Galab & Rao, 2003; Ghate, 2007; Swain & Wallentin, 2009). The women members of the SBLP have shown better performance than the male members of the groups in various parts of India (Sinha, Parida, & Baurah, 2012) and even have a better repayment performance of the credit amount (Puhazhendi & Badatya, 2002). There are basically two methods discussed for measuring empowerment i.e. Process based and outcome based method (Kabeer, 2001; Li et al., 2011; Malhotra, Schuler, & Boender, 2002). The outcome method is more popular and uses direct indicators to measure the variable (Hashemi et al., 1996; Li et al., 2011). Many researchers have used the factors like freedom to take decision, freedom to move, economic empowerment and social empowerment (Chakrabarti & Biswas, 2012; Swain, 2012). Outcome methods are more concerned about the gender inequality and they try to measure it in addition to the other variables like social and economic aspects (Kabeer, 2001). Microfinance services disbursed to the women is beneficial not only for them but for the whole family (Pitt et al., 2006). Microfinance has also emerged as an important tool to eradicate poverty by promoting various ways and means of equal distribution of income (Arun, Imai, & Sinha, 2006). NABARD's step of introducing the bank linkage programme to these SHGs provided them greater opportunity to contribute to their family income and improving the status of the family.

The Government started the Integrated Rural Development Programme, which was formulated to target the poorest section of the rural population by providing them facilities at subsidized rate in 1978 (Garikipati, 2008; Mader, 2013). But it was not a successful programme as it was not able to produce satisfying results (NABARD, 2014). Failure of such programmes lead to the introduction of alternatives for the benefit of poor. Thus, there was strong need for an improved programme with more features and wide coverage which could suit the poor and needy section of the society. Government of India has always tried to focus on the poor population of the country by making special policies for them. Nationalisation of banks in 1969, Priority sector lending, and establishment of Regional Rural Banks in 1987 are some of the major steps taken by the government for providing the opportunities to the rural poor for availing financial services (Karmakar, 2008; Seibel, 2007). Microfinance programme should be such that it promotes the habit of saving and inculcate skills of entering into income generating activities. SHGs have also the potential to improve socio economic status of the members mainly through investment in microenterprises that ultimately helps in poverty reduction (Sivachithappa, 2013; Suprabha, 2014). Particularly in India, NABARD has introduced two models of microfinance i.e. SHG Bank Linkage Programme (SBLP) and MFI Bank Linkage Programme. SHG Bank Linkage Programme was started as a pilot project by NABARD in 1992 (Sinha, Parida & Baurah, 2012). Under SHG Bank Linkage Programme, it was decided to link at least 500 SHGs with the banks. But at the end of 1993 only 225 SHGs could be actually linked. Still, it was marked as a great success and an innovation in Indian financial system. SHG bank linkage program is dominating the microfinance sector with high success rate (Bansal, 2003; Kropp & Suran, 2002; Swain & Floro, 2010; Varman, 2005). The microcredit provided under this scheme is free from collaterals and is based on collective group performance which improves the sustainability of the SHGs. After 6 months of stable performance of SHGs, the groups can be credit linked to the banks. The ratio of credit to saving amount is 4: 1. This means that group can borrow four times the amount of their saving (Swain, 2012). In India, microfinance programmes has shown positive impact on members especially with reference to their economic and social status (Garikipati, 2008; Puhazhendi & Badatya, 2002; Sharma, 2008; Sinha et al., 2012).

SHGs are formed in a village by the initiatives of the NGOs, or by banks so that they can save on collective basis and can disburse loan of small amounts out of the collected amount. Most of the NGOs play an important role in the formation and promotion of SHGs and provide full assistance and guidance to the rural people, teaching them the working and importance of these groups. NGOs are good at forming better relations with people and solving the problems of high transaction costs and most importantly the requirement of collateral for availing credit. NGOs are also trying to provide perfect conditions for the promotion of microenterprises (Padhi, 2003). Most of the SHGs mainly follow the model in which Groups are formed by NGOs and financed by banks (Swain & Varghese, 2013). SBPL model is greatly supported by Government of India. It has made a huge contribution in upliftment of the poor through Microfinance. Microfinance has outreached a number of people by providing financial services to them (Basu & Srivastava, 2005a). Formal financial sector has also started taking an active lead in promoting microfinance. Commercial banks, RRBs and NGOs are making great contribution in the SHG bank linkage programme.

In India there are three sub types of SHG bank linkage model as defined by NABARD which are stated as below:

1. **SHGs formed and financed by banks**: In this model, the SHGs are formed and created solely by bank. The financial support in the form of savings, credit and other financial services are also provided by the banks. It is in fact a bank's initiative to promote SHGs.
2. **SHGs formed by NGOs and financed by banks**: In this model NGOs play a role of Self-Help Promoting Institutions (SHPIs) for the formulation of SHGs. All other things pertaining to financial services are provided by the banks.
3. **SHGs formed by NGOs and financed by NGOs with the help of banks**: In this model an NGO acts as a financial intermediary. These NGOs borrow money from banks and then disburse it to SHGs.

Figure 2 shows the different models of microfinance introduced by NABARD in India.

Figure 2. Models of Microfinance in India
Source: Author's work based on NABARD's SHG- Bank Linkage Model

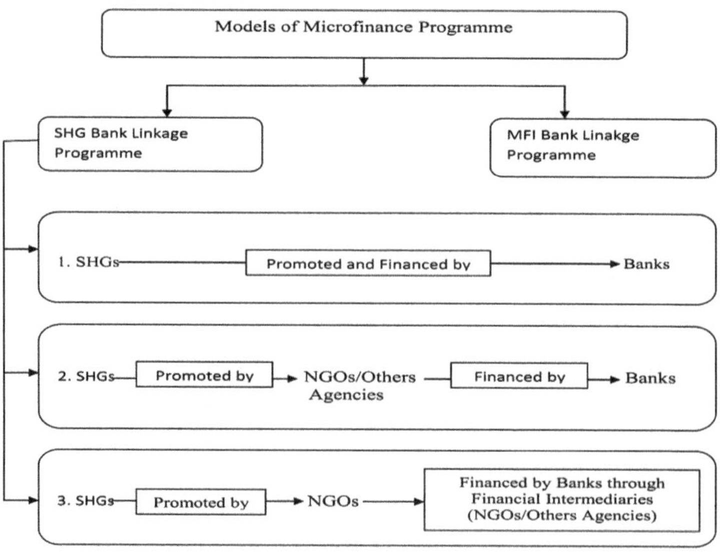

Microfinance Institution (MFI) Bank Linkage Model: Under this model, banks finance the mainstream Microfinance Institution (MFI). Banks provide financial assistance to MFI so that these MFIs can further provide financial assistance to SHGs and other marginal borrowers. These financial services include savings, loans, insurance and remittance management. Analysing the trend of number of SHGs linked with banks, loan disbursed to these SHGs and refinance assistance provided to them during certain years provides us an idea of progress of SHG Bank Linkage Programme in India. It also convinces us about the growing relevance of such programme in Indian economy. Looking at the data the fact is reassured that in Indian financial system linking the poor with the formal financial institutions is the need of the hour.

Table 1. Status of Microfinance in India since 1999

Year End March	During the Year	
	Number of SHGs Linked	Bank Loans (Amount in Lakhs)
1998-99	18678	3300
1999-00	81780	13600
2000-01	149050	28800
2001-02	197653	54500
2002-03	255882	102200
2003-04	361731	185600
2004-05	539365	299400
2005-06	620109	449900
2006-07	1105749	657000
2007-08	1227770	884900
2008-09	1609586	1225400
2009-10	1586822	1445300
2010-11	1196134	1454800
2011-12	1147878	1653500
2012-13	1219821	2058500
2013-14	1366421	2401700
2014-15	1626238	2728231
2015-16	1832323	3728690
2016-17	1898120	3878116
2017-18	2261132	4718587
2018-19	2698400	5831763

Source: NABARD

Figure 3. The bar graph showing the growth of loan disbursed through SHG Bank Linkage Programme
Source: Based on data retrieved from NABARD

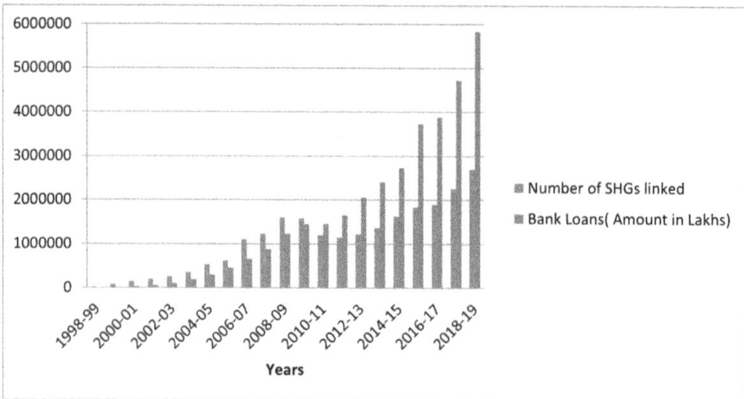

The Above data is also shown with the help of graph.

The graph shows that there has been a steady growth in the number of SHGs and amount of loan disbursed to the SHG members.

The government of India has launched many schemes and programmes for the promotion of microfinance along with the help of NABARD. Livelihood projects are initiated by government like Micro Enterprise Development Programme (MEDPs) and Livelihood and Enterprise Development Programmes (LEDPs) for SHGs. Other schemes for the promotion of women SHGs in the backward regions are implemented with the help of NABARD. The Micro Credit Innovation Department of NABARD is working for the promotion of SHG Bank Linkage Programme. SHG Bank Linkage Programme also provides interest subsidy when the clients make repayment of loan before due date. This motivates the clients or the members to make timely repayment of loan taken for different purpose.

The Bibliometric Analysis in the Present Scenario

In the field of qualitative research, the techniques of bibliometric analysis are getting great attention as well as importance as through bibliometric analysis one can synthesize the data which is available in the previous literature. With the help of bibliometric techniques, a meaningful as well as logical depiction of the research already done can be portrayed. Most prolific authors working in that field with their area in that field work, most cited publications and journal of publications can be seen at one particular place. This gives us an idea about the research already being done in this area and prominent authors working in this field, alongside we understand

Table 2. Top 20 Documents

S. No.	Documents	Authors	Year	Source	Citations
1	Indicators of sustainable development for industry: A general framework	Azapagic, A., Perdan, S.	2000	Process Safety and Environmental Protection 78(4), pp. 243-261	369
2	Tackling the down side: Social capital, women's empowerment and micro-finance in Cameroon	Mayoux, L.	2001	Development and Change 32(3), pp. 435-464	281
3	Micro-finance evangelism, 'destitute women', and the hard selling of a new anti-poverty formula	Rogaly, B.	1996	Development in Practice 6(2), pp. 100-112	139
4	Effectiveness of community health financing in meeting the cost of illness	Preker, A.S., Carrin, G., Dror, D., (...), Hsiao, W., Arhin-Tenkorang, D.	2002	Bulletin of the World Health Organization 80(2), pp. 143-150	92
5	Efficiency of microfinance institutions: A data envelopment analysis	Haq, M., Skully, M., Pathan, S.	2010	Asia-Pacific Financial Markets 17(1), pp. 63-97	85
6	The economics of avoiding dangerous climate change. An editorial essay on the Stern Review	Barker, T.	2008	Climatic Change 89(3-4), pp. 173-194	70
7	Renewable energy: Prospects and trends in Bangladesh	Hossain, M.F., Hossain, S., Uddin, M.J.	2017	Renewable and Sustainable Energy Reviews 70, pp. 44-49	48
8	Do protected areas and conservation incentives contribute to sustainable livelihoods? A case study of Bardia National Park, Nepal	Thapa Karki, S.	2013	Journal of Environmental Management 128, pp. 988-999	46
9	The Paradox of Sustainability: Reflections on NGOs in Bangladesh	Devine, J.	2003	Annals of the American Academy of Political and Social Science 590, pp. 227-242	45
10	Women's empowerment and micro-finance programmes: strategies for increasing impact	Mayoux, L.	1998	Development in Practice 8(2), pp. 235-241	44
11	Questioning the future of NGOs in microfinance	Dichter, T.W.	1996	Journal of International Development 8(2), pp. 259-269	40

continued on following page

Table 2. Continued

S. No.	Documents	Authors	Year	Source	Citations
12	How shall we examine and learn about public-private partnerships (PPPs) in the health sector? Realist evaluation of PPPs in Hong Kong	Wong, E.L.Y., Yeoh, E.-K., Chau, P.Y.K., (...), Cheung, A.W.L., Fung, H.	2015	Social Science and Medicine 147, pp. 261-269	36
13	Financial resources for the circular economy: A perspective from businesses	Aranda-Us6n, A., Portillo-Tarragona, P., Marín-Vinuesa, L.M., Scarpellini, S.	2019	Sustainability (Switzerland) 11(3),888	34
14	An evolutionary analysis of green finance sustainability based on multi-agent game	Cui, H., Wang, R., Wang, H.	2020	Journal of Cleaner Production 269,121799	28
15	Dynamic capabilities and environmental accounting for the circular economy in businesses	Scarpellini, S., Marín-Vinuesa, L.M., Aranda-Us6n, A., Portillo-Tarragona, P.	2020	Sustainability Accounting, Management and Policy Journal 11(7), pp. 1129-1158	27
16	Linking Subsistence Activities to Global Marketing Systems: The Role of Institutions	Kolk, A.	2014	ournal of Macromarketing 34(2), pp. 186-198	27
17	Surgery for degenerative cervical myelopathy: a patient-centered quality of life and health economic evaluation	Witiw, C.D., Tetreault, L.A., Smieliauskas, F., (...), Massicotte, E.M., Fehlings, M.G.	2017	Spine Journal 17(1), pp. 15-25	26
18	Informing policy makers about future health spending: A comparative analysis of forecasting methods in OECD countries	Astolfi, R., Lorenzoni, L., Oderkirk, J.	2012	Health Policy 107(1), pp. 1-10	25
19	Things are different today: the challenge of global systemic risks	Renn, O., Lucas, K., Haas, A., Jaeger, C.	2019	Journal of Risk Research 22(4), pp. 401-415	24
20	Rural microfinance service delivery: Gaps, inefficiencies and emerging solutions	Parikh, T.S.	2006	2006 International Conference on Information and Communication Technology and Development, ICTD2006 4085536, pp. 223-232	24

Source: Compiled from SCOPUS Database

the future orientation of the researchers in that field. The research publications in the field of 'sustainability and microfinance' were extracted using the Scopus database which is regarded as one of the prestigious as well as comprehensive peer reviewed research repository in the field of social sciences. We used the 'keyword' "sustainability and microfinance" for searching the query and 154 papers have been extracted from the Scopus database for 27 years that is 1995 to 2021. It is

Table 3. The 27 Years Citation Table

S.No	Years	Documents	Citations
1	2021	20	11
2	2020	20	93
3	2019	17	121
4	2018	10	66
5	2017	8	105
6	2016	6	25
7	2015	6	56
8	2014	14	61
9	2013	4	54
10	2012	8	72
11	2011	3	3
12	2010	5	112
13	2009	4	8
14	2008	1	70
15	2007	4	27
16	2006	3	59
17	2005	2	11
18	2004	2	16
19	2003	2	48
20	2002	1	92
21	2001	2	287
22	2000	6	384
23	1999	0	0
24	1998	2	50
25	1997	1	10
26	1996	2	179
27	1995	1	0

Table 4. Top 10 Source by Documents

S.No	Source	Documents	Citations
1	International Journal of Social Economics	4	42
2	Journal of Cleaner Production	4	54
3	Sustainability Switzerland	4	46
4	Development in Practice	3	183
5	Iop Conference Series Earth and Environmental Science	3	4
6	Energies	2	5
7	Humanomics	2	13
8	Indian Journal of Agricultural Economics	2	3
9	Journal Fur Entwicklungspolitik	2	1
10	Journal of African Business	2	3

Source: Compiled from SCOPUS Database

Table 5. Documents by Author

S.No	Author	Documents	h-Index
1	Mayoux, L.	23	11
2	Aranda-Usón, A.	50	25
3	Marín-Vinuesa, L.M.	19	7
4	Mohiuddin, M.	43	10
5	Parvin, S.S.	2	2
6	Portillo-Tarragona, P.	18	11
7	Scarpellini, S.	53	24
8	Taiwo, J.N.	19	4
9	Abdullah, R.	5	4
10	Adewunmi, A.O.	1	1
11	Adjie, A.R.	1	0
12	Agbaeze, E.K.	24	4
13	Aiyepola, P.O.	1	1
14	Alam, G.M.	36	13
15	Alam, J.	6	2
16	Alam, K.M.	11	5
17	Albastaki, N.K.	1	0
18	Ali, S.S.	7	1
19	Amara, A.B.H.	2	0
20	Ameur, H.B.	34	7

Source: Compiled from SCOPUS Database

important to mention that the search was only limited to the articles published in Journals that too only in the field of Business and Management and Accounting. The following top 20 documents from the extracted dataset are listed which are having highest citations. The highest cited articles cover the thematic areas of sustainable development, women's empowerment and micro-finance, microfinance as an anti-poverty formula, financing needs of community health, efficiency of microfinance, finances for Renewable energy and sustainable livelihoods.

The Table 3 shows documents published and cited from 1995 to 2021 on the theme of sustainability and microfiance.

The table 4 shows the top ten journals publishing in the area of sustainability and microfinance.

The Table 5 shows the authors publishing in this area with their h-index.

Table 6. Documents By Affiliation

S.No	Affiliation	Documents	Citations
1	University of Washington	3	57
2	University of Sussex	3	65
3	Tshwane University of Technology	2	3
4	Indian Institute of Technology Indian School of Mines, Dhanbad	2	22
5	Universidad de La Rioja	2	61
6	Universidad de Zaragoza	2	61
7	National University of Singapore	2	4
8	Universität Kassel	2	42
9	Universiti Malaya	2	10
10	University of Cambridge	2	88
11	Thompson Rivers University	2	4
12	Université Laval	2	4
13	University of Chittagong	2	9
14	Addis Ababa University	2	8
15	Institute of Development Studies, Brighton	2	19
16	Covenant University	2	0
17	National Council of Applied Economic Research	1	5
18	Atma Jaya University	1	22
19	Ministry of Education	1	0
20	Indian Association for Savings and Credit	1	3

Source: Compiled from SCOPUS Database

Table 7. Documents by Country or Territory

S.No	Country	Documents	Citations
1	India	22	63
2	United Kingdom	20	1060
3	United States	18	249
4	China	11	77
5	Indonesia	8	38
6	Canada	6	36
7	Germany	6	77
8	Malaysia	6	22
9	Spain	6	84
10	South Africa	5	6
11	Australia	4	92
12	Bangladesh	4	61
13	France	4	36
14	Netherlands	4	52
15	Nigeria	4	2

Source: Compiled from SCOPUS Database

Table 6 shows the universities who have published highest number of documents on "sustainability and microfinance".

Table 7 shows the documents published region wise with their citations where India has published highest number of articles.

CONCLUSION

Microfinance institutions are involved in nurturing and formation of SHGs. But the sustainability of these institutions depends upon the funds provided by the donors and the concessions provided by the government. Loans under this programme provide additional purchasing power to the borrowers for meeting their consumption, investment and production needs (Kropp & Suran, 2002). It helps in promoting social cohesion among the rural people or the members of the programmes. Providing microfinance services has become an important part of achieving the objectives of financial inclusion (Ledgerwood, Earne, & Nelson, 2013). Microfinance helps in promoting financial inclusion by providing access to micro financial services to small and new entrepreneurs in rural sectors of the economy. The sustainability of the SHGs helps to promote growth of micro-entrepreneurs. Important strategies are to be formulated on the part of the Government and promoting agencies that would surely help for achieving regional balances. Microfinance is bringing a drastic change in the lives of the participants, most importantly the women; thereby leading to the development of the nation socially and economically. Thus, it becomes necessary for a researcher to ponder upon the impact of this programme on the poor masses of the country.

REFERENCES

Adams, D. W., & Von Pischke, J. (1992). Microenterprise credit programs: Deja vu. *World Development, 20*(10), 1463–1470. doi:10.1016/0305-750X(92)90066-5

Aghion, B. A., & Morduch, J. (2004). *The economics of microfinance*. Oxford Press.

Arun, T., Imai, K., & Sinha, F. (2006). Does the microfinance reduce poverty in India? Propensity Score Matching based on a National-Level Household Data. *Economics Discussion Paper, The University of Manchester*.

Bansal, H. (2003). SGH-bank linkage program in India: An overview. *Journal of Microfinance/ESR Review, 5*(1), 21-50.

Basu, P., & Srivastava, P. (2005a). Exploring possibilities: Microfinance and rural credit access for the poor in India. *Economic and Political Weekly*, 1747–1756.

Basu, P., & Srivastava, P. (2005b). Scaling-up microfinance for India's rural poor. *World Bank Policy Research Working Paper*, 3646.

Buckley, G. (1997). Microfinance in Africa: Is it either the problem or the solution? *World Development, 25*(7), 1081–1093. doi:10.1016/S0305-750X(97)00022-3

Chakrabarti, S., & Biswas, C. S. (2012). An exploratory analysis of women's empowerment in India: A structural equation modelling approach. *The Journal of Development Studies, 48*(1), 164–180. doi:10.1080/00220388.2011.615920

Dasgupta, R., & Rao, K. D. (2003). Microfinance in India: Issues, challenges and policy options. *Savings and Development*, 203-237.

Fernandes, A. (2006). History and spread of the self-help affinity group movement in India. *Occasional Paper, 3*(6).

Fisher, T., Sriram, M., & Harper, M. (2002). *Beyond micro-credit: Putting development back into micro-finance*. Oxfam.

Garikipati, S. (2008). The impact of lending to women on household vulnerability and women's empowerment: Evidence from India. *World Development, 36*(12), 2620–2642. doi:10.1016/j.worlddev.2007.11.008

Ghatak, M. (1999). Group lending, local information and peer selection. *Journal of Development Economics, 60*(1), 27–50. doi:10.1016/S0304-3878(99)00035-8

Ghatak, M., & Guinnane, T. W. (1999). The economics of lending with joint liability: Theory and practice. *Journal of Development Economics, 60*(1), 195–228. doi:10.1016/S0304-3878(99)00041-3

Ghate, P. (2007). *Indian Microfinance: The challenges of rapid growth*. SAGE Publications India. doi:10.4135/9788132101574

Goetz, A. M., & Gupta, R. S. (1996). Who takes the credit? Gender, power, and control over loan use in rural credit programs in Bangladesh. *World Development, 24*(1), 45–63. doi:10.1016/0305-750X(95)00124-U

Hashemi, S. M., Schuler, S. R., & Riley, A. P. (1996). Rural credit programs and women's empowerment in Bangladesh. *World Development, 24*(4), 635–653. doi:10.1016/0305-750X(95)00159-A

Hermes, N., & Lensink, R. (2007). Impact of microfinance: A critical survey. *Economic and Political Weekly*, 462–465.

Hulme, D., & Mosley, P. (1996). *Finance for the poor or poorest?: Financial innovation, poverty and vulnerability*. University of Reading, Department of Economics and Department of Agricultural Economics.

Husain, Z., Mukerjee, D., & Dutta, M. (2014). Self-help groups and empowerment of women: Self-selection, or actual benefits? *Journal of International Development, 26*(4), 422–437. doi:10.1002/jid.2815

Joshi, D. P. (2006). *Social Banking: Promise, performamce, and potential*. Foundation Books. doi:10.1017/UPO9788175968271

Kabeer, N. (2001). Conflicts over credit: Re-evaluating the empowerment potential of loans to women in rural Bangladesh. *World Development, 29*(1), 63–84. doi:10.1016/S0305-750X(00)00081-4

Kaladhar, K. (1997). Microfinance in India: Design, structure and governance. *Economic and Political Weekly*, 2687–2706.

Karmakar, K. (2008). Microfinance revisited. In K.G., Karmarkar (Ed.). Microfinance in India (pp.33-54).New Delhi: SAGE Publications.

Khandker, S. R. (2005). Microfinance and poverty: Evidence using panel data from Bangladesh. *The World Bank Economic Review*, *19*(2), 263–286. doi:10.1093/wber/lhi008

Kropp, E. W., & Suran, B. (2002). *Linking banks and (financial) self help groups in India-An assessment.* Paper presented at the Seminar on SHG-bank Linkage Programme. New Delhi, Nabard.

Ledgerwood, J. (1998). *Microfinance handbook: An institutional and financial perspective*. World Bank Publications. doi:10.1596/978-0-8213-4306-7

Ledgerwood, J., Earne, J., & Nelson, C. (2013). *The new microfinance handbook: A financial market system perspective*. World Bank Publications. doi:10.1596/978-0-8213-8927-0

Levine, R. (1997). Financial development and economic growth: Views and agenda. *Journal of Economic Literature*, *35*(2), 688–726.

Li, X., Gan, C., & Hu, B. (2011). The impact of microcredit on women's empowerment: Evidence from China. *Journal of Chinese Economic and Business Studies*, *9*(3), 239–261. doi:10.1080/14765284.2011.592352

Littlefield, E., Morduch, J., & Hashemi, S. (2003). Is microfinance an effective strategy to reach the Millennium Development Goals? *Focus Note*, *24*, 1–11.

Mader, P. (2013). Rise and fall of microfinance in India: The Andhra Pradesh crisis in perspective. *Strategic Change*, *22*(1-2), 47–66. doi:10.1002/jsc.1921

Maksudova, N. (2010). *Macroeconomics of microfinance: How do the channels work?* (CERGE-EI Working Paper Series 423).

Malhotra, A., Schuler, S. R., & Boender, C. (2002). Measuring women's empowerment as a variable in international development.

Mathew, E. (n.d.). *Does repayment indicate the success of micro-finance programme?* (172). Institute for Social and Economic Change. http://www.isec.ac.in/WP%20-%20172.pdf

Mishra, S. (2004). [Beyond Micro Credit: Putting development back into micro-finance, Thomas Fisher, M.S. Sriram]. *Indian Economic Review*, *39*(2), 401–406.

Montgomery, R. (1996). Disciplining or protecting the poor? Avoiding the social costs of peer pressure in micro-credit schemes. *Journal of International Development*, *8*(2), 289–305. doi:10.1002/(SICI)1099-1328(199603)8:2<289::AID-JID368>3.0.CO;2-2

Otero, M. (1999). Bringing development back, into microfinance. *Journal of Microfinance/ESR Review*, *1*(1), 8-19.

Padhi, B. (2003). Mainstreaming microfinance: Bridging ngo-banker divide. *Economic and Political Weekly*, 4832–4836.

Pathak, B. V. (2003). *Indian Financial System* (1st ed.). Pearsion Education.

Pitt, M. M., & Khandker, S. R. (1998). The impact of group-based credit programs on poor households in Bangladesh: Does the gender of participants matter? *Journal of Political Economy*, *106*(5), 958–996. doi:10.1086/250037

Pitt, M. M., Khandker, S. R., & Cartwright, J. (2006). Empowering women with micro finance: Evidence from Bangladesh. *Economic Development and Cultural Change*, *54*(4), 791–831. doi:10.1086/503580

Planning Commission of India. (2012). *Poverty Estimates for 2011-12*. Government of India Press Information Bureau. New Delhi.

Puhazhendi, V., & Badatya, K. (2002). *SHG-Bank linkage programme for rural poor–An impact assessment*. Paper presented at the seminar on SHG bank linkage programme. New Delhi, Nabard, Mumbai.

Rahman, A. (1999). Micro-credit initiatives for equitable and sustainable development: Who pays? *World Development*, *27*(1), 67–82. doi:10.1016/S0305-750X(98)00105-3

Rajasekhar, D. (1996). Problems and prospects of group lending in NGO credit programmes in India. *Savings and Development*, *20*(1), 79–104.

RBI. (2006). *Report of working group to suggest measures to assist distressed farmers*. RBI. https://rbidocs.rbi.org.in/rdocs/PublicationReport/Pdfs/78889.pdf

RBI. (2008). *Policy Environment. In Report on Trend and Progress of Banking in India. Mumbai*. RBI. https://rbidocs.rbi.org.in/rdocs/Publications/PDFs/RTP0809PRD_Full.pdf

Reddy, A. A., & Malik, D. P. (2011). A review of shg-bank linkage programme in India. *Indian Journal of Industrial Economics and Development*, *7*(2), 1–10.

Sankaran, M. (2005). Micro credit in India: An overview. *World Review of Entrepreneurship, Management and Sustainable Development*, *1*(1), 91–100. doi:10.1504/WREMSD.2005.007755

Seibel, H. D. (2001). *SHG Banking: A financial technology for reaching marginal areas and the very poor*. University of Cologne.

Seibel, H. D. (2007). *The role of microfinance in rural microenterprise development*. University of Cologne.

Shankar, S., & Asher, M. (2011). The microfinance sector in India: Which way now? *ASCI Journal of Management*, *40*(2), 1–20.

Sharma, H. (2008). Functioning and impact of microfinance: Evidence from Himachal Pradesh. Reforming Indian agriculture: Towards employment generation and poverty reduction. *Essays in honour of GK Chadha,* 269-290.

Singh, S. (2015). The effects of microfinance programs on women members in traditional societies. *Gender, Place and Culture*, *22*(2), 222–238. doi:10.1080/0966369X.2013.855627

Sinha, P., Parida, P. C., & Baurah, P. (2012). The impact of NABARD's self help group-bank linkage programme on poverty and empowerment in India. *Contemporary South Asia*, *20*(4), 487–510. doi:10.1080/09584935.2012.737306

Sivachithappa, K. (2013). Impact of micro finance on income generation and livelihood of members of self help groups–A case study of Mandya District, India. *Procedia: Social and Behavioral Sciences*, *91*, 228–240. doi:10.1016/j.sbspro.2013.08.421

Suprabha, K. (2014). Empowerment of self help groups (shgs) towards microenterprise development. *Procedia Economics and Finance*, *11*, 410–422. doi:10.1016/S2212-5671(14)00208-1

Swain, R. B. (2012). Differential impact of microfinance delivery mechanism on vulnerability. *Applied Economics Letters*, *19*(8), 721–724. doi:10.1080/13504851.2011.597716

Swain, R. B., & Wallentin, F. Y. (2009). Economic or non-economic factors–What empowers women? *Econ Papers.*

Tatikonda, N., & Suresh, P. (2013). Rural credit system in India - problem and prospects. In R. K. Miryala (Ed.), *Changing Paradigms of Rural Management.* Zenon Academic Publishing.

United Nation. (1995). *Report of the world summit for social development.*

Vatta, K. (2003). Microfinance and poverty alleviation. *Economic and Political Weekly*, *38*, 432–433.

Verhelle, C., & Berlage, L. (2003). *Determinants of microfinance group performance: an empirical analysis of self-help groups in India. MSE paper*. Department of Economics.

Young, S. (2010). The "moral hazards" of microfinance: Restructuring rural credit in India. *Antipode*, *42*(1), 201–223. doi:10.1111/j.1467-8330.2009.00737.x

Yunus, M. (2003). *Expanding microcredit outreach to reach: The Millennium Development Goal–Some Issues for Attention*. Paper presented at the International seminar on attacking poverty with microcredit, Dhaka

Zeller, M. (1998). Determinants of repayment performance in credit groups: The role of program design, intragroup risk pooling, and social cohesion. *Economic Development and Cultural Change*, *46*(3), 599–620. doi:10.1086/452360

Chapter 5
Who Loses in Financial Inclusion?

Peterson K. Ozili
https://orcid.org/0000-0001-6292-1161
Central Bank of Nigeria, Abuja, Nigeria

ABSTRACT

Financial inclusion involves the provision of basic formal financial services to members of society. Policy efforts and collaboration with the private sector have helped to increase the level of financial inclusion in many countries. Such efforts give rise to net winners and net losers from financial inclusion efforts. This chapter identifies the net losers from financial inclusion efforts. The lesson from the net losers identified in this study is that being 'banked' is only a necessary condition to enjoy the benefits of financial inclusion. Being 'banked' is not a sufficient condition to enjoy the benefits of financial inclusion. A banked adult can be a net loser from financial inclusion despite being banked. This has wider implications for understanding the challenges to sustained financial inclusion.

INTRODUCTION

Increasing the level of financial inclusion is good for society. Greater financial inclusion means that adults will have greater access to basic financial products and services which they can use to meet their day-to-day financial needs, raise capital to start a business, accumulate savings in a secure financial system, and to insure themselves against risks (Ozili, 2021a; Čihák, Mare, and Melecky, 2021). Greater financial inclusion in the form of more access to basic financial products and

DOI: 10.4018/978-1-6684-5647-7.ch005

services will bring unbanked adults into the formal financial sector and give them an opportunity to live a more financially secure and stable life.

Many developed and developing countries have used policy efforts, policy tools and collaboration with the private sector to increase access to formal financial services for unbanked adults. After granting access to formal financial services, people make decisions that are either welfare-enhancing or welfare-destructive. In the end, financial inclusion will give rise to 'net winners' and 'net losers. The net winners are those who gain more than they lose from participating in the formal financial sector. Examples of net winners include wealthy individuals, middle-class citizens, government, banks, non-bank financial institutions, the central bank and the tax authorities (Oz-Yalaman, 2019; Ozili, 2022a; Shihadeh et al, 2018, etc). The net losers are those who experience huge losses, and the loss erode any gains that have been made from participating in the formal financial sector.

This chapter focuses on the net losers from financial inclusion. Few studies in literature have examined the negative effects of financial inclusion while many studies show overwhelming evidence about the positive benefits of financial inclusion (Ahmad, Green and Jiang, 2020; Ozili, 2021a; Čihák, Mare, and Melecky, 2021; Ozili, 2020). There are no studies in the literature that examine the losers from financial inclusion. Even in the critical literature, some studies have examined several challenges of financial inclusion such as the potential of financial inclusion to encourage indebtedness (Natarajan et al, 2021); concerns that financial inclusion can lead to the financialisation of poverty (Mader, 2018), and formal lenders violating privacy laws by commercializing the private data of banked adults (De Koker and Jentzsch, 2013; Ozili, 2022b). Despite these challenges identified in the critical literature, the financial inclusion literature has not clearly identified the losers in a financially inclusive society. This study addresses this issue by identifying in clear terms the losers from financial inclusion.

The study contributes to the financial inclusion literature. It contributes to the literature that examine the challenges to financial inclusion. Studies in this literature identified several challenges of financial inclusion (see, for example, Milana and Ashta, 2020; Mani, 2016; Ozili, 2021b; Kulkarni and Ghosh, 2021). This paper adds to the literature by showing that some banked adults, despite being banked, may not be better off in welfare terms, and this presents a challenge to financial inclusion. The rest of the chapter is structured as follows. Section 2 presents the background to the chapter. Section 3 presents the losers from financial inclusion. Section 4 concludes.

LITERATURE REVIEW

There is a consensus that financial institutions, technology companies and regulators are major stakeholders of financial inclusion. Financial institutions and technology companies use financial technology to offer financial products and services to banked customers to increase financial inclusion while regulators ensure that customers are treated fairly in the process (Ozili, 2018). Although financial inclusion efforts have been largely successful in developed countries, the progress made towards financial inclusion in developing countries has been very slow especially in some African countries and in some Latin America countries due to a number of issues that hinder access to basic and affordable financial services (Beck et al., 2015).

The literature points out some issues with financial inclusion that make it doubtful that financial inclusion will realise its potential benefits. Studies such as Llewellyn (2021) identified four barriers to financial inclusion, namely, (i) structural factors such as inadequate financial infrastructure, (ii) institutional constraints such as weak institutions, (iii) demand factors such as low demand for basic financial services due to lack of bank branch presence in communities, and (iv) educational limitations such as limited financial literacy. Sharizan, Redzuan and Rosman (2021) show that developing countries such as Malaysia, witness some hindrance to financial inclusion which are lack of financial education, lack of proper documentation and lack of financial literacy. Ozili (2021b) argues that although the financial inclusion agenda has good intentions, financial inclusion brings benefits that disappear after a few years, it promotes the use of transaction accounts, and digital financial inclusion efforts bear a resemblance to a campaign against having cash-in-hand. Varghese and Viswanathan (2018) point out that financial institutions may be reluctant to serve small value and unprofitable customers that have irregular income because financial institutions view financial inclusion as a business opportunity.

Chen and Divanbeigi (2019) note that despite the commitment of the development community to increase access to finance, financial inclusion rates worldwide are still unsatisfactory. In their study, they assessed whether regulatory quality improves financial inclusion outcomes using data from several countries. They find that countries that have low regulatory quality have low levels of financial inclusion. Beck, Senbet and Simbanegavi (2015) show that foreign banks from emerging markets, including Africa, have contributed to greater financial inclusion, but foreign banks from Europe and U.S have not contributed to greater financial inclusion and this is because financial inclusion is not a major issue in Europe and U.S. López and Winkler (2019) show that high and rising levels of financial inclusion might contribute to a destabilizing credit boom, and that policy makers will face the challenge of ensuring that high levels of financial inclusion does not lead to destabilizing credit boom.

Arun and Kamath (2015) point out that having a bank account does not guarantee long-term participation in the formal financial system, as households can move in and out of the formal financial system over time. They suggest that effort should be made to bring the unbanked into the banking sector, and banks should put in much effort to retain and engage current bank customers to prevent them from becoming un-banked/under-banked. Chen and Jin (2017) point out that limited access to credit can cause financial vulnerability for households and lead to economic loss in a country. They studied the use of formal credit and informal credit in China. They find that 53.21 percent of households used informal credit, and only 19.77% used formal credit. The findings suggest that informal credit is more prevalent in China due to many households being at a social and economic disadvantage in China. In a related study, in the context of India, Ghosh and Vinod (2017) find that gender differences matter for financial inclusion. They find that female-headed households were less likely to access formal financial services, and more likely to access informal financial services compared to households that were headed by males. The studies reviewed above shows that financial inclusion causes some issues for banked customers and households.

LOSERS IN FINANCIAL INCLUSION

Banked Adults Who Are Financially-Illiterate

An adult who is banked can be financially-illiterate. Financial illiteracy is the inability to manage one's personal finance (Shambare and Rugimbana, 2012). It occurs when people lack the basic money acquisition skills, money saving skills, money management skills and basic financial risk management skills needed to participate in the formal financial sector (Albastiki and Hamdan, 2019; Turner, Klein and Stein, 2016; Shambare and Rugimbana, 2012). Banked adults who are financially illiterate will not enjoy the full benefits of financial inclusion. They will be at the losing end depending on the degree of their financial illiteracy. The reason why banked adults who are financially illiterate will be at the losing end of financial inclusion is because they can own bank accounts but they lack financial knowledge on how to use the bank accounts to improve their welfare in a sustainable way. Their financial illiteracy can lead them to make bad financial decisions and welfare-destructive decisions despite being banked (Turner, Klein and Stein, 2016). For example, banked adults who are financially illiterate can utilize the wrong type of financial products and services when searching for financial products and services to meet a particular need. Banked adults who are financially illiterate can open multiple bank accounts that they do not really need, thereby incurring huge account maintenance fees that ultimately worsen their welfare in the formal financial sector. Banked adults who are financially illiterate can easily become over-indebted (Kiesel and Noth, 2016), as they will likely borrow money from formal lending institutions just because credit is available and accessible without first assessing whether they have the ability to repay the loan from their own personal financial resources. Empirical studies, such as Gathergood (2012) and Gutiérrez-Nieto et al (2017), show a positive relationship between financial illiteracy and over-indebtedness. This suggests that banked adults who are financially illiterate adults are more likely to experience more losses from financial inclusion than the perceived benefits as they are more prone to becoming over-indebted and more likely to make financial mistakes and bad financial decisions. Financial illiteracy is a barrier to financial inclusion because it prevents banked adults from enjoying the full benefits of formal financial services. One reason why financial illiteracy among banked adults persist is because most financial inclusion efforts in many countries end at formal account ownership. Once citizens own a formal bank account, it is often assumed that financial inclusion goals have been achieved. Financial inclusion efforts need to go beyond formal account ownership. It should consider the extent of financial services usage as well as active formal accounts.

Banked Adults Who Are Extremely Poor

It is important to first distinguish between 'banked adults who are poor' and 'banked adults who are extremely poor'. On one hand, 'banked adults who are poor' are adults who have irregular low income and put small deposit in their formal account or bank account. On the other hand, 'banked adults who are extremely poor' are adults who have no income but put small deposit in their formal account.

Banked adults who are extremely poor will hardly enjoy any significant benefit from financial inclusion. This is because banked adults who are extremely poor have no income and have only small deposit in their account from which formal financial institutions will debit to collect transaction fees and account maintenance fees. Formal financial institutions, including banks, often describe these category of adults as 'unprofitable customers. In practice, we know that banks impose income thresholds as a part of the eligibility criteria to access formal credit. These income thresholds make it almost impossible for banked adults who are extremely poor to access formal credit due to their lack of income or little account inflow or deposit. By formal credit, I mean loans that are issued by regulated financial institutions. Although banked adults who are extremely poor will have access to savings and deposit products, they are unlikely to have access to formal credit because of their extreme poverty status.

Some may argue that banked adults who are extremely poor can access credit facilities from Fintech lenders who do not require documentation or income thresholds, thereby enabling them to bypass banks and formal lending institutions (Agarwal et al, 2020; Bernards, 2019; Ozili, 2018). A counter argument is that many Fintech lenders often embed sophisticated technology into their digital lending applications. The technology allows the Fintech lender to run a quick credit worthiness check on customers' accounts using the account number supplied by the potential poor borrower.

The purpose of running the credit worthiness check is to determine whether the borrower is eligible to access Fintech loans based on the credit history information and other information about the borrower's account activity. The result of such credit worthiness checks is often unfavorable to banked adults who are extremely poor, thereby making it difficult for them to access Fintech credit because they fall short of Fintech lending criteria.

Banked Adults Who Use Only Deposit Account Services

Another category of banked adults who lose from financial inclusion are banked adults that only use basic deposit account services. These banked adults are only interested in keeping their money in their formal accounts as deposit. They are not interested in accessing other formal financial services offered by financial institutions even when the services are advertised to them. They are not interested in using available investment and savings products even if the cost is low. They are not interested in mortgage finance products even if the cost of a mortgage is very low. They only care about the safe-keeping benefit of deposit account services. They only care about keeping their money in the bank as deposit and collecting it whenever they want. Despite the safe-keeping benefit they enjoy, this category of banked adults loses from financial inclusion because the money they keep as deposit in their formal account may not earn interest. Moreover, the deposits are often subject to deductions in the form of bank charges, which reduces the value of customer deposits. Banks can also use the deposits placed with them to lend to others and make a decent profit (Ozili, 2022c), while depositors do not get a share of the profit that banks make from using depositors' fund for lending purposes. This means that owning only a deposit account actually benefits banks and other financial institutions in many ways, meanwhile, it offers very little benefit to depositors. In fact, apart from the safe-keeping benefit of owning a deposit account, banked adults who choose to own only a deposit account loses from financial inclusion because they are unable to use other available financial services, such as investment and savings products, to increase their income.

People Who Are Involuntarily Banked

There are people who never wanted to be in the formal financial sector. They were either coerced or forced by their employers or the State to open a formal account or risk losing their expected income if they do not open a formal account or bank account. The fear of losing one's expected income or other benefits will make them open a formal account involuntarily. After involuntarily owning a bank account, many people who are involuntarily banked, especially those in the low-income group, often withdraw their funds immediately they receive inflows from their employers or the State. The implication of this behaviour for financial inclusion is that this category of banked adults will not use existing savings products or loan products which the formal sector provides. People who are involuntarily banked will be less interested in using existing savings products or loan products because they did not see the need for these financial products in the first place. Rather, they are more concerned about using their bank account to receive inflow and withdraw it immediately before banks begin to collect charges from their account. This behaviour is often caused by a general lack of trust in banks. People who are involuntarily banked do not trust banks. They believe that banks charge high fees even on small deposits thereby reducing the value of customer deposit.

The Informal Economy Loses From Financial Inclusion

The informal economy refers to market-based value-creating activities which are not taxed, registered, or regulated by the government and are therefore difficult to measure (Restrepo-Echavarria, 2014). The informal economy is visible in the form of survivalist business activities that are conducted from pavements, pedestrian malls, transport stations, road traffic, streets and from abandoned buildings (Smit and Musango, 2015). The informal economy has a bad reputation for conducting economic activities outside regulatory oversight, reducing government revenue collection, and for increasing corruption (Sakuhuni, 2014; Ouédraogo, 2017; Neef, 2002; Hoa, 2019). But the informal economy also has benefits that need to be acknowledged. Some benefits of the informal economy include lower prices of goods and services and job creation for people who cannot gain formal employment (Sakuhuni, 2014; Ketchen Jr et al, 2014; Alter Chen, 2005). People may not be able to gain formal employment either because they are too young, uneducated, unfit or unqualified for employment in the formal economy. These categories of people often rely on the informal economy to find a means of livelihood. Most of the jobs they find in the informal economy are jobs that rely on cash-based transactions.

Greater financial inclusion will reduce the size of the informal economy and lead to a reduction in cash-based activities in order to bring informal economic activities into the formal economy. The government can reduce the amount of cash in circulation, which can make cash become limited in supply and scarce. Prolonged scarcity of cash will shrink the informal economy and displace workers in the informal economy. The consequence is loss of jobs for people who rely on the informal economy to survive. As a result, the informal economy loses from financial inclusion.

CONCLUSION

Financial inclusion will give people access to basic banking products and services which they can use to improve their welfare. However, despite the potential benefits of financial inclusion, there will always be net winners and net losers from financial inclusion. This paper identified some net losers from financial inclusion. It showed that the net losers from financial inclusion are banked adults who are financially-illiterate, banked adults who are extremely poor, people who are employed in the informal economy and people who are involuntarily banked. The implication is that while efforts are being made to bring basic financial services to unbanked adults, policymakers have to deal with the problem of banked adults who lose out on the full benefits of financial inclusion. There is a need for policy makers to identify the losers from financial inclusion and reduce the number of losers from financial inclusion. Initiatives that are introduced to expand financial inclusion should be one that reduce the number of losers from financial inclusion in order to ensure that financial inclusion achieve its maximum benefits for all members of society. It is recommended that policymakers should provide mechanisms to ensure that those who lose out on the full benefits of financial inclusion are encouraged to increase their participation in the formal financial sector, and any existing barriers to financial inclusion should be removed. Future studies can examine the net winners in financial inclusion. Future studies can also identify the compensation that can be given to losers from financial inclusion to compensate them for the net loss they experience in the formal financial sector.

REFERENCES

Agarwal, S., Qian, W., & Tan, R. (2020). Financial inclusion and financial technology. In Household finance (pp. 307-346). Palgrave Macmillan. doi:10.1007/978-981-15-5526-8_9

Ahmad, A. H., Green, C., & Jiang, F. (2020). Mobile money, financial inclusion and development: A review with reference to African experience. *Journal of Economic Surveys*, *34*(4), 753–792. doi:10.1111/joes.12372

Albastiki, N., & Hamdan, A. (2019, September). Financial illiteracy and entrepreneurship success: literature review. In *European Conference on Innovation and Entrepreneurship*. Academic Conferences International Limited.

Alter Chen, M. (2005). *Rethinking the informal economy: Linkages with the formal economy and the formal regulatory environment* (No. 2005/10). WIDER Research Paper.

Arun, T., & Kamath, R. (2015). Financial inclusion: Policies and practices. *IIMB Management Review*, *27*(4), 267–287. doi:10.1016/j.iimb.2015.09.004

Beck, T., Senbet, L., & Simbanegavi, W. (2015). Financial inclusion and innovation in Africa: An overview. *Journal of African Economies*, *24*(suppl_1), i3–i11. doi:10.1093/jae/eju031

Bernards, N. (2019). Fintech and Financial Inclusion. In T. M. Shaw, L. C. Mahrenbach, R. Modi, & X. Yi-chong (Eds.), *The Palgrave Handbook of Contemporary International Political Economy* (pp. 317–329). Palgrave Macmillan. doi:10.1057/978-1-137-45443-0_20

Chen, R., & Divanbeigi, R. (2019). *Can Regulation Promote Financial Inclusion?* World Bank Policy Research Working Paper, No. 8711.

Chen, Z., & Jin, M. (2017). Financial inclusion in China: Use of credit. *Journal of Family and Economic Issues*, *38*(4), 528–540. doi:10.100710834-017-9531-x

Čihák, M., Mare, D. S., & Melecky, M. (2021). Financial Inclusion and Stability: Review of Theoretical and Empirical Links. *The World Bank Research Observer*, *36*(2), 197–233. doi:10.1093/wbro/lkaa006

De Koker, L., & Jentzsch, N. (2013). Financial inclusion and financial integrity: Aligned incentives? *World Development*, *44*, 267–280. doi:10.1016/j.worlddev.2012.11.002

Gathergood, J. (2012). Self-control, financial literacy and consumer over-indebtedness. *Journal of Economic Psychology*, *33*(3), 590–602. doi:10.1016/j.joep.2011.11.006

Ghosh, S., & Vinod, D. (2017). What constrains financial inclusion for women? Evidence from Indian micro data. *World Development*, *92*, 60–81. doi:10.1016/j.worlddev.2016.11.011

Gutiérrez-Nieto, B., Serrano-Cinca, C., & de la Cuesta González, M. (2017). A multivariate study of over-indebtedness' causes and consequences. *International Journal of Consumer Studies*, *41*(2), 188–198. doi:10.1111/ijcs.12324

Hoa, N. T. (2019). How large is Vietnam's informal economy? *Economic Affairs*, *39*(1), 81–100. doi:10.1111/ecaf.12328

Ketchen, D. J. Jr, Ireland, R. D., & Webb, J. W. (2014). Toward a Research Agenda for the Informal Economy: A Survey of the Strategic Entrepreneurship Journal's Editorial Board. *Strategic Entrepreneurship Journal*, *8*(1), 95–100. doi:10.1002ej.1175

Kiesel, K., & Noth, F. (2016). When Debt spells Sin: Does Religiosity guard against Over-Indebtedness? In *Annual Conference 2016 (Augsburg): Demographic Change* (No. 145774). Verein für Socialpolitik/German Economic Association.

Kulkarni, L., & Ghosh, A. (2021). Gender disparity in the digitalization of financial services: Challenges and promises for women's financial inclusion in India. *Gender, Technology and Development*, *25*(2), 233–250. doi:10.1080/09718524.2021.1911022

Llewellyn, D. T. (2021). *Introduction: financial inclusion-an overview of key issues*. Inclusive Financial Development.

López, T., & Winkler, A. (2019). Does financial inclusion mitigate credit boom-bust cycles? *Journal of Financial Stability*, *43*, 116–129. doi:10.1016/j.jfs.2019.06.001

Mader, P. (2018). Contesting financial inclusion. *Development and Change*, *49*(2), 461–483. doi:10.1111/dech.12368

Mani, M. (2016). Financial inclusion in South Asia—Relative standing, challenges and initiatives. *South Asian Survey*, *23*(2), 158–179. doi:10.1177/0971523118783353

Milana, C., & Ashta, A. (2020). Microfinance and financial inclusion: Challenges and opportunities. *Strategic Change*, *29*(3), 257–266. doi:10.1002/jsc.2339

Natarajan, N., Brickell, K., Guermond, V., Lawreniuk, S., & Parsons, L. (2021). Challenging the financial inclusion-decent work nexus: Evidence from Cambodia's over-indebted internal migrants. *Global Public Policy and Governance*, *1*(3), 361–381. doi:10.100743508-021-00026-7

Neef, R. (2002). Aspects of the informal economy in a transforming country: The case of Romania. *International Journal of Urban and Regional Research*, *26*(2), 299–322. doi:10.1111/1468-2427.00381

Ouédraogo, I. M. (2017). Governance, corruption, and the informal economy. *Modern Economy*, *8*(02), 256–271. doi:10.4236/me.2017.82018

Oz-Yalaman, G. (2019). Financial inclusion and tax revenue. *Central Bank Review*, *19*(3), 107–113. doi:10.1016/j.cbrev.2019.08.004

Ozili, P. K. (2018). Impact of digital finance on financial inclusion and stability. *Borsa Istanbul Review*, *18*(4), 329–340. doi:10.1016/j.bir.2017.12.003

Ozili, P. K. (2020). Theories of financial inclusion. In *Uncertainty and challenges in contemporary economic behaviour*. Emerald Publishing Limited. doi:10.1108/978-1-80043-095-220201008

Ozili, P. K. (2021a). Financial inclusion research around the world: A review. *The Forum for Social Economics*, *50*(4), 457–479. doi:10.1080/07360932.2020.1715238

Ozili, P. K. (2021b). Financial inclusion: a strong critique. In *New Challenges for Future Sustainability and Wellbeing* (pp. 1–16). Emerald Publishing Limited. doi:10.1108/978-1-80043-968-920211002

Ozili, P. K. (2022a). Can central bank digital currency increase financial inclusion? Arguments for and against. In *Big Data Analytics in the Insurance Market* (pp. 241–249). Emerald Publishing Limited. doi:10.1108/978-1-80262-637-720221013

Ozili, P. K. (2022b). Digital financial inclusion. In *Big Data: A Game Changer for Insurance Industry* (pp. 229–238). Emerald Publishing Limited. doi:10.1108/978-1-80262-605-620221015

Ozili, P. K. (2022c). Fault lines in financial inclusion. perspectives on global development and technology. *Perspectives on Global Development*, *21*(3), 188–201. doi:10.1163/15691497-12341624

Restrepo-Echavarria, P. (2014). Macroeconomic volatility: The role of the informal economy. *European Economic Review*, *70*, 454–469. doi:10.1016/j.euroecorev.2014.06.012

Sakuhuni, R. C. (2014). Causes, Benefits and Costs Of Informal Economy: Evidence From Zimbabwe. *Researchjournali's Journal of Commerce*, *2*(4), 1–9.

Shambare, R., & Rugimbana, R. (2012). Financial literacy among the educated: An exploratory study of selected university students in South Africa. *Thunderbird International Business Review*, *54*(4), 581–590. doi:10.1002/tie.21485

Sharizan, S., Redzuan, N. H., & Rosman, R. (2021). Issues and challenges of financial inclusion among low-income earners in rural areas of Malaysia. *Turkish Journal of Economics*, *8*(Special Issue), 277–299. doi:10.26414/A2376

Shihadeh, F. H., Hannon, A. M., Guan, J., Ul Haq, I., & Wang, X. (2018). Does financial inclusion improve the banks' performance? Evidence from Jordan. In Global Tensions in Financial Markets (Research in Finance, Vol. 34). Emerald Publishing Limited.

Smit, S., & Musango, J. K. (2015). Towards connecting green economy with informal economy in South Africa: A review and way forward. *Ecological Economics*, *116*, 154–159. doi:10.1016/j.ecolecon.2015.04.022

Turner, J. A., Klein, B. W., & Stein, N. P. (2016). Financial Illiteracy Meets Conflicted Advice: The Case of Thrift Savings Plan Rollovers. *The Journal of Retirement*, *3*(4), 47–65. doi:10.3905/jor.2016.3.4.047

Varghese, G., & Viswanathan, L. (2018). Financial inclusion: Opportunities, issues and challenges. *Theoretical Economics Letters*, *8*(11), 1935–1942. doi:10.4236/tel.2018.811126

Chapter 6
Proceed With Caution:
Protecting the Economic Well-Being of Women Using Microfinance – Egyptian Microfinance Case Study

Shymaa Bedaiwy
https://orcid.org/0000-0003-0092-9672
University of Massachusetts, Boston, USA

ABSTRACT

Microfinance had a clear mission of serving the least privileged. However, 45 years after Muhammad Yunus introduced the first microloans, the global microfinance market has become increasingly commercialized, with high tendencies toward for-profit organizations, in contrast to how it was originally introduced within the realm of not-for-profits. Microfinance is now a multi-billion-dollar financial industry. Microcredit is adopted as an efficient tool to achieve sustainable development goals. This chapter is analyzing how the current Egyptian microfinance regulations can contribute to the achievement of SDGs. The analysis shows that Egypt has developed and enacted a law that is meeting the international standards of microfinance global best practice; however, there is room for ensuring the microfinance institutions are following their social justice mission by regulating other microcredit services beyond financing income-generating activities. The chapter concludes that more regulations are needed to ensure that MFIs are reaching out to women micro-entrepreneurs and doing them no harm.

DOI: 10.4018/978-1-6684-5647-7.ch006

INTRODUCTION

Microfinance, since its evolution, had a clear mission of serving the least privileged. However, 45 years since Muhammad Yunus introduced the first microloans, primarily targeting Bangladeshi women, the global microfinance market is no longer exclusively the purview of Non-Governmental Organizations (NGOs) with a clear social mission; for-profits are also providing microfinance products. The microfinance market has become increasingly commercialized, with a significant increase in the microcredit market share of for-profit organizations compared to NGOs. Besides NGOs, microfinance institutions (MFIs) include for-profit banks and investment firms. It is now a multi-billion dollar financial industry. In 2015, the World Bank estimated that the microfinance industry loans reached $60 to $100 billion globally, acquiring an estimated 200 million clients, most of whom live in acute poverty.

Muhammad Yunus, the founder of Grameen Bank, the Bank for the Poor, the godfather of microcredit and what is known as microfinance, was awarded the Nobel Peace Prize in 2006 for his work "to help poor people escape from poverty by providing loans on terms suitable to them and by teaching them a few sound financial principles so they could help themselves." (nobelprize.org, n.d.-b). In 2019, the Nobel Prize for Economic Science was awarded to three economists, Abhijit Banerjee, Esther Duflo, and Michael Kremer, for "their experimental approach to alleviating global poverty" (nobelprize.org, n.d.).org, n.d.-a). Two of them are known for a long history of experimental research evaluating microcredit and criticizing its celebrated role in alleviating poverty (Rajadhyaksha, 2019). From 2006 to 2019, the Microfinance industry witnessed revolutionary developments and raised many concerns about its effectiveness in helping the poor.

The concept of lending small amounts of money to poor people to aid business development, and other purposes, has a long history. The idea of lending to others informally predated microcredit and the services of what is known as MFIs (Roodman, 2012). However, "the advent of modern microfinance has been credited to several pilot projects that occurred roughly simultaneously, most famously Muhammad Yunus' experiments. He started with microcredit in 1976 with $27.00 from his own pocket and eventually became the Grameen Bank." (Wong & Richards, 2014) p.383. The terms Microcredit and Microfinance are interchangeable because microcredit was the first financial product offered to the poor (Khandker, 1998).

Moreover, Roodman (2012) claims that Microcredit, as Yunus presented it, was targeting poor rural women in the first place. Since then, Microcredit has proliferated. Other financial services, such as micro-savings and micro-insurance, were provided to the poor, which later constructed what we now know as Microfinance (Morduch, 1999). Microcredit or Microfinance has been seen as an effective tool to alleviate poverty and create jobs for decades.

Microfinance is a tool that aims to provide the unbankable poor with financial products to empower them and alleviate poverty (AbuDeif, 2016; Khandker, 1998; Mahmoud Ali & Ghoneim, 2019; Taha, 2012). The unbankable populations lack access to regular financial banking services due to the lack of required and adequate collaterals or physical outreach of banks in remote areas where the poor live (Hamid & Nisser, 2017).

The microfinance promise is to serve the poor on both ends, economically and socially, by providing the poor with financial products (such as credit, savings, insurance, and remittance) that meet their needs and capabilities as well (Morduch, 1999). The provision of microcredit to the poor paved the way for other financial products to be customized to the poor's capabilities. However, MFIs either prefer (or self-limit) their services to only credit, although other financial services are demanded by the poor and would, if adequately provided, help them enhance their living conditions, such as micro-savings and micro-insurance (Duvendack et al., 2011). The unique characteristics of the unbankable, being illiterate and primarily concentrated in remote and rural areas, required MFIs to follow a unique operations model, unlike other conventional financial services providers. In one model, since microfinance clients are usually illiterate, MFIs depended heavily on verbal communication with potential clients. Also, MFIs would recruit their loan officers from the same areas/communities they serve; the outreach depends heavily on word of mouth and the trusted networks of local communities.

With microcredit preceding its respective government regulations, internationally, the importance of social responsibility within the microfinance market began to evolve through self-regulation. As MFIs came under increased inspection, national associations/networks were developed to exchange information, identify and recognize best practices, and develop codes of conduct (Moussa, 2007). Such organizations included the Association of Microfinance Institutions in Uganda, Sa-Dhan in India, and ProDesarrollo in Mexico. A leading international program has emerged, providing standards for the social responsibility of MFIs. The program was 'Smart Campaign, the Universal Standards for Social Performance Management and Microfinance Transparency' (promoted by the NGO-investor network Consultative Group to Assist the Poor (CGAP) and the non-profit ACCION) (Mader, 2017).

The Microfinance Leaders Retreat, also known as The Pocantico Declaration, was organized by Boulder Institute of Microfinance, CGAP, and Deutsche Bank at the Pocantico Conference Center of New York. The Boulder Institute, founded in 1995, is a nonprofit organization that provides research on microfinance. The declaration's signatures include representatives from The Grameen Foundation, Deutsche Bank, the Inter-American Development Bank, and CGAP.

In March 2009, the Center for the Financial Inclusion at ACCION International, along with CGAP of the World Bank, synthesized the declaration distilling the main points into Six Clients Protection Principles (CPPs) (Forster, Lahaye, & Mckee, 2009). Later, in 2011, a seventh principle was added to the campaign expanding the scope of CPPs to cover multiple financial products other than microcredit and highlighting the concept of non-discrimination (Smart, n.d.).

CPPs call on MFIs to "adopt appropriate product design schemes and adequate delivery channels with the characteristics of the clients taken into consideration; prevent the over-indebtedness of clients; provide transparent information on the financial products in a simple sufficient way to the clients; adhere to responsible pricing judgment for the financial services; treat clients fairly and respectfully; protect clients' data; and construct an efficient complaints resolution mechanism" (Smart, n.d.). The CPPs are reinforcing the idea of sustaining the business of MFIs and protecting clients from harm.

The Smart Campaign was identified as the most visible international standard for MFIs, and the World Bank has also promoted and built its basic Microfinance regulations model following those standards (Afonso, Morvant-Roux, Guérin, & Forcella, 2017). The seven principles of the Smart Campaign are outlined in the Campaign focus on social responsibility. The standards are

1. appropriate product design and delivery;
2. prevention of over-indebtedness;
3. transparency;
4. responsible pricing;
5. fair and respectful treatment of customers;
6. privacy, security, and integrity of client data; and
7. mechanisms for complaint resolution.

The limitations of self-regulatory frameworks are not the content of the standards but the lack of specificity within the standards and the assumption that MFIs will adhere to the social performance standards and principles on their own. These factors urged governments to enact laws and regulations to organize microfinance markets domestically.

With the expansion of the services provided and the types of MFIs, governments started to consider regulating and supervising microfinance activities by developing and enacting laws concerned with microfinance. Before governmental regulations prevailed, microfinance markets were self-regulated. MFIs would gather under a network or a national NGO umbrella to exchange lessons learned and information to document the best practices (Moussa, 2007). The primary purpose of microfinance regulation is to protect the MFIs from defaulting and the clients from abuse. Microfinance clients are generally marginalized, illiterate or have primary education, and lack proper social protection networks. In addition to the fact that microfinance is a double-bottom development tool, economic and social regulations should balance the two ends to eliminate mission drifts of MFIs and empower clients (Schicks, 2012). Sound regulations would consider clients' protection both theoretically and practically.

Mission drift in Microfinance is when the mission of an MFI tilts more often towards profit-making at the cost of helping the poor graduate out of poverty. Muhammad Yunus claims that better-off clients tend to crowd out poor clients in the market (Mersland & Strøm, 2010). MFIs struggle to achieve sustainability and their social mission (Bali Swain & Wallentin, 2017; Kar & Bali Swain, 2018). Reaching out to the poor in the remote areas they live in adds a burden to operations costs an MFI may have, in addition to lending to the poor is risky too. Mission drift is widely measured by two main indicators. The first indicator is the breadth of outreach which represents the number of clients served by MFIs, and the depth of outreach, which represents the average loan size (Kar & Bali Swain, 2018; Mersland & Strøm, 2010; Quayes, 2020; Vanroose & D'Espallier, 2013). Mission drift happens when MFIs serve less percentage of the targeted population and increase the average loan size offered, which means that MFIs are not serving the poor in the first place, which contradicts the Microfinance promise.

This chapter will review the law and regulations of Microfinance in Egypt. It also presents the market reports from the first published March 2016 to the latest publicly available report on the Egyptian Financial Regulatory Authority (FRA) website, dated December 2021. The review highlights concerns in the market and how the regulations address such concerns. Also, the chapter will bring to the reader's attention the best practices and literature documented regarding issues related to Sustainable Development Goals (SDGs), particularly SDG 1 and SDG 8, with a special focus on women. The chapter will focus on microcredit only, and the author translated all laws and regulations statements from Arabic to English. All data reported are extracted from the FRA reports.

MICROFINANCE IN EGYPT

Egypt has had microfinance activities running since the 1950s in many forms. It started in the agriculture sector by providing farmers with small loans via the Principal Bank for Development and Agriculture, a government-owned bank. In 1977, the Ministry of Social Solidarity introduced the "Productive Families" project targeting low-income families to provide them with microcredit, given that they have one government employee as a grantor (Barsoum, 2006). NGOs championed microfinance for a very long time, especially for women, until the early 2000s when for-profit companies entered the market (Moussa, 2007). The first all-women microcredit program was established in 1981 when most women had no national ID cards. The program was criticized, and loan repayment was questioned. However, all women repaid their loans successfully (Bibars, 2019). MFIs were not regulated under one umbrella for so long. NGO-MFIs were regulated and supervised by the Ministry of Social Solidarity (MoSS) under the MoSS mandate to regulate all NGOs. For-profit MIFs were regulated and supervised by the Ministry of Investment (MoI) (Sanabel, 2010). Although both MFI NGOs and MFI companies (for-profits) were providing the same service exactly, microcredit, they were regulated by two different entities (Moussa, 2007), which leaves the actual microfinance provision unregulated, and sources of reliable data on the market needed to track its trends are missing.

Some Egyptian NGOs launched their microcredit programs in the 1980s with the support of USAID (Waly, 2010), and they expanded their programs and grew to be pioneers in the Egyptian Microfinance Market. Since their expansions coincided with the lack of a regulatory authority, no formal report has accurately assessed Egypt's market volume. Calls for regulating Microfinance activities started to appear in almost all documents and reports on financial sector reform in Egypt (Moussa, 2007; Nasr, 2006; Sanabel, 2010).

In 2004, a law on Small and Medium Enterprise (SME) Development was enacted and delegated the role of coordinating the efforts of SMEs to the Social Fund for Development (SFD). However, it was not enough because it ignored the micro-enterprise contribution to the economy back then (Moussa, 2007). Later, SFD was merged with the newly established Micro-Small-Medium Enterprise Development Agency (MSMEDA) (Egypt Today, 2017).

In 2014, the Egyptian Government enacted the first Microfinance activities law No. 141 for the year 2014, which delegated the FRA to regulate the market (AbuDeif, 2016). FRA is an independent governmental authority that reports to the cabinet and regulates Non-Banking Financial Services, including insurance, factoring, and the stock market (FRA, n.d.). The Egyptian Microfinance Law No. 141 of the year 2014 defines microfinance as any non-banking finance provided for income generation that does not exceed a total of EGP 100,000, one hundred thousand Egyptian pounds ($ 4,000) (AbuDeif, 2016). While other financial services could be used for other purposes, such as personal expenses or mitigating the effects of a crisis, the Egyptian microfinance definition limits the purpose of financial provision to clients to income-generating activities only, which means that other forms of finance provided by MFIs to their clients are illegal, this might include lending for personal expenses or consumer lending. In October 2020, the government ratified amendments to the Microfinance Act (Law 141/2014) to expand the outreach of Micro-Small-Medium Enterprise (MSME) financing further and changed its title to be exclusive for financing MSME, and increased its cap to EGP 200,000 ($8,157).

Category	Active Portfolio
NGO(A)	equal to and more than EGP 50 million
NGO(B)	equal to and more than EGP 10 million
NGO(C)	less than EGP 10 million
Companies	Registered for-profit-companies

FRA regulates MFIs be they NGOs or companies. The regulations FRA adopted for microfinance divided MFIs into four categories (see Table 1).

All licensed MFIs are required to report to FRA and FRA develops quarterly market reports. Reporting is crucial for adopting sound regulations to help the market's sustainability and protect clients. Thanks to FRA, Egypt now has solid quarterly reports to rely on, and all licensed MFIs are listed on FRA's website with their contacts for the first time.

FRA published the first formal report on Microfinance in June 2016 and made all its quarterly reports public on its website. Before FRA's reports, the market depended on Sanabel (regional network for microfinance) and SFD's (known later as MESMEDA). However, both organizations were member-centered and reported on their members only. Before FRA's reports, Sanabel in 2010 reported that active clients in Egypt reached 1.3 million active clients and around EGP 990 million. The figures were reported from the 14 MFI members of Sanabel, who included the largest MFIs in Egypt; all were NGOs. Later on, after enacting the law, they were categorized under NGOs-A and NGOs-B. The first report of FRA in 2016 reported active clients of all licensed MFIs reported to be 1.5 million clients with EGP 3.6 billion served by 709 licensed MFIs through 1,356 branches and offices. FRA regulates MFIs be they NGOs or for-profit Companies. Thanks to FRA, we now have solid quarterly reports to rely upon, and those reports are made public on their website.

MICROFINANCE AND ENDING POVERTY

SDG 1 is exclusively dedicated to ending poverty. While women are being assigned a triple societal role of production, reproduction, and community management (Drolet, 2011), which might cause women to be burdened with personal expenses that they lack access to proper funds to cover (A. Taha & Ajlouni, 2018). One of the personal expenses highlighted in different pieces of literature is marriage expenses (Rogaly, Castillo, & Serrano, 2004) (Bali Swain & Wallentin, 2017) (WorldBank, 2018). This complexity means that women also need a safe source of finance to cover other expenses rather than income-generating activities.

The New Woman Foundation released a study in 2020 highlighting reasons for rural women applying for micro-loans. The results showed that other than financing business, 23.4 percent of women borrow to cover marriage expenses, versus 22.2 percent of men. Also, 21.3 percent of women borrow to pay other debts, versus 18 percent of men (Elantary & Ezzat, 2020). Lack of personal finance products increases the chances of women resorting to informal finance to meet their financial needs.

Tackling the percentage of microfinance clients borrowing to pay other debts brings to the discussion the importance of regulating credit information. With the growth of average loan size happening in the market, as highlighted earlier, examining how the microfinance law considers issues related to market stability and prevention of over-indebtedness is crucial. The SMART campaign highlighted the importance of a client's ability to repay the loan as a criterion to assess the market's capacity to prevent over-indebtedness. It urged regulators and MFIs to implement policies and internal systems to improve credit information sharing (Bedaiwy & Peter, 2022). For years, the credit registry system at the Central Bank of Egypt (CBE) was only accessible to banks, and it had a minimum of EGP 20,000 ($ 800) till 2005 for reporting (Nasr, 2006). Article 7 of Law No. 141 addressing Egyptian Microfinance obliged MFIs to participate in a credit score system and delegated the regulation of this obligation to FRA to ensure the capacity of the clients to repay their finance is widely available for MFIs so that they can build sound judgment on whom to lend.

Article 22 of FRA's NGOs-MFIs regulations obligated MFIs to run a credit score check on each client applying for a loan that is equal to or more than EGP 1,500 ($ 60) without acquiring written consent from the client as long as the MFI follows the data protection protocols. The regulation required MFIs to run their credit check to a credit score system that is independent and certified by the Central Bank of Egypt (CBE). In 2005 iScore, the full-scaled private credit bureau, was established to increase access to creditworthiness information. To date, iScore is the only independent credit system company registered and licensed to run credit checks at the CBE. FRA also obligated MFIs to report their client data to the credit score system and any legal actions they may take against a defaulting client monthly. However, the lending decision remains an exclusive right of MFI boards to take, despite the credit score report of clients. The credit risk assessment is an internal decision of the MFI, not related to the result of the credit check in this case.

With FRA enforcing MFIs to report to the credit score system, the credit scoring system in Egypt witnessed an unprecedented expansion thanks to the Microfinance law. The data (Nasr, 2006) presented on the expansion in credit scores after establishing the iScore showed an exponential significance for loans lower than EGP 10,000 ($ 250). Therefore, expanding the credit score database to loans equal to or more than EGP 1,500 ($ 60) contributes significantly to the overall financial health of the Egyptian market. FRA, in its NGOs-MFIs regulations article 20, listed important points to be considered by MFIs while deciding about the loan application, the decision whether to lend to the client or not. The article explicitly stated that MFIs should be considering avoiding over-indebtedness and consider the client's capacity to repay loans, the client's history with the lending MFI itself, the average debt-to-income ratios, the client's cash flow, and the number of active loans a client might be having simultaneously with other MFIs. Although this regulation is only a recommendation for MFIs to consider when deciding whom to lend, it is a great step toward cultivating the culture of avoiding over-indebtedness at MFIs and helping with the transition towards building sound lending policies and decisions, especially for category NGOs-C. This category is known for its spread in rural areas. This article, among others, shows how much Egyptian law aligns with the internationally identified best practices.

In addition to the NGOs-MFIs regulations, FRA developed a guideline on client protection to help expand the knowledge around microfinance best practices among key stakeholders, including MFIs. Principle no. 4 of the Egyptian Microfinance Client Protection Guidelines is titled: Comprehensive Finance Policies Considerate of Clients' Financial Status. It elaborated on Article 22 of the NGO regulations and highlighted that the credit score check applies to individual and group lending. It explained that MFIs are to decide the capacity of the client to repay the loan based on her credit score as reported from the credit score system. In case of a rejected loan application, the MFI shall provide the contact information of the organization running the credit score system to the client so she can resolve her issue and enhance her credit score. It also required MFIs to keep the credit score reports in the client files.

The principle combined Articles 20 and 22 of the NGOs regulations explicitly mentioning group lending. This principle is an excellent step in building a credible and reliable credit score system. Given that NGOs launched their microcredit programs way before the law was enacted, as explained earlier, and most women clients were given microcredit even without having a national ID (Bibars, 2019), the law comes in to synchronize the data from multiple NGOs and clean it up.

It is crucial for FRA to enforce the credit score-sharing mechanism and tighten the criteria for client selections to make sure they are not over-indebted. It is worth mentioning that FRA reports ignore the cases of clients double-lending from different institutions and, in some cases, triple-lending or more. FRA can at least report publicly the percentage of double-lending to give a more accurate understanding of the market dynamics and encourage MFIs to reach more eligible and in need, unbankable clients, particularly women.

With companies and NGOs providing microfinance services in the market, it is worrying to see a decline in the number of NGO clients. Companies' share of clients increased higher than the shares of the three tiers of NGOs. In the first five years of the law's enactment between 2014 and 2019, reports show that companies were witnessing the most considerable increase in their market share. NGOs category B were reported to have a decrease of -20.23 percent in market share compared to the same reporting period of 2018. This expansion is only for a year. The five-year progress report shows that companies increased their average loan size by 1.04 percent in 2019 compared to 2016, when FRA started publicly reporting on the market. The trend of a growing market share of for-profit companies against NGOs continues. It is worth mentioning that in the first public report FRA released in March 2016, for-profit companies' market share was around 10 percent. In December 2021, it reached 57.37 percent. This growth enforces that the market is tiling towards commercialization. Companies' average loan size grew from EGP 3,329 in 2016, with a market share of 10.28 percent, to EGP 10,000 in 2021, with a market share of 57.37 percent.

MICROFINANCE AND DECENT WORK

SDG 8 on Decent Work adopted "Promote sustained, inclusive and sustainable economic growth, full and productive employment and decent work for all" in its targets 8.3, there is an explicit promotion for supporting MSMEs, while target 8.5 highlighted equality between men and women. Law No. 141 on Microfinance Activities determined the purpose of the financing provided to clients for income-generating activities only with a maximum amount of EGP 100,000, later amended to EGP 200,000 in October 2020. The rationale for specifying the purpose of getting finance solely for income-generating activities is to help the client repay the loan and make the MFI sustainable. With the limited resources the poor may have, it is to their benefit to enforce the idea of having the finance to fund income-generating activities to help them not only repay the loan but also sustain a source of income to enhance their living conditions (Mahmoud Ali & Ghoneim, 2019). Women are less privileged than men and carry triple-role responsibilities in society, production, reproduction, and community-manage (Drolet, 2011). Therefore encouraging women to finance income-generating activities will help them better manage their resources and prevent them from over-indebtedness.

In Egypt, there are two types of lending mechanisms MFIs have and report on to FRA: Individual Loans (ILs) and Group Loans (GLs). ILs are usually offered to clients individually, while GLs are offered to solidarity groups, where a group of 3-5 members comes together in one group to act as a grantor for each other in case of any member defaults. Usually, GLs are dominated by women, and FRA reports indicate that women represent more than 90 percent of the clientele of the GLs. AbuDeif (2016) stated that ILs generally have higher monetary value and lengthier repayment periods. It could start with an amount of EGP 500 ($ 20) to EGP 25,000

($ 1,000) and could be repaid in monthly installments over a minimum period of 4 months and up to 2 years. GLs could start with EGP 50 ($ 2) to EGP 1,500 ($ 60) per woman and could be repaid weekly over a period ranging between 10 to 40 weeks. The microfinance activities law put a ceiling of EGP 100,000 ($ 5,500) per individual client. Most of the literature confirms that GLs are offered to women (AbuDeif, 2016; Farag, 2011; Moussa, 2007). Those are also the two lending mechanisms reported by FRA.

Tracking the progress of the two lending mechanisms as reported by FRA, ILs are given to individuals financing their business/enterprise. It usually requires one or two persons to act as the borrower's guarantors (AbuDeif, 2016). In March 2016, FRA reported that ILs clients represent more than 45 percent of active clients with more than 69 percent of the portfolio and an average loan size of EGP 3,488.

On the other hand, GLs clients were 54 percent of active clients, mostly women, with only 30 percent portfolio and an average loan size of EGP 1,314. In December 2021, ILs clients were reported to represent 64.27 percent of active clients with 85.66 percent of the portfolio with a higher average loan size of more than EGP 10,000. GLs clients of the same reporting period had 35.73 percent of active clients with 14.34 percent of the portfolio and an average loan size of EGP 3,110. This shows that the market favors ILs over GLs and offers higher loan sizes to ILs than GLs.

Figure 1.

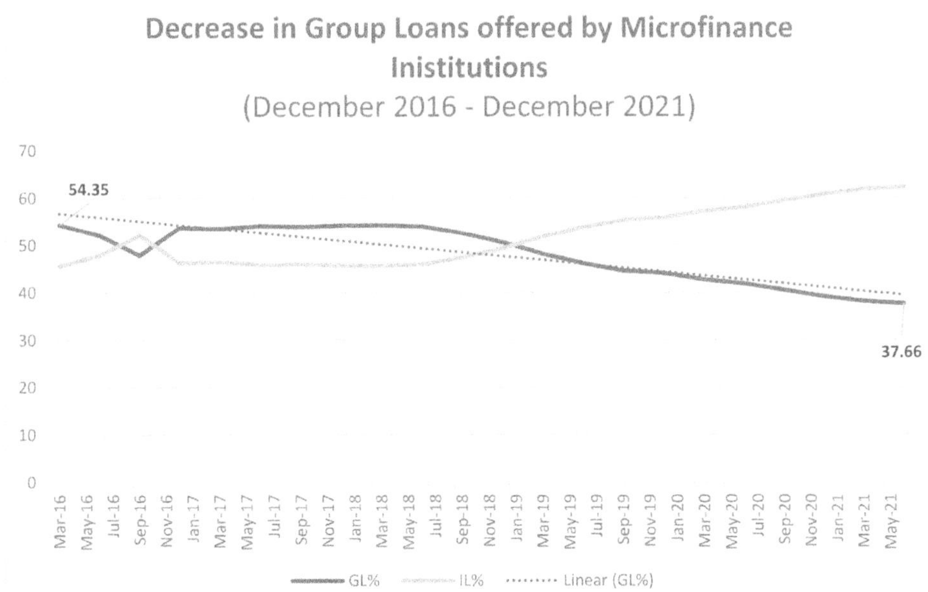

Figure 1 shows a market trend of decline in the percentage of GLs. It shows that women are being crowded out of the market. GLs being dominated by poor women is not only leaving unbankable women behind, but also the increase in the average loan size shows that the microfinance market in Egypt is tilting towards mission drift both in the breadth of outreach which is represented here in the declining number of poor women clients, and the depth of outreach, which is represented here in the increase of the average loan size offered to women.

Muhammad Yunus expressed his worry about the commercialization of MFIs and called them loan sharks on the opinion page of the New York Times on January 14, 2011. He explained that he mainly thought of microcredit to help the poor and eliminate the presence of loan sharks who benefited from the poor. He said: "In 1983, I founded Grameen Bank to provide small loans that people, especially poor women, could use to bring themselves out of poverty. At that time, I never imagined that one day microcredit would give rise to its own breed of loan sharks" (Negley & Yunus, 2011). The accelerated increase in interest rates turned MFIs into commercial institutions and drifted their social mission of helping the poor in the first place. Yunus explained that the main reason behind the emergence of such a phenomenon in 2005 was the lack of wholesale funds to lend the poor. MFIs resorted to banks and commercial institutions to get funds, transmitting the financial burden to the poor (Yunus, 2011). As we know it now, microfinance was initially introduced as a tool to help the poor graduate out of poverty. However, with profiting from the poor, MFIs are losing their focus on the original mission.

Figure 1 shows that the percentage of GLs declined from 54.35 percent in 2016 to 37.66 percent by the end of 2021. Some may argue that the decline in GLs is not necessarily significant over the years, yet, the linear analysis shows a clear declining trend in expanding microfinance services to poor women over the years. Since the Microfinance law in Egypt limited the purpose of finance to be for income-generating activities only, this decline in the percentage of GLs also highlights the fact that opportunities for financing women-led micro-enterprises are also shrinking for the poor who are interested in developing and expanding their micro-enterprise. Target 8.3 of SDG 8 states: "Promote development-oriented policies that support productive activities, decent job creation, entrepreneurship, creativity and innovation, and encourage the formalization and growth of micro-, small- and medium-sized enterprises, including through access to financial services." With the clear tendencies of the microfinance market in Egypt towards the declining number of GLs, mainly targeting micro-entrepreneurs, a rising concern comes questioning meeting the achievement of target 8.3. Moreover, the only indicator under this target is 8.3.1 "Proportion of informal employment in total employment, by sector and sex" knowing that GLs in Egypt serve women clients mostly, as per FRA reports, it also raises a concern about the availability of appropriate funds for women micro-entrepreneurs to maintain, develop, and expand their micro business.

CONCLUSION

Egypt has extremely promising social and economic development plans, and women are at their heart. Two of the most significant national initiatives, Haya Karima (which translates into decent life) and the National Family Development Project, acknowledge the role of microfinance and financial inclusion as the main pillars of success. Egypt also adopted its sustainable development strategy titled Egypt 2030, which aligns with the 17 SDGs. Microfinance activities and financing micro-enterprises are still regulated under FRA with law no.14 of 2014. The law needs special consideration to ensure that MFIs' social missions comply with the broader government initiatives and that MFIs assume their original role of alleviating poverty. NGOs championed providing microfinance products, and microcredit is still the market's most prevailing product. FRA excellently aligns Egyptian Microfinance regulations with the best practices documented worldwide. Moreover, FRA issued a separate document highlighting client protection measures within the regulations. However, following the progress reports FRA published quarterly, it is easy to tell that the market is being commercialized.

Commercialization of the market raises many questions regarding reaching the real poor and accomplishing the social mission of Microfinance as it originally started. The growth of for-profits over NGOs in the market would urge NGOs to serve higher tiers of clients to maximize their profit and survive the competition with for-profits (Pedrini & Ferri, 2016; Wong & Richards, 2014). Also, with NGOs championing the market since its early development, the most highly trained calibers and outreach officers are NGO staff. Therefore, FRA might consider developing a training program focused on the social mission of Microfinance and obliging for-profits staff to receive the training and abide by it as part of their licensing process.

Egypt is rated the second-largest Arab Microfinance market (Sanabel, 2010). The market has only been regulated for the last eight years, showing a strong political will to enlarge and sustain the Microfinance market and raise country-wide financial inclusion rates. A nationwide survey is highly needed to get a sense of average interest rates and also the capacities of MFIs, in general, to adjust regulations as needed.

Most importantly, a transparent report on the overlap of borrowers should be publicly available with the quarterly report by FRA to assess the gap in reaching clients and direct investors in disadvantaged areas. The availability of information opens room for cooperation with the Central Bank of Egypt to raise financial inclusion rates in Egypt.

When it comes to assigning the role of microfinance in achieving the SDGs, Microfinance proved successful in many countries and cases in alleviating poverty and enhancing people's lives, highlighted under SDG1: End Poverty. However, women are burdened with triple roles in the community, and Egypt is no exception. Studies proved that women borrow to cover some personal expenses. The current microfinance law in Egypt limits microcredit to financing income-generating activities only. This limitation pushes women to borrow from informal resources, unregulated and unmonitored. Informal lending is irresponsible compared to formal and regulated lending. Therefore, microfinance law might consider expanding the regulations to other purposes than financing income-generating activities to protect women from borrowing from informal resources. Such change will make information on double-borrowing available, which ensures that women are not overly indebted and encourages MFIs to reach out to eligible clients.

Regarding SDG 8, dedicated to promoting decent work, in its targets, the goal highlighted the role of promoting and supporting micro-enterprise development in social and economic development and the availability of equal opportunities for men and women. The latest data showed that women are being crowded out of the market while there is a market share increase in for-profit companies. Market commercialization also shows that women do not have equal opportunities as men, and microfinance regulations need to recognize the urgency to reach out to more women.

The commercialization of the microfinance market in Egypt raises many questions regarding the social justice issues related to poverty alleviation. Microfinance best practices were globally identified, recognized, and adopted to prevent profiting from the poor. Therefore, microfinance regulations in Egypt need such suggested reforms and revisions under the umbrella of national social and economic development projects to ensure that microfinance is a catalyst of success for those entities and is doing no harm to its clients.

REFERENCES

Abdelmoumni, F., Ackerman, C., Barry, N., Chao-Beroff, R., Choudhury, S., Counts, A.. … Stauffenberg, D. v. (2008). *The Pocantico Declaration*. Retrieved from https://www.smartcampaign.org/storage/documents/Pocantico_Declaration.pdf

AbuDeif, S. (2016). *The Role of Microfinance in alleviating unemployment in Egypt: Quantitative study*. Retrieved from www.amarabac.com

Afonso, J. S., Morvant-Roux, S., Guérin, I., & Forcella, D. (2017). Doing Good by Doing Well? Microfinance, Self-Regulation and Borrowers' Over-indebtedness in the Dominican Republic. *Journal of International Development, 29*(7), 919–935. doi:10.1002/jid.3244

Bali Swain, R., & Wallentin, F. Y. (2017). The Impact of Microfinance on Factors Empowering Women: Differences in Regional and Delivery Mechanisms in India's SHG Programme. *The Journal of Development Studies, 53*(5), 684–699. doi:10.1080/00220388.2016.1205732

Barsoum, G. (2006). Who gets credit? The gendered division of microfinance programs in Egypt. *Canadian Journal of Development Studies, 27*(1), 51–64. doi: 10.1080/02255189.2006.9669120

Bedaiwy, S., & Peter, D. (2022). An evaluation of Egyptian microfinance laws and regulations preventing overindebtedness of women. *Journal of International Development*, 1–16. doi:10.1002/jid.3633

Bibars, I. (2019). *Transforming Society ~ How micro-credit helped women in Egypt have a choice*. Retrieved October 29, 2019, from http://www.transformingsociety.co.uk/2019/07/02/how-micro-credit-helped-women-in-egypt-have-a-choice/

Drolet, J. (2011). Women, micro credit and empowerment in cairo, Egypt. *International Social Work, 54*(5), 629–645. doi:10.1177/0020872810382681

Duvendack, M., Palmer-Jones, R., Copestake, J. G., Hooper, L., Loke, Y., & Rao, N. (2011). What is the evidence of the impact of microfinance on the well-being of poor people? *Systematic Reviews.*

Egypt Today. (2017). *MSMEDA provides LE 215M to micro, small projects in 2017*. Retrieved November 7, 2019, from https://www.egypttoday.com/Article/3/38247/MSMEDA-provides-LE-215Mto-micro-small-projects-in-2017

Elantary, S., & Ezzat, M. (2020). *Increasing Rural Women Financial Inclusion.* Retrieved from https://nwrcegypt.org/ليلد-لومشلا-ىلاملا-ةدايزو-صرف-لمعلا-لل/

Farag, N. M. (2011). *Microfinance and Poverty Alleviation A Case Study of Al-Darb Al-Ahmar District in Cairo*. The American University in Cairo.

Forster, S., Lahaye, E., & Mckee, K. (2009). *Implementing the Client Protection Principles A Technical Guide for Investors*. Academic Press.

Hamid, A. L. I., & Nisser, I. (2017). Microfinance and Women's Empowerment in Egypt. *International Journal of Business and Economic Affairs*, *2*(1). Advance online publication. doi:10.24088/ijbea-2017-21007

Kar, A. K., & Bali Swain, R. (2018). Competition, Performance and Portfolio Quality in Microfinance Markets. *European Journal of Development Research*, *30*(5), 842–870. doi:10.105741287-018-0135-6

Khandker, S. (1998). *Fighting poverty with microcredit: experience in Bangladesh.* Retrieved from https://www.cabdirect.org/cabdirect/abstract/19991800156

Mader, P. (2017). How Much Voice for Borrowers? Restricted Feedback and Recursivity in Microfinance. *Global Policy*, *8*(4), 540–552. doi:10.1111/1758-5899.12474

Mahmoud Ali, I. A., & Ghoneim, H. (2019). The effect of microfinance on income inequality: Perspective of developing countries. *Journal of Economics and Management*, *35*(1), 40–62. doi:10.22367/jem.2019.35.03

Mersland, R., & Strøm, R. Ø. (2010). Microfinance Mission Drift? *World Development*, *38*(1), 28–36. doi:10.1016/j.worlddev.2009.05.006

Morduch, J. (1999). The Microfinance Promise. *Journal of Economic Literature*, *37*(4), 1569–1614. doi:10.1257/jel.37.4.1569

Moussa, M. (2007). *Regulation and Supervision of Microfinance in Egypt*. Retrieved from https://www.arabic.microfinancegateway.org/sites/default/files/mfg-en-paper-regulation-and-supervision-of-microfinance-in-egypt-2007_0.pdf

Nasr, S. (2006). *Access to Finance and Economic Growth in Egypt*. The World Bank. Retrieved from http://siteresources.worldbank.org/INTEGYPT/Resources/Access_to_Finance.pdf

Negley, K., & Yunus, M. (2011). Sacrificing Microcredit for Megaprofits. *NYTimes*. Retrieved November 3, 2019, from https://www.nytimes.com/2011/01/15/opinion/15yunus.html?_r=1

nobelprize.org. (n.d.). *Abhijit Banerjee – Facts – 2019*. Retrieved April 6, 2021, from https://www.nobelprize.org/prizes/economic-sciences/2019/banerjee/facts/

Pedrini, M., & Ferri, L. M. (2016). Doing Well by Returning to the Origin. Mission Drift, Outreach and Financial Performance of Microfinance Institutions. *Voluntas, 27*(6), 2576–2594. doi:10.100711266-016-9707-2

Rajadhyaksha, N. (2019). *Opinion | The microfinance mess.* Retrieved April 20, 2021, from https://www.livemint.com/opinion/columns/opinion-the-microfinance-mess-11575825705818.html

Rogaly, B., Castillo, A., & Serrano, M. R. (2004). Building assets to reduce vulnerability: Microfinance provision by a rural working people's union in Mexico. *Development in Practice, 14*(3), 381–395. doi:10.1080/0961452042000191213

Roodman, D. (2012). *Due diligence: An impertinent inquiry into microfinance.* Retrieved from https://books.google.com/books?hl=en&lr=&id=CxGnCoLkt4QC&oi=fnd&pg=PR1&dq=roodman+2012&ots=NTVMDHicF-&sig=MLil7-sDtXEZ0yObnV1sdst_7Xw

Sanabel. (2010). *Country Profile (Egypt).* Retrieved from http://www.sanabelnetwork.org/SanabelFiles/Publications/TransparencyPublications/Sanabel_Profile_Egypt_Eng.pdf

Schicks, J. (2012). *The Over-Indebtedness of Microfinance Customers-An Analysis from the Customer Protection Perspective* [Dissertation].

Smart. (n.d.). *Campaign Mission & Goals - The Smart Campaign - Keeping Clients First in Financial Inclusion.* Retrieved May 13, 2019, from https://www.smartcampaign.org/about/campaign-mission-a-goals

Taha, S. G. A. (2012). *The effectiveness of microcredit programmes on alleviating poverty and empowering women* [Unpublished thesis].

Waly, G. (2010). *Microfinance in Egypt: An Overview.* Retrieved October 29, 2019, from https://www.fra.gov.eg/content/efsa2_ar/pool_extra_efsa/UG18915UG18916.pdf

Wong, K., & Richards, D. (2014). Commercialization and Microfinance Interest Rates: Usury or Just Prices? *Journal of Markets & Morality, 17*(2), 381–404.

World Bank. (2018). *Women Economic Empowerment Study.* Author.

Yunus, M. (2011). *Sacrificing Microcredit for Megaprofits.* Academic Press.

Chapter 7
The Holistic Metamorphosis of Rural Lives Through Microfinance:
A Perspective

Manpreet Arora
https://orcid.org/0000-0002-4939-1992
School of Commerce and Management Studies, Central University of Himachal Pradesh, Dharamshala, India

ABSTRACT

Microfinance has been associated with playing a radical role in transforming any economy, especially where the goals are to uplift the disadvantaged sectors. It is also considered to be an important tool for helping poor people in order to fulfil their basic needs. It has got an immense capability to safeguard the vulnerable by its ripple effects from certain financial risks and poverty. Some call it a "poverty vaccine" for people living in rural areas. It also aims at assisting the various communities, economically as well as the socially excluded, focus on asset creation as well as for creating source of income. The holistic metamorphosis of rural lives is possible through the microcredit interventions, and the instances are plenty. In this pandemic, where the economies are facing huge economic crises, the rural vulnerable and the excluded sections have suffered the most. In this phase of transformation, the microfinance intervention with re-oriented objectives can again prove to be an effective tool for reviving the economy as a whole.

DOI: 10.4018/978-1-6684-5647-7.ch007

INTRODUCTION

Microfinance and micro-credit are frequently used interchangeably and are treated as synonyms, although microfinance encompasses deposits, loans, payment services, and insurances for the poor (De Aghion, Armendáriz & Morduch, 2007). Microfinance has been associated with playing a radical role in transforming any economy especially where the goals are to uplift the disadvantaged sectors. It is also considered to be an important tool for helping poor people in order to fulfil their basic needs. It has got an immense capability to safeguard the vulnerable by its ripple effects from certain financial risks and poverty. Some call it a "poverty vaccine" for people living in rural areas. It also aims at assisting the various communities economically as well as socially excluded focus much on asset creation as well as for creating source of income. The holistic metamorphosis of rural lives is possible through the microcredit interventions and the instances are plenty. In this pandemic where the economies are facing huge economic crises the rural vulnerable and the excluded sections have suffered the most. In this phase of transformation, where the world witnessed pandemic Covid-19, which eventually shattered the economies, again the microfinance intervention with re-oriented objectives can prove to be effective tool for reviving the economies worldwide. This chapter focuses on the Holistic metamorphosis of rural lives through microfinance.

BACKGROUND

There are certain peculiarities of every rural community therefore the tools for the development of rural communities are always somewhat different from other demographics. As per the encyclopedic entry of National Geographic the rural area is defined as; "A rural area is an open swath of land that has few homes or other buildings, and not very many people". Further the density of rural areas in terms of population is also very low. Most of the rural communities are smaller in size and the density of population is comparatively less than the urban population. Rural communities most of the time shows homogeneity of language, culture (Asante et al.,2005), traditions, ways of living and customs etc. Rural communities are known for living near the nature and following sustainable living practices (National Geographic Encyclopedia). In most parts of the world the rural communities do not have access to fast communication and they generally rely on agriculture and allied activities. Rural community has been defined as an area which is not fully developed and not civilized. Rural community is defined to be that the geographic area which is located outside towns and cities thereby not having access to modern amenities of life fully. Agriculture is the primary source of living in the rural areas.

The rural communities are also associated with activities which are close to nature. In west rural areas are also regarded as country because of the reason that residents are close to wildlife and natural resources of the country.

The Indian rural society is characterized by the unit called as village. The people living in villages carry the agriculture, small businesses and allied activities for their living (Shah, 2012). . The distinctive framework of villages is of castes and social casteism is a dominant factor of villages in India (Singer & Cohen, 1968). Social Institutions based on social and economic relations can be found in all these villages. The peculiar characteristic of the rural society is that ethnicity, religion and caste composition of village is largely determined by its nature as well as its structure. Dominant trade of Indian rural society is agriculture (Mukherjee, 1957). Possession of land carries social as well as prestigious value for the land holders of farmers. In addition to those who possess land for agriculture, there is a considerable part of population which is landless laborers as well as tenants of land which also depend upon agriculture. The Indian society is broadly divided into three parts that is tribal, rural and urban society based upon geographical surroundings and socio-cultural characteristics. There are many issues as well as challenges associated with rural development in India like education, health and sanitation, availability of credit, employment opportunities, and facilities for agricultural extension and research (Karmakar, (Ed.), 2008; Panda & Majumder, 2013; Mearns, 1999). According to ILO the rural economy carries a significant potential of creating decent as well as productive jobs around the world. It has significant potential of contributing towards sustainable development and economic growth. In all over the world still a drastic deficit of decent work opportunities can be found. In the 2030 agenda of sustainable development, one of the simplest but effective policies for eradication of poverty in the rural economies is to promote decent work. These goals are also stated in 2030 agenda of sustainable development and are getting increased attention towards rural development, agriculture-oriented activities and food security. Investments in innovations and employment generating activities through microfinance have a lot of potential in achieving these 2030 sustainable development goals of decent work and creation of employment.

THE HOLISTIC METAMORPHOSIS OF RURAL LIVES THROUGH MICROFINANCE

Microfinance and micro-credit are frequently used interchangeably and treated as synonyms, although microfinance encompasses deposits, loans, payment services, and insurances for the poor (De Aghion, Armendáriz & Morduch, 2007). Several microfinance services are available in various developing nations across the world.

The impact of microfinance is studied by people across the world and the impacts are not just economic they are even social, cultural, and multi-dimensional (Vatta, 2003, Arora & Singh, 2015). The benefits of microfinance are wider (Arora & Singh, 2018). It is not only regarded as a tool for poverty reduction but if it is strategically used it can transform the lives of especially those who are living in the rural areas (Arora & Singh, 2022, Arora & Singh, 2018). If we talk particularly of rural microfinance in India's various states. Their ideas are, at their core, the same. i.e., to provide rapid and simple lending to the poor without the need for collateral, but there are some structural peculiarities in the organizational and legal framework that distinguish them. They are classified as follows:

- SHG Model,
- Grameen Model,
- Co-operative Model, and
- For-profit Model.

Among the four versions mentioned, the SHG Model is the most popular in India.

Self- Help Group Model

The rural poor who do not have any collateral or a guarantee in order to avail credit from local moneylenders, who take advantage of them by charging exorbitant interest rates are generally very vulnerable. Lack of formal credit for the poor increases their risk in bad times like pandemic or any other external shocks prevalent in the economy. SHG is an attempt to liberate the impoverished from this vicious loop of intricacy. It is regarded as a better platform for the poor and vulnerable to organise themselves around regular saving and lending habits, as well as engage in some income-generating activities (Arora & Singh, 2018). Generally this model fosters skill development and paves way towards successful micro, small, medium and cottage industry or ventures. It also has the capability of inducing the pace of start-ups. The concept of self-help group focuses on establishing a pool of capital by the members from their savings which help them to run some money earning activities. This concept has deep down impacts like, building resilience, planning activities, leadership abilities and women empowerment (Arora & Singh, 2018) along with poverty reduction, employment generation and connecting the most vulnerable with the mainstream. As members manage their salaries, production activities, and marketing of the product and make spending decisions, a sense of responsibility develops among them, particularly among women. They learn the peculiarities of market. They understand the mechanism of demand and supply which helps them to economically grow. The homogeneous nature of the group members enables them to create solidarity among themselves in the event of an emergency and emerge strong in the event of a community misfortune.

What Is a Self- Help Group?

A self-help group, according to the National Bank for Agriculture and Rural Development (NABARD), is a group of nearly 10-20 poor people who come together in order to address their common concerns. They voluntarily contribute to a shared fund on a regular basis, mobilise their funds, and invest in micro-enterprises.

SHG is a self-governed, peer-controlled small and informal association of the poor, mainly from socio economically homogeneous families, that is formed around savings and credit operations. SHG members meet weekly or monthly to discuss issues and challenges of the groups and share information in order to find a solution to shared challenges. Members of the group work together in order to find solutions to their economic and social problems, which push them into the dearth of poverty and economic suffering.

Objectives of SHGs

The concept of self-help group is based on the premise of creating a platform where people especially women from rural backgrounds who do not have access to modernity's and have the zeal to become self sufficient come together with their thrifts and contribute as group saving which is further invested in income earning activities (Nair, 2005; Karmakar, 1999; Reddy & Reddy, 2012; Deininger & Liu, 2013, Arora & Singh, 2016). The major objectives served by SHGs are following:

- To serve as a platform for people who are extremely poor and lack access to traditional financial institutions.
- To help members learn how to work together and cooperate in a group setting.
- To provide members with a savings system that meets their needs and further gives them opportunity to become self-dependent.
- To provide a cost-effective delivery mechanism to its members in exchange for a minor credit.

Formation and Development of SHGs

Any informal community-based organization's long-term practicability depends on using a meticulous and methodical approach. From the stage of conception to achieving the stage of maturity, SHGs like other organisations go through several stages. Forming, storming, norming, and performing are four separate developmental stages. In the initial stages of forming a self help group, a local individual who is already well-known among the poor villages and is willing to step forward at first, assists the poor in forming a group. Generally initiators of the group are having good reputation in the village and other potential members trust him or her. He is commonly referred as a facilitator. The facilitator teaches and convinces the other potential investors/ members, the various advantages of saving and investment i.e small tokens of money contributed in a pool generally referred to as thrift. Self-help Promoting Agencies (SHPI) in India is either government agencies or are frequently some NGO's, or a microfinance institution (MFI), a bank, or a government agency like the District Rural Agency which encourage the villagers to form a self help group. The next stage is of basically the norming phase where the process of sensitization takes place, in which all the group members are encouraged to practise and bring into action the self-help principles. The total emphasis of group action over all the individual activity is fostered into the group members' perceptions. During this stage, any existing dispute or misunderstanding of opinions among the group members is permitted to be expressed so that if anyone has doubts and apprehensions they come out and if somebody wants to leave the group it also becomes clear. The group's decision-making abilities are assessed at the end of this stage. After spending some time together and discussing about the activities which can be performed by the group it develops group norms at this point, and group unity takes hold. As individualistic goals or objectives are totally replaced by collectiveness, the group becomes more cohesive and development-oriented; the focus of the group now is on earning activities and on the development of living standard of group members. Discussions among the members as well as self help group promoting institutions and other entities involved in group formation smoothes out the diversions of thoughts which generally prevail in the initial stages of the group formation. After this actually the group becomes functional and they indulge into earning activities. We can call it a Performing Stage. With the support of collective action, leadership is established, roles are clarified, and the group operates in a cohesive manner to fulfil its purpose. Because SHGs are informal groups, a minimum of 10 members is required to form a group, and the maximum number of members cannot exceed 20. A gathering of more than 20 people is legally required to register. According to NABARD just one individual from each household is allowed to join the organisation, allowing more families to participate in the movement. Members are usually from the same town or village, which facilitates communication. They share the same social and economic circumstances. It promotes effective communication among the members. A group without a leader cannot sustain for long period of time. The group's members democratically elect the group's leader, generally the one who has diverse knowledge or has market understanding. The leader is in charge of organizing group meetings and presiding over their activities. She or he keeps track of the group's data and assists with banking and other economic and social contacts. The group meets once a week or at least once a month. It allows members to better comprehend one other's problems. Meeting attendance is required for all members. The group bylaws are also agreed upon which help in regulating the working of the group. They decide on the meeting's date and location, and all of the participants' savings are collected during the meeting. The members share and debate the issues they are facing. For all the transactions, simple and unambiguous accounts are kept. If none of the group members can keep the account up to date, the group seeks outside assistance. Mostly the NGO's have interventions in linking the group with the banks in India. So representatives from NGO's or Self help group promoting institutions assist and make the group learn certain activities like taking production decisions, how to market the product, how to keep the accounts, how to maintain the register of the contributions savings etc. NGO employees occasionally assist the group in keeping track of various records. To minimise any misunderstandings or mistrust among the members, all truncations are only documented during group meetings.

Savings and Lending Mechanism

The prime focus of every self-help group is on savings and thrift (Nair, 2005; Suguna, 2006; Khatibi & Indira, 2011; Thangamani & Muthuselvi, 2013). The members of the group generally begin saving a small sum on a regular basis so as to cover up their working capital needs. They learn to create liquidity so that the in hand opportunities are not lost. It teaches members to save money and to be disciplined in their financial decisions, which will aid them in managing bank debts. Once the group is functional and works for at least six months, the focus is on making it a formal SHG and it is linked with the financial system and registered. After one or two meetings, the SHG passes a resolution in the group meeting, which is signed by all members, to open a savings bank account in the SHG's name. The SHG allows at least three members to handle the account jointly, with any two of them being able to do so. The bank receives the resolution, along with the completed application form and a copy of the SHG's rules and regulations. The SHG is then given a passbook for a savings bank account. The mechanism of internal lending is also there in order to help in the financial needs of the group members. After saving for a minimum of two to three months, the group begins lending to its members from the common savings pool at a predetermined interest rate. The terms and conditions for loan advancement are predetermined. Intra-group loans are generally offered for both production and consumption, with interest rates ranging from two to four percent each month (NABARD). Once the group gets a formal shape and is registered it becomes eligible for external lending from commercial banks or financial institutions. The SHG seeks external borrowing from a bank after six months, when the members have demonstrated a saving habit and have learnt to handle, consume, and reimburse their loans. The bank evaluates the group's accomplishment based on factors such as group size, meeting regularity, saving collection within the group, savings use, loan recoveries, and so on. The bank makes a loan in the name of the SHG after determining the group's sustainability. The loan amount is usually one to four times the group's savings, but it might be more if the bank is pleased with the SHG's strength.

The members of the team are also eligible for getting a second loan. They consider a loan applicant's eligibility based on the requirement and purpose of the expenditure. The objective can range from purchasing assets for income-generating activities to meeting instantaneous necessities such as sickness, wedding ceremony, and so on. As part of the communal fund, the interest earned is placed in the account. The group is still liable for repaying the external credit as a whole. The SHG agrees to a miniature and standard payback calendar. Obstinate failure to pay is discouraged by peer load, peer support, and peer monitoring. Every member is trained that the money does not belong just to him, but also to the other members of the business. The promotional organization possibly will arrange training programmes for the group's common income-generating activities.

Operational Models

In India, three SHG-credit linkage models are operational. Below are some of them:

1. Model I: In this model, SHGs are founded, guided, and financed directly by banks.
2. Model II (SHG-Bank Linkage Model): In this model, SHGs are directly financed by banks, such as commercial banks (CBs), both public and private; regional rural banks (RRBs), and cooperative banks (Co-op. banks). Facilitators include NGOs and government entities such as the DRDA. They provide training on a variety of revenue-generating activities.
3. Model III (MFI-Bank Linkage Model): In this model, microfinance institutions (MFIs) obtain bulk loans from banks in order to on-lend to SHGs and other small borrowers.

Microfinance Institutions (MFIs)

Although the deliverance mechanisms and conduits employed by micro credit providers varied in structure and nature, a huge variety of institutions, both formal and informal, provide financial services to the poor in India as well as the world. Some of the organisations are entirely focused on the needy; others give such services to the poor in addition to standard banking services to all types of consumers. MFIs, according to the NABARD Task Force, are financial institutions that provide small amounts of money, credit, and other financial services and products to the poor in rural, semi-urban, and urban regions in order to help people improve their income and living conditions.

MFIs include organisations such as NGOs, Federations of SHGs, Mutually Aided Cooperative Societies (MACS), state and national co-operatives, and Non-Banking Financial Companies (NBFCs) that provide specific financial services to the poor, at least at the entry level. Microfinance service providers are banks that offer microfinance in addition to their regular banking services (Arora & Singh, 2017). NABARD and the Small Industries Development Bank of India (SIDBI) are apex level microfinance service providers, whereas Rashtriya MahilaKosh (RMK) is an apex level microfinance institution. NABARD also refinances the banks that provide SHGs with microfinance.

Progression of the SHG Bank Linkage Programme in India

With an outreach of 13.87 crore families, the SHG-BLP programme has undoubtedly turned out to be a model of success for a microfinance programme around the world, providing social, economic, and financial support to the rural poor, particularly women.

Advancement of Savings Linkage of SHGs With Banks in India (2018-19 to 2020-21)

As the deposits of SHGs' rise, they become more eligible for bank/financial institution advances, which ultimately increase the amount of capital/money they may invest in their businesses. Table 1 and Figure 1 show the results of SHG savings linkage in terms of absolute numbers and percentage share during 2018-19 to 2020-21. Comparative data by region reveals that, in terms of the number of SHGs holding bank accounts, there was a positive trend across all regions in 2020-21. The Central Region had the highest rate of development, at 19 percent, while the Western Region had the lowest rate of development, at 5 percent. The Northern Region had the most elevated development of 193 percent, followed by the Western Region (85 percent), North Eastern Region (73 percent), Southern Region (45 percent), Focal Region (24 percent), and the Eastern Region had the most lowered development of 17 percent.

When it comes to the percentage share of savings related SHGs, the Southern Region has the highest percentage share at 35.3 percent; however, this lowered down 0.7 percent when we look at the figures of 2019-20. The Eastern Region continued to

Table 1. Region-wise progress of Savings linked SHGs with Banks (2018-19 to 2020-21) (Amount in lakhs)

S.No.	Regions	2018-19		2019-20		2020-21	
		No. of SHGs	Savings Amount	No. of SHGs	Savings Amount	No. of SHGs	Savings Amount
1.	Northern Region	5,48,624	62,453	5,77,122	59,550	6,09,808	1,74,345
2.	North Eastern Region	5,23,469	40,407	5,56,899	48,141	6,33,714	83,126
3.	Eastern Region	26,54,358	6,01,155	28,11,130	6,64,333	31,22,424	7,74,912
4.	Central Region	10,62,759	1,33,230	11,35,083	1,71,217	13,45,575	2,11,870
5.	Western Region	13,88,615	2,05,275	14,73,853	2,01,880	15,50,178	3,74,023
6.	Southern Region	38,36,418	12,89,928	36,89,236	14,70,085	39,61,703	21,29,485
	Total	**1,00,14,243**	**23,32,448**	**1,02,43,323**	**26,15,205**	**1,12,23,400**	**37,47,761**

Source: NABARD - National Bank for Agriculture and Rural Development
https://www.nabard.org

have the second highest share (27.8%), with a small increase over the previous year (27.4 percent). The Western region is at the third place, with a share of 13.8 percent in 2020-21, which shows a slight decrease from the previous year (14.4 percent).

Savings Outstanding With SHGs

Aggregate savings with SHG reveals its vigour and demonstrates abstinence discipline, both of which are essential to satisfy individual crises or life cycle requirements. Savings is the most important deciding element whilst applying for a bank loan or a mortgage from any financial institution. SHG savings outstanding increased by 43 percent from Rs. 26152.05 crore to Rs. 37477.61 crore as of 31 March 2021 in India, enlisting a significant growth of 43 percent for the year 2019-20, with all areas registering a positive growth. The states like Chhattisgarh, Assam, Meghalaya, Tripura, Punjab, Andhra Pradesh, Puducherry, Dadra Nagar Haveli, Lakshadweep, and Maharashtra are among the 10 states/UTs that have higher development rates than the national average. Figure 2 shows the average savings per SHG by region. From Rs. 25531 in 2019-20 to Rs. 33392 in 2020-21, the average saving has increased by 31%. The average savings has increased for every region, with the Northern Region leading the way with a 177 percent increase from Rs. 10381 to Rs. 28590, followed by the Western Region (76 percent) and the North Eastern Region (76 percent) (52 percent). The Southern and North Eastern regions have the highest and lowest average savings per SHG, respectively. Punjab has the highest savings outstanding among the States/UTs, at Rs. 2 lakhs per SHG.

Credit Disbursement by Banks

Table 2 shows the comparative data of bank loans dispersed to SHGs for the three fiscal years (2018-19 to 2020-21). In the fiscal year 2020-21, banks disbursed Rs. 58070.68 crore to 28.87 lakh SHGs, compared to Rs. 77659.34 crore to 31.46 lakh SHGs in the previous fiscal year (NABARD). This resulted in a negative trend of 8.22% and 25.22% in terms of loans to SHGs and the amount dispensed individually, respectively. During 2020-21, in the Southern Region highest disbursement was there, amounting to Rs. 37860.63 crore to 13.37 lakh SHGs, while in the Northern Region the lowest amount was disbursed totalling to Rs. 37860.63 crore to 13.37 lakh SHGs (Rs. 940.45 crore to 0.68 lakh SHGs).In comparison to the previous year, credit disbursement decreased in the Southern (-31%), Eastern (-16.67%), and Northern, North Eastern, and Central areas, while it increased in the Northern, North Eastern, and Central regions. Significant states such as Chhattisgarh, West Bengal, Himachal Pradesh, Jammu and Kashmir, Andhra Pradesh, Karnataka, and Maharashtra saw a considerable drop, which could be attributed to the pandemic's effect. Figure 3 shows a similar assessment of SHG credit linkage by region during the last three years (2018-19 to 2020-21). According to the data, there was a significant increase in 2019-20, and the credit linkage returned to 2018-19 levels in 2020-21.

With the exception of the Northern and North Eastern Regions, all other Regions have seen a decline in credit-linked SHGs. The Eastern area surpassed the Southern region in the level of SHGs credit linked throughout the year 2020-21, despite a 4 percent reduction, but this is due to a 10.6 percent decrease in the latter. In the Northern, North Eastern, Central, and Western Regions, the percentage of credit linked SHGs remained below 12%. As shown in Table 2, the average loan size per SHG decreased by Rs. 45733 in 2020-21 (Rs. 201118) compared to 2019-20. (Rs. 246851). With the exception of the Northern Region, the average loan size per SHG has shrunk in the remaining regions. For the years 2020-21, the average loan size is highest in the Southern area, followed by the North Eastern Region and the Western Region.

Nine States/UTs, namely Madhya Pradesh, Uttarakhand, Jharkhand, Manipur, Meghalaya, Haryana, Himachal Pradesh, Jammu and Kashmir, and Punjab, enlisted an increase in average loan size, while three States, namely Assam, Mizoram, and Rajasthan, maintained the status quo, and the remaining States enrolled lower average loan disbursements. Andhra Pradesh, Kerala, Tamil Nadu, Telangana, and Gujarat saw a considerable drop in average loan size, which had a significant impact on the overall average loan size.

Table 2. Region-wise Status of Bank Loan Disbursed to SHGs during 2018-19 to 2020-21

Region	2018-19			2019-20			2020-21		
	No. of SHGs	Total Loans Disbursed	Average Loan Disbursed	No. of SHGs	Total Loans Disbursed	Average Loan Disbursed	No. of SHGs	Total Loans Disbursed	Average Loan Disbursed
Northern	55,922	62,664	1,12,056	62,905	84,694	1,34,637	67,658	94,045	1,39,001
North Eastern	27,086	29,001	1,07,070	37,807	57,893	1,53,128	68,116	1,03,651	1,52,168
Eastern	9,09,375	11,97,079	1,31,638	11,23,517	17,85,075	1,58,883	11,24,578	14,87,551	1,32,276
Central	85,135	72,199	84,805	1,11,074	1,04,249	93,856	1,28,617	1,05,428	81,971
Western	1,46,674	1,84,565	1,25,833	1,74,218	2,49,327	1,43,112	1,61,159	2,30,331	1,42,921
Southern	14,74,208	42,86,256	2,90,750	16,36,481	54,84,696	3,35,152	13,37,266	37,86,063	2,83,120
Total	26,98,400	58,31,763	2,16,119	31,46,002	77,65,935	2,46,851	28,87,394	58,07,068	2,01,118

(Total loan disbursed in Rs. Lakh/ Average loan disbursed in Rs. Per SHG)
Source: NABARD - National Bank for Agriculture and Rural Development
https://www.nabard.org

Credit Outstanding

As of March 31, 2021, there were 57.80 lakh credit-linked SHGs with loans totalling Rs. 103289.71 crore. Figure 4 shows the number of SHGs with outstanding loans by region, as well as their percentage share of total loans outstanding as of 31 March 2021. As of March 31, 2021, 51.50 percent of the 112.23 lakh SHGs in the SHG-BLP were credit tied to banks. The Eastern Region has the highest percentage of SHGs with outstanding bank credits, at 72.12 percent, followed by the Southern Region (64.10 percent). Furthermore, when compared to the best two regions, the performance of other regions is extremely low. When it comes to the percent share of SHGs with loans outstanding as of 31 March 2021, the Southern Region (43.93 percent) and Eastern Region (38.96 percent) have the highest percentages, while the Northern (2.48 percent) and North Eastern Region (2.84 percent) lag far behind. Figure 4 depicts the percentage of SHGs with outstanding bank loans per state as of March 31, 2021. In general, 51.5 percent of the 112.23 lakh SHGs with savings account connections, or 57.80 lakh SHGs, have bank loans outstanding. Eight states have credit linkage rates that are higher than the national average. Bihar leads the way with 85.7 percent of its SHGs having outstanding debts, followed by West Bengal (85.6 percent) and Telangana(79.6 percent).The best-performing states are primarily from the Northern, Eastern, and Southern regions, with the Southern states dominating the list. Figure 5 shows the average loan outstanding per SHG per state as of March 31, 2020 and March 31, 2021. In 25 states, the average credit size has shrunk since 31 March 2020, compared to the position on 31 March 2020. Punjab has experienced the greatest decline (68%) followed by New Delhi (57%) and Chandigarh (56 percent). In terms of average loan size growth compared to the outstanding at the end of the previous year, Dadra Nagar Haveli (51 percent), Sikkim (28 percent), and Tripura (22 percent) are the top three states. The best three states in terms of average loan outstanding per SHG are Andhra Pradesh, Telangana, and Karnataka.

CONCLUSION

Microfinance has been associated with playing a radical role in transforming any economy especially where the goals are to uplift the disadvantaged sectors. It is also considered to be an important tool for helping poor people in order to fulfill their basic needs. It has got an immense capability to safeguard the vulnerable by its ripple effects of from certain financial risks and poverty. Some call it a "poverty vaccine" for people living in rural areas. It also aims at assisting the various communities economically as well as socially excluded focus much on asset creation as well as for creating source of income. The concept propounded by Mohammad Yunus started from Bangladesh which spread to most of the nations of the world and showed remarkable efforts on the lives of excluded and most vulnerable sections of the society talking particularly about developing economies like India. Programmes focusing on self-help groups have contributed a lot in developing the socio-economic status of rural people.

To prove microfinance as an effective tool of intervention in this world crises where during pandemic the developing economies were hit worst for it requires focusing on disbursement of quick loans for helping people to meet their financial needs and provide extensive portfolios of loans in order to uplift the rural poor.

The holistic metamorphosis of rural lives is possible through the microcredit interventions and the instances are plenty. In this pandemic where the economies are facing huge economic crises the rural vulnerable and the excluded sections have suffered the most. In this phase of transformation again the microfinance intervention with re-oriented objectives can again prove to be effective tool for reviving the economy as a whole.

REFERENCES

Arora, M., & Singh, S. (2015). An Evaluation of the Non Performing Assets of Public and Private Sector Banks Under the SHG Bank Linkage Programme. *Indian Journal of Finance*, *9*(6), 41–50. doi:10.17010/ijf/2015/v9i6/71161

Arora, M., & Singh, S. (2016). Disbursement of credit under the SGSY scheme: A comparison of SHGs' swarozgaris and individual swarozgaris. *Indian Journal of Finance*, *10*(11), 54–63. doi:10.17010/ijf/2016/v10i11/104918

Arora, M., & Singh, S. (2017). Role of Financial Institutions in Promoting Microfinance through SHG Bank Linkage Programme in India. *Pacific Business Review International*, *10*(4), 50–58.

Arora, M., & Singh, S. (2018a). Impact Assessment of Self-Help Group Bank Linkage Programme on Women Empowerment in the State of Himachal Pradesh. Academic Press.

Arora, M., & Singh, S. (2018b). Microfinance, Women Empowerment, and Transformational Leadership: A Study of Himachal Pradesh. *International Journal on Leadership*, *6*(2), 23.

Arora, M., & Singh, S. (2018c). The Impact of SHG Bank Linkage Programme on the Members of Self Help Groups: An Empirical Investigation in the State of Himachal Pradesh. *Sumedha Journal of Management*, *7*(1), 34–46.

Arora, M., & Singh, S. (2022). Microfinance for achieving Sustainable Development Goals: Pondering Over Indian Experiences for the Preservation of Magnificent African Natural Resources. In *Microfinance and Sustainable Development in Africa* (pp. 82–102). IGI Global. doi:10.4018/978-1-7998-7499-7.ch004

Asante, M. K., Brandon, G., Hall, R. L., Gaston, J. R., Maultsby, P. K., Philip, J. E., & Williams, S. W. (2005). *Africanisms in American culture*. Indiana University Press.

David, K. B., Aborode, A. T., Olaoye, D. Q., Enang, N. V., Oriyomi, A. K., & Yunusa, I. (2021). Increased risk of death triggered by domestic violence, hunger, suicide, exhausted health system during COVID-19 pandemic: Why, how and solutions. *Frontiers in Sociology*, *6*, 648395. doi:10.3389/fsoc.2021.648395 PMID:34169112

De Aghion, B. A., Armendáriz, B., & Morduch, J. (2007). *The economics of microfinance*. Academic Press.

Deininger, K., & Liu, Y. (2013). Evaluating program impacts on mature self-help groups in India. *The World Bank Economic Review*, *27*(2), 272–296. doi:10.1093/wber/lhs028

Elgar, F. J., Stefaniak, A., & Wohl, M. J. (2020). The trouble with trust: Time-series analysis of social capital, income inequality, and COVID-19 deaths in 84 countries. *Social Science & Medicine*, *263*, 113365. doi:10.1016/j.socscimed.2020.113365 PMID:32981770

Karmakar, K. G. (1999). *Rural credit and self-help groups: Micro-finance needs and concepts in India*. Sage Publications India Pvt Ltd.

Karmakar, K. G. (Ed.). (2008). *Microfinance in India*. SAGE Publications India.

Khatibi, F. S., & Indira, M. (2011). Empowerment of women through self help groups and environmental management: Experiences of NGOs in Karnataka State, India. *Journal of Human Ecology (Delhi, India)*, *34*(1), 29–40. doi:10.1080/09709274.2011.11906366

Kiers, J., Seinhorst, J., Zwanenburg, M., & Stek, K. (2022). Which Strategies and Corresponding Competences Are Needed to Improve Supply Chain Resilience: A COVID-19 Based Review. *Logistics*, *6*(1), 12. doi:10.3390/logistics6010012

Kiran, E. (2020). Prominent Issues About the Social Impacts of Covid 19. *Gaziantep University Journal of Social Sciences, 19*, 752-766.

Kitamura, Y., Karkour, S., Ichisugi, Y., & Itsubo, N. (2020). Evaluation of the economic, environmental, and social impacts of the COVID-19 pandemic on the japanese tourism industry. *Sustainability*, *12*(24), 10302. doi:10.3390u122410302

Madhavi, B. H., & Wickramarachchi, R. (2022, September). Strategic Decision Making for a Resilient Supply Chain during a Pandemic. In *2022 International Research Conference on Smart Computing and Systems Engineering (SCSE)* (Vol. 5, pp. 303-308). IEEE. 10.1109/SCSE56529.2022.9905209

Mearns, R. (1999). *Access to land in rural India: policy issues and options* (Vol. 2123). World Bank Publications. doi:10.1596/1813-9450-2123

Mueller, J. T., McConnell, K., Burow, P. B., Pofahl, K., Merdjanoff, A. A., & Farrell, J. (2021). Impacts of the COVID-19 pandemic on rural America. *Proceedings of the National Academy of Sciences of the United States of America*, *118*(1), 2019378118. doi:10.1073/pnas.2019378118 PMID:33328335

Mukherjee, R. (1957). *The dynamics of a rural society*. Popular Prakashan. doi:10.1515/9783112582305

Nair, A. (2005). *Sustainability of microfinance self help groups in India: would federating help?* (Vol. 3516). World Bank Publications. doi:10.1596/1813-9450-3516

Neff, L. M. (2020). Hidden hunger: Food insecurity in the age of coronavirus. *The American Journal of Clinical Nutrition, 112*(5), 1160–1161. doi:10.1093/ajcn/nqaa279 PMID:33095254

O'Sullivan, D., Rahamathulla, M., & Pawar, M. (2020). The impact and implications of COVID-19: An Australian perspective. *The International Journal of Community and Social Development, 2*(2), 134–151. doi:10.1177/2516602620937922

Oronce, C. I. A., Scannell, C. A., Kawachi, I., &Tsugawa, Y. (2020). Association between state-level income inequality and COVID-19 cases and mortality in the USA. *Journal of General Internal Medicine, 35*(9), 2791-2793.

Panda, S., & Majumder, A. (2013). A review of rural development programmes in India. *International Journal of Research in Sociology and Social Anthropology, 1*(2), 37–40.

Prawoto, N., Priyo Purnomo, E., & Az Zahra, A. (2020). *The impacts of Covid-19 pandemic on socio-economic mobility in Indonesia*. Academic Press.

Reddy, K. R., & Reddy, C. S. (2012). *Self help groups in India. A study on quality and sustainability.* Enable Publication.

Saccone, D. (2021). Can the Covid19 pandemic affect the achievement of the 'Zero Hunger' goal? Some preliminary reflections. *The European Journal of Health Economics, 22*(7), 1025–1038. doi:10.100710198-021-01311-2 PMID:33934264

Sarkis, J. (2020). Supply chain sustainability: Learning from the COVID-19 pandemic. *International Journal of Operations & Production Management, 41*(1), 63–73. doi:10.1108/IJOPM-08-2020-0568

Shah, A. M. (2012). *The structure of Indian society: Then and now*. Routledge India. doi:10.4324/9780203085370

Shahed, K. S., Azeem, A., Ali, S. M., & Moktadir, M. (2021). A supply chain disruption risk mitigation model to manage COVID-19 pandemic risk. *Environmental Science and Pollution Research International*, 1–16. doi:10.100711356-020-12289-4 PMID:33400113

Singer, M. B., & Cohn, B. S. (Eds.). (1968). *Structure and change in Indian society* (Vol. 47). Transaction Publishers.

Sombultawee, K., Lenuwat, P., Aleenajitpong, N., & Boon-itt, S. (2022). COVID-19 and Supply Chain Management: A Review with Bibliometric. *Sustainability, 14*(6), 3538. doi:10.3390u14063538

Suguna, B. (2006). *Empowerment of rural women through self-help groups*. Discovery Publishing House.

Thangamani, S., & Muthuselvi, S. (2013). A study on women empowerment through self-help groups with special reference to Mettupalayam Taluk in Coimbatore District. *Journal of Business and Management*, *8*(6), 17–24.

Timotius, E., Sunardi, O., Soenandi, I. A., Ginting, M., & Sabini, B. (2022). Supply chain disruption in time of crisis: a case of the Indonesian retail sector. *Journal of International Logistics and Trade*.

Vatta, K. (2003). Microfinance and poverty alleviation. *Economic and Political Weekly*, *38*, 432–433.

Wang, H., Dill, S. E., Zhou, H., Ma, Y., Xue, H., Sylvia, S., Smith, K., Boswell, M., Medina, A., Loyalka, P., Abby, C., Friesen, D., Rose, N., Guo, Y., & Rozelle, S. (2021). Health, economic, and social implications of COVID-19 for China's rural population. *Agricultural Economics*, *52*(3), 495–504. doi:10.1111/agec.12630 PMID:34149132

Chapter 8
Local Peoples' Perceptions on Microfinance in Nepal:
A Structural Equation Modelling Approach

Seema Kumari Sah
Quest International College, Nepal

Niranjan Devkota
https://orcid.org/0000-0001-9989-0397
Kathmandu Model College, Tribhuvan University, Nepal

Udaya Raj Paudel
Quest International College, Nepal

Sahadeb Upretee
Central Washington University, USA

Surendra Mahato
Nepal Commerce Campus, Tribhuvan University, Nepal

Devid Kumar Basyal
https://orcid.org/0000-0002-8363-8581
La Grandee International College, Nepal

Purnima Lawaju
Quest International College, Nepal

Sabina Bohaju
Quest International College, Nepal

Krishna Dhakal
Quest International College, Nepal

DOI: 10.4018/978-1-6684-5647-7.ch008

ABSTRACT

Microfinance has been evolving as an indispensable tool of poverty eradication and rural improvement. At present, almost all the commercial banks have delved into the microfinance foray and offer various lucrative schemes designed for the rural poor, specifically to carry out their own small economic activities. This chapter attempts to study the perception of the people in the microfinance business of Janakpur, Nepal. This study is taken from explanatory research design and collected data using a structure questionnaire, and the sample taken is 283 users of microfinance. SEM was used to test the hypothesis. It is found that microfinance needs to focus more on training assessment, better compensation structure, and women-friendly policies for the workforce. This study reveals that though all have delved into microfinance, a lot of effort is still required to pave the way for microfinance in Janakpur, Nepal.

INTRODUCTION

Microfinance is a method of providing a wide range of financial services to the poor based on market forces and commercial approaches, such as savings mobilization, credit disbursement, money transfer, and microinsurance (Dhungana, 2021). It covers both formal and informal financial institutions that provide small-scale financial services to rural people. In the age-old banking industry, microfinance is a relatively new innovation. In Nepal's rural areas, microfinance is an effective tool for poverty reduction (Mansori et al., 2020). Microfinance institutions have helped to alleviate poverty in the country by providing microfinance to the poor. Making microfinance institutions more affordable to the poor is a top priority for the world (Dhungana, 2021).

Savings and credit cooperatives (SACCOs) and small farmer cooperatives (SFCs) abound, Banks and financial institutions (BAFIA) regulate microfinance institutions in Nepal, which are governed by the Cooperative Act (1992) (Kayastha, 2013). The Financial Intermediary Act (1998) regulates the activities of non-governmental financial intermediaries (FINGEs). The processes for obtaining services from various microfinance modalities vary. As a result, a single umbrella act is required to make microfinance simple, understandable, and accessible(Kandil, 2018).

Microfinance is now widely recognized as a strong tool for poverty reduction and women's empowerment, as well as a promising source of funding for banks, financial institutions, and non-governmental organizations (Shrestha et al., 2019). Nepal's microfinance industry faces both opportunities and challenges. This industry faces numerous challenges, including lack of accessibility, unhealthy competition, seasonal migration, political ignorance, and the exclusion of vulnerable groups (Guérin et al., 2015). Poverty in Nepal, combined with opportunities, is paving the way for the growth of this sector and providing a large market for microfinance. On this basis, the industry offers numerous opportunities, including economic growth stimulation, women empowerment, increased volume, accessibility and outreach, and scope economics, among others (Karn, 2018).

Today, most countries are globally integrated the need for sustainable development has gained great importance and popularity around the globe. Nepal is progressing towards globalization through an integrated economy and the slogan of sustainable development (Karn, 2018). The people perception about microfinance in Nepal despite the fact that all nationalized banks have delved into microfinance, this shows that much work remains to be done to pave the way for microfinance in the commercial banking sector (Mansori et al., 2020). Banks undoubtedly provide a variety of microfinance services, but the question is how many target beneficiaries are aware of these services and how many use them. The poor are reluctant to approach banks for their financial needs due to the long procedural formalities involved in obtaining credit from them. They prefer to raise money in less formal, but more convenient, ways (Dhungana, 2021). Furthermore, banks need collateral, which the poor are unable to provide.

In order to alleviate poverty in Nepal, the government established microfinance banks, institutions, and cooperatives. In Nepal's rural areas, microfinance banks have been providing microcredit, savings, informal education, first-aid health services, training, and skill growth (Dhungana, 2021). Microfinance is a form of lending that provides "the little" money. It aids in the improvement of the poor and severe poor's situation by increasing income and benefit, thus lifting them out of poverty and raising their living standards (Karn, 2018). To retain and develop their revenue portfolio, microfinance institutions should focus on other income-generating activities (i.e., micro-enterprise).

Microfinance is the hot topics of Nepal and the role of government is the important for the effective development of the microfinance (Kumari, 2021). People perception about the microfinance in Janakpur is all about providing loans to poor people as they have not more aware and known about the benefits of microfinance. Borrowers should be given training, mentoring, and consultancy services so that micro entrepreneurs can spend their money at the right time and in the right place (Toindepi, 2016). The risk mapping approach can be an effective tool for determining how people perceive risk to their livelihoods. Projects aimed at improving the livelihoods of poor rural communities must take into account the factors that influence how people perceive their problems (Shrestha et al., 2019). Thus, the study will facilitate the development of appropriate educational programs to close the knowledge gap among people and to prepare them for an objective of the people perception among local. This is critical because that requires special attention and local people have adequate knowledge of it to ensure its long-term viability about microfinance (Uluwaduge & Senathiraja,

2019). So, the people feel difficult to be put collateral in the microfinance in bank and take loan to invest in market.

Several questions have emerged in the context of microfinance on the local people perception of Janakpur, Nepal. They are: (i) What is the present situation of the local people user in microfinance? (ii) What are the factors affecting the perception of local people about microfinance? (iii) What sort of the challenges that is faced by the local people about microfinance in Janakpur, Nepal? and (iv) What will be the appropriate managerial solution for the effective management of microfinance in Janakpur, Nepal? Therefore, a proper study is required to explore this question in the context of Nepal financial sector and to reveal these questions to microfinance uses of local people in context of Nepal. Hence, this study aims to people perception about microfinance in Janakpur, Nepal. It is aimed to address the above-mentioned questions.

RESEARCH METHOD

Theoretical Framework

The research plan is the theoretical structure, theoretical need for a diverse range of individuals in terms of perception, behaviors, norms, values, behavioral purposes, and so on has been made clear. microfinance provide low-income people with microloans and the ability to become self-sufficient by promoting saving and credit activities. (Effendi et al., 2020; Kumar & Das, 2019). It helps people who have no collateral to put up as security for loans but who have local skills and a strong desire to engage in economic activities for self-employment and income generation (Varpio et al., 2020).

For this theory, the theory of reasoned action model appears to be the best fit for this review. Theory of reasoned Action is a well-known and trustworthy principle that has been used in management research for many years, including banking and finance (Kumar & Das, 2019). The theory of logical action and the theory of rational action are the most influential and commonly used models of the attitude-behavior relationship (Tucker et al., 2019). Norms, beliefs, views, behaviors, and, ultimately, social expectations are all part of this model. Also consider the following three factors: Subjective expectations, behavioral behaviors, and perceived behavioral regulation (Hummel & Schlick, 2016; Effendi et al., 2020). The aim of this model is to explain the relationship between attitudes and behaviors in human behavior. It is primarily used to forecast how people will act based on their prior attitudes and behavioral intentions (Hummel & Schlick, 2016). Because the purpose helps to predict the probability of consumers making a purchase within a given period and acts as a proxy for actual behavior, Theory of Reasoned Action is used in this study with the variable of customer decisions included (Effendi et al., 2020).

The aim of this model is to explain the relationship between attitudes and behaviors in human behavior. It is primarily used to forecast how people will act based on their prior attitudes and behavioral intentions (Hummel & Schlick, 2016). Because the purpose helps to predict the probability of consumers making a purchase within a given period and acts as a proxy for actual behavior, Theory of Reasoned Action is used in this study with the variable of customer decisions included (Effendi et al., 2020).

Micro-finance is considered as a significant vehicle for socio-economic transformation of women in the developing countries like Nepal. So, the government focus on the development of microfinance for the development, the perception of the people is important to understand as this model helps to understand the behavior about the microfine to the people.

Conceptual Framework

The conceptual structure describes the condition of knowledge by means of a literature review in general identifies and summarize the state of knowledge and the methodological basis of the research project identify gaps in our understanding of a phenomenal or problem (Varpio et al., 2020). Microfinance has a growing industry of Nepal. There are several models describing the perception of people about microfinance for providing sound conceptual framework. The researcher has used five model based on theory of planned behavior.

According to the perception of the people about microfinance the different model have been used like: Theory of Reasoned Action Model, Social Entrepreneurship Intention Model, Social Cognitive Theory Model, Technology Acceptance Model (Ashraf, 2019). TRA model helps to find that it is to better understand an individual's voluntary behavior by looking at the underlying basic motivation for doing something (Kasser, 2009). The theory is often used as a theory of comprehension of communication discourse. Social entrepreneurship intention model is applied to investigate Microfinance Institutes' perceptions of Social Entrepreneurship (SE), as well as the application of the Positive Theory of Social Entrepreneurship (PTSE) in microfinance and the identification of special social entrepreneurial characteristics in microfinance (Rawhouser et al., 2019). TAM model helps to aims to discover the various factors that influence employees' attitudes and acceptance of CBS (Rocco & Plakhotnik, 2009; Rawhouser et al., 2019). Social cognitive model is related to the behavior this helps to identify the perception about the microfinance of local people do (Adhikari, 2021). Therefore, in the sense of "Emotion and feelings " this model helps to find the perceive about the microfinance to local people.

Figure 1. Conceptual Framework

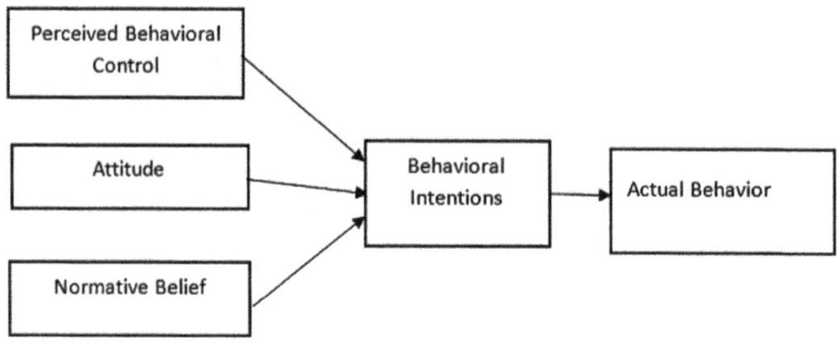

According to research on local people attitudes and behavior towards microfinance in Janakpur has been main focus. The development of this conceptual framework was grounded upon the behavioral intention model or theory of reasoned action. Attitude is characterized as the psychological feeling and the positive or negative assessment of an individual's behavior (Chen & Tung, 2014). Personal beliefs and religion, prior experiences, perceptions and opinions of family and peers, social position, and economic conditions are all intrinsic and extrinsic elements that might influence an individual's decision to act in a certain way (Mansori et al., 2020).

This model has explained about three key aspects such as intentions, conditions and origins for systematic and sustainable management of microfinance. It says that the customer attitude explains about the participation in the microfinance (Arora & Meenu, 2012). There are several models describing the about the people attitude to involve in microfinance for providing sound conceptual framework. In the conceptual framework, the dependent variable is actual behavior and independent variable is normative belief, perceived behavioral control, and attitude. we have mediator variable named is behavioral intention. A mediator variable mediates the interaction between the independent and dependent variable. Intention is a proxy for actual action that can be used to predict the likelihood of customers making a purchase within a given time frame (Maulana et al., 2018). Intentions predict future conduct, whereas actual behavior portrays previous occurrences.

Attitude and Behavior Intention About Microfinance

Attitude is characterized as the psychological feeling and the positive or negative assessment of an individual's behavior (Chen & Tung, 2014; Rawhouser et al., 2019). Customers regarded microfinance to be less burdensome than traditional microfinance because it did not impose large fees. The behavior assessment is positive or negative by a person. According to (Possner et al., 2021) when people have a more positive stance, so they have more positive and vice versa behavioral intentions. It claims that microfinance, such as that which has used charity funds to absorb operational costs, has succeeded in bringing the price down to more accessible levels (Zheng & Zhang, 2021).

H1. Local people attitude towards microfinance has positive and significant impact toward behavior intention

Normative Belief and Behavioral Intentions

Normative views are personal beliefs that are accepted by specific persons or groups that determine whether or not a certain behavior is appropriate. Norms are statements that are prescriptive or proscriptive, as the women are important for the improvement of microfinance and development as social networks play an important role in enforcing them through sanctioning (Maulana et al., 2018). Women are organized into a network of organizations via microfinance programs (Heacock, 2015). By improving their social capital and endowing them with normative influence, women's participation in microfinance groups can improve their individual agency and facilitate collective empowerment. are all factors to consider (Ajzen, 1985; Kumar & Das, 2019). Microfinance institutions play an important role in encouraging micro and small business owners to think about and care for not only their company's growth but also the environment (Nugroho et al., 2017).

H2: Belief about how microfinance should influence a person normative belief towards behavioral intentions.

Behavior Intention Positively Affect Actual Behavior

Behavioral intention is one of the most important indicators of an individual's actual behavior. Intention is a mental representation of a person's actions (Maulana et al., 2018). Several intrinsic and extrinsic factors, such as personal views and faith, prior experiences, perceptions and opinions of family and peers, social standing, and economic conditions, can affect an individual's behavior to act in a certain way (Mansori et al., 2020). Intention is a proxy for real action that helps estimate the chance of consumers making a purchase within a particular time frame (Chowk, 2020).

H3: Positive behavior intention towards using microfinance should positively affect actual behavior

Perceived Behavioral Control (PBC) Positively Affect Behavioral Intention

PBC is impacted by self-efficacy, compatibility, and resource enabling situations, and it is favorably associated to behavioral intention and also refers to the ability to sign up for a microfinance service (Tahmasebi & Askaribezayeh, 2021). Because intentions have been eliminated, this would be directly tied to microfinance participation behavior. PBC as a predictor of intention. Perceived behavioral control refers to a person's belief that a certain activity is problematic (Ashraf, 2019). People may not be able to control external and internal influences such as time, money, opportunity, and so on. As a result, the more people who have influence over the opportunities and resources to engage in a particular activity, the more likely that behavior will occur and explains that the people action determined by the behavioral intention {Formatting Citation}. Microfinance has been identified as the most significant financial intervention in the fight against poverty. It gives hope to the poor who have the skills to manage their financial resources but are unable to better their living conditions due to a lack of funds (Maulana et al., 2018). As the people are involved in informal sources is also because of lack of awareness about microcredit services as many people are seeking the help from the informal source as this helps to predict the youth intention for the microcredit (Kandil, 2018).

H4: Perceived behavioral control (PBC) positively affects behavioral intention about microfinance

Variable and Each Definition

The different variables that are taken in the study of peoples' perception on micro-finance are shown in table 1.

Study Area, Population and Sample Size

The study area chosen for the study is Janakpur which is conducted by using explanatory design. Janakpur is a sub-metropolitan city in Nepal's Province No. 2's Dhanusha District of Nepal. The geographic coordinates of Janakpur are: latitudes 26°43'43.8'' N and longitudes 85°55'34.6'' E and has an area of 91.97 square kilometers at a height of 90 meters above sea level (Dhungana et al., 2016). Janakpur is the Terai's third-largest city (after Biratnagar and Birgunj) and Nepal's seventh-largest city. The Janakpur Dham Sub-Metropolis is organized into 25 wards and is approximately 450 kilometers from the federal capital Kathmandu. Between Janakpur and India,

Table 1. Variable and Each Definition

Construct	Observed Variables	Variable Notation	Description
Normative Belief	Close friend	NB1	Engagement in microfinance
	Colleagues	NB2	Engagement in microfinance service
	Parents	NB3	Engagement in microfinance service
	Siblings	NB4	Use of microfinance
	People	NB5	Microfinance services
	Siblings important	NB6	Engagement in microfinance service
	People importance	NB7	Use of microfinance services
Perceived Behavior Control	Political condition	PBC1	Condition of politics motivate to use microfinance
	Control	PBC2	Self-control of microfinance
	Confidence about microfinance	PBC3	Microfinance practice
	Effective usage	PBC4	Effective usage of microfinance
	Knowledge of system	PBC5	Knowledge about use of system
	System by government	PBC6	Government facilities
	Efficient services	PBC7	Support by government
Attitude	Profitable	AT1	Experience of using microfinance
	Desirable	AT2	Desirable of using microfinance services
	Pay on deposit	AT3	high pay on deposit
	Cost	AT4	Charge on transaction cost
	Complicated	AT5	Complication on transaction
	Pleasant	AT6	Pleasant of using microfinance
	Wise	AT7	Worth of using microfinance
	Favorable	AT8	Benefit of using microfinance
Behavioral Intentions	Perception	BI1	Interest on microfinance
	Adaptation	BI2	Adopt of microfinance
	Recommendation	BI3	Strong recommendation to others
	Choose microfinance	BI4	Like to adopt microfinance
	Decision on adaptation	BI5	Selection of microfinance is right
	Microcredit facility	BI6	Obtain microcredit on future
	Adopt of microfinance in future	BI7	Adopt in future
Actual Behavior	Complicated	AB1	Difficult in understanding
	Collateral need	AB2	Collateral requirements
	Substitute	AB3	Better for microcredit
	Uncertain	AB4	Transaction are uncertain so plan to participate
	Compatibility	AB5	Compatibility of religious values
	Perception	AB6	Perception about microfinance

Nepal Railways used to run. And aside from dwelling, the surface is almost entirely flat which make the live of local people easy (Bartington et al., 2017).

It is also known as Janakpur Dham or Janakpur. Janakpur is Nepal's largest sub-metropolitan city and one of the country's fastest growing cities. The city features a lot of parks, private schools, colleges, and internet service providers, as well as superior health care facilities (Dhungana et al., 2016). Janaki temple is the center of attraction of tourist and also Mithila art, railways but because of lack of infrastructural development and services there is difficult to attract them (Mor et al., 2016) . As for per the development finance need is necessary as to provide the financial support microfinance helps in development of the Janakpur as they provide the loan to local people and awareness program to them so that they can invest in business and mobilize the economy (Jha et al., 2011) As people are also aware about the development because due to railways it helps to easy access of the services in near future. So, local people can get loan from microfinance and invest in business which helps to development of economy (Bartington et al., 2017). Researcher's purpose for selecting the area is to acquire the information on how local people is practiced about microfinance and how they perceived about microfinance in Janakpur as the working system and culture differ as the places differ and how the local people are taking advantage of microfinance in Janakpur place. A complete of 283 respondents were selected from Janakpur using probability sampling technique.

Instrument and Procedure of Data Collection, and Data Analysis

The primary tools utilized in this study are structured questionnaires with observations. Testing instruments include estimators (instance, survey or scale) that are designed to collect information from research subjects on a topic of concern (Trigueros, 2017). Structure questionnaire was the most research instrument employed in this study. A structure questionnaire has been developed and the structured questionnaire are set in the kobo toolbox and then the process of data collection started where devised to conduct survey on local people perception about microfinance Janakpur, Nepal. Quantitative data was extracted through interview and questionnaire set for the survey. Primary data from questionnaire survey are collected. The researchers have linked questionnaire so as to satisfy the varied objectives mentioned above within the study. Both public and personal questions were to collect data. Probability sampling is chosen for this study where cluster sampling is chosen. The interview consisted of total of 283 respondents as the sample size determination is of known population. The questionnaire, expert judgment and observation have been included in this analysis.

The questionnaire was in the form of 5-point Likert scale, subjective questions and multiple choice. The main source of the research is primary data collection.

It is carried out using descriptive analysis, which consists of a mean, median, and style analysis, as well as inferential analysis, which consists of structural equation modeling based on numerous latent constructs. Every piece of data acquired from the field is evaluated in order to make sense of the research and come to specific conclusions and discoveries (Oyedokun,2019). For data analysis, applications such as STATA and SPSS AMOS were used, as well as Microsoft Excel for data entry and research tallying. Data analysis was performed using descriptive analysis and inferential analysis. Descriptive analysis was used to understand the socio demographic characters, its impact on local people perception of microfinance of Janakpur and to analyze the challenges faced by people during the microfinance's services and its managerial solutions descriptive analysis was performed. Inferential analysis includes the descriptive analysis, exploratory factor analysis, confirmatory analysis, measurement model, path analysis and mediation analysis.

RESULT AND ANALYSIS

Socio-demographic Analysis

General information about the polled perception of microfinance is covered by socio-demographic analysis like age, sex, occupation, work experience, and educational level were all taken into consideration. Individual characteristics of the population that are expressed statistically, such as age, gender, marital status, educational level, and work experience, are the focus of socio-demographic data (Adam, 2020). Table 2 shows the socio-demographic characteristics of respondents in this study, respectively.

Determinants for Perception of Local People About Microfinance

The various factors about local people perception about microfinance are described in order to know about the present information about microfinance. Five variables are mentioned below i.e., Normative belief, Attitude, Behavioral intention, Actual Behavior and perceive behavior control. These variables are measured in five scale under Likert scale (1= strongly agree, 2= Agree, 3= Neutral, 4= Disagree, 5= strongly Disagree) (see table 3). Table 3 shows that normative belief, attitude, perceived behavioral control, behavioral intention and actual behavior are the major determinants for perception of local people about microfinance.

Table 2. Socio-Demographic characteristics

Variables	Category	Frequency	Percentage
Sex	Male	185	65%
	Female	98	35%
Age	below 20	9	3.22%
	31-40	117	41.93%
	41-50	62	21.91%
	51-60	10	3.53%
	above 60	1	0.35%
Education Level	SLC/see	58	20.79%
	Bachelor	204	72.04%
	Master	19	6.71%
	above master	2	0.71%
Family occupation	Business	81	28.62%
	Government Job	52	18.37%
	Industrial Worker	68	24.03%
	Student	34	12.01%
	Others	48	16.96%
Members in Household	2	8	2.83%
	3	42	14.84%
	4	54	19.08%
	5	102	36.04%
	Above 6	77	27.21%
Employed Member in Household	1	67	23.64%
	2	165	58.30%
	3	43	15.19%
	4	5	1.77%
	Above 5	3	1.06%
Income	10000-20000	75	26.50%
	21000-30000	119	42.05%
	31000-40000	75	26.50%
	Above 40000	14	4.95%
Training Related to Microfinance	Yes	153	54.06%
	No	130	45.4%

Table 3. Perception of Local People about Microfinance

		1	2	3	4	5
Normative belief						
a.	My parents think I should involve in microfinance services	0.35%	3.53%	7.77%	73.49%	14.84%
b.	My siblings that are important to me would think I should engage in microfinance services	1.06%	1.41%	8.48%	80.91%	8.12%
c.	People important to me would think I should use microfinance services	0.70%	2.12%	9.8%	78.44%	8.83%
Attitude						
a.	Using microfinance service is profitable	2.82%	1.41%	46.28%	46.64%	2.82%
b.	Using microfinance service is valuable	0.70%	2.82%	40.98%	48.40%	7.06%
c.	Choosing microfinance is beneficial	1.06%	3.53%	35.68%	53..00%	6.713%
Perceived Behavioral Control						
a.	The political conditions in the country motivates me to use microfinance	3.88%	3.88%	30.74%	59.36%	2.12%
b.	I have enough knowledge to use microfinance services	2.47%	8.83%	27.91%	58.30%	2.47%
c.	The government supports microfinance practice	1.77%	6.00%	29.32%	62.19%	0.70%
Behavioral Intentions						
a.	I am interested to adopt microfinance in the future	1.76%	1.41%	19.78%	169.96%	7.06%
b.	I like to adopt microfinance	0.35%	2.82%	21.55%	68.55%	5.65%
c.	I will make an effort to obtain microcredit in future	0%	3.18%	24.73%	63.60%	8.48%
Actual Behavior						
a.	Collateral requirements or need of security affect my usage of microcredit in microfinance	2.82%	6.71%	27.91%	58.65%	3.88%
b.	Microfinance is a good substitute of my microfinance contract	1.06%	4.59%	31.095%	53.%	63.25%
c.	Behavior of people influence the perception about microfinance	0.70%	5.30%	33.21%	53.0%	7.77%

Source: Field Study

Challenges on Local People Perception

The study modal response reveals 92.93% of respondents have challenges to understand about microfinance and remaining the remaining 7.07% faced no challenges. In this study it shows that majority of local people in Janakpur face challenges to understand about microfinance. The challenges that microfinance face in empowering micro and small business owners to be concerned about not only their own business growth but also the environmental sustainability of their surroundings have prompted microfinance to improve their services and provide environmental training to their employees, particularly in incorporating eco-friendly factors into credit analysis of prospective investors and monitoring business customers (Dhungana et al., 2016).

Our study shows that the respondents are facing various challenges like difficult to understand, complicated, uncertain, trustworthy, higher interest rate and others. It is revealed that 30.74% of people face challenge of difficult to understand, 24.03% find it complicated, 7.77% face challenge of uncertain. 7.42% has faced challenge of trust, 20.85% face challenge of high interest rate and remaining 2.12% face other challenges. According to our study the challenges that affect the most is difficult to understand the system.

The study also reveals that the most responsible institutes for the challenges for the microfinance are government and local politics as 112 respondents i.e., 39.57% and 81 respondents i.e., 28.62% finds government and local politics responsible for the above challenges respectively. As the majority respondent i.e,196 (69.25%) of the respondent find that the challenges have moderate impact on microfinance, it is concluded that the impact of the challenges in microfinance is moderate. the very low impact of challenges on microfinance according to the research with respondent. According to the previous researcher microfinance and microcredit schemes have negative consequences in that they assist the moderately poor more than the destitute, and so their impact varies by income category (better- off benefit more from microcredit) (M. Hossain, 2021) and the study says the impact of microfinance is moderate on the challenges.

Managerial Solution

Microfinance institution devise a variety of novel solutions, including group lending, sufficient incentives, and collateral substitutes (Hockerts, 2017). Nonfinancial services may be provided to address the lending methodology, which has a substantial impact on product design, client selection, application and approval processes, loan repayment, monitoring, and portfolio management (Effendi et al., 2020). The microfinance has many challenges and to solve there are challenges to solve those challenges are like grabbing the market opportunities, providing the training to the local people, learning managerial skill, brining managerial skill and technology and others.

From the study, it is found that providing training to the people and aware them about microfinance is the best way to tackle with the challenges as majority of the respondent chose it. According to others study it shows that to solve the challenges there are microfinance devise a variety of novel solutions, including group lending, sufficient incentives, and collateral substitutes (Rizzo & Columna, 2020). The majority of respondent 51.94% i.e., 174 respondents find government responsible for betterment of microfinance. Similarly, 10.95%, choose individual, 15.54% choose society, 14.84% choose local politics and remaining 19% chose others as the responsible parties for betterment of microfinance.

Pandemic Effect on Microfinance: As local governments have gained key responsibility for social security mechanisms, the urgency of the COVID-19 response has sparked new sorts of cross-sectoral and multi-scalar interaction between administrative units involved in coordinating responses (Janssens et al., 2021). The issue that this covid-19 pandemic has brought to light is that governance experiences vary greatly across different regions of the world — indeed, that the same policies, such as lockdowns, will play out very differently for the middle classes and the impoverished (Dutta & Fischer, 2021). The study shows that the effect of pandemic is high according to 216 respondent and only 67 respondent says there is no impact of covid-19 on microfinance among the total number of respondents 283. This shows that the covid -19 has a major impact on microfinance with majority.

Effect that Respondent Have Faced About Microfinance: As the microfinance and social efficacy is related to each other and covid -19 shows that the financial efficiency of MFIs is reduced as a result of the pandemic's impact; however, the social efficiency of MFIs is raised as a result of COVID-19's influence (Dutta & Fischer, 2021) . According to our research the effect caused due to COVID-19 during the lockdown situation as some of the problem are train the local people about microfinance and aware them about the system and conditions of microfinance, Difficult to understand the system during knockdown of the microfinance, to collect interest as the interest is to be paid during pandemic, financial problem, make policy for proper analysis of client property, Difficult in knowing the system during knockdown of the microfinance due to pandemic, Technology advancement, Political parties act like he was a boss of that area, corruption in the area, Cannot get more of the deposit, Unmanages system, weak governance, flexible staff, pandemic-induced impact decreases the financial efficiency of microfinance however, the social efficiency is increased under the impact of COVID-19 to explore potential channels through which efficiency is influenced by the COVID-19 outbreak, Shortage of the transportation to receive the microfinance institutions, Shift in the system of the time, Problem contact to the bank during the lockdown time.

Managerial Solution: To mitigate the negative impact of the Covid-19 on the microfine, microfinance must adopt insurance coverage, treat service providers more like workers, and provide safety safeguards, among other things (Dutta & Fischer, 2021). Microfinance can use a process approach to help them achieve their objectives and manage the risks associated with their operations (Brickell et al., 2020). According to our study some of the managerial solution for the microfinance are decreasing the interest rate for the growth of the microfinance activities. Because of Covid-19, like whole economy, Microfinance have also been affected in many ways.

Our study has suggested provide training to the local people about microfinance institutions, provide discount to the customers during lockdown, provide the information about finance related work and give different facilities regarding microfinance bank, analysis the market situation, analysis the people behavior and others, relaxing some aspects of the traditional microfinance model, targeting microcredit products better, and lending for activities beyond entrepreneurial activities that leads to substantial welfare gains, make awareness program about microfinance so that they get knowledge about them, merge with the small cooperative or microfinance to make a capital, use of new technologies during lock down, provide different scheme to the people so that we can bounce back the market as to get easy interest rate, lowering the transaction cost and make the system of loan simple for the poor and needy people as some of the possible solution.

Inferential Analysis

By taking a random sample of data from a population to describe and make decisions about that community, inferential analysis aids in the examination of sample data in order to anticipate and estimate future justices. It is based on the phenomenon accumulation of population- specific data to explain and make population decision (Allua & Thompson, 2009). It includes six sections for the analysis. The first section discusses about descriptive statics, the second section includes expletory analysis. The third section comprises of confirmatory factor analysis along with measurement model on the fourth section. The fifth section include path ad mediation analysis

Summary Statistics

There are 283 respondents from which we have collected data from Janakpur. The mean of the respondents is from 3.5194 to 3.9894 and the median is 3. Skewness and kurtosis measures are frequently used to describe the shape of a distribution and Kurtosis is a measure of the "peak" of probability distribution. They've been used in normality tests and studies (Kallner, 2018). The result shows that the value of skewness of data lies from -1.958 to -0.236. All construct lies above -3 and below 0. As per Kallner (2018), it shows that it has a negative skewness i.e., the tail of the left side is the distribution is longer. Likewise, in the kurtosis the values lie above 0.614 to 8.905 which lies between -10 to +10. As per Kallner (2018), it represents that the distribution has high peak kurtosis and has leptokurtic distributions. This indicates that the data of this study is normally distributed.

Exploratory Analysis

Exploratory factor analysis is a statical method to minimize a large set of sample observed to a small proposition of "outcomes" representing the general existence of group of variables (Gaskin, 2021). The first measure is of the Kaiser-Meyer-Olkin measure of sampling adequacy and the value we have here is 0.703. Gaskin (2021) states that 0.5 is acceptable although a value above 0.6 is preferred. As far as the Bartlett's test of Sphericity, the obtained p-value or the significance level is 0.000 which normally we would record as less than 0.05 which represents there is sufficient correlation. This shows that want to have a statistically significant value for Bartlett's Test of Sphericity so value below 0.05.

Common Method Bias (CMB)

A study with significant common method bias is one in which a single factor explains the majority of the variance. There are a few different tests that can be used to test for a common method bias (Gaskin, 2021) and in our study we have used Harmon's single factor test. In this total common bias method, the SPSS have extracted five factors and the cumulative percentage is 21.382% which is less than 50%. Hence, it suggests that CMB does not affect our data.

Measurement Model

The measurement model quantifies the relations between hypothetical frameworks that could perhaps be known but not measurable elements and observed variables that, in the form of a linear mixture, represent a particular imaginary construct (Lam & Maguire, 2012). Measurement model deals with the concern of validity and reliability which is done by checking convergent and discriminant validity. Hamid et al. (2017) defined the criteria of AVE>0.5, CR >0.7 and CR>AVE to be fulfilled for the study to demonstrate convergent validity and the criteria of AVE>ASV &

Table 4. Measurement Model

Construct	Indicator	Factor Loading	Cronbach's Alpha	CR	AVE	MSV
Normative Belief	NB3	0.779	.803	0.818	0.604	0.020
	NB5	0.906				
	NB7	0.849				
Attitude	AT1	0.853	.806	0.809	0.587	0.103
	AT3	0.859				
	AT5	0.798				
Perceived Behavior Control	PBC1	0.813	.805	0.808	0.584	0.017
	PBC3	0.861				
	PBC5	0.862				
Behavioral Intentions	BI2	0.871	.810	0.814	0.595	0.045
	BI4	0.862				
	BI6	0.799				
Actual Behavior	AB2	0.817	.810	0.814	0.595	0.103
	AB4	0.836				
	AB6	0.865				

Table 5. Latent Construct Correction

	BI	NB	AT	PBC	AB
BI	**0.771**				
NB	0.086	**0.777**			
AT	0.127	0.142	**0.766**		
PBC	-0.132	0.082	0.105	**0.764**	
AB	0.211	0.044	0.321	0.078	**0.771**

MSV and to be fulfilled for the study to demonstrate discriminant validity. In the table, as all constructs has fulfilled the criteria for convergent validity discriminant validity. Similarly, Cronbach's alpha is also measured which should be above 0.7 for the data to be acceptable. The result shows that all values of Cronbach's alpha are greater than 0.7. It implies that the study has good internal consistency among variable. Table 4 the validity and reliability of data which insists that data is suitable for further analysis. Table 5 displays the square root of AVE together with the inter-construct correlation matrix.

Table 6. Model Fit Results

Name	Results	Acceptable Values	Judgment of Model Fit
Chi- square/df (CMIN/df)	7.697	<5	No good fit
Root Mean Squared Residual (RMR)	0.061	<0.08	Good fit
Goodness of Fit Index (GFI)	0.546	>0.8	No Good fit
Comparative Fit Index (CFI)	0.620	>0.9	No Good fit
Turker-Lewis Index (TLI)	0.531	>0.9	Good fit
Incremental Fit Index (IFI)	0.925	>0.9	Good fit
Root Mean Square Error of Approximately (RMSEA)	0.054	<0.08	Good fit

Table 7. Hypothesis Testing

Hypothesis	Estimate	S. E.	C.R.	P Value	Significant/ Insignificant	Conclusion
H01: Attitude ®Behavior intentions	-.025	.027	.287	.774	Insignificant	Rejected
H02: Normative belief ®Behavior intentions	1.010	.086	2.867	.004	Significant	Accepted
H03: Behavior Intentions ®Actual behavior.	-.101	.022	-1.078	.281	Insignificant	Rejected
H04: Perceived behavior Control ®Behavior intentions.	.1000	.831	2.578	.010	Significant	Accepted

Confirmatory Factor Analysis

Confirmatory factor analysis is the multivariate statical process which is used to test how the measured variables the number of construct (Kumari, 2021). For the confirmatory factor analysis several values such as CMIN/df, RMR, GFI, CFI, TLI, IFI and RMSEA results are measured and compared with the acceptable value of the table. Hair et al., (2010) has identified the acceptable value which is shown in the table. From the comparison, it is found that RMR, TLI, IFI,

Figure 2. Path Analysis of Latent, Observed and Error Variables

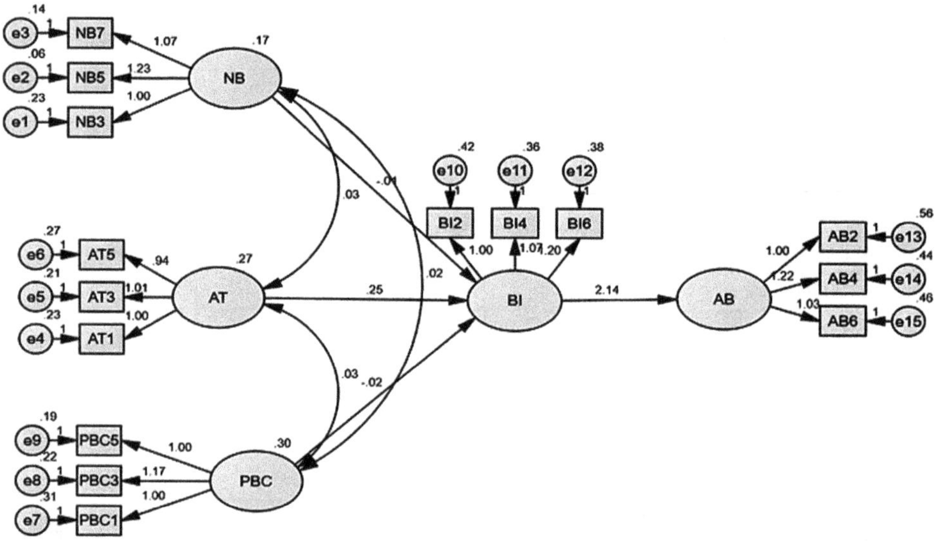

RMSEA have good fit for the model whereas CMIN/df, GFI, CFI doesn't meet the criteria of good fit (see table 6). These results indicate that the model is fit for the study purpose.

Hypothesis Testing

A hypothesis is a precise, testable declaration of what the researchers predict will be the effect of the study (White-Davis et al., 2018). Table 7 shows that only two hypotheses i.e., H01 (Normative belief and Behavior intentions) and H04 (Perceived behavior Control and Behavior intentions) has P-value less than 0.05. It means that only these two hypotheses are accepted which means there are significant relationship between dependent (Behavior intentions) and independent variables (Normative belief and Perceived behavior Control). Similarly, the remaining hypothesis i.e., H01 and H03 are rejected which implies that the relationship between Attitude and Behavior intentions, Behavior Intentions and Actual behavior is insignificant. Mediation Analysis is also used to analyze the effect of the mediating variables which is examined through SOBEL test (Jones et al., 2021). Our study reveals that the mediating variable (Behavior Intention) has mediating effect on the relationship between the dependent i.e., Actual behavior and independent variables i.e., Perceived Behavior Control, Attitude and Normative Belief as the P value for all the relationships is less than 0.05.

DISCUSSION

This discussion part consists the overall outcome or results to be discussed that we came to find out from data presentation and analysis in this chapter. Tables and figures are presented in the descriptive analysis where as various statical technique and SEM model analysis is present in the inferential analysis

The first section of this chapter deals with the descriptive analysis in which socio-demographic characteristics of respondents were analyzed. The result shows that there are 64.66% of male and 35.34% of female people are customer of microfinance. similarly, the respondents are coming under the age group 31-40 years which is 117 respondents among the 283 total respondents. Likewise looking at the employment status of the residents in the household among the total member of family is 2 has majority of member working with 58.3%. the people and customer of the microfinance involvement education level is bachelor with 72.04%. looking at the family occupation are people involved in more in business than other sector with the higher percent 28.75%. Looking at the training side to the people the more people are involved in training with 153 respondents with 283 total. This shows thar people are involved in training but they are nor experiencing in the practical use. This shows that the people who are using the training helps them to use the new innovation and technology with ease (Shrestha et al., 2019). Microfinance has used the distributor network concept, which relies on key business partners' distribution capabilities (Mansori et al., 2020). The above study says that the member involved in microfinance are have less number and are more business than other field and the people are more educated in bachelor and shows that the educated people can grasp more opportunities in the market than the uneducated (Tahmasebi & Askaribezayeh, 2021).

Likewise, the study is mainly concerned with the perception of the people about microfinance and to identify the perception the variable is introduced like attitude, perceived variable control, behavioral intention, actual behavior, normative belief. From the above analyzed part we came to know that normative belief of the people this show that the people should involve in microfinance and take the service of microfinance. the attitude towards the microfinance of people is positive as this helps to know that services are profitable, valuable and beneficial to the people of Janakpur. The perceived behavior control is self-efficacy the reflect one's belief and confidence and according to analyze the political condition and government support the microfinance practice with majority respondents among the 283 people. Behavioral intention shows the technology adaptation of the microfinance and this show the people want to involve in future also and recommend others to use the microfinance with the latest technology use. Normative beliefs represent 'expectancies,' while motivations to comply represent 'values' in the belief-based measure of subjective norms (Tahmasebi & Askaribezayeh, 2021). The underlying logic is that the intention to behave in a particular way is determined by the expected utilities (both personal and social) of the action in question. This helps to know the people, friend helps to know that the use of microfinance is good as it indicate positive response (Ashraf, 2019)The actual behavior is the intention of the people as this shows the collateral requirement in microfinance affect the usage of the facility and shows the behavior of people influence microfinance performance. Though aggregate t shows the people are likely to use the microfinance process.

Here in this study, it mainly deals with the problem that people faced during the use of microfinance and show the challenges about microfinance. According to analyze that shows it is difficult to understand the people perception about microfinance with majority 92.93%. The major responsible for challenges are government and local politics with 28.62% and 39.57% of majority. The major responsible for challenges is difficult to understand the people perception and vice versa. Likely there are many challenges and the impact of the challenges of the microfinance are moderate and also shows that the betterment of these challenges are the local bodies and government. Corporate governance is also the one which helps to improve the challenges of the microfinance and sometime it also not sufficient to improve the challenges (Maulana et al., 2018) as staff and their education will have a favorable impact on the microfinance industry in particular, as well as the country's overall economy (Hossain, 2021). Close monitoring and relationships with borrowers, they argued, appear to be critical for early detection of loan difficulties. A tight interaction between microfinance and other government organizations that give development assistance to the rural poor may be regarded critical to the success of the microfinance plan (Hockerts, 2017). And also, it shows that COVID-19has impact on microfinance. As a result of the economic consequences of COVID-19, credit-taking will likely increase in terms of the number of borrowers and loan amounts, and that the lack of social safety nets will lead to women's bodily and emotional "depletion" as they try to service these loans through increased (un) paid work burdens (Brickell et al., 2020). Microfinance, over-indebtedness, and the COVID-19 pandemic are all exacerbating social reproduction challenges that will stymie progress toward gender equality and long-term development (Hossain, 2021). As the microfinance and social efficacy is related to each other and covid -19 shows that the financial efficiency of MFIs is reduced as a result of the pandemic's impact; however, the social efficiency of MFIs is raised as a result of COVID-19's influence (Dutta & Fischer, 2021)

As there are challenges and to solve these issues the problem there are managerial solution introduced like wise to lessen the negative impact of the Covid-19 on the microfine, microfinance must, among other things, embrace insurance coverage, treat service providers more like workers, and provide safety protections (Dutta &

Fischer, 2021). The findings shed light on the Toindepi in terms of cleanliness and safety, many microfinance institutions have launched hygiene and safety training programs (Hossain, 2021). Microfinance has devised a variety of innovative solutions, including group lending, sufficient incentives, and collateral substitutes. They may also provide non-financial services to help with the problem's settlement (Brickell et al., 2020). Microfinance can use a process-oriented approach to solving problems.

The third section of this chapter depicted inferential analysis in which the mean, standard deviation, minimum and maximum values of the variables considered in conceptual framework were generated. SEM is used to analysis local people perception on mic with the help of five factor used in thus study. Result obtained confirmed that the model fitness criteria fulfilled in all condition. The Kaiser-Meyer-Olkin or KMO for this study is found to be 0.775 which is considered to be significant or positively corelated. The Sig is 0.00 which shows that the data is fit for the further process. The goodness of model is test by the help of model fit indicators. We EFA under which KMO Barletta analysis the value is said to be suitable if it is more than 0.7 and extraction need to be more than 0.5 and all factors of each construct have more than 0.5. likewise in rotated matrix it estimates the correlation between each of the variable and estimated component. In CFA model fit is done. Similarly, measurement model, path analysis and mediation analysis are done in this chapter. The AT and BI, BI and AB has insignificant relationship because P-value is more than 0.05 where insignificant mean that null hypothesis is fail to reject. It indicates there is no relationship between the attitude and behavior intention, behavior intention and actual behavior. NB and BI, PBC and BI has significant relationship because it has P- value less than 0.05, it indicates there is relationship between normative belief and behavior intention, perceived behavior control and behavior intention. This indicates that local people of Janakpur have a more favorable perception towards microfinance.

CONCLUSION

The key aim of this analysis is to know the perception of local people about microfinance. Different literature has been examined to include confirmation of facts and figures, evaluate the research gap and recommend more focus area primary and secondary sources to achieve the targets. Because of their potential contribution to the establishment of viable financial markets in rural regions for families, particularly those who previously had appropriate access to financial services, microfinance institutions have gained increased attention in the development literature. These banks have recently transitioned to a credit-plus age, expanding their scope of operations to include savings and insurance. However, there is a case to be made that these institutions should place a greater focus on delivering financial services to the lowest of the poor, matching demand requirements. Both of these developments point to the need for the industry to adopt more adaptable and cost-effective regulation methods. The result shows that there are 64.66% of male and 35.34% of female people are customer of microfinance. similarly, the respondents are coming under the age group 31-40 years which is 117 respondents among the 283 total respondents. Likewise looking at the employment status of the residents in the household among the total member of family is 2 has majority of member working with 58.3%. SEM is used to analysis local people perception on mic with the help of five factor used in thus study. Result obtained confirmed that the model fitness criteria fulfilled in all condition. The Kaiser-Meyer-Olkin or KMO for this study is found to be 0.775 which is considered to be significant or positively corelated. The Sig is 0.00 which shows that the data is fit for the further process. The goodness of model is test by the help of model fit indicators.

REFERENCES

Ab Hamid, M. R., Sami, W., & Sidek, M. M. (2017, September). Discriminant validity assessment: Use of Fornell & Larcker criterion versus HTMT criterion. *Journal of Physics: Conference Series, 890*(1), 012163. doi:10.1088/1742-6596/890/1/012163

Abidoye, R. B., Junge, M., Lam, T. Y., Oyedokun, T. B., & Tipping, M. L. (2019). Property valuation methods in practice: evidence from Australia. *Property Management.*

Abu-Bader, S., & Jones, T. V. (2021). Statistical mediation analysis using the sobel test and hayes SPSS process macro. *International Journal of Quantitative and Qualitative Research Methods.*

Adam, A. M. (2020). Sample size determination in survey research. *Journal of Scientific Research and Reports, 26*(5), 90–97. doi:10.9734/jsrr/2020/v26i530263

Adhikari, S. (2021). Role of gender diversity on banking performance in Kathmandu Valley. *Quest Journal of Management and Social Sciences, 53*(9), 1689–1699.

Ajzen, I. (1985). From intentions to actions: A theory of planned behavior. *Action Control*, 11–39. doi:10.1007/978-3-642-69746-3_2

Allua, S., & Thompson, C. B. (2009). Inferential Statistics. *Air Medical Journal, 28*(4), 168–171. doi:10.1016/j.amj.2009.04.013 PMID:19573763

Ashraf, M. A. (2019). Theory of islamic entrepreneurship: A conceptual paper. *International Journal of Entrepreneurship*, *23*(3), 1–12.

Bartington, S. E., Bakolis, I., Devakumar, D., Kurmi, O. P., Gulliver, J., Chaube, G., Manandhar, D. S., Saville, N. M., Costello, A., Osrin, D., Hansell, A. L., & Ayres, J. G. (2017). Patterns of domestic exposure to carbon monoxide and particulate matter in households using biomass fuel in Janakpur, Nepal. *Environmental Pollution*, *220*(8), 38–45. doi:10.1016/j.envpol.2016.08.074 PMID:27707597

Bjerner, J., Theodorsson, E., Hovig, E., & Kallner, A. (2009). Non-parametric estimation of reference intervals in small non-Gaussian sample sets. *Accreditation and Quality Assurance*, *14*(4), 185–192. doi:10.100700769-009-0490-2

Brickell, K., Picchioni, F., Natarajan, N., Guermond, V., Parsons, L., Zanello, G., & Bateman, M. (2020). Compounding crises of social reproduction: Microfinance, over-indebtedness and the COVID-19 pandemic. *World Development*, *136*, 105087. doi:10.1016/j.worlddev.2020.105087 PMID:32834384

Chen, M. F., & Tung, P. J. (2014). Developing an extended theory of planned behavior model to predict consumers' intention to visit green hotels. *International Journal of Hospitality Management*, *36*, 221–230. doi:10.1016/j.ijhm.2013.09.006

Chowk, B. (2020). Microfinance as an instrument for economic and social benefits to women : Andréa parent centre for microfinance Nepal centre for microfinance Nepal. *Knowledge Services for Institutions Serving the Poor.*

Dhungana, B. R. (2021). Impact of micro-finance on women : A case of Lekhnath municipality of Nepal impact of micro-finance on women : A case of Lekhnath municipality of Nepal. *The Lumbini Journal of Business and Economics*, *3*(2), 76–84.

Dhungana, B. R., Singh, J. K., Acharya, D., Gautam, S., & Paudyal, P. (2016). Perceived usefulness of a microfinance intervention on health awareness and practices in Nepal. *Frontiers in Public Health*, *3*(1), 1–7. doi:10.3389/fpubh.2015.00289 PMID:26835443

Dutta, A., & Fischer, H. W. (2021). The local governance of COVID-19: Disease prevention and social security in rural India. *World Development*, *138*, 105234. doi:10.1016/j.worlddev.2020.105234 PMID:33106724

Effendi, I., Murad, M., Rafiki, A., & Lubis, M. M. (2020). The application of the theory of reasoned action on services of Islamic rural banks in Indonesia. *Journal of Islamic Marketing*, *12*(5), 951–976. doi:10.1108/JIMA-02-2020-0051

Gaskin, C. J., & Happell, B. (2014). On exploratory factor analysis: A review of recent evidence, an assessment of current practice, and recommendations for future use. *International Journal of Nursing Studies, 51*(3), 511–521. doi:10.1016/j.ijnurstu.2013.10.005 PMID:24183474

Guérin, I., Morvant-Roux, S., & Villarreal, M. (2014). *Microfinance, Debt and Over-Indebtedness. Juggling with Money*. Routledge.

Hair, J. F., Gabriel, M., & Patel, V. (2014). AMOS covariance-based structural equation modeling (CB-SEM): Guidelines on its application as a marketing research tool. *Brazilian Journal of Marketing, 13*(2).

Heacock, L., Weissbrot, J., Raad, R., Campbell, N., Friedman, K. P., Ponzo, F., & Chandarana, H. (2015). PET/MRI for the evaluation of patients with lymphoma: Initial observations. *AJR. American Journal of Roentgenology, 204*(4), 842–848. doi:10.2214/AJR.14.13181 PMID:25794075

Hockerts, K. (2017). Determinants of social entrepreneurial intentions. *Entrepreneurship Theory and Practice, 41*(1), 105–130. doi:10.1111/etap.12171

Hossain, M. (2021). The effect of the Covid-19 on sharing economy activities. *Journal of Cleaner Production, 280*, 124782. doi:10.1016/j.jclepro.2020.124782 PMID:33106734

Hummel, K., & Schlick, C. (2016). The relationship between sustainability performance and sustainability disclosure – Reconciling voluntary disclosure theory and legitimacy theory. *Journal of Accounting and Public Policy, 35*(5), 455–476. doi:10.1016/j.jaccpubpol.2016.06.001

Hummel, K., & Schlick, C. (2016). The relationship between sustainability performance and sustainability disclosure – Reconciling voluntary disclosure theory and legitimacy theory. *Journal of Accounting and Public Policy, 35*(5), 455–476. doi:10.1016/j.jaccpubpol.2016.06.001

Janssens, W., Pradhan, M., de Groot, R., Sidze, E., Donfouet, H. P. P., & Abajobir, A. (2021). The short-term economic effects of COVID-19 on low-income households in rural Kenya: An analysis using weekly financial household data. *World Development, 138*, 105280. doi:10.1016/j.worlddev.2020.105280

Jha, A., Ranjan, S., Pradhan, P. K., & Jha, T. (2011). Challenges of setting up psychiatric services in Nepal: Lessons from the first year of Janakpur Project. *Asian Journal of Psychiatry, 4*(4), 297–299. doi:10.1016/j.ajp.2011.10.004 PMID:23051166

Kandil, M. (2018). Investigating determinants of youth's intentions of seeking microcredit in the post-conflict era. *The Electronic Library, 34*(1), 1–5.

Karn, S. K. (2018). Challenges and opportunities of microfinance in Nepal. *International Journal of Social Sciences and Management, 5*(3), 72–75. doi:10.3126/ijssm.v5i3.20612

Kasser, T. (2009). Psychological need satisfaction, personal well-being, and ecological sustainability. *Ecopsychology, 1*(4), 175–180. doi:10.1089/eco.2009.0025

Kayastha, R. (2013). Current issues of microfinance in Nepal. *Yokohama Journal of Social Sciences, 18*(3), 71–83.

Kumar, S., & Das, S. (2019). An extended model of theory of planned behaviour: Entrepreneurial intention, regional institutional infrastructure and perceived gender discrimination in India. *Journal of Entrepreneurship in Emerging Economies, 11*(3), 369–391. doi:10.1108/JEEE-09-2018-0089

Kumari, J. A. P. (2021). The impact of the dimensions of microfinance on poverty reduction : Confirmatory factor analysis (CFA) via individual measurement models. *International Journal of Postharvest Technology and Innovation, 8*(2), 112–121.

Lam, T. Y., & Maguire, D. A. (2012). Structural equation modeling: Theory and applications in forest management. *International Journal of Forestry Research.* doi:10.1155/2012/263953

Mansori, S., Safari, M., & Mohd Ismail, Z. M. (2020). An analysis of the religious, social factors and income's influence on the decision making in Islamic microfinance schemes. *Journal of Islamic Accounting and Business Research, 11*(2), 361–376. doi:10.1108/JIABR-03-2016-0035

Manzano-León, A., Camacho-Lazarraga, P., Guerrero-Puerta, M. A., Guerrero-Puerta, L., Alias, A., Aguilar-Parra, J. M., & Trigueros, R. (2021). Development and validation of a questionnaire on motivation for cooperative playful learning strategies. *International Journal of Environmental Research and Public Health, 18*(3), 960. doi:10.3390/ijerph18030960 PMID:33499224

Maulana, H., Razak, D. A., & Adeyemi, A. A. (2018). Factors influencing behaviour to participate in Islamic microfinance. *International Journal of Islamic and Middle Eastern Finance and Management, 11*(1), 109–130. doi:10.1108/IMEFM-05-2017-0134

Meenu, S. A. (2012). Microfinance interventions and customer perceptions: a study of rural poor in Punjab. *Decision, 39*(1).

Nitzl, C., & Chin, W. W. (2017). The case of partial least squares (PLS) path modeling in managerial accounting research. *Journal of Management Control, 28*(2), 137–156. doi:10.100700187-017-0249-6

Nugroho, L., Utami, W., Akbar, T., & Arafah, W. (2017). The challenges of microfinance institutions in empowering micro and small entrepreneur to implementating green activity. *International Journal of Energy Economics and Policy*, *7*(3), 66–73.

Possner, A., Bruns, S., & Musshoff, O. (2021). A Cambodian smallholder farmer's choice between microfinance institutes and informal commercial moneylenders: The role of risk attitude. *Agricultural Finance Review*. doi:10.1108/AFR-07-2020-0105

Rawhouser, H., Cummings, M., & Newbert, S. L. (2019). Social impact measurement: Current approaches and future directions for social entrepreneurship research. *Entrepreneurship Theory and Practice*, *43*(1), 82–115. doi:10.1177/1042258717727718

Rizzo, T. L., & Columna, L. (2020). Theory of planned behavior. Routledge Handbook of Adapted Physical Education, 326–346. doi:10.4324/9780429052675-25

Rocco, T. S., & Plakhotnik, M. S. (2009). Literature reviews, conceptual frameworks, and theoretical frameworks: Terms, functions, and distinctions. *Human Resource Development Review*, *8*(1), 120–130. doi:10.1177/1534484309332617

Shrestha, S., Parajuli, S., & Paudel, U. R. (2019). Communication in banking sector: A systematic review. *Quest Journal of Management and Social Sciences*, *1*(2), 272–284. doi:10.3126/qjmss.v1i2.27445

Simkhada, N. R. (2013). Problems and prospects of the cooperative sector in Nepal for promoting financial inclusion. *Enterprise Development & Microfinance*, *24*(2), 146–159. doi:10.3362/1755-1986.2013.014

Tahmasebi, A., & Askaribezayeh, F. (2021). Microfinance and social capital formation- a social network analysis approach. *Socio-Economic Planning Sciences, 76*(8), 100978. doi:10.1016/j.seps.2020.100978

Toindepi, J. (2016). Investigating a best practice model of microfinance for poverty alleviation conceptual note. *International Journal of Social Economics*, *43*(4), 346–362. doi:10.1108/IJSE-05-2014-0091

Tucker, M., Jubb, C., & Yap, C. J. (2019). The theory of planned behaviour and student banking in Australia. *International Journal of Bank Marketing*, *38*(1), 113–137. doi:10.1108/IJBM-11-2018-0324

Uluwaduge, P., & Senathiraja, R. (2019). Micro Finance Institutions Through Entrepreneurship. *Sri Lankan Experience the Lens of Social.*, *05*(1), 49–71.

Varpio, L., Paradis, E., Uijtdehaage, S., & Young, M. (2020). The distinctions between theory, theoretical framework, and conceptual framework. *Academic Medicine*, *76*(6), 989–994. doi:10.1097/ACM.0000000000003075 PMID:31725464

Zheng, C., & Zhang, J. (2021). The impact of COVID-19 on the efficiency of microfinance institutions. *International Review of Economics & Finance*, *71*, 407–423. doi:10.1016/j.iref.2020.09.016

Chapter 9
The Impact of COVID-19 on the Indian Microfinance Industry and Its Sustainability

Satheesh Pandian Murugan
Arumugam Pillai Seethai Ammal College, India

Shivaprasad G.
CMS Business School, India

Dhanalakshmi A.
Acharya Bangalore Business School, India

Sriram V. P.
https://orcid.org/0000-0002-7105-0713
Acharya Bangalore Business School, India

Kanchan Rajput
ISBR Research Centre, Bengaluru, India

Mahesh B. N.
Surana College, Peenya, India

Chandan Chavadi
https://orcid.org/0000-0002-7214-5888
Presidency Business School, Presidency College, Bengaluru, India

Dhanabalan Thangam
https://orcid.org/0000-0003-1253-3587
Presidency Business School, Presidency College, Bengaluru, India

Shaila Kedla
Acharya Institute of Graduate Studies, India

DOI: 10.4018/978-1-6684-5647-7.ch009

ABSTRACT

The COVID-19 pandemic has interrupted operations throughout the world. It also forced all the industries towards unprecedented changes of their business operations, and in some cases, it pushes the businesses to shut down their operations either partially or fully. The microfinance industry is one of the sectors that was affected badly by the pandemic. As a result, microfinance institutions were forced to do some considerable changes to their domestic processes and make tricky decisions to decrease their loan issue process while the loan is required mostly by the borrowers or dropping employees' salaries. In the same way, microfinance customers were also affected. It forced business units to close their operations, and as a result, it condensed revenue generation. Customers also faced the tortuous brunt from the interrupted business support which were frequently incompatible and inadequate for public support. As a result, few customers have realized better income generation during the pandemic.

INTRODUCTION

The covid-19 pandemic crisis causes danger to all sectors, including health and economic sectors across the globe. As a result, it is a challenge for the weaker section of people in developing economies. This section includes farmers, artisans, Informal workers, and micro and agro entrepreneurs, and all of these people got affected by rigorous financial in connection with covid-19 related safety measures such as lock-down and social distancing taken to dissolve the occurrence. Meanwhile, the weaker section of people is resilient, and many of them depend on microfinance support for their survival. Microfinance services support clients with a margin of suppleness to manage the urgent situation when overtly funded security nets fall short. This Covid-19 pandemic collapsed all the sectors and industries, of which the microfinance sector is one. Especially its impact on the Indian microfinance industry is more. Further, this sector also faced a faced huge crisis after the demonetization process initiated by the Indian Government. As micro and small loans are serving a lot to large number of people who runs micro and small medium enterprises, predominantly in unorganized employment domains (Singh et al, 2021). Thus, Microfinance institutions playing key roles in business lending, have to be prepared to seize moderate risk for enhanced financial returns and customers who require non-securitized loans to carry out their livelihood activity. According to the MFIN report 2021-22, the microfinance sector has been serving 3.44 crore customers by providing Rs. 74,371 crores worth of loans and other products. It means, on average Rs 22,000 has been issued as a loan for all the microfinance accounts, further, it has the potential to increase the loan amount by 6 percent year on year. As far as the return on investment is concerned, this sector has a strong position in the social as well as economic returns. As a result, this industry has deployed a huge amount of money to a large number of customers, for prompting their livelihoods (MFIN, 2022). The MFIN report also reveals that the industry has received Rs. 42,250 crores as liability and Rs.16, 200 crores as equity, and it is 33% more than the preceding year. It also understands from the same that the requirement for the loans has been increasing every year along with higher lenders' trust. This industry is following the principle of 'secure contact, reliance, and financing sustainable livelihoods. On one side this sector supports micro and small medium enterprises and businesses; on the other side, it creates huge employment opportunities in the organized and unorganized sectors. It was also stated in the report that, even at the time of the pandemic this sector offers 2.5 lakhs employment opportunities to the individuals working in the field, it also conducts online meetings with customers to tenacity their doubts connected to business and personal sustainability, finance related, meeting of government rules and regulations about the pandemic, and other personal support related to Covid-19 health management. This sector also offers employment as well as business support to the customers who have taken the loan, other than their company employment. As a result, more than 3.5 crore customers have benefited from this process. In such a way that this sector has sanctioned income-generating loans to individuals for transforming personal as well as family members. Thus the microfinance industry has contributed a lot to personal, social, and economic ways, however, Covid-19 has collapsed drastically. The Covid controlling measures such as lockdown and social distance have killed almost all the businesses, but the worst case was those who are with smaller or no financial reserves and functioned highly cash oriented. It also buckled the micro and small medium enterprises worst. As a result, the pandemic has ultimately diminished the earning capacity of the business, and their impacts have been reflected on the microfinance customers, as they were not able to repay the loans (Singh, Brown, Chelekis, Apostolidis & Dey 2022).). This chain has also become a menace to the existence of the microfinance industry, even though the government is taking steps to regularise its business operations through deferment of loans. Though microfinance institutions have their requirement and credit needs, the post-Covid-19 period has put this industry under pressure with a sudden rise the income generating loans and more repayment periods. The situation has paved a way for the new way of mergers and acquisitions in the sector with the more financial restructuring. The pretentious income flow of businesses in turn pretentious their microfinance business entities and therefore the banking and financial institutions are at a high level of risks such as unemployment, business shutdown, and so on. As a result, the problems of unorganized sectors have existed at all levels of the industry to date; it has also affected the workers in various big cities, business proprietors in various cities and towns, and rural areas.

Due to this issue, Microfinance Company people are anticipated to face a somber financial crisis during Covid-19; as a result, space between income and functional expenditures is mounting with diminished financial reserves. Such adverse issues can minimize financial circulation; however it may not be a problem for long-standing microfinance institutions or the company with strong and steady financial backup, but is adequate to trouble micro and small size of microfinance institutions (Astawa, Astara, Mudana & Dwiatmadja 2021). Further, the microfinance institutions with constant financial flow, entrenched technology support, and brawny hold on the society have more potential to stay alive during and after the covid-19 pandemic. However, the operations of the microfinance industry are not only got affected, but it has affected gradually the other large financial institutions operating like the microfinance institutions such as private and public commercial banks, and other investors. Even in the year 2008, the entire world witnessed a financial crisis due to the financial disorder that happened in the United States real estate and financial sector. However its impact has moved only to the banking and real estate industry, and the rest of the industries were operating normally. But, the Covid-19 pandemic is not like that; it has collapsed all the industries more radically and caused sudden consequences, and stretched swiftly to all sectors (Zheng & Zhang, 2021). As a result, this pandemic halts the entire economic cycle immediately of the disgusting demand and supply of the market simultaneously. Ultimately, this effect has stopped the operations of Micro, Small, Medium, and even larger enterprises, and forced them to use substitute channels to disseminate information about the goods and services to the customers and clients. As a result, many micro and small enterprises including microfinance institutions have been unable to cope with this situation, and have suspended their business operations, shut down their financial activities, and made the workers and owners lead their life without jobs and income. The same kind of situation also stressed microfinance institutions to face the internal confronts to continue their mainstay business process during the government-initiated shutdowns, lockdowns, and social isolation rules (Sawada & Sumulong, 2021).

With this backdrop, the present chapter intended to disclose the impacts made by the covid-19 on the microfinance industry and its various stakeholders.

MICROFINANCE INDUSTRY DURING COVID-19 – GLOBAL OUTLOOK

The covid-19 crisis has affected the microfinance industry badly throughout the world; however, the Indian microfinance industry has managed itself better than the microfinance industries functioning in the rest of the world. Though the performance of the Indian microfinance industry looks good during the pandemic, it was not free from numerous problems for the microfinance industry. The problems include credit disbursement, collection of loans and EMIs, repayment problems, the problem of contacting clients, and restructuring of internal operational systems and workflow. Ultimately its impact has reflected on the performance of microfinance institutions in different ways in different regions of the world. Even though the impacts are not depending on the locations of the microfinance industry in connection with the pandemic prevalence, however, it has been depending on the kinds of services provided, and the internal operations followed. For providing loans, microfinance institutions used to accumulate savings and depend on deposits. Many microfinance institutions in the Sub-Saharan African region depend on the deposits for making loans and such kinds of institutions were affected deeply, but such kinds of issues have not been witnessed in India, because the Indian microfinance institutions have not authorized to take deposits (Ufua et al, 2022).

Indian microfinance institutions are using digital technologies in their business operations capable to move forward with advanced ways of communication with the customers and carry out the business digitally without any kind of delay. However, there are countries in the world such as Central Asian countries, some African counties, Latin America, and Central American countries that were affected worst, as these countries have been following conventional business practices such as meeting the clients in person, material contract with clients were rigorously distressed by the movement restrictions due to the pandemic (Bisht, Trusson, Siwale & Ravishankar, 2021). Regarding this issue, the Consultative Group to Assist the Poor (CGAP) and the rating agency Micro Finanza Rating (MFR) joined together and conducted a study with 400 microfinance institutions from June to December 2020. The key findings of the study reveal that from 2019 to 2020, the credit risk of the microfinance institutions assesses the risk in the underlying credit portfolios by integrating the portfolio at risk after one month (30 days) (PAR30), the write-off and restructured ratio have been increased by 45% on an average. Microfinance institutions operating in Sub-Saharan Africa revealed that there was the highest credit risk point found in 2020 (Ampaw et al, 2022). The same has been presented in figure 1.

It is noted that not all the microfinance institutions indicated extra financial support during the pandemic crisis, around 55% of microfinance institutions in Central Asia (ECA) and Europe region reported no additional needs for credit, and 23% of microfinance institutions revealed that their financial needs have reduced. Where in the case of the Middle East and North Africa, Sub-Saharan Africa, Latin America, and the Caribbean regions about 31% of the microfinance institutions have revealed that there were funding needs that are between 25% and 50% more than what had been planned before the Covid-19 pandemic. Irrespective of the sternness and occurrence of the covid-19 pandemic, microfinance institutions have taken appropriate steps to solve the crisis. Thus microfinance institutions have made different modifications to

Figure 1.
Source: www.cgap.org

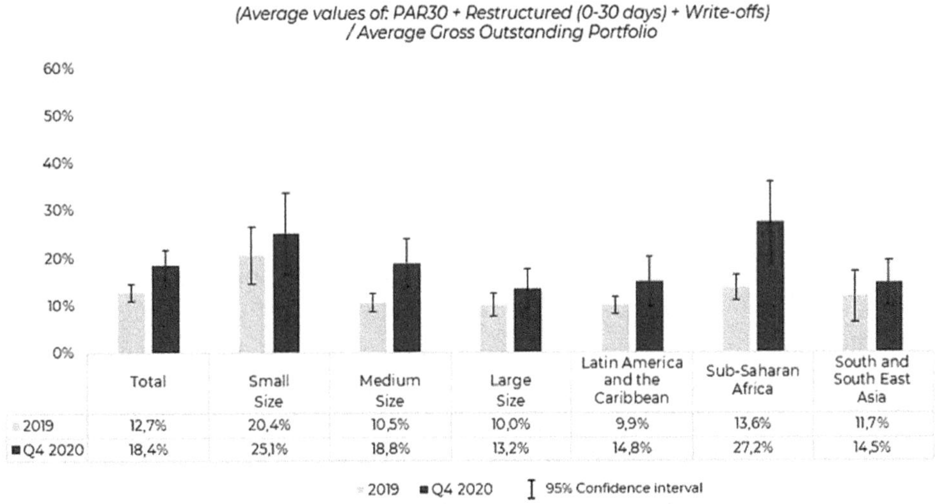

their business operations, risk management techniques, and customer relationship management practices. Thus, many microfinance institutions have executed their business process strategies, predicament management, scrutinizing committees, and consulted with shareholders and other stakeholders.

Even though various confronts and problems have happened due to the pandemic crisis, there are productive outcomes have also happened in the microfinance sector. Due to the pandemic crisis, microfinance institutions have been forced to go with digital transformations, and thus pandemic enables them to operate the business in the new digital environment (Benni, 2021). Through this transformation, microfinance institutions have realized the virtual business world and thereby it has promoted competitive advantages in their operations. On the other side, this pandemic also stimulated microfinance institutions to explore new opportunities in the markets and to develop and promote new financial products. In a manner, this pandemic will support a lot the resilience of the microfinance institutions in the days to come (Bai, Quayson & Sarkis, 2021).

IMPACT OF THE COVID 19 PANDEMIC ON THE MICROFINANCE INSTITUTIONS

As the Covid-19 pandemic started to occupy the countries, it forced them to move towards lockdown. As a result irrespective of the size and nature, all the business units have stopped their operations, excluding vital and medical services. However, the micro, small, and medium enterprises were affected, as they highly depend upon finance for their day to operations. This, in turn, unfavorably affected their bankers and microfinance institutions: Before the announcement of lockdowns, microfinance institutions have largely depended on corporeal relations with clients and had been following the door-to-door business services and collections and loan disbursements. In such a situation, this lockdown and business shutdown harmed cash collections and loan disbursements, as the governments restricted the people and business movements during the early times of the pandemic. As a result, around 99% of the microfinance accounts come under moratorium in May 2020 (Vampa, 2021). Thus it has been confirmed that the repayment would not happen for the next three months. As the customers were already under financial pressure even to fulfill their basic obligations, ultimately this impact has affected microfinance institutions and put them under financial issues. However, at the beginning of 2021, Indian microfinance institutions received huge demand for financial needs from 62 million customers, located in 620 districts in 28 states and eight Union Territories. As a result, though the pandemic has prevailed, the industry has estimated a business portfolio worth Rs 2.35 trillion. Thus, the pandemic is impacted the microfinance industry in one way, it also has opened a positive door for microfinance institutions in another way. The detailed impacts of covid-9 on the microfinance industry have happened in two ways, one on the clients and the other on microfinance institutions (Kumar, Sahu & Kumar, 2021). They are explained as follows;

BRUNT OF COVID-19 ON CLIENTS

It is easy to understand that almost 85% of microfinance customers or clients have been got affected directly or indirectly by the pandemic. Governments' covid-19 safety measures have affected the clients directly and forced them to shut down or close their business operations for the time being due to various personal causes such as physical condition or safety of the family. On the other side, this pandemic also created some indirect impact, by disrupting the business processes, and supply chains and diminishing the requirement for some of the goods and services produced by the microfinance customers (Onuka & Oroboghae, 2022). Apart from this it also has created so many issues on Business permanence, Business concert, Employees and Salaries, and Future Outlook.

On Business Permanence

Covid-19 has changed the entire business operations differently and forces business organizations to change their working style like working from home. Even the business units are considered essential for the society forced to alter their business style along with social distancing procedures and augmented hygienic requirements. On the other side, many numbers of businesses such as street vendors, saloons, and beauty shops, have stopped their business operations, and consequently got affected worst. Petty shops, grocery shops, all sorts of markets, personal and common transports, the construction industry, and workers have been forced to close their operations or asked to reduce their business operations considerably (Abed, 2021). However, some of the sectors like agricultural sectors, have been free from such controlling activities, and their direct and instantaneous brunt was less marked, however, it is a provisional phenomenon due to the characteristics of agriculture and the period between production and sales. This pandemic also paved the way for business people in so many ways, such as conducting business activities through a new types of platforms such as digital and online (Boiral, Brotherton, Rivaud, & Guillaumie, 2021).

Thus the business people have practiced more domestic changes to do business in new ways. However, the businesses which are unable to accommodate the new ways of doing business due to their nature have continued the business with sanitized and social distancing. Business units that have manifold operations cost better than one process business enterprises because not every business line had to suspend or dawdling down at a similar time or a similar rate. Further, there are a considerable percentage of business people, for some microfinance institutions getting 22% of their client base, who pendant their business activities willingly out of fear of getting contaminated or due to their circumstances. However, it is exciting to note that even though the conditions may be hard, and in some cases, the probability of resuming the business or recurring to the pre-pandemic levels of performance may be little, the number of business closes among microfinance customers is very little. Because the majority of business owners are running the business hopefully, try to prolong though the way of doing is likely to be diverse (Alshater, Atayah, & Khan, 2022).

On Business Concert

CGAP and MFR survey report reveals that, though many microfinance customers have got affected badly by this pandemic, a small number of customers mentioned that they have not experienced a reduction in sales, and in return, against this very few numbers customers affirmed that there is an augment in business. However, many of the micro, small, and medium enterprises have faced issues of reduction in revenue considerably, due to the decline in sales, even though customers are in different sectors such as hospital and medical industry, real estate, manufacturing industries, information, and communication technology, and home-based handmade businesses have realized a slighter decrease in income. To face this adverse situation and to continue to exist in the business, many numbers of microfinance customers start to use financial support steps implemented by the governments. However, these supportive steps have their limitations, conditions, and time, and thus supportive steps or measures are not suitable for many businesses such as micro-enterprises, and small-scale entrepreneurs because these measures were constructed to fit the medium and larger size businesses (Kurter, & Husseini, 2021). Further, in some cases, government assistance is available for such kinds of micro-entrepreneurs, but they are not able to furnish suitable and sufficient data, as there is no clarity in the existing programs.

On Employees and Salaries

Many of the micro-enterprises do not have employees, as they have been utilized the family members for the same. Thereby they can save income from the business. On the other hand, well-established companies have provided holidays to their employees along with salaries. Some companies and organizations have transformed their working style to work from home, and some of the government units and their supported programs provided salaries even during the pandemic. However, the employees who have been working in private institutions such as school and college teachers were in the worst situation as their salary has been reduced to continue their employment. The worst part here is a one-third of microfinance customers have come under this category and they found it difficult to repay the loan even after the moratorium period (Zheng & Zhang, 2021).

On the Future Outlook

Most microfinance customers have thought that once the pandemic-related safety measures have lifted, their financial situation will back to pre covid-19 situation, though this confidence is not absolute. Many customers also anticipated that the government will provide supportive measures to stabilize the financial system during the evolution period. However, there is also a conviction that the financial recovery may be extensive and sluggish. The more negative viewpoint on the prospected revival is more difficult among the entrepreneurs in the urban side than in the rural area. But still, more entrepreneurs are worried about their business sustainability. As a result, they are not able to measure their capacity to resume their business operations and they have also not been able to forecast what kind of support will be suited more (Yeboah, Antoh, & Kumi, 2022). However, the CGAP and MFR survey report reveals that around 25% of the customers mentioned that they won't borrow loans in the future due to financial uncertainty and the wounded incurred during the pandemic.

INSTITUTIONAL BRUNT OF COVD-19 ON MICROFINANCE

The effect of the covid-19 pandemic on microfinance organizations has been sensible and most microfinance institutions altered themselves to change rapidly according to the new circumstance. It is also heard that none of the microfinance institutions has experienced significant financial losses that would compel them to leave the business or put them near the precarious edge of bankruptcy. This situation exhibits the status of microfinance institutions for managing an emergency and the flexibility of their functional and administration structures.

Portfolio Performance

Not like microfinance institutions in different countries that experienced significant crumbling of portfolio value, the Indian microfinance institutions could maintain the risk levels and even develop them further corresponding to the pre-covid-19 time frame. Microfinance institutions in countries like Herzegovina, Bosnia, and Macedonia have remained constant and their portfolios demonstrated remarkable execution. Microfinance institutions in many countries experienced development in their business Standard, for some circumstances regardless, replicating the PAR30 during the pandemic yet this addition was from a low beginning Standard number, for example from 2.2% to 4.6% as definite by one microfinance institution (Bika, Subalova & Locke, 2022). However more PAR30 results have been recorded by some microfinance institutions in north India, but again, these greater numbers reflect crediting by these affiliations which base on new organizations and starting stage associations whose ability to get by during the crisis is a ton lower than that of extra spread out adventures. However, PAR30 estimations itemized by microfinance institutions are not upsetting and don't depict a huge rot in the idea of their portfolios. And these larger numbers mirror the idea of loaning by these microfinance institutions which center around new companies and beginning phase organizations whose capacity to make due during the emergency is a lot lower than that of additional laid out ventures. In précis, PAR30 measurements detailed by Microfinance institutions are not disturbing and don't illustrate a significant decay of the nature of their portfolios. Nonetheless, this underlying end should be qualified in some measure in two ways. In the first case, numerous controllers permitted the rescheduling of credits under the pandemic alleviation programs and permitted the incorporation of these rescheduled advances as a feature of the customary portfolio, successfully regarding them as performing credits. This anyway these credits may not be performing, hence the accessible measurements on PAR given by MFIs, albeit precise and accurately determined by the administrative prerequisites, may not mirror the genuine nature of their portfolios (Adhariani, 2022). The genuine nature of the portfolio may be realized after the moratoria terminate which will occur generally speaking before the year's over. Second, surveying the full effect of the pandemic on the monetary circumstance of the borrowers is still too soon. Numerous borrowers had the option to exploit different help estimates proposed by the legislatures and the Microfinance institutions themselves and had the option to meet their monetary responsibilities and continue to take care of their advances. This might change when such help measures are presently not accessible soon.

Demand for Credit

To be expected, the interest for advances and loans has diminished, particularly toward the start of the pandemic when the circumstance was very muddled about the future and there was little craving concerning the clients to draw more credit. The circumstance anyway shifts from one microfinance institution to another, and nation to nation. Some Microfinance establishments have encountered a critical decline in credit applications during the pandemic time frame, and they don't see an inversion of that pattern. The credit payment of new advances diminished considerably by 62% and something else for a few Microfinance establishments in correlation with the pre-pandemic time frame and comparable period the earlier year. However, most Microfinance organizations see considerable expansion for new advances, particularly in the long stretch of June and July when the economies began to re-open and there was greater clearness about the market interest and business open doors. Be that as it may, this new interest is unique from the interest previously. Credits that are mentioned are for more modest sums and they are prevalently for working capital purposes to take care of the ongoing working expenses. Barely any credits are looked for venture and business extension, which is predictable with the proceeded vulnerability of the ongoing circumstance and the business viewpoint for the not-so-distant future. Notwithstanding, since banks have diminished loaning, Microfinance institutions might have the option to catch another section of independent ventures subsidized up to the point provided by banks (The Hindu,2022).

Credit Rationing

Poor by clients for new advances is additionally coupled in certain occurrences with deliberate credit apportioning by Microfinance institutions due to three reasons. Some Microfinance organizations viewed themselves as liquidity obliged and needed to restrict the dispensing of credits mentioned to match their capacity to finance the new advances. Regardless of whether the Microfinance institutions had adequate liquidity to subsidize new advances, some have acquainted limits on payment to bring down the credit risk during questionable times. Furthermore, most Microfinance institutions have changed their financial risk evaluation strategies and methodology which prompted more tough credit appraisal and a rejection of specific business exercises that might be viewed as riskier according to the perspective of the covid-19effect (Kizza & Samali, 2022).

Product Offer

In the overall understanding, Microfinance institutions didn't change their financial products offered by them, even though they might have changed a portion of their elements and qualification models, for instance by offering interest-free periods for the initial three months of the credit. Some of the Microfinance institutions presented new financial products that were explicitly intended for and persuaded by the ongoing emergency. These were generally transient liquidity products to assist the customers with conquering temporary money deficiencies and business needs. This was the situation when the governments and social interest organizations presented exceptional crisis loaning schemes for micro and small companies during the Covid-19 outbreak. At times Microfinance institutions were qualified for receiving financial support from such projects (Yeboah, Antoh & Kumi, 2022).

Working With Clients

Microfinance institutions have changed their communication pattern with customers decisively during the covid-19 outbreak. The failure to make site visits to the places for offering and collecting loans made a need to open up a new mode of communication platform digitally which has been utilized by most of the Microfinance institutions as of now somewhat and has now been extended. They also began to utilize different digital communication platforms such as Whatsapp, Google meets Zoom, Skype, and the like. Through these applications, they have sent and received credit application forms through smartphones. Further, they have changed specific techniques and necessities to match what is going on, for instance, it ensures paperless financial transactions through electronic archives when it is viable and permitted. Though it is looking like a challenge to say for those who are not willing to change the communication process. However, microfinance institutions needed to roll out various domestic improvements in their business operations and processes; however, customers had additionally to figure out how to impart utilizing new apparatuses. Even though people have smartphones, it is difficult to expect that each customer will know how to convey the necessary records in the computerized structure or have the option to digitally sign the credit reports and documents electronically (Gabbiadini et al, 2021).

Risk Management

Many of the Microfinance institutions chose to change and alter their business operations to reduce business risk and manage the business better manner amongst the Covid-19. Changes incorporated the utilization of time for issuing and collecting loans, the decline in the credit limit, and changes connected with new financial regulations directing business operations. The new risk management strategies may reject specific kinds of business operations or reduce their operation in some part of the credit portfolio. However, some Microfinance institutions chose not to change the policies related to risk management, until the tragedy is over (Thomas, & Kumar, 2021).

Internal Operations

Microfinance institutions throughout the world were forced to follow lockdown and social separating guidelines which have considerably influenced their business operation plans. As they have to follow the work-from-home guidelines, all of which required a significant change in their work and communication patterns. As a result, many of the microfinance institutions shut down their usual office and moved to a collaborating space for gatherings, depending generally on telecommuting. Telecommuting and a virtual joint effort were especially hard for credit officials who are having direct and personal contact with customers. Further, these institutions kept on working out of their workplaces needed to oblige the prerequisites of social separation and with protective measures like masks, hand gloves, sanitizers, and other preventative measures (Gabbiadini et al, 2021). Yet another change was made with online credit applications and online loan instalment frameworks that would permit customers to apply for credit and make payments through digital platforms. At present, microfinance institutions start to offer internet-based credit applications and repayment solutions even though more work needs to be developed in this regard. Some of the Microfinance institutions in India that initiated the digital business process before Covid-19 lined up with the conventional credit application procedure and saw an expansion in the utilization of the digitalized applications during the pandemic (Thomas, & Kumar, 2021).

Financial Management

Though the pandemic has shaken the entire business, the performance of the Indian Microfinance institutions looks good; however, some institutions have had initial problems with liquidity which was one of the significant problems in the beginning. Against the same, some Microfinance institutions began the financial year with a good liquidity position and didn't encounter liquidity deficiencies. Simultaneously, poor credit demand facilitated the strain on liquidity. While some microfinance institutions ran into liquidity deficiencies issues to get financing under marked agreements with the investors who were hesitant to dispense cash during the Covid-19, meantime the investors had fostered a unique liquidity pattern that gave transient monetary help to the microfinance organizations (Ngumo, Collins & David, 2020).

Cost Reduction

Few Microfinance institutions in India demonstrated that they had to decrease their functional expenses to have the option to endure the emergency and to be in great monetary standing. The cost cuts included disposal of certain costs, for example, preparing and proficient turn of events, bringing down wage levels, furloughing, or laying off staff, and deferring making specific ventures till after the pandemic (Elzahi Saaid Ali, 2022; Ngumo, Collins & David, 2020).

Impact on the Future Operations

The pandemic has affected microfinance institutions and their future. As a result, they are needed to reach normal operations to get typical appearances that won't be what they used to be. The changes made by the pandemic are probably to stay with microfinance institutions and make them continue their business processes more digital than before (Gott, 2022). Thus the pandemic has formed a new way of credit creation and delivery by transforming conventional business processes into modern and digital.

STAKEHOLDERS RESPONSES TO THE CRISIS CAUSED BY THE PANDEMIC

Organizations on all levels are responded to the arising wellbeing emergency offering different help components inside their area of capability and authority.

Microfinance Institutions

Though the microfinance institutions are working in specific circumstances and organizational climates, they could able to react against Covid-19 emergency times. However they have not been using all the methods and approaches the same, but they have implemented changes in Domestic Business Operations, loaning procedures,

Loan reforms and Emergency loan sanctions, customers relationship, supporting customers to revive themselves and their business, risk management procedures, cash management, and other related measures.

Domestic Business Operations

Microfinance institutions needed to adjust their domestic business operations according to the prevailing emergency. For the same, some of the actions have been incorporated. They are:

Execution of a Business Progression Plan: Microfinance institutions frequently disregarded and failed to remember the methodology tracked down their utilization during the emergency to change the association to the new circumstances and reassign liabilities diversely that during typical tasks.

Shifting Online Work Platform: The majority of the microfinance institutions in India have moved to online and digital work platforms, by forcing the staff to do the job digitally. Indeed, even with the facilitating of limitations on association and maintaining individual distance. Thus, microfinance institutions keep on working on the digital platform even though some decided to get back to the individual and personal contact with customers gradually.

Workplace Safety and Preventive Measures: Covid-19 also forced the companies to go with new kinds of safety and preventive measures including wearing a face mask, applying sanitizers, social distancing, clean and hygienic workplace, and coordination with stakeholders (Tehulu, 2022).

Lending Process

The new loan issuing process has been tightened and several loans sanctioned have also been restricted by the microfinance institutions. It is due to the dual effect of less customer demand for loans and a reduction in credit supply due to the mounting risks of a pandemic. However some new types of loans have also been designed by the microfinance institutions and need to manage the existing loans constant basis, otherwise, it will create a challenge to the business process, loaning procedures, and financial management systems (Karibo, 2022). The following are the most common adjustments done by microfinance institutions with respect to lending:

Online Credit Applications and Credit Endorsements: Due to the pandemic outbreak most microfinance institutions had initiated online business processes such as issuing applications through digital mode and receiving cash through electronic payments; thus the pandemic promoted digital credit applications and avoided other forms of the application process. As result microfinance institutions and clients start to embrace the digital way of doing banking.

Online Loan Distributions and EMI Collections: Microfinance institutions forced to adopt the digital process in their business to pay out cash and allow cash settlement of loans had to rapidly expand digital business options using digital banks, smartphones, or other card payments.

Digital Business Monitoring: Due to the government social distance protocol, in-person and onsite supervision was impossible; as a result, microfinance institutions start to use various digital communication platforms to monitor customers and their capacity to pay back their loans. In such a process various contemporary technologies such as Whatsapp, Google Meet, Zoom, Skype, and Viber, are most suitable for smartphones as most customers have a smartphone with video potential.

Restructuring of Loans and Urgent Lending

Loan rescheduling was a common aspect followed by microfinance institutions during the early months of the pandemic, as well as launching new products for emergency lending. In connection with this the following measures were adopted by the majority of the microfinance institutions:

Restructuring of and a Moratorium on Loans: Microfinance institutions launched different forms of moratorium schemes on repayment and restructuring of the loan, as a result, there were variations have been existing in the execution. While some of the microfinance institutions offered to restructure loan facilities to all customers, the mainstream took a more restricted move towards offering a moratorium on a case-by-case base, and as a result, loans have been restructured to those who requested. The majority of the loan rescheduling happened on a basis of the departure of the microfinance institutions with an option to demand repayments as early as the customers restarted their business (Dandapat & Das, 2022).

Launch of New Financial Products: Microfinance institutions restricted considerably their new loan sanctioned volume, while some microfinance institutions launched new financial products to combat the Covid emergency and to maintain their customers with cash during the pandemic. However such new financial products' demand was not up to mark among the customers as they may not be eager to take on extra burden in the uncertain period.

Customer Communication

Microfinance business is popular for its relationship with customers, and it is happening through onsite communication with customers. The communication might have been personal and friendly before the pandemic, but it forced us to move from an onsite to a virtual platform by using digital technologies (Dandapat & Das, 2022). For the same many microfinance institutions used two approaches, as follows:

Credit Officer Interactions: Credit officers used to interact with their customers to ascertain their condition during the pandemic. In many cases, clients were getting in touch at least once, and frequently, credit officers uphold regular communication with their customers during the pandemic.

Customer Opinion Surveys: Microfinance institutions conducted an opinion survey among customers to study about confronts and to provide better measures based on the range of the exertions faced by customers.

Conducting Awareness Programmes for Clients and Their Businesses

Although, microfinance institutions did not provide support for business development services to their customers, conducted awareness programs through online training and webinars on various contemporary business areas. While some microfinance institutions were also providing coaching and mentoring services to their customers to aid them to move forward. Even though it did not happen homogeneously and consistently, numerous microfinance institutions provided pertinent information about various business financing opportunities and other relevant supportive programs available with State and Central governments to ensure that customers take benefit of such financial assistance programs (Masanyiwa, Chusi & Haji, 2022).

Risk Management

Microfinance institutions have introduced transformations in their risk appraisal process even though not every alteration was yet established as bureaucrat rules and regulations. The policy transformations mostly related to the disclosure of a business to possible risks shaped by the Covid such as the impending effects of social distancing on the capability to run a business or the place of a business. These provisional changes will be incorporated into the usual rules and regulations when these perils are understood better and can be calculated.

Liquidity Management

Despite the early pandemic fears, only a few microfinance institutions have reported that were in cash problems, they had to diminish it, if not suspend lending and diminish expenses in the short period. Meantime, microfinance institutions were capable to collect finance from their lenders and investors under the existing contracts; others had to enter into rough discussions to take delivery of funding. Larger microfinance institutions were capable to attain cash support from local banks to plaster their cash deficiency to pay wages and other existing expenses. Those microfinance institutions that were unable to accumulate the essential finance had to initiate more radical measures like plummeting staff remuneration. On the other hand, most microfinance institutions fell into financial crisis in a comparatively strapping liquidity situation which aids them to continue to exist against the pandemic with no major negative impacts (Masanyiwa, Chusi & Haji, 2022).

Other Measures

Besides the above-revealed cases are the most ordinary responses to the crisis caused by Covid-19, as a result, every microfinance institution has used various essential measures towards the context of a country as well as the requests of the confined authorities. In many cases, the majority of the microfinance institutions acted autonomously or through their national associations, wrote letters to their respective government agencies, and requested support for their financial institutions as well as their customers.

Microfinance Investors

The reactions of the investors towards microfinance look like an assorted one because it took an unadventurous move towards lending microfinance institutions to those lenders which presented supplementary financial support along with other help during Covid-19 (Czura, Englmaier, & Spantig, 2022). In a manner various compassionate measures were initiated by the lenders and financiers consisting of the following:

Prolongation of financial support to microfinance institutions and continuing former agreements: even though it is not common, the majority of the investors desire to continue the pending promises to microfinance institutions, without additional due diligence and inspection, as they needed funding support.

Rearrangement arrears: In many cases, the lenders and investors of microfinance have been ready to renegade settlement of due by microfinance institutions, caused by Covid-19. Further microfinance institutions which are not made repayments within the stipulated time; the investors approved to dangle delayed payment fines and rearrange the arrears for a future date. Apart from these measures, necessary technical support is also provided to the microfinance customers by the investors, to make stronger their capability to endure and pay back loans to microfinance institutions (Czura, Englmaier, & Spantig, 2022).

Regulators

Reserve bank of India and other financial regulatory bodies introduced provisional policies relating to risk management and lending to regulate the loan issuing and repayment procedures to manage unexpected conditions created by the pandemic. Those policy measures include moratorium, interest rate reduction, and so on (Jain, 2022). The same has been explained in the following manner.

Provisional moratorium on settlement of Loans: Like other countries, the Reserve Bank of India also issued provisional moratorium policies to help the borrowers to postpone repayment of loans for six months during Covid-19. In connection with this microfinance institutions made effort to disseminate the information about the moratorium. This moratorium has been provided as an option and left to the discretion of the borrowers, to take a decision. In many of the countries moratorium option has been issued only for the repayment of bank loans not for microfinance institutions. But, in India, the moratorium option has been provided to the microfinance institutions too, and it has been treated as a provisional relief to the needy people.

New-fangled Risk Management Policies and Credit Risk Categorization: Reserve bank of India has changed its policies related to Banking and Financial Institutions including microfinance institutions to modify the categorization of loans based on the customers who repay the loan dues lately, due to the pandemic. Such policies have facilitated microfinance institutions to categorize the performance of the portfolios into two categories as directly and not directly pretentious by the pandemic.

Governments

During the time of the pandemic, every country's government has assumed different types of policies to safeguard the public against the spread of Covid-19 and thereby ensured a secure environment in the domestic and working places. Meantime, governments provided monetary support and assistance to maintain businesses to prolong their business operations (Balanagalakshmi & Kumari, 2022). The most common government supportive measures comprise the following:

Deferment of Levies: Due to the pandemic all the business units have got affected severely and lost their income too. So the governments of various countries postponed the tax payment period to reduce the financial burden of business, and the same has also been followed by the government of India. This has given an option to the microfinance institutions to pay the tax either on time or afterward.

Redundancy Benefits: The government of India has initiated the unemployment allowance scheme for various segments of people. This scheme was much useful for workers who were made outmoded or furloughed, but still, this action was not much constructive to the microfinance institutions and their clients.

KEY CHALLENGES TO EMERGING FROM THE PANDEMIC CRISIS

Finally, the three-year virus war called covid-19 has come to an end. As we are approaching the end of 2022, the virus has started to lose its control slowly and lessening its grip on the financial system of the countries, however, in many countries, Covid-19 cases represent that the pandemic is not over. Governments of various countries are initiating different economic promotional activities with a variety of amount of restrictions and boundaries to turn the economy towards the new normal. The government of India has also taken a lot of initiatives to regularise the economy by reducing the issue caused by the covid-19. Thus the measures taken by the Government of India help the microfinance institutions and customers to move back to the pre-covid-19 environment and it also aids them to adjust themselves to cope-up with the post-covid-19 environment (Onuka, & Oroboghae, 2022). Though the Government of India is taking so many measures to save the microfinance institutions and customers, still there are several confronts such as monetary, Business, and personal in front of microfinance institutions and customers.

Challenges to Microfinance Clientele

Irrespective of developed, developing, and underdeveloped countries, Covid-19 has affected all economies and created so many challenges to all sectors, microfinance is one among them. Confronts faced by the microfinance clientele turn their capability to resume their business process and activities and to clear bank loans and other monetary obligations mounted up during the Covid-19 (Aziz, Iqbal, Murtza, Gill & Cheema, 2022). The following are some of the challenges in front of the entrepreneurs are expected to meet:

Monetary Challenges

Repayment of loans to banking and other financial institutions: Though banking, financial, and microfinance institutions facilitate repayment rearrangement either on their own or by the ruling of government regulations, there were no arrears clemency schemes for the microfinance clientele those who are still accountable for their existing loans to banking, financial and microfinance institutions. Though the rearrangement of loans is helpful in the present, it lifts the cost of debt to the clientele and pushes them into a difficult situation to settle up the loans, particularly when the business resurgence is unsure.

Challenges for facing other financial commitments: The government of India established deferment of various payments related to the government such as income and other taxes, payments to the social security schemes, and the like. However the rescheduled payments, and loans, do not decrease or reduce the requirement to pay, instead, it is increasing the financial pressure additionally on individual and business businesses to start to resume their operations, and reduced the ability to make profits than pre-covid-19 (Aziz, Iqbal, Murtza, Gill & Cheema, 2022).

Challenges to the Business Concerns

Resuming Business Processes: resuming the stopped business process is not such an easy task and it may require numerous forms of effort and time. Resuming the business process may be easy and trouble-free for some business people and they may start their business as early as possible once the pandemic precincts are lifted, they may also be capable to go back to the pre-pandemic circumstances. This is possible only for the services industries such as cafeterias, hotels, beauty salons, and so on. Though these businesses start their business operations, they need to transform the way of doing business, as they need to bring into line themselves with precautionary measures. On the other side, some kinds of businesses and other revenue-generating activities are not possible to resume and force the entrepreneurs to stop the business process either partially or completely or to start a new line of business (Patra, Reddy, Reddy & Reddy, 2022).

Reinstatement of Customer Base and ensuring Business Relations: Pandemic has forced business people to transform their business practices in a new way by observing the government rules for ensuring the safety of customers. As a result, almost all sorts of businesses start to embrace online business, although the size of the business is micro and small. As a result, they lost their offline customer base and are in a situation to gain a new customer base. It may be hard for business people to get back the previous customers. In the same way, the old supply chain associations need to alter due to the crisis.

Acclimatize the Business to New Business Environment: Covid-19 has not only changed business, but also the mindset of the people. The majority of the entrepreneurs thought that they have capable to prolong their business process as earlier it was before covid-19; however, it may not be possible for all business people. As the covid-19 has transformed the way people think, communicate, and buy, it is also expected that this transformation to prolong and progress in the days to come, rather than turn back to the precedent business practices.

Personal Challenges

Challenges to upgrade personal Skills to face the Virtual and Digital World: Pandemic has changed the way of doing business, and forced business people to upgrade their skills to incorporate and use information communication technology and shift business processes from offline to online. In a country like India still, the majority of the people are in lower level educational qualifications and this may be confronting for those business people and customers, as it is hard to pivot towards new technology-based business operations.

Fear of Failure to Start New Business: Covid-19 has threatened all the sectors to move forward, as it has more possibility of failure and incurring extra costs in unsure times. As a result, starting a new business may be more exigent for the new as well as existing entrepreneurs, as they have to borrow more money to start a new or get their existing business going again. Though these issues are real and general, some businesses people ready to prolong their business process and are willing to take the risk of resuming their existing business operations (Rameshkumar, 2022).

Challenges to Microfinance Institutions

All the industries were got affected by Covid-19, and the Microfinance industry is one among them and it had faced more crises, however, the majority of the microfinance institutions can deal with the crisis caused by the pandemic. They also have emerged from the crisis successfully, not free from some of the challenges. The following are some of the challenges to face by microfinance institutions in the days to come.

Functional Issues

Though the pandemic forced all businesses to embrace digital platforms for their survival, still many industries are not able to introduce digitalization in their business, the microfinance industry one among them. Many parts of India still have not digitalized their business process due to various reasons such as higher investment, training requirements, and so on. Moreover, the policies related to risk management need to be attuned to describe the new types of perils connected with the covid-19 which compel certain boundaries to various business processes and make some of the business activities more uncovered to the risk in case of the pandemic. Apart from this, the operational style of the businesses need to reorder and regulate to meet the recent challenges of social distancing, and sanitization of working places which may necessitate reorganization of the organizational spaces in the working places and transformations in the work schedules such as client meeting, visits to the field (Singh, Chamola, Kumar, Verma, & Makkar, 2022).

Market Challenges

Due to the adverse and worst conditions created by the covid-19, the majority of the business houses have been under the financial trap, and it has reduced the credit demand aftermath of Covid-19, as the business people remained more cautious and engaged in business. Further, this pandemic forced the borrowers to shift to other financial platforms such as fin techs to fulfill their financial requirements, as it is equipped better for virtual processes and it has incarcerated parts of the microfinance industry during covid-19.

Financial Challenges

Covid-19 has created so many challenges to the microfinance industry; the financial challenges are one among them. Due to the pandemic, the interest rate of the loans is expected to increase to balance the augmented financial risk associated with the business. Further, all the business concerns are trying to transform their business to digital, and it forces the businesses to increase investments in information and communication technologies, and this issue also increased the cost of microfinance institutions. However access to finance after the pandemic seems not such an easy task, due to the economy recovering slowly from the crisis, as a result extending financial support to the microfinance industry is considered a perilous proposition.

Strategic Challenges

The pandemic changes the way of doing business and interrupt the linear strategies of the microfinance industry and made them redesign their business objectives, vision, and business positioning in the new socio and economic environment after Covid-19. As a result microfinance institutions faced numerous confronts such as access to finance, direct and indirect borrowing, guarantees, and augmented credit mechanisms or other financial amenities.

Application of Digital Technology Platforms: this global pandemic forced the microfinance industry to invest more in digital technology platforms to facilitate internal as well as external business. Since the microfinance institutions are realizing the financial benefits from the loans developed at low cost, it may not be possible for the microfinance institutions for upgrading their existing operational systems as their internal financial capability is not sufficient to create the requisite investments (Uddin, Jamil, & Khan, 2022).

Payment systems: the government of India is forcing the banking, and non-banking financial institutions to follow the national payment system to ensure fraudless financial transactions, serve customers better, and ensure inclusive financial systems. However, the majority of the microfinance institutions are not linked with the national payment system, and as a result, ultimately become a failure.

POLICY RECOMMENDATIONS AND ACTIONS NEED TO BE TAKEN

It is understood from the previous sections that the pandemic has collapsed the entire world as well as all the business sectors. To rejuvenate and recover society as well as the economy from this crisis need to take some actions and policy measures to alleviate the consequences of Covid-19 and we must address the issues at all levels such as the microfinance industry, customers, and society.

Recommendations to Microfinance Associations

Regional as well as national microfinance associations need to play an important role to advocate for the essential support for microfinance institutions as well as the customers. Microfinance associations need to work with regional and national government agencies and regulators, to settle the functional, economic, strategic, and regulatory support to microfinance institutions to continue their services in the post-Covid without problems. Microfinance associations should also extend operational aid to microfinance institutions to align themselves to install and utilize digital technologies to speed up the business process. Microfinance institutions need to concentrate more on knowledge management area to tackle the days to come. They also try to learn from the present happenings and thereby enhance their capability based on the best things that emerged from the pandemic. Policymakers need to concentrate more on microfinance-related research and development aspects so that the requirements, confronts and opportunities available to the microfinance institutions after Covid-19 can be understood better.

Recommendations to Investors

The role played by microfinance investors is crucial during and after the pandemic, as their investment policies decide the functional ability of microfinance institutions against the pandemic. They have invested the lower interest during pandemics. In the same way, microfinance investors need to alter their financial indications and benchmarks to their accounts to do changes in the concert of the portfolio after the pandemic. They also need to redesign and renew their existing contracts on funding and ensure the required financial support to microfinance institutions to uphold unimpeded business processes.

Recommendations to Governments and Policymakers

Both the governments and policymakers are having more responsibility to support the smooth functioning of the microfinance industry at the national level after the pandemic. Governments need to redesign the current credit guarantee scheme to support microfinance institutions in the post-Covid financial environment. Thereby microfinance institutions can help their customers with new credit programs for needy people such as rural business people, day to day business people. Policymakers need to alter the existing legal regulations to permit customers to provide the necessary documents to enter into the contracts. Need to make changes in the existing microfinance institutions' risk measurement framework to ensure sufficient financial support. Policymakers also made the microfinance institutions enrol themselves in the national payment system to the smooth progress of online business dealings with their customers.

CONCLUSION

Microfinance industry act as an instrument and it has been extending financial support to the needy people especially to the poor, marginalised and unprivileged people. It has change the lifestyle of people by means of ensuring the financial support. Such a wonderful microfinance industry is currently in a difficult situation due to covid-19 pandemic. This pandemic has affected the microfinance industry negatively, due to this situation, this industry unable to raise fund from the debt market, and found difficult to move ahead. To support the microfinance industry, government of India has launched some of the constructive measures to get better the financial needs. It has provided 4.10 billion USD worth of financial support for microfinance industry, non-banking financial institutions, and for housing finance companies. By this way it is expected to lubricate the functioning of microfinance industry, thereby it will help to move forward in the new normal. Further, thorough this financial support microfinance industry will support its customers to recommence their business as well as economic activities. Thereby it is expected that the demand for the loans and repayment of the loans will be increase in the days to come, there by the business performance of this industry expected to improve.

REFERENCES

Abed, S. S. (2021). A literature review exploring the role of technology in business survival during the Covid-19 lockdowns. *The International Journal of Organizational Analysis*.

Adhariani, D. (2022). Microfinance and the role of accounting in supporting family-resilience-based women's empowerment. *Qualitative Report*, *27*(2), 366–384. doi:10.46743/2160-3715/2022.4249

Alshater, M. M., Atayah, O. F., & Khan, A. (2022). What do we know about business and economics research during COVID-19: A bibliometric review. *Economic Research-Ekonomska Istraživanja*, *35*(1), 1884–1912. doi:10.1080/1331677X.2021.1927786

Ampaw, E. M., Nte-Adik, N. M., Azaare, J., Adu-Sackey, A., Essah, B. O., & Amuzu, G. (2022). Embracing mobile financial inclusion in the wake of Covid-19 pandemic: The mediating role of cognitive and affective-based trust embeddedness. *International Journal of Technology and Management Research*, *7*(1), 1–22. doi:10.47127/ijtmr.v7i1.148

Astawa, I. P., Astara, I. W. W., Mudana, I. G., & Dwiatmadja, C. (2021). Managing Sustainable Microfinance Institutions in the Covid-19 Situation through Revitalizing Balinese Cultural Identity. *Quality - Access to Success*, 131–137.

Aziz, A., Iqbal, J., Murtza, M. H., Gill, S. A., & Cheema, I. Y. (2022). Effect of Covid-19 pandemic on women entrepreneurial sustainability: the role of Islamic microfinance institutions. *Journal of Economic and Administrative Sciences*.

Bai, C., Quayson, M., & Sarkis, J. (2021). Covid-19 pandemic digitization lessons for sustainable development of micro-and small-enterprises. *Sustainable Production and Consumption, 27*, 1989-2001.

Balanagalakshmi, B., & Kumari, S. S. (2022). Impact of Covid on Micro Finance Institutions. *ECS Transactions*, *107*(1), 10431–10438. doi:10.1149/10701.10431ecst

Benni, N. (2021). *Digital finance and inclusion in the time of Covid-19: Lessons, experiences and proposals*. Food & Agriculture Org.

Bika, Z., Subalova, M., & Locke, C. (2022). Microfinance and small business development in a transitional economy: Insights from borrowers' relations with microfinance organisations in Kazakhstan. *The Journal of Development Studies*, *58*(1), 183–203. doi:10.1080/00220388.2021.1956472

Bisht, N. S., Trusson, C., Siwale, J., & Ravishankar, M. N. (2021). Enhanced job satisfaction under tighter technological control: The paradoxical outcomes of digitalisation. *New Technology, Work and Employment*, ntwe.12222. doi:10.1111/ntwe.12222

Boiral, O., Brotherton, M. C., Rivaud, L., & Guillaumie, L. (2021). Organizations' management of the COVID-19 pandemic: A scoping review of business articles. *Sustainability*, *13*(7), 3993. doi:10.3390u13073993

Czura, K., Englmaier, F., Ho, H., & Spantig, L. (2022). Microfinance loan officers before and during Covid-19: Evidence from India. *World Development*, *152*, 105812. doi:10.1016/j.worlddev.2022.105812 PMID:35035030

Dandapat, A., & Das, P. (2022). Role of Microfinance to Promote the Growth of Unorganized Manufacturing Enterprises in India: An Analysis. In Microfinance to Combat Global Recession and Social Exclusion (pp. 131-146). Palgrave Macmillan.

Elzahi Saaid Ali, A. (2022). The Regulatory and Supervisory Frameworks of Microfinance from Islamic Perspective: The Case of Sudan. In Empowering the Poor through Financial and Social Inclusion in Africa (pp. 73-86). Palgrave Macmillan.

Gabbiadini, A., Baldissarri, C., Durante, F., Valtorta, R. R., De Rosa, M., & Gallucci, M. (2021). Corrigendum: Together Apart: The Mitigating Role of Digital Communication Technologies on Negative Affect during the Covid-19 Outbreak in Italy. *Frontiers in Psychology*, *12*, 701130. doi:10.3389/fpsyg.2021.701130 PMID:34122291

Gott, G. (2022). Microcredit and the Financial Frontiers of Racial Neoliberalism. *Journal of Law and Political Economy*, *2*(2). Advance online publication. doi:10.5070/LP62258228

Jain, S. (2022). Impact of Covid-19 on Financial Performance of Micro-Financing Institutions in India. *Journal of Management & Entrepreneurship, 267.*

Karibo, F. B. (2022). *Determinants Of Financial And Operational Sustainability: Empirical Evidence from Microfinance Institutions (MFIS) in Ethiopia* (Doctoral dissertation).

Kizza, J., & Samali, N. (2022). Microfinance risk management, social mission and financial performance during the Covid-19 pandemic in Uganda. *American Journal of Finance*, *7*(2), 13–22. doi:10.47672/ajf.1017

Kumar, P., Sahu, S. K., & Kumar, R. (2021). An Analysis of Role of Microfinance Institutions In Inclusive Growth. *Kuwait Chapter of the Arabian Journal of Business and Management Review*, *10*(4), 161–167. doi:10.12816/0059989

Kurter, O., & Husseini, İ. A. (2021). Evaluation of Strategic Management Issues Related To The Microfinance Industry And Small And Medium Enterprises In Afghanistan. *Uluslararası Finansal Ekonomi ve Bankacılık Uygulamaları Dergisi*, *2*(2), 34–67.

Masanyiwa, Z. S., Chusi, T. N., & Haji, A. U. (2022). Determinants for Sustainability of Microfinance Institutions in North "A" District in Zanzibar. *Open Journal of Business and Management*, *10*(4), 1583–1600. doi:10.4236/ojbm.2022.104083

MFIN. (2022). *Building an Inclusive India*. https://mfinindia.org/assets/upload_image/publications/AnnualReports/AR%202021-22%20-%20Web.pdf

Ngumo, K. O. S., Collins, K. W., & David, S. H. (2020). *Determinants of financial performance of microfinance banks in Kenya*. arXiv preprint arXiv:2010.12569.

Onuka, I. O., & Oroboghae, O. R. (2022). The Impact of the Covid-19 Pandemic on Microfinance Banks Customers in Nigeria. *Journal of Asian Business Strategy*, *12*(1), 35–48. doi:10.55493/5006.v12i1.4598

Patra, R. K., Reddy, K. S. C., Reddy, K. M., & Reddy, T. N. K. (2022). A Study on the Scope of E-Commerce Industry in Covid 19 Situation: A Review of Literature on Indian Incorporations. *Journal of Positive School Psychology*, *6*(3), 9258–9261.

Rameshkumar, N. (2022). Impact of Covid-19 among Micro, Medium and Small Enterprises–A Case Study in Coimbatore District. *International Journal of Multidisciplinary Educational Research*, *11*(3), 92–97.

Sawada, Y., & Sumulong, L. (2021). Macroeconomic impact of Covid-19 in developing. *Asia*.

Singh, D. R., Sunuwar, D. R., Shah, S. K., Sah, L. K., Karki, K., & Sah, R. K. (2021). Food insecurity during Covid-19 pandemic: A genuine concern for people from disadvantaged community and low-income families in Province 2 of Nepal. *PLoS One*, *16*(7), e0254954. doi:10.1371/journal.pone.0254954 PMID:34288965

Singh, P., Brown, D. M., Chelekis, J., Apostolidis, C., & Dey, B. L. (2022). Sustainability in the beer and pub industry during the Covid-19 period: An emerging new normal. *Journal of Business Research*, *141*, 656–672. doi:10.1016/j.jbusres.2021.11.066 PMID:36540607

Singh, S., Chamola, P., Kumar, V., Verma, P., & Makkar, N. (2022). Explaining the revival strategies of Indian MSMEs to mitigate the effects of Covid-19 outbreak. *Benchmarking*.

Tehulu, T. A. (2022). Capital adjustment process and credit growth of microfinance institutions: Evidence from Sub-Saharan Africa. *Cogent Economics & Finance, 10*(1), 2111791. doi:10.1080/23322039.2022.2111791

The Hindu. (2022). *Microfinance lenders should not charge usurious rates of interest, RBI says in revised norms for the sector*. Available at: https://www.thehindu.com/news/national/microfinance-lenders-should-not-charge-usurious-rates-of-interest-rbi-says-in-rev ised-norms-for-the-sector/article65224515.ece

Thomas, J. R., & Kumar, J. (2021). Microfinance Sector and the Supportive Role of Regulator in its Transformation: A Case Study from India. In Financial Inclusion in Emerging Markets (pp. 219-235). Palgrave Macmillan. doi:10.1007/978-981-16-2652-4_11

Uddin, M. A., Jamil, S. A., & Khan, K. (2022). Indian MSMEs amidst the Covid-19 Pandemic: Firm Characteristics and Access to Finance. *Academic Journal of Interdisciplinary Studies, 11*(3), 71–71. doi:10.36941/ajis-2022-0069

Ufua, D. E., Olujobi, O. J., Tahir, H., Al-Faryan, M. A. S., Matthew, O. A., & Osabuohien, E. (2022). Lean Entrepreneurship and SME Practice in a Post Covid-19 Pandemic Era: A Conceptual Discourse from Nigeria. *Global Journal of Flexible Systems Management*, 1-14.

Vampa, D. (2021). Covid-19 and territorial policy dynamics in Western Europe: Comparing France, Spain, Italy, Germany, and the United Kingdom. *Publius, 51*(4), 601–626. doi:10.1093/publius/pjab017

Yeboah, T., Antoh, E. F., & Kumi, E. (2022). Strategic responses of microfinance institutions to the Coronavirus disease (Covid-19) crisis in Ghana. *Development in Practice, 32*(1), 112–127. doi:10.1080/09614524.2021.1991890

Zheng, C., & Zhang, J. (2021). The impact of Covid-19 on the efficiency of microfinance institutions. *International Review of Economics & Finance, 71*, 407–423. doi:10.1016/j.iref.2020.09.016

Chapter 10
Exploring Factors Influencing Growth of MSMEs in Factor-Driven and Efficiency-Driven Economies

Mohammad Izzuddin Mohammed Jamil
https://orcid.org/0000-0002-2967-7870
Universiti Brunei Darussalam, Brunei

ABSTRACT

The growth of micro, small, and medium-sized enterprises (MSMEs) is important as MSMEs constitute the main drivers of economic growth, particularly in the emerging economies of factor-driven and efficiency-driven economies. MSMEs represent an estimate of 90% of business organisations and more than half of job creation worldwide, and the growing global workforce means that growth of MSMEs are often a high priority for governments. However, despite attempts to support nurture and vitalise the growth of MSMEs, MSMEs located in emerging economies are often subjected to more hostile environments compared to their counterparts in developed economies, such as the lack of access to micro-finance and underdeveloped educational institutions. The lack of micro-finance is especially detrimental as MSMEs without creditworthy history could not apply for finance. This research synthesizes growth factors from literature in order to identify and examine the factors influencing growth of MSMEs in the emerging economies of factor-driven and efficiency-driven economies.

DOI: 10.4018/978-1-6684-5647-7.ch010

INTRODUCTION

Micro, Small and Medium-sized Enterprises (MSMEs) are organisations with sales, assets, or employees that fall below a specific threshold (Aybar-Arias et al., 2003). An MSME is defined differently in each economy and certain size requirement must be satisfied, as well as the industry. The major criteria that often determine whether an organisation is an MSME or a large-sized organisation is its number of employees, and the consideration of its total sales turnover or entire balance sheet (Aybar-Arias et al., 2003; Decker, Schiefer & Bulander, 2006, August). Around the world, MSMEs are in three distinct stages of economic development: factor-driven, efficiency-driven and innovation-driven economies. Factor-driven and efficiency-driven economies are part of developing or emerging economies, while innovation-driven economies consist of developed economies.

The most important MSMEs are the ones located in the emerging economies of factor-driven and efficiency-driven economies. Many emerging economies have been dealing with structural vulnerabilities such as persisting social and economic disparities, war and forced displacement, falling public trust, climate change consequences, and environmental fragility (Khan, 2000). However, despite attempts to support nurture and vitalise the growth of MSMEs, MSMEs in emerging economies still face various challenges that hinders growth, more so in factor-driven economies. Factor-driven economies are the least developed in the stages of economic development as they are dominated by subsistence agriculture and extraction businesses, with a heavy reliance on unskilled labour and natural resources (Hadidi & Kirby, 2015). MSMEs located in emerging economies are often subjected to more hostile environments compared to their counterparts in developed economies such as the lack of access to micro-finance and underdeveloped educational institutions (Welter et al., 2012). As a result, they are subjected to a high failure rate upon its early years of operations. Thus, growth of MSMEs are important for emerging economies as they are the key to overcoming poverty and a source of innovation and sustainable growth.

The most significant reason as to why MSMEs are important is that they outnumber large corporations by a significant proportion in any given national economy, and thus employs many more people (Lee, 2009). In Chile, an efficiency-driven economy, over 98.5% of organisations are categorised as MSMEs (Tan, 2009). In efficiency-driven Tunisia, self-employed people account for around 28% of total non-farm employment, while organisations with less than 100 employees account for approximately 62% of total employment (Rijkers, Arouri, Freund & Nucifora, 2014). MSMEs in the United States, an innovation-driven economy account for half of all jobs, but only 40% of Gross Domestic Product (GDP) (Berger, 2006). For instance, MSMEs in innovation-drive Australia account for

98% of all enterprises, create one-third of total GDP, and employ 4.7 million people (Ahmad & Seet, 2009).

The most significant benefit of encouraging small-scale industries and MSMEs is that they create jobs without requiring considerable government intervention. Both urban and rural growth are aided by MSMEs. The successful growth of MSMEs will up the ante of economic growth. Economic growth is the most effective tool for eliminating poverty and raising living standards in emerging nations. As a result, both the rate and pattern of growth are important in alleviating poverty. An effective poverty reduction plan must include efforts to encourage rapid and sustained economic growth as a fundamental component. Thus, growth of MSMEs has become one of the major research areas by both traditional and contemporary researchers in the century. Growth of MSMEs is important as MSMEs constitute the main drivers of economic growth, particularly in the emerging economies of factor-driven and efficiency-driven economies. MSMEs represent an estimate of 90% of organisations and more than half of job creation worldwide (Khan, 2000), and the growing global workforce means that growth of MSMEs are often a high priority for governments.

This chapter aims to develop a conceptual model of internal and external factors influencing the growth of MSMEs in the emerging economies of factor and efficiency-driven economy. While there are countless researches into growth of MSMEs, most of them are broad and generalised to the extent that questions must be asked if they are applicable for emerging economies. For example, studies on growth factors in the innovation-driven United States may not be applicable in factor-driven and efficiency-driven economies (Berger, 2006). Secondly, this chapter offers one of the most important growth factors; Information Technology (IT) capabilities as a moderating variable. With the rapid growth of technology due to Industry 4.0, it is vital to study the effects of IT capabilities on growth for MSMEs to keep up with current trends and have competitive advantage. Third, this chapter gathers the most important growth factors that have the strongest influence on growth; by devoting precious resources by managers into these areas, MSMEs can experience tremendous growth. Empirical testing of this framework would provide guidance to managers in emerging economies of factor-driven and efficiency-driven economies. Fourth, studies on MSMEs have been conducted in many industries and contexts but none have so far studied in the context of factor-driven and efficiency-driven economies. In fact, academic studies on the three stages of economic development of factor-driven, efficiency-driven and innovation-driven economies are rare and have only begun to surface (Acs, Desai, Hessels, 2008). Sixth, some studies on growth factors on organisations are generalised and broad, while others are empirically catered for larger corporations (Lieberson & O'Connor, 1972). As a result, these studies may not be applicable for MSMEs as MSMEs have an entirely different characteristics from large corporations such as meagre value of assets, small number of employees, low sales turnover, as well as lack of goodwill and reputation. Finally, although researchers have made good progress in the understanding of growth in MSMEs, it is the mixed results that have casted a shadow of ambiguity over this field of study. For example, it has been discovered that the elements driving growth in Thailand include MSMEs characteristics, customer and market, business practises, resources and financing, and external environment (Chittithaworn, Islam, Keawchana, & Yusuf, 2010). On the other side, the main constraints limiting MSMEs' growth in Kosovo include a lack of access to capital, competition, corruption, globalisation, rules and regulations, management competency, a shortage of trained labour, and a lack of investment in innovation, technology, and marketing (Soini, & Veseli, 2011). As indicated by these, the factors might change greatly depending on the place, particularly because economically established and growing countries have distinct features, and this research attempts to focus on the most critical growth drivers.

The content of this chapter is organised into sections based on growth literature; the first section explains the dependent variable of growth of MSMEs in terms of sales turnover and employees, followed by the discussion on the independent variables of characteristic of entrepreneurs, managerial skills, access to micro-finance and government macroeconomic policies. Then, the chapter discusses the moderating role of Information Technology (IT) capabilities in the proposed framework. Most importantly, the chapter showcases the proposed theoretical framework followed by the managerial and policy implications of this conceptual chapter. The chapter then closes off with a conclusion.

GROWTH

Growth is simply defined as the increase in size of firms (Beck, Demirgüç-Kunt, Laeven & Levine, 2005). Growth is a term that is often used to describe business performance and success, and the words 'Growth', 'Performance', and 'Success' are often used interchangeably (Pasanen, 2003). Researchers obtain insights into the drivers of firm growth (Nichter & Goldmark, 2009; Shepherd & Wiklund, 2009) as well as the key drivers of economies by researching the causes of firm growth (Shepherd & Wiklund, 2009). Growth is proof of the entrepreneur's investment and self-fulfillment for an individual entrepreneurial business (Autere & Autio, 2000), and it is also a requirement of survival for new and small enterprises, since growing firms are proven less sensitive to failure than non-growers (Nichter & Goldmark, 2009; Autere & Autio, 2000).

Definitions of growth are often defined by their indicators, and there are many indicators that can be used to measure the growth of MSMEs. Some authors make use of multiple indicators to measure growth in their researches, while others make use of one indicator (Shepherd & Wiklund, 2009; Autere & Autio, 2000). Growth can be measured in terms of two of most widely used and reliable aspects; namely growth of MSME in terms of sales turnover, and growth of MSMEs in terms of number of employment (Shepherd & Wiklund, 2009). This is followed by the second most widely used indicator, which is growth in terms of assets and equity/capital employed (Shepherd & Wiklund, 2009). It should be noted that there are other advanced indicators being used such as conversion rates in website analytics, and return on investment (Hall, 2011), market share, market capitalisation, number of outlets or branches (Daunfeldt, Elert, & Johansson, 2014), customer retention rate and cost per acquisition (Locke, 2004). However, advanced indicators are rarely used by researchers due to its complicated method of measurement, as well as the lack of transparency due to unwillingness of organisations to show or publish certain information due to sensitivity (Khanna & Palepu, 1999). These indicators are also refuted for its reliability, owing to the lack of empirical researches in literature to validate advanced metrics and their infancy nature means that the primary researches will be exploratory and time-consuming in nature. Thus, researchers have generally agreed that sales revenue and number of employees are a useful indicator when measuring growth of MSMEs.

Growth of MSMEs contribute up to 40% of GDP in emerging economies and consist of 60% of GDP and 70% of total employment in low-income countries (Keskġn, Ġentürk, Sungur & Kġrġġ, 2010, June). Owing to the underdeveloped infrastructure of emerging economies, growth of MSMEs are found to slow in efficiency-driven economies and even slower in factor-driven economies, compared to developed economies (Wang, 2016; Acs, Desai & Hessels, 2008). Thus, growth of MSMEs must be prioritised in emerging economies, and in the context of this research, growth of MSMEs are defined as the increase in sales turnover and the increase in number of employees.

CHARACTERISTICS OF ENTREPRENEURS

Characteristics of an entrepreneur is the forefront of an MSME's internal resources (Moorthy et al., 2012; Mohd Shariff & Ali, 2020; Trang, 2016). It is the entrepreneurial skills of the owner that makes it possible for MSMEs to generate growth and development of new ventures, especially in emerging economies (Sharu & Guyo, 2013). Because the owner has considerable influence over an MSME's strategies, tactics and operations, decision-makings are centralized around the owner and a suitable personality and behaviours are needed for an MSME to succeed (Moorthy et al., 2012; Trang, 2016). However, the broad nature on the phrase 'characteristics of entrepreneurs' mean that there have been mixed results on whether characteristics of entrepreneurs have a positive correlation to MSME growth or otherwise.

Generally, there are two school of thoughts for studies on characteristics of entrepreneurs; those who are studying from the perspective of an entrepreneur's personality traits and attitudes (Isaga, 2018), and those who are studying the background of an entrepreneur (Trang, 2016). Wijewardena et al. (2008) have found that there is a strong relationship between owner or managers' mentality and personality traits to financial performance, which inevitably spell their growth. Shah et al. (2013) found that personality traits fosters entrepreneurial culture of innovation (Kozubíková, Čepel & Zlámalová, 2018) and risk-taking (Isaga, 2018), increasing the likelihood of growth.

Background of an entrepreneur is brought about by education, and Brown (2007) has emphasized heavily on entrepreneurship being embedded to all levels of education. Education is found to have a positive correlation with growth (Brown 2007; Trang, 2016). Zhou et al. (2009) have found that organisational determinants such as attributes and strategies have the most influence on growth of an organisation. In fact, to a lesser extent, individual determinants such as personality traits and growth motivation have an influence on growth (Zhou et al. 2009; Trang, 2016). It is not enough to have the determination and willpower from personality traits to be entrepreneur, skills and knowledge from education such as management and technical capabilities are needed to ensure the smooth running of an MSME.

Aside from personality traits that embodies willpower of entrepreneurship and the background of possessing relevant knowledge and intelligence, it is found that experiences of running an organisation has an influence on growth of MSMEs (Trang, 2016). Individuals that have prior experiences starting-up and running own organisations are found to have a competitive advantage (Li Jr & Fu, 2009). Having business experience implies that an induvial are well-versed in running a business (Li Jr & Fu, 2009; Vixathep, 2014; Tan & Tay, 1995). Entrepreneurs who have been in business for a while are aware of the shifting trends and demands (Vixathep, 2014). This understanding leads to the creation of effective goods that appeal to the target market. A personal experience-based business has the benefit of knowing that there are people willing to buy what you're selling. The experience allows to effortlessly communicate with consumers (Li Jr & Fu, 2009; Vixathep, 2014).

However, care must be taken that entrepreneurs learn from their experiences (Martin & Smith, 2010; Lamont, 1972). The issue of whether entrepreneurs truly gain from experiences has been one of the vital subjects of business research. On the off chance that they do gain, what do they learn? The significance of learning and figuring how to avoid repeating mistakes is a crucial characteristic (Lamont, 1972). To address this, researchers present a theoretical model comprised of four components: experience, learning, information and business execution (Martin &

Smith, 2010; Lamont, 1972). From these components, entrepreneurs can successfully learn from their failures.

Thus, in the context of this conceptual research, this chapter offers a more holistic and contemporary definition on characteristics of entrepreneurs; a combination of personality traits and attitudes, education level, and the ability to learn experiences. An entrepreneur aiming grow their enterprises must have the necessary willpower and determination, the right level of knowledge and intelligence, and have learnt valuable lessons from past experiences. In summary, the majority of authors have found that the various dimensions for characteristics of entrepreneurs have significant influence on growth of MSMEs.

MANAGEMENT SKILLS

Another crucial factor that determines the success of an MSME is management skills and capacities. It is important to note that owners and managers are of separate entity, and management skills are skills related to managers rather than entrepreneurs/owners. Management skills are defined as sets of knowledge, skills, and competencies that can make MSMEs more efficient in providing their goods and services (Olawale and Garwe, 2010). Singh et al. (2008) have highlighted that management skills are necessary for MSMEs to survive and are a crucial internal factor achieving growth for MSMEs. The lack of management skills is a barrier to growth and is one of the factors that can lead to failure. Empirical-wise, Pasanen (2007) have found that the growth pattern of MSMEs is positively correlated with their managerial capacities. Organisations and MSMEs that displays a shortage of core competences due to managerial incompetence is one of the main challenges facing MSMEs everywhere (Bhide, 1996). Management skills however focuses on the competences that managers must possess. A skill also embodies the capacity to carry out a certain behavioral activity or to carry out a specific cognitive process that is functionally connected to a specific task (Peterson & Van Fleet, 2004). Other examples of managerial skills that is found to have a positive impact on growth include planning, communication, problem-solving and motivation (Bouazza, Ardjouman & Abada, 2015). Possessing great communication skills is crucial for a manager as it can determine how well information is shared throughout a team, ensuring that the group acts as a unified and coherent workforce can influence growth of MSME (Khoshnodifar et al., 2016). How well a manager communicates with the rest of the team also determines how well outlined procedures can be followed, how well the tasks and activities can be completed, and thus, how successful an MSME will be. Planning is also a vital aspect within an MSME as it refers to one's ability to organize activities in line with set guidelines while still remaining within the limits of the available resources such as time, money, and labour (Osiyevskyy et al., 2013). A good manager must have the ability to tackle and solve the frequent problems that can arise in a typical workday. Problem-solving in management involves identifying a certain problem or situation and then finding the best way to handle the problem and get the best solution. The ability to motivate is another important skill in an MSME as it helps bring forth a desired behaviour or response from the employees or certain stakeholders that can even exceed limitations (Moen et al., 2016). Dimensions of management skills are varied among researchers, though most authors are focused on management styles that is related to methods of running an organisation. To summarise, management skills must consist of technical, human, and conceptual skills and it is imperative that MSMEs hire competent and skillful managers that can help steer employees towards achieving objectives.

Managers need technical skills for a variety of reasons, including the ability to teach, lead, and assess subordinates doing specific jobs. An early definition of supervision was as an educational process in which someone with specific knowledge and competence accepts responsibility for educating someone with less knowledge and skill (Tajaddini, Mujtaba & Bandenezhad, 2010; Norman, Tharmmaphornphilas, Needy, Bidanda & Warner, 2002). The implication appears to be that managers must have a thorough understanding of the technique or approach in order to instruct their employees.

The human skills comprise of cooperation, conflict resolution, communication, and establishing an organisational atmosphere (Mujtaba & Kaifi, 2011). Human skills comprise behavioral principles, interpersonal connections, motivation, and communication (Alam, Gale, Brown & Khan, 2010). Human skills are required if managers are to offer performance feedback, coach and counsel subordinates, and overall create a constructive work environment (Pant & Baroudi, 2008; Alam, Gale, Brown & Khan, 2010). Human abilities also incorporate interpersonal skills. The phrase refers to an employee's capacity to cooperate effectively with others in the workplace (Mujtaba & Kaifi, 2011). Communication and listening abilities, as well as attitude and deportment, are all examples of interpersonal skills.

Finally, conceptual abilities are defined as the capacity to perceive an organisation as a whole or from a systemic perspective (Mujtaba & Kaifi, 2011). They are mental talents that enable a manager to comprehend the interactions among the many work units within the organisation, the impact of changes on any one element of the system, and how the organisation fits into the system (Mujtaba, Javed & Nguyen, 2013). Without which, managers will feel overwhelmed at the workload of organising the various units in the organisation. Thus, management skills influence MSME performance.

ACCESS TO MICROFINANCE

For MSMEs to start-up, they require the necessary finance to build their business operation from the ground up. Access to finance would not only help them commence business but helps them to grow, prosper and expand their operations in terms of sales and firm size (Brown, Earle & Lup, 2005). Furthermore, MSMEs with greater access to capital are more able to effectively exploit growth and investment opportunities (Beck et al, 2006). However, it is important to note that, finance can either be self-financed by own savings and family or via financial institutions such as banks.

One of the most significant impediments to MSMEs' growth is financial restraints caused by a lack of capital to launch their businesses (Beck & Demirguc-Kunt, 2006; Ndiaye et al., 2018; Quartey et al., 2017; Wang, 2016). According to the World Bank, financial constraints are one of the most frequently cited barriers to MSME growth in developing and emerging economies (Mthimkhulu & Aziakpono, 2015). According to the World Bank's enterprise-level survey, MSMEs in developing and emerging countries have limited access to credit from financial institutions when compared to large corporations (Kuntchev et al., 2012).

Furthermore, the smaller the size of the organisation, the less likely it is to secure the finances required to develop; as a result, it confronts more financial issues and uses less external borrowing than larger enterprises (Lawless et al., 2015; Nikaido et al., 2015). This is because banks and financial institutions are often hesitant to lend to start-ups and MSMEs because they are perceived as the riskiest of investments (Thompson Agyapong, Mmieh & Mordi, 2018; Brown, Earle & Lup, 2005; Ngugi & Bwisa, 2013); MSMEs frequently lack credit worthiness to demonstrate a history of being able to payback on time, and the low collaterals and small quantity of assets are insufficient to act as security, discouraging financial institutions from lending.

In literature, in order to adapt to today's context as well due to increasing business competition, a new form of finance have been introduced; micro-finance (De Aghion, Armendáriz & Morduch, 2007). Micro-finance is a relatively new term design specifically for start-ups and small businesses, and the term 'finance' has started to become inapplicable for MSMEs due to a number of reasons (Beck, 2015); some small enterprises are not registered, and is part of informal economy, in which conventional banks not willing to lend, and lack of credit history further discourages financial institutions from lending.

The distinction between microfinance and banking is in their scope, since microfinance assists individuals who require loans with few or no assets, whereas banks provide loans to clients who have collateral (Armendariz & Labie, 2011). Microfinance is an individual-focused financial service that gives funds to needy individuals or small enterprises who do not have access to traditional resources. Microfinance has lower risk-adjusted capital costs, no collateral, and more leverage than traditional banks (Milana & Ashta, 2012). While the amount is not as much as the usual conventional finance, micro-finance provide that necessary means by which inexperienced and beginners of enterprises to jumpstart in order to provide the necessary goods and services, and in the long run, promotes growth of MSMEs. It can be seen that most micro-finance are studied in the context of developing and emerging economies, and Microfinance Companies play an important role in rural areas. Thus, micro-finance plays a crucial role in economic growth and development in developing and emerging economies.

Countless studies have found that micro-finance have an influence on performance and growth of MSMEs (Ashamu, 2014; Babagana, 2010; Mugori, 2012). Microfinance is significant because it gives resources and money to the financially disadvantaged, such as individuals who cannot obtain checking accounts, lines of credit, or loans from regular banks. Without microfinance, these people may be forced to rely on high-risk loans or payday advances, or even borrow money from family and friends. Microfinance enables people to invest in their enterprises, and hence in themselves. Micro-finance is also found to have encouraged entrepreneurial activity and intention, due to graduates and aspiring entrepreneurs being encouraged at the prospect (Zhiri, 2017).

However, hindering the progress of micro-finance are its barriers and challenges; key findings indicate that both internal and external variables increase the likelihood of a crisis (Sainz-Fernandez, Torre-Olmo, López-Gutiérrez & Sanfilippo-Azofra, 2015). We identify many characteristics that minimise the chance of a crisis (business success, national economic development, political stability, and the presence of a private credit bureau). A paper demonstrates that microfinance banking in Nigeria faces enormous challenges due to inadequacies in infrastructure, social misconceptions, a poor legal and regulatory framework, unbridled competition from other financial institutions, abandonment of core microfinance functions, and a scarcity of qualified manpower. Acha Ikechukwu, A., & Acha, I. (2012).

Micro-finance is found to improve financial performance (Kanyugi, 2011); when MSMEs develop, they require finances to finance fixed asset expansion and enhance working capital. As a result, SMEs demand long-term loans in ever-increasing quantities in order to acquire raw materials, suppliers, and carry out operations required to aid the manufacturing process. One study even contributed to sustainable growth, citing micro-finance to sustain growth of small businesses (O Oni, Imam Paiko & Koholga, 2012). However, to ensure sustainability in growth of MSMEs, it is recommended that governments conduct periodic intervention to regulate the micro-finance, in order to ensure that micro-finance reaches to any and all socio-economic background especially in rural areas; the distribution of micro-finance is unfortunately not equal.

Overall, majority of researchers have found that external factor of access to micro-finance to be positively correlated to growth of MSMEs (Goto & Negash 2016; Muiruri, 2014; Yusufu, Suleiman & Saliu, 2020). Generally, conventional finance is more difficult to obtain than micro-finance, and it has been found that the lack of access to credit is a major impediment to inhibiting the growth of micro enterprises (GOK 2005). The lack of access to external financing is considered a major challenge to the growth of MSMEs, and it has accounted for high rates of failure among those MSMEs (Ropega, 2011). Entrepreneurs with the greatest of ideas and entrepreneurial characteristics would not be able to mobilise its resources and capital should they not find the necessary finance to start-up their MSME. Unfortunately, financial institutions and banks in general are unwilling to lend to aspiring entrepreneurs (Boata, Gerdes & Risk, 2019). This is because many lenders find it impossible to assess the relevant risks of an investment, and the existence of high degree of uncertainty and lack of assurance gives them further reasons to not lend (Abraham & Schmukler, 2017). Thus, a business plan is critical for securing financial support. This is also proven by Nichter and Goldmark (2009) where credit access favours large corporations due to their superior assets, while MSMEs face problems and difficulties to their development as a consequence of lack of access to finance.

From a general point-of-view, MSMEs in both emerging and developed economies have experienced less access to external financing (Bouazza, Ardjouman, & Abada, 2015). As a result, MSMEs are more restrained in their operations and growth compared to large corporations. A recent study done by Beck et al. (2006) in developing and emerging countries provides further evidence that MSMEs face greater financing obstacles than large corporations do. Ayyagari et al. (2006) show that financing, crime, and political instability directly affect the rate of growth of MSMEs, with financing being the most significant constraint affecting MSME growth. Above all, Rocha. et al (2010) analyze the most binding constraint on MSME growth in developing and emerging countries: they find that each country faces a different set of constraints and that these constraints also vary by firm characteristics, especially firm size. However, across all countries, access to financing is among the most binding obstacle while other obstacles appear to matter much less affecting growth of MSMEs. Thus, micro-finance circumvents the issues that conventional finance has, and the provision of micro-finance is essential for growth of MSMEs. As a result, it is vital to include the external factor of access to micro-finance as factor impacting MSMEs' development in the developing and emerging economies of factor and efficiency-driven countries.

GOVERNMENT MACROECONOMIC POLICIES

The Legal, Regulatory and Political Framework constitutes a government's administrative agencies that have the authority to conduct control and order via policies, ultimately responsible for the creation and the nature of a business ecosystem in an economy (Saleh & Ndubisi, 2006). This includes interest rates, laws and regulations, government expenditure on infrastructure, taxation system, circulation of money supply in an economy and others. Thus, this falls outside the control of MSMEs. Lumpkin and Dess in 1996 have noted that the growth of MSMEs are affected by their business climate or environment. This includes the macroeconomic framework that consists of government policies of an economy in which an ecosystem is determined, affecting the MSMEs competing in the ecosystem. It goes without saying that an unfavorable business climate has negative affect on MSME growth. Competition is considered healthy and favourable as it encourages innovation among organisations and the prevention of monopoly and dominant corporations (Brown; 2007).

From macroeconomic point-of-view, taxation plays a vital role in determining entrepreneurship. Davidsson, Achtenhagen & Naldi (2010) has found that an unfavorable tax system, such as high corporation tax may hamper the growth of MSMEs. A high-income tax will discourage MSMEs from employing employees in order to save costs owing to their small organisational size and low amount of equity. There have been instances where government encourages the establishment of monopoly, especially in scenarios that requires consistent delivery of a product or service that has a very high up-front cost (Beecher, 2001). Such examples of products are electric and water utilities as it is often costly to build new electric plants or dams, so in order to stay economically viable, monopolies must be allowed to control prices to pay for these costs. In addition, rules and regulations regarding entry to an industry must be exercised and relaxed in order to allow smooth entry of MSMEs willing to compete (Doern, 2009). Lenient policies must be implemented to ensure less bureacucracy and paperworks on start-ups entering an industry, as complicated rules and regulations can heavily hamper growth of MSMEs.

Finally, corruption in an economy affects entrepreneurial activity. Krasniqi (2007) showed that corruption is a major source of the rise in unfair competition. He further emphasized that the cost of complying with regulations and increased tax rates increases MSMEs' expenses while limiting their growth. Likewise, St-Jean et al. (2008) noted that unfair competition from the informal sector, cumbersome regulations, and tax rates are the main obstacles on MSME growth.

A study done by International Finance Corporation (IFC; 2013) on 45,000 organisations in developing and emerging countries, found that the top obstacles to their operations are a poor investment climate, especially red tape, high tax rates, and competition from the informal sector, and inadequate infrastructure, especially with an insufficient or unreliable power supply. Informal economy constitutes of black market, which is a major hindrance for MSMEs in developing and emerging countries (Skenderi, Islami, & Mulolli, 2017). Thus, policies must include low tax rates, the elimination of unfair competition from black market, elimination of corruption, relaxing of barriers to entry, the abolishment of monopoly and the lowering of bureaucratic red tapes can influence MSME growth.

INFORMATION TECHNOLOGY (IT) CAPABILITIES

In this age of technological breakthroughs and inventions, the technological capability of an organisation is another crucial internal factor influencing growth of MSMEs. In layman terms, IT capabilities are considered methods, tools and technology encompassing hardware and software format for strengthening the competitiveness of MSMEs (Romijn, 2001). Due to rapid advancement of technology and the increased level of competition in any industry, it is essential for MSMEs to get ahead of industry average via utilization of IT in a process known as technological innovation (Lester & Tran, 2008; Romijn, 2001). Innovation is a key driver of productivity and long-term growth and can help solve social challenges at the lowest possible cost.

However, innovation is not possible without the necessary technological capability (Lester & Tran, 2008). In other words, technology sparks innovation in MSMEs, and innovative companies are able to respond by utilising internal knowledge and insights about existing products or services, allowing to adapt to dynamic changes required by the customer within their niche market (Levy & Powell 2005, 22). Innovation relies on bringing together different types of research and utilizing this knowledge to design new products; therefore, innovation greatly relies on research and development investments. Due to increase in IT capability encouraging the rate of innovation in MSMEs, researches have stated that there is significant relationship between IT capability and growth of MSMEs (Kmieciak et al., 2012; Lester, & Tran, 2008). Performance in terms of productivity had also been enhanced by IT (Moorthy, 2012), while information and communication technologies such as internet use and web presence for business purposes and social media were positively associated with MSME success (Bala & Feng, 2019).

MSMEs must have the ability to undertake all four aspects (Avgerou, Smith, & Van den Besselaar, 2008) known as the 4C; computing, connectivity, content and capacity. Computing: initial investments on technology are prohibitively costly for most start-ups, shared access is unavoidable (Kredel & Weispfenning, 1988). Technological investments are difficult to operate, and even experts spend a significant amount of time maintaining their computers, worrying about upgrades, security, and hardware compatibility. Connectivity: while mobile telephony is increasing across the world, it remains costly, restricted, and ineffective for MSMEs when it comes to data connectivity, thus warranting the use of social media instead (Jorfi, Nor, & Najjar, 2011). Content: many languages lack meaningful information, and the majority of that content is irrelevant to the local context, thus filtering is needed to remove irrelevant information and prevent information overload (Rahimnia & Hassanzadeh, 2013). Capacity: in order to harness the potential of ICT, users must be literate in IT, particularly digital literacy (Jamil & Almunawar, 2021) and information literacy (Koltay, 2011) in order to be creative (Avital & Te'Eni, 2009). By fulfilling the 4C dimensions, IT brings the benefits of increasing productivity of entrepreneurs and managers, thus has the capability to play a crucial role in enhancing relationship between growth factors and growth of MSMEs, and this paper proposes IT capabilities as moderating variable.

CONCEPTUAL FRAMEWORK

From the above discussion as well as the basis of the academic literature on factors influencing growth, this paper proposes a conceptual framework as shown in Figure 1, where it is assumed that growth of MSMEs is affected by two internal factors and two external factors. The internal factors consist of characteristics of entrepreneurs and management skills, while the external factors consist of access to micro-finance and government policies. These make the four dependent variables. This framework posits that growth of MSMEs are applicable in emerging economies of factor-driven and efficiency-driven economies where business environments are often considered hostile and possess a lack of ecosystem that allows entrepreneurship to flourish. This paper composed a holistic approach to Characteristics of Entrepreneurs that have three dimensions; a combination of personality traits and attitudes, education level, and the ability to learn experiences. Management skills have three different skills: human, technical, and conceptual skills. Access to micro-finance incorporates two elements such as institutional framework that allows free-flowing information, and diversification of sources of finance. Government macroeconomic policies encompass the various conditions that enables MSME-friendly ecosystem, particularly low tax rates, the elimination of unfair competition from black market, elimination of corruption, relaxing of barriers to entry, the abolishment of monopoly and the lowering of bureaucratic red tapes. It is believed that the stronger the internal and external growth factors, the higher the growth of MSMEs in terms of sales and number of employees. Moreover, the paper also composes Information Technology capabilities as a moderator in the relationship between growth factors and growth of MSMEs, where it is assumed that the presence of four

Figure 1. Conceptual Framework of Factors influencing Growth of Micro, Small and Medium-sized Enterprises in the Emerging Economies of Factor-driven and Efficiency-driven Economies.

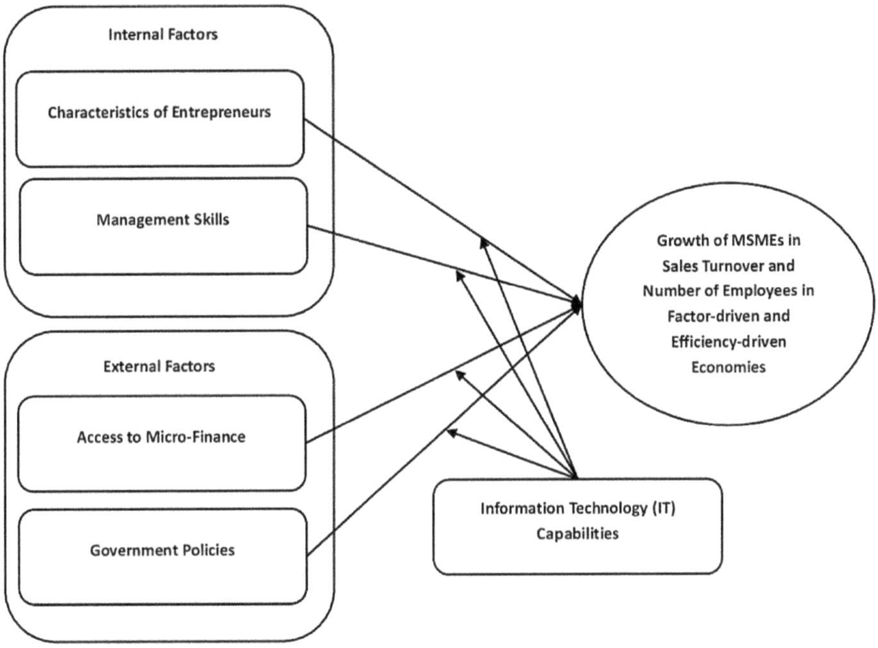

dimension of Information Technology capabilities; computing, connectivity, content and capacity will boost the relationship between internal and external growth factors and growth of MSMEs.

MANAGERIAL AND POLICY IMPLICATIONS

The framework identifies the factors influencing growth of MSMEs in terms of sales turnover and number of employees. Practising managers looking to enhance their sales figure and manpower will find that the framework's internal factors are within their control and is the key to growth. Factor-driven and efficiency-driven economies face hostile environments such as lack of access to micro-finance and underdeveloped educational institutions as critical elements that aggravate the high failure rate of MSMEs in the early years of their operations. The managerial implication is that this research will benefit MSMEs in emerging economies as understanding which factors that are crucial for growth serves as a guideline on how to grow their enterprises in order to survive in nowadays' uncertain, competitive and dynamic business environment. The scarcity of resources faced by owners and managers of MSMEs meant that monetary investment must be devoted to the correct growth factors due to opportunity cost. The various growth factors found in academia may cause confusion as to which factor must resources be devoted to, and this research helps to filter down and identify which factors are the most crucial. The policy implication here is that by identifying the factors that encourages growth of MSMEs, MSME-friendly policies can be implemented by governments in order to foster an entrepreneurial ecosystem and promote economic growth. Specifically, the external factors of access to micro-finance and government policies are key to enhancing the growth of MSMEs, which in turn mean more income for the government. In conjunction with industry 4.0, it is the objective of emerging economies to advance and diversify the economy by encouraging the growth of MSMEs, and it is the aim of both factor-driven and efficiency-driven economies to transition towards the third stage of economic development of innovation-driven economy, where economies are considered the most economically advanced.

CONCLUSION

In today's economy, growth of MSMEs are essential. They account for a major portion of employment generation in every modern economy, and they make substantial contribution to GDP growth. Growth of MSMEs increase the level of competition in any industry, promoting innovation of products. Growth of MSMEs are especially important in the emerging economies of factor-driven and efficiency-driven economies, where economic development is sorely needed. This paper has taken the various factors that are empirically proven to have an influence on growth of MSMEs and synthesise them into a single framework. This research had proposed a theoretical framework that has essentially identifies factors influencing growth of MSMEs, especially in the emerging economies of Factor-driven and Efficiency-driven Economies. Internal factors consist of characteristics of entrepreneurs and management skills, while external factors consist of government policies and access to micro-finance. These factors are the most important as it is found that these variables are the most empirically studied and discussed, and thus have the strongest effect on growth of MSMEs. These factors enhance sales turnover and number of employees, and this paper proposed information technology capabilities as a moderator for more profound effect on growth. This paper believes that this research offers more insight and contributes into growth literature and an empirical study of this paper can ascertain the validity of this framework.

REFERENCES

Abraham, F., & Schmukler, S. L. (2017). Addressing the SME finance problem. *World Bank Research and Policy Briefs*, (120333).

Acha Ikechukwu, A., & Acha, I. (2012). Microfinance banking in Nigeria: Problems and prospects. *International Journal of Finance and Accounting*, *1*(5), 106–111.

Acs, Z. J., Desai, S., & Hessels, J. (2008). Entrepreneurship, economic development and institutions. *Small Business Economics*, *31*(3), 219–234. doi:10.100711187-008-9135-9

Ahmad, N. H., & Seet, P. S. (2009). Understanding business success through the lens of SME founder-owners in Australia and Malaysia. *International Journal of Entrepreneurial Venturing*, *1*(1), 72–87. doi:10.1504/IJEV.2009.023821

Alam, M., Gale, A., Brown, M., & Khan, A. I. (2010). The importance of human skills in project management professional development. *International Journal of Managing Projects in Business*, *3*(3), 495–516. doi:10.1108/17538371011056101

Armendariz, B., & Labie, M. (Eds.). (2011). *The handbook of microfinance*. World Scientific. doi:10.1142/7645

Ashamu, S. O. (2014). The impact of micro-finance on small scale business in Nigeria. *Journal of Policy and Development Studies*, *9*(1), 179–193. doi:10.12816/0011191

Autere, J., & Autio, A. (2000). Is entrepreneurship learned? Influence of mental models on growth motivation, strategy, and growth. In *Academy of Management Conference* (pp. 47-68). Academic Press.

Avgerou, C., Smith, M. L., & Van den Besselaar, P. (2008). *Social dimensions of information and communication technology policy*. Springer. doi:10.1007/978-0-387-84822-8

Avital, M., & Te'Eni, D. (2009). From generative fit to generative capacity: Exploring an emerging dimension of information systems design and task performance. *Information Systems Journal*, *19*(4), 345–367. doi:10.1111/j.1365-2575.2007.00291.x

Aybar-AriasC.Casino-MartinezA.Lopez-GraciaJ. (2003). Capital structure and sensitivity in SME definition: a panel data investigation. *Available at* SSRN 549082. doi:10.2139/ssrn.549082

Azam, S. F., & Abdullah, M. A. (2015). Differential roles between owner and manager in financial practice that contributes to business success: An analysis on Malaysian small business. *Academic Journal of Interdisciplinary Studies*, *4*(1 S2), 123-123.

Babagana, S. A. (2010). Impact assessment of the role of micro finance banks in promoting small and medium enterprises growth in Nigeria. *International Journal of Economic Development Research and Investment*, *1*(1), 42–53.

Bala, H., & Feng, X. (2019). Success of small and medium enterprises in Myanmar: Role of technological, organizational, and environmental factors. *Journal of Global Information Technology Management*, *22*(2), 100–119. doi:10.1080/1097198X.2019.1603511

Beck, T. (2015). *Microfinance*. Independent Evaluation Group.

Beck, T., & Demirguc-Kunt, A. (2006). Small and medium-size enterprises: Access to finance as a growth constraint. *Journal of Banking & Finance*, *30*(11), 2931–2943. doi:10.1016/j.jbankfin.2006.05.009

Beck, T., Demirguc-Kunt, A., & Levine, R. (2005). SMEs, growth, and poverty: Cross-country evidence. *Journal of Economic Growth*, *10*(3), 199–229. doi:10.100710887-005-3533-5

Beecher, J. A. (2001). Privatization, Monopoly, and Structured Competition in the Water Industry: Is there a role for regulation? *Environmental consequences of privatising water services in Germany*, 327-339.

Berger, A. N. (2006). Potential competitive effects of Basel II on banks in SME credit markets in the United States. *Journal of Financial Services Research*, *29*(1), 5–36. doi:10.100710693-005-5106-3

Bhide, A. (1996). The questions every entrepreneur must answer. *Harvard Business Review*, *74*(6), 120.

Bianchi, A. (1993). Who's most likely to go it alone? *Inc.*, *15*(5), 58.

Boata, A., Gerdes, K., & Risk, D. C. (2019). *European regulatory changes will make banks less willing to lend to SMEs*. Euler Hermes Global.

Bouazza, A. B., Ardjouman, D., & Abada, O. (2015). Establishing the factors affecting the growth of small and medium-sized enterprises in Algeria. *American International Journal of Social Science*, *4*(2), 101–115.

Brown, J. D., Earle, J. S., & Lup, D. (2005). What makes small firms grow? Finance, human capital, technical assistance, and the business environment in Romania. *Economic Development and Cultural Change*, *54*(1), 33–70. doi:10.1086/431264

Brown, R. (2007). Promoting entrepreneurship in arts education. *Entrepreneurship in the creative industries: an international perspective*, 126-141

Carver, C. S. (2012). *Self-awareness*. Academic Press.

Chit, M. M. (2019). Financial information credibility, legal environment, and SMEs' access to finance. *International Journal of the Economics of Business*, *26*(3), 329–354. doi:10.1080/13571516.2019.1645379

Davidsson, P., Achtenhagen, L., & Naldi, L. (2010). *Small firm growth*. Now Publishers Inc. doi:10.1561/0300000029

De Aghion, B. A., Armendáriz, B., & Morduch, J. (2007). *The economics of microfinance*. Academic Press.

Decker, M., Schiefer, G., & Bulander, R. (2006, August). Specific challenges for small and medium-sized enterprises (SME) in M-business. In *Proceedings of the International Conference on E-Business (ICE-B 2006)* (pp. 169-174). INSTICC Press.

Doern, R. (2009). Investigating barriers to SME growth and development in transition environments: A critique and suggestions for developing the methodology. *International Small Business Journal*, *27*(3), 275–305. doi:10.1177/0266242609102275

Doh, S., & Kim, B. (2014). Government support for SME innovations in the regional industries: The case of government financial support program in South Korea. *Research Policy*, *43*(9), 1557–1569. doi:10.1016/j.respol.2014.05.001

Elena, M., Chavez, E., Kramer, R., Rangel, A. C., Garcia, E. M., & Santillan, A. G. (2015). Empirical evidence on locus of control among owner and manager and its relation to success firms. *Journal of Emerging Trends in Economics and Management Science*, *6*(3), 177–184.

Goto, M., & Negash, F. A. (2016). The Effect of Micro Finance Institutions in Growth and Development Small Business. 經濟學研究, *66*(2), 67-90.

Hadidi, H. E., & Kirby, D. A. (2015). Universities and innovation in a factor-driven economy: The Egyptian case. *Industry and Higher Education*, *29*(2), 151–160. doi:10.5367/ihe.2015.0248

IFC. (2010). *Scaling-Up SME Access to Financial Services in the Developing World*. Financial Inclusion Experts Group.

Isaga, N. (2018). The relationship of personality to cognitive characteristics and SME performance in Tanzania. *Journal of Small Business and Enterprise Development*, *25*(4), 667–686. doi:10.1108/JSBED-02-2017-0067

Jamil, M. I. M., & Almunawar, M. N. (2021). Importance of Digital Literacy and Hindrance Brought About by Digital Divide. In *Encyclopedia of Information Science and Technology* (5th ed., pp. 1683–1698). IGI Global. doi:10.4018/978-1-7998-3479-3.ch116

Jorfi, S., Nor, K. M., & Najjar, L. (2011). Assessing the impact of IT connectivity and IT capability on IT-business strategic alignment: An empirical study. *Computer and Information Science*, *4*(3), 76. doi:10.5539/cis.v4n3p76

Kanyugi, I. N. (2011). *The impact of micro-finance credit on the financial performance of SMEs in Kenya* [Doctoral dissertation].

Keskġn, H., Ġentürk, C., Sungur, O., & Kġrġġ, H. M. (2010, June). The importance of SMEs in developing economies. In *2nd International Symposium on Sustainable Development* (pp. 183-192). Academic Press.

Khan, M. M. H. (2000). *Rural poverty in developing countries: Issues and policies*. International Monetary Fund.

Khanna, T., & Palepu, K. (1999). *Emerging market business groups, foreign investors, and corporate governance*. Academic Press.

Khoshnodifar, Z., Ghonji, M., Mazloumzadeh, S. M., & Abdollahi, V. (2016). Effect of communication channels on success rate of entrepreneurial SMEs in the agricultural sector (a case study). *Journal of the Saudi Society of Agricultural Sciences*, *15*(1), 83–90. doi:10.1016/j.jssas.2014.04.001

Koltay, T. (2011). The media and the literacies: Media literacy, information literacy, digital literacy. *Media Culture & Society*, *33*(2), 211–221. doi:10.1177/0163443710393382

Kozubíková, L., Čepel, M., & Zlámalová, M. (2018). *Attitude toward innovativeness based on personality traits in the SME sector. Czech Republic case study*. Management & Marketing-Challenges for the Knowledge Society. doi:10.2478/mmcks-2018-0013

Krasniqi, B. A. (2007). Barriers to entrepreneurship and SME growth in transition: The case of Kosova. *Journal of Developmental Entrepreneurship*, *12*(01), 71–94. doi:10.1142/S1084946707000563

Kredel, H., & Weispfenning, V. (1988). Computing dimension and independent sets for polynomial ideals. *Journal of Symbolic Computation*, *6*(2-3), 231–247. doi:10.1016/S0747-7171(88)80045-2

Lamont, L. M. (1972). What entrepreneurs learn from experience. *Journal of Small Business Management, 10*, 36.

Lee, K. H. (2009). Why and how to adopt green management into business organizations? The case study of Korean SMEs in manufacturing industry. *Management Decision*, *47*(7), 1101–1121. doi:10.1108/00251740910978322

Lester, D. L., & Tran, T. T. (2008). Information technology capabilities: Suggestions for SME growth. *Journal of Behavioral and Applied Management*, *10*(1), 72–88. doi:10.21818/001c.17169

Levy, M., & Powell, P. (2003). Exploring SME internet adoption: Towards a contingent model. *Electronic Markets*, *13*(2), 173–181. doi:10.1080/1019678032000067163

Li Jr, F. F., & Fu, K. (2009). *Factors Influencing the Growth of Small and Medium Sized Firms in Different Growth Stages-A Study of Four Chinese SMEs*. Academic Press.

Lieberson, S., & O'Connor, J. F. (1972). Leadership and organizational performance: A study of large corporations. *American Sociological Review*, *37*(2), 117–130. doi:10.2307/2094020 PMID:5020209

LockeS. (2004). ICT adoption and SME growth in New Zealand. Available at SSRN 3284905.

Lumpkin, G. T., & Dess, G. G. (1996). Clarifying the entrepreneurial orientation construct and linking it to performance. *Academy of Management Review*, *21*(1), 135–172. doi:10.2307/258632

Makri, E., Spiliotopoulos, D., Vassilakis, C., & Margaris, D. (2020). Human behaviour in multimodal interaction: Main effects of civic action and interpersonal and problem-solving skills. *Journal of Ambient Intelligence and Humanized Computing*, *11*(12), 5991–6006. doi:10.100712652-020-01846-x

Martin, F., & Smith, R. (2010). What is it that entrepreneurs learn from experience? *Industry and Higher Education*, *24*(6), 505–512. doi:10.5367/ihe.2010.0016

McClelland, D. (1961). *The achieving society. Van Nostrand*. doi:10.1037/14359-000

Milana, C., & Ashta, A. (2012). Developing microfinance: A survey of the literature. *Strategic Change*, *21*(7-8), 299–330. doi:10.1002/jsc.1911

Moen, Ø., Heggeseth, A. G., & Lome, O. (2016). The positive effect of motivation and international orientation on SME growth. *Journal of Small Business Management*, *54*(2), 659–678. doi:10.1111/jsbm.12163

Mohd Shariff, M. N., Peou, C., & Ali, J. (2010). Moderating effect of government policy on entrepreneurship and growth performance of small-medium enterprises in Cambodia. *International Journal of Business and Management Science, 3*(1), 57–72.

Moorthy, M. K., Tan, A., Choo, C., Wei, C. S., Ping, J. T. Y., & Leong, T. K. (2012). A study on factors affecting the performance of SMEs in Malaysia. *International Journal of Academic Research in Business & Social Sciences, 2*(4), 224.

Mugori, W. M. (2012). *The effects of access to micro-finance on the financial performance of small and medium enterprises owned by youths in Nairobi Kenya* [Doctoral dissertation]. University of Nairobi.

Muiruri, P. M. (2014). *The Role of Micro-Finance Institutions to the Growth of Micro and Small Enterprises (MSE) in Thika. Empirical Review of NonFinancial Factors.*

Mujtaba, B. G., Javed, M., & Nguyen, L. D. (2013). Management skills of Pakistanis: a comparison of technical, human and conceptual differences. *Advances in Management and Applied Economics, 3*(3), 129.

Mujtaba, B. G., & Kaifi, B. A. (2011). Management skills of Afghan respondents: A comparison of technical, human and conceptual differences based on gender. *Journal of International Business and Cultural Studies, 4*, 1.

Ngugi, J., & Bwisa, H. (2013). Factors influencing growth of group owned small and medium enterprises: A case of one village one product enterprises. *International Journal of Education and Research, 1*(8), 1–14.

Nichter, S., & Goldmark, L. (2009). Small firm growth in developing countries. *World Development, 37*(9), 1453–1464. doi:10.1016/j.worlddev.2009.01.013

Norman, B. A., Tharmmaphornphilas, W., Needy, K. L., Bidanda, B., & Warner, R. C. (2002). Worker assignment in cellular manufacturing considering technical and human skills. *International Journal of Production Research, 40*(6), 1479–1492. doi:10.1080/00207540110118082

OECD/ERIA. (2018). *SME Policy Index: ASEAN 2018: Boosting Competitiveness and Inclusive Growth.* OECD Publishing. Retrieved from https://asean.org/wp-content/ uploads/2018/08/Report-ASEAN-SME-Policy-Index-2018.pdf

Olawale, F., & Garwe, D. (2010). Obstacles to the growth of new SMEs in South Africa: A principal component analysis approach. *African Journal of Business Management, 4*(5), 729–738.

Olu, O. J. O. (2009, November). Impact of microfinance on entrepreneurial development: The case of Nigeria. In The international conference on economics and administration, faculty of administration and business (pp. 536-545). Academic Press.

Oni, E., Imam Paiko, I., & Koholga, O. (2012). *Assessment of the contribution of micro finance institutions (MFIs) to sustainable growth of small and medium scale enterprises (SMEs) in Nigeria*. Academic Press.

Osiyevskyy, O., Hayes, L., Krueger, N. F., & Madill, C. (2013). *Planning to Grow? Exploring the Effect of Business Planning on the Growth of Small and Medium Enterprises (SMEs)*. Social Science Research Network. https://papers.ssrn.com/abstract=2392921

Pant, I., & Baroudi, B. (2008). Project management education: The human skills imperative. *International Journal of Project Management*, *26*(2), 124–128. doi:10.1016/j.ijproman.2007.05.010

Pasanen, M. (2003). *In search of factors affecting SME performance: The case of Eastern Finland*. Kuopion Yliopisto.

Pekmezovic, A., & Walker, G. (2016). The global significance of crowdfunding: Solving the SME funding problem and democratizing access to capital. *Wm. & Mary Bus. L. Rev.*, *7*, 347.

Peterson, T. O., & Van Fleet, D. D. (2004). The ongoing legacy of RL Katz: An updated typology of management skills. *Management Decision*, *42*(10), 1297–1308. doi:10.1108/00251740410568980

Popescu, L., Iancu, A., Avram, M., Avram, D., & Popescu, V. (2020). The role of managerial skills in the sustainable development of SMEs in Mehedinti County, Romania. *Sustainability*, *12*(3), 1119. doi:10.3390u12031119

Rahimnia, F., & Hassanzadeh, J. F. (2013). The impact of website content dimension and e-trust on e-marketing effectiveness: The case of Iranian commercial saffron corporations. *Information & Management*, *50*(5), 240–247. doi:10.1016/j.im.2013.04.003

Rahman, A., Rahman, M. T., & Belas, J. (2017). Determinants of SME finance: evidence from three central European countries. *Review of Economic Perspectives*.

Rijkers, B., Arouri, H., Freund, C., & Nucifora, A. (2014). Which firms create the most jobs in developing countries? Evidence from Tunisia. *Labour Economics*, *31*, 84–102. doi:10.1016/j.labeco.2014.10.003

Romijn, H., & Albu, M. (2001). *Explaining innovativeness in small high-technology firms in the United Kingdom.* Eindhoven Centre for Innovation Studies, The Netherlands Working Paper.

Ropega, J. (2011). The reasons and symptoms of failure in SME. *International Advances in Economic Research, 17*(4), 476–483. doi:10.100711294-011-9316-1

Sainz-Fernandez, I., Torre-Olmo, B., López-Gutiérrez, C., & Sanfilippo-Azofra, S. (2015). Crisis in microfinance institutions: Identifying problems. *Journal of International Development, 27*(7), 1058–1073. doi:10.1002/jid.3129

Saleh, A. S., & Ndubisi, N. O. (2006). *SME development in Malaysia: Domestic and global challenges.* Academic Press.

Salovey, P., & Grewal, D. (2005). The science of emotional intelligence. *Current Directions in Psychological Science, 14*(6), 281–285. doi:10.1111/j.0963-7214.2005.00381.x

Shah, S. F. H., Nazir, T., Zaman, K., & Shabir, M. (2013). Factors Affecting the Growth of Enterprises: A Survey of the Literature from the Perspective of Small- and Medium-Sized Enterprises. *Journal of Enterprise Transformation, 3*(2), 53–75. doi:10.1080/19488289.2011.650282

Sharu, H., & Guyo, W. (2015). Factors influencing growth of youth owned small and medium enterprises in Nairobi County, Kenya. *International Journal of Scientific Research, 4*(4), 973–987.

Shepherd, D., & Wiklund, J. (2009). Are we comparing apples with apples or apples with oranges? Appropriateness of knowledge accumulation across growth studies. *Entrepreneurship Theory and Practice, 33*(1), 105–123. doi:10.1111/j.1540-6520.2008.00282.x

Singh, R. K., Garg, S. K., & Deshmukh, S. G. (2008). Strategy development by SMEs for competitiveness: A review. *Benchmarking, 15*(5), 525–547. doi:10.1108/14635770810903132

Skenderi, N., Islami, X., & Mulolli, E. (2017). The Impact of Informal Economy in the Development of SMEs-Evidence from Kosovo (2008-2012). *International Journal of Management, Accounting and Economics, 4*(5), 2383–2126.

Sridhar, R., Sachithanandam, V., Mageswaran, T., Purvaja, R., Ramesh, R., Senthil Vel, A., & Thirunavukkarasu, E. (2016). A Political, Economic, Social, Technological, Legal and Environmental (PESTLE) approach for assessment of coastal zone management practice in India. *International Review of Public Administration, 21*(3), 216–232. doi:10.1080/12294659.2016.1237091

St-Jean, E., Julien, P. A., & Audet, J. (2008). Factors associated with growth changes in" gazelles. *Journal of Enterprising Culture, 16*(02), 161–188. doi:10.1142/S0218495808000089

Tajaddini, R., Mujtaba, B. G., & Bandenezhad, M. (2010). Management skills of Iranians: A comparison of technical, human and conceptual differences based on gender, age and longevity in management ranks. *Labour and Management in Development, 10*.

Tan, H. (2009). *Evaluating SME support programs in Chile using panel firm data.* World Bank Policy Research Working Paper, (5082).

Tan, W. C., & Tay, R. S. (1995). Factors contributing to the growth of SMEs: The Singapore case. *Journal of Enterprising Culture, 3*(02), 197–210. doi:10.1142/S0218495895000106

Thompson Agyapong, G., Mmieh, F., & Mordi, C. (2018). Factors influencing the growth of SMEs: The case of Ghana. *Thunderbird International Business Review, 60*(4), 549–563. doi:10.1002/tie.21945

Timmons, J. A., & Spinelli, S. (1994). *New venture creation: Entrepreneurship for the 21st century*. Irwin Homewood.

Trang, T. K. (2016). Key success factors of SME entrepreneurs: Empirical study in Vietnam. *International Journal of Business and Management, 11*(1), 136.

Vixathep, S. (2014). Entrepreneurship, government policy and performance of SMEs in Laos (No. 28). Graduate School of International Cooperation Studies, Kobe University.

Wang, Y. (2016). What are the biggest obstacles to growth of SMEs in developing countries?–An empirical evidence from an enterprise survey. *Borsa Istanbul Review, 16*(3), 167–176. doi:10.1016/j.bir.2016.06.001

Welter, F., Smallbone, D., Slonimski, A., Linchevskaya, O., Pobol, A., & Slonimska, M. (2012). Enterprising families in a hostile environment for entrepreneurship (No. 2012-1). Jönköping International Business School.

Wijewardena, H., Nanayakkara, G., & De Zoysa, A. (2008). The owner/manager's mentality and the financial performance of SMEs. *Journal of Small Business and Enterprise Development, 15*(1), 150–161. doi:10.1108/14626000810850892

Yaron, J., Benjamin, M. P., & Piprek, G. L. (1997). *Rural finance: Issues, design, and best practices* (Vol. 14). World Bank.

Yusufu, O. S., Suleiman, O., & Saliu, H. T. (2020). Effect of micro finance bank on the growth of Small and Medium Enterprises in Nigeria. *KIU Interdisciplinary Journal of Humanities and Social Sciences*, *1*(2), 127–142.

Zhiri, D. D. (2017). Impact of micro-finance services on performance of small and medium scale enterprises (SMEs) In Zaria metropolis. *International Journal of Scientific Research in Social Sciences & Management Studies*, *2*(1), 49–65.

Zhou, H., Wit, G. D., A, H. Z., & B, G. D. W. (2009). *EIM Research Reports reference number*. https://www.un.org/en/development/desa/population/publications/pdf/popfacts/popfacts_2010-6.pdf

Compilation of References

Ab Hamid, M. R., Sami, W., & Sidek, M. M. (2017, September). Discriminant validity assessment: Use of Fornell & Larcker criterion versus HTMT criterion. *Journal of Physics: Conference Series*, *890*(1), 012163. doi:10.1088/1742-6596/890/1/012163

Abdelmoumni, F., Ackerman, C., Barry, N., Chao-Beroff, R., Choudhury, S., Counts, A.. ... Stauffenberg, D. v. (2008). *The Pocantico Declaration*. Retrieved from https://www.smartcampaign.org/storage/documents/Pocantico_Declaration.pdf

Abdullah, W. M. Z. B. W., Zainudin, W. N. R. A. B., Ismail, S. B., Haat, M. H. C., & Zia-Ul-Haq, H. M. (2021). The Impact of Microfinance on Households' Socioeconomic Performance: A Proposed Mediation Model. *The Journal of Asian Finance. Economics and Business*, *8*(3), 821–832.

Abed, S. S. (2021). A literature review exploring the role of technology in business survival during the Covid-19 lockdowns. *The International Journal of Organizational Analysis*.

Abidoye, R. B., Junge, M., Lam, T. Y., Oyedokun, T. B., & Tipping, M. L. (2019). Property valuation methods in practice: evidence from Australia. *Property Management*.

Abraham, F., & Schmukler, S. L. (2017). Addressing the SME finance problem. *World Bank Research and Policy Briefs*, (120333).

Abu-Bader, S., & Jones, T. V. (2021). Statistical mediation analysis using the sobel test and hayes SPSS process macro. *International Journal of Quantitative and Qualitative Research Methods*.

AbuDeif, S. (2016). *The Role of Microfinance in alleviating unemployment in Egypt: Quantitative study*. Retrieved from www.amarabac.com

Acha Ikechukwu, A., & Acha, I. (2012). Microfinance banking in Nigeria: Problems and prospects. *International Journal of Finance and Accounting*, *1*(5), 106–111.

Acheampong, G. (2018). Microfinance, gender and entrepreneurial behaviour of families in Ghana. *Journal of Family Business Management*, *8*(1), 38–57. doi:10.1108/JFBM-09-2017-0028

Acs, Z. J., Desai, S., & Hessels, J. (2008). Entrepreneurship, economic development and institutions. *Small Business Economics*, *31*(3), 219–234. doi:10.100711187-008-9135-9

Adam, A. M. (2020). Sample size determination in survey research. *Journal of Scientific Research and Reports, 26*(5), 90–97. doi:10.9734/jsrr/2020/v26i530263

Addae-Korankye, A. (2020). Historical emergence of microfinance and the microfinance sector in Ghana. *Business Management Dynamics, 10*(2), 1.

Addae-Korankye, A., & Abada, A. (2017). Microfinance and women empowerment in Madina in Accra, Ghana. *Asian Economic and Financial Review, 7*(3), 222–231. doi:10.18488/journal.aefr/2017.7.3/102.3.222.231

Addai, B., 2017. Women empowerment through microfinance: Empirical evidence from Ghana. *Journal of finance and accounting, 5*(1), pp.1-11.

Adhariani, D. (2022). Microfinance and the role of accounting in supporting family-resilience-based women's empowerment. *Qualitative Report, 27*(2), 366–384. doi:10.46743/2160-3715/2022.4249

Adhikari, S. (2021). Role of gender diversity on banking performance in Kathmandu Valley. *Quest Journal of Management and Social Sciences, 53*(9), 1689–1699.

Adusei, M. (2021). Interest Rate and the Social Performance of Microfinance Institutions. *The Quarterly Review of Economics and Finance, 80*, 21–30. doi:10.1016/j.qref.2021.01.009

Adusei, M., & Adeleye, N. (2021). Start-up microenterprise financing and financial performance of microfinance institutions. *Journal of Small Business and Entrepreneurship*, 1–24. doi:10.1080/08276331.2020.1842047

Afonso, J. S., Morvant-Roux, S., Guérin, I., & Forcella, D. (2017). Doing Good by Doing Well? Microfinance, Self-Regulation and Borrowers' Over-indebtedness in the Dominican Republic. *Journal of International Development, 29*(7), 919–935. doi:10.1002/jid.3244

Agarwal, S., Qian, W., & Tan, R. (2020). Financial inclusion and financial technology. In Household finance (pp. 307-346). Palgrave Macmillan. doi:10.1007/978-981-15-5526-8_9

Ahmad, A. H., Green, C., & Jiang, F. (2020). Mobile money, financial inclusion and development: A review with reference to African experience. *Journal of Economic Surveys, 34*(4), 753–792. doi:10.1111/joes.12372

Ahmad, N. H., & Seet, P. S. (2009). Understanding business success through the lens of SME founder-owners in Australia and Malaysia. *International Journal of Entrepreneurial Venturing, 1*(1), 72–87. doi:10.1504/IJEV.2009.023821

Ajzen, I. (1985). From intentions to actions: A theory of planned behavior. *Action Control*, 11–39. doi:10.1007/978-3-642-69746-3_2

Akhter, J., & Cheng, K. (2020). Sustainable empowerment initiatives among rural women through microcredit borrowings in Bangladesh. *Sustainability, 12*(6), 2275. doi:10.3390u12062275

Al Mamun, A., & Hayat, N. (2019). Microcredit and microenterprises performance in Malaysia. [IJABE]. *International Journal of Applied Behavioral Economics*, *8*(2), 1–13. doi:10.4018/IJABE.2019040101

Alam, P. and Azad, I., 2021. Impact of Microfinance on income and employment of women in Jigjiga, Ethiopia. *Int. J. Econ. Bus. Adm*, 373-381.

Alam, P. and Azad, I., 2021. Impact of Microfinance on income and employment of women in Jigjiga, Ethiopia. *Int. J. Econ. Bus. Adm*, pp.373-381.

Al-Amin, M. and Mamun, H.A.R., 2022. Exploring the impact of microfinance on socio-economic development: Empirical evidence from Balunnaghar Village. *International Journal of Social Science and Human Research ISSN (print)*, 2644-0679.

Alam, M., Gale, A., Brown, M., & Khan, A. I. (2010). The importance of human skills in project management professional development. *International Journal of Managing Projects in Business*, *3*(3), 495–516. doi:10.1108/17538371011056101

Alaoui, Y. L., & Tkiouat, M. (2017). Assessing the Performance of Microfinance Lending Process Using AHP-Fuzzy Comprehensive Evaluation Method: Moroccan Case Study. *International Journal of Engineering Business Management*, *9*, 1–11. doi:10.1177/1847979017736692

Albastiki, N., & Hamdan, A. (2019, September). Financial illiteracy and entrepreneurship success: literature review. In *European Conference on Innovation and Entrepreneurship*. Academic Conferences International Limited.

Alfaro, G. L. N. (1999). *Sostenibilidad y Alcance en Instituciones Financieras de Desarrollo Pa ra la Micro y Pequena Empresa: Un Modelo Aplicado a Tres Casos de Estudio (Ademi Inc., Bancosol, S.A. y Génesis Empresarial)*. INCAE, Cento de Políticas Pủblicas.

Alhassan, Y., Salia, S., & Nwagbara, U. 2022. Microfinance Impact on Microbusiness Development in Africa: Evidence from a Control Group Experiment in Ghana. In Microfinance and Sustainable Development in Africa (pp. 1-26). IGI Global.

Alhassan, Y., Kuagbela, F., Nurokina, C. D., & Appiah, B. (2022). *The Role of Microfinance in Africa: A Review of Outcomes from Ghana and Nigeria*. Microfinance and Sustainable Development in Africa.

Alhassan, Y., Kuagbela, F., Nurokina, C. D., & Appiah, B. (2022). *The Role of Microfinance in Africa: A Review of Outcomes From Ghana and Nigeria*. Microfinance and Sustainable Development in Africa.

Alhassan, Y., & Nwagbara, U. (Eds.). (2021). *Microfinance and Sustainable Development in Africa*. IGI Global.

Alhassan, Y., Nwagbara, U., & Salia, S. (2022). Analysis of Factors That Affect the Use of Microfinance for Microbusiness Development in Ghana. In *Microfinance and Sustainable Development in Africa* (pp. 103–126). IGI Global. doi:10.4018/978-1-7998-7499-7.ch005

Allet, M. (2014). Why Do Microfinance Institutions Go Green? An Exploratory Study. *Journal of Business Ethics*, *122*(3), 405–424. doi:10.100710551-013-1767-2

Allua, S., & Thompson, C. B. (2009). Inferential Statistics. *Air Medical Journal*, *28*(4), 168–171. doi:10.1016/j.amj.2009.04.013 PMID:19573763

Al-Mamun, A., Wahab, S. A., Mazumder, M. N. H., & Su, Z. (2014). Empirical investigation on the impact of microcredit on women empowerment in urban Peninsular Malaysia. *Journal of Developing Areas*, *48*(2), 287–306. doi:10.1353/jda.2014.0030

Alnaa, S. E. (2017). Microcredit to rural women, intra-household power play and employment creation in Northern Ghana. *Journal of Interdisciplinary Economics*, *29*(2), 197–213. doi:10.1177/0260107916688388

Al-shami, S. A., Al Mamun, A., Rashid, N., & Al-shami, M. (2021). Microcredit Impact on Socio-Economic Development and Women Empowerment in Low-Income Countries: Evidence from Yemen. *Sustainability*, *13*(16), 9326. doi:10.3390u13169326

Al-Shami, S. S. A., Razali, R. M., & Rashid, N. (2018). The effect of microcredit on women empowerment in welfare and decisions making in Malaysia. *Social Indicators Research*, *137*(3), 1073–1090. doi:10.100711205-017-1632-2

Alshater, M. M., Atayah, O. F., & Khan, A. (2022). What do we know about business and economics research during COVID-19: A bibliometric review. *Economic Research-Ekonomska Istraživanja*, *35*(1), 1884–1912. doi:10.1080/1331677X.2021.1927786

Alter Chen, M. (2005). *Rethinking the informal economy: Linkages with the formal economy and the formal regulatory environment* (No. 2005/10). WIDER Research Paper.

Alvi, E., & Senbeta, A. (2012). Does foreign aid reduce poverty? *Journal of International Development*, *24*(8), 955–976. doi:10.1002/jid.1790

Ampaw, E. M., Nte-Adik, N. M., Azaare, J., Adu-Sackey, A., Essah, B. O., & Amuzu, G. (2022). Embracing mobile financial inclusion in the wake of Covid-19 pandemic: The mediating role of cognitive and affective-based trust embeddedness. *International Journal of Technology and Management Research*, *7*(1), 1–22. doi:10.47127/ijtmr.v7i1.148

Anderson, F. 2019. *Assessment of the role of microfinance on women empowerment in Nsawam* [Doctoral dissertation, University of Cape Coast].

Angelucci, M., Karlan, D., & Zinman, J. (2015). Microcredit impacts: Evidence from a randomized microcredit program placement experiment by Compartamos Banco. *American Economic Journal. Applied Economics*, *7*(1), 151–182. doi:10.1257/app.20130537

Annim, S. K. (2018). Outreach and the poverty-reducing effect of microfinance in Ghana. *Enterprise Development & Microfinance*, *29*(2), 145–171. doi:10.3362/1755-1986.17-00020

Armendariz, B., & Labie, M. (Eds.). (2011). *The handbook of microfinance*. World Scientific. doi:10.1142/7645

Arora, M., & Singh, S. (2018a). Impact Assessment of Self-Help Group Bank Linkage Programme on Women Empowerment in the State of Himachal Pradesh. Academic Press.

Arora, M., & Singh, S. (2015). An Evaluation of the Non Performing Assets of Public and Private Sector Banks Under the SHG Bank Linkage Programme. *Indian Journal of Finance*, *9*(6), 41–50. doi:10.17010/ijf/2015/v9i6/71161

Arora, M., & Singh, S. (2016). Disbursement of credit under the SGSY scheme: A comparison of SHGs' swarozgaris and individual swarozgaris. *Indian Journal of Finance*, *10*(11), 54–63. doi:10.17010/ijf/2016/v10i11/104918

Arora, M., & Singh, S. (2017). Role of Financial Institutions in Promoting Microfinance through SHG Bank Linkage Programme in India. *Pacific Business Review International*, *10*(4), 50–58.

Arora, M., & Singh, S. (2018b). Microfinance, Women Empowerment, and Transformational Leadership: A Study of Himachal Pradesh. *International Journal on Leadership*, *6*(2), 23.

Arora, M., & Singh, S. (2018c). The Impact of SHG Bank Linkage Programme on the Members of Self Help Groups: An Empirical Investigation in the State of Himachal Pradesh. *Sumedha Journal of Management*, *7*(1), 34–46.

Arora, M., & Singh, S. (2022). Microfinance for achieving Sustainable Development Goals: Pondering Over Indian Experiences for the Preservation of Magnificent African Natural Resources. In *Microfinance and Sustainable Development in Africa* (pp. 82–102). IGI Global. doi:10.4018/978-1-7998-7499-7.ch004

Arun, T., & Kamath, R. (2015). Financial inclusion: Policies and practices. *IIMB Management Review*, *27*(4), 267–287. doi:10.1016/j.iimb.2015.09.004

Asad, A., Hameed, W. U., Irfan, M., Jiang, J., & Naveed, R. T. (2020). The Contribution of Microfinance Institutes in Women-Empowerment and role of Vulnerability. *Revista Argentina de Clínica Psicológica*, 223–238.

Asante, M. K., Brandon, G., Hall, R. L., Gaston, J. R., Maultsby, P. K., Philip, J. E., & Williams, S. W. (2005). *Africanisms in American culture*. Indiana University Press.

Ashamu, S. O. (2014). The impact of micro-finance on small scale business in Nigeria. *Journal of Policy and Development Studies*, *9*(1), 179–193. doi:10.12816/0011191

Ashraf, M. A. (2019). Theory of islamic entrepreneurship: A conceptual paper. *International Journal of Entrepreneurship*, *23*(3), 1–12.

Astawa, I. P., Astara, I. W. W., Mudana, I. G., & Dwiatmadja, C. (2021). Managing Sustainable Microfinance Institutions in the Covid-19 Situation through Revitalizing Balinese Cultural Identity. *Quality - Access to Success*, 131–137.

Autere, J., & Autio, A. (2000). Is entrepreneurship learned? Influence of mental models on growth motivation, strategy, and growth. In *Academy of Management Conference* (pp. 47-68). Academic Press.

Avgerou, C., Smith, M. L., & Van den Besselaar, P. (2008). *Social dimensions of information and communication technology policy*. Springer. doi:10.1007/978-0-387-84822-8

Avital, M., & Te'Eni, D. (2009). From generative fit to generative capacity: Exploring an emerging dimension of information systems design and task performance. *Information Systems Journal, 19*(4), 345–367. doi:10.1111/j.1365-2575.2007.00291.x

Awojobi, O. N. (2019). Microcredit as a strategy for poverty reduction in Nigeria: A systematic review of literature. *Global Journal of Social Sciences, 18*(1), 53–64. doi:10.4314/gjss.v18i1.5

Aybar-AriasC.Casino-MartinezA.Lopez-GraciaJ. (2003). Capital structure and sensitivity in SME definition: a panel data investigation. *Available at* SSRN 549082. doi:10.2139/ssrn.549082

Azam, S. F., & Abdullah, M. A. (2015). Differential roles between owner and manager in financial practice that contributes to business success: An analysis on Malaysian small business. *Academic Journal of Interdisciplinary Studies, 4*(1 S2), 123-123.

Aziz, A., Iqbal, J., Murtza, M. H., Gill, S. A., & Cheema, I. Y. (2022). Effect of Covid-19 pandemic on women entrepreneurial sustainability: the role of Islamic microfinance institutions. *Journal of Economic and Administrative Sciences.*

Babagana, S. A. (2010). Impact assessment of the role of micro finance banks in promoting small and medium enterprises growth in Nigeria. *International Journal of Economic Development Research and Investment, 1*(1), 42–53.

Bai, C., Quayson, M., & Sarkis, J. (2021). Covid-19 pandemic digitization lessons for sustainable development of micro-and small-enterprises. *Sustainable Production and Consumption, 27,* 1989-2001.

Bakhtiari, S. (2011). Microfinance and poverty reduction: Some international evidence. *International Business and Economics Research Journal (IBER), 5(12.* Banerjee, A., Duflo, E., Glennerster, R. and Kinnan, C., 2015. The miracle of microfinance? Evidence from a randomized evaluation. *American Economic Journal. Applied Economics*, 7(1), 22–53.

Bala, H., & Feng, X. (2019). Success of small and medium enterprises in Myanmar: Role of technological, organizational, and environmental factors. *Journal of Global Information Technology Management, 22*(2), 100–119. doi:10.1080/1097198X.2019.1603511

Balanagalakshmi, B., & Kumari, S. S. (2022). Impact of Covid on Micro Finance Institutions. *ECS Transactions, 107*(1), 10431–10438. doi:10.1149/10701.10431ecst

Bali Swain, R., & Wallentin, F. Y. (2017). The Impact of Microfinance on Factors Empowering Women: Differences in Regional and Delivery Mechanisms in India's SHG Programme. *The Journal of Development Studies, 53*(5), 684–699. doi:10.1080/00220388.2016.1205732

Bank of Ghana (2011). Operating Rules and Guidelines for Microfinance Institutions. Notice to Banks, Non-Bank Financial Institutions and the General Public. *Notice No: BG/GOV/SEC/2011/04*

Barder, O. M. 2009. What is poverty reduction? *Center for Global Development Working Paper*, (170).

Barsoum, G. (2006). Who gets credit? The gendered division of microfinance programs in Egypt. *Canadian Journal of Development Studies*, *27*(1), 51–64. doi:10.1080/02255189.2006.9669120

Bartington, S. E., Bakolis, I., Devakumar, D., Kurmi, O. P., Gulliver, J., Chaube, G., Manandhar, D. S., Saville, N. M., Costello, A., Osrin, D., Hansell, A. L., & Ayres, J. G. (2017). Patterns of domestic exposure to carbon monoxide and particulate matter in households using biomass fuel in Janakpur, Nepal. *Environmental Pollution*, *220*(8), 38–45. doi:10.1016/j.envpol.2016.08.074 PMID:27707597

Bateman, M. (2012). The role of microfinance in contemporary rural development finance policy and practice: Imposing neoliberalism as 'best practice'. *Journal of Agrarian Change*, *12*(4), 587–600. doi:10.1111/j.1471-0366.2012.00376.x

Beck, T. (2015). *Microfinance*. Independent Evaluation Group.

Beck, T., & Demirguc-Kunt, A. (2006). Small and medium-size enterprises: Access to finance as a growth constraint. *Journal of Banking & Finance*, *30*(11), 2931–2943. doi:10.1016/j.jbankfin.2006.05.009

Beck, T., Demirguc-Kunt, A., & Levine, R. (2005). SMEs, growth, and poverty: Cross-country evidence. *Journal of Economic Growth*, *10*(3), 199–229. doi:10.100710887-005-3533-5

Beck, T., Senbet, L., & Simbanegavi, W. (2015). Financial inclusion and innovation in Africa: An overview. *Journal of African Economies*, *24*(suppl_1), i3–i11. doi:10.1093/jae/eju031

Bedaiwy, S., & Peter, D. (2022). An evaluation of Egyptian microfinance laws and regulations preventing overindebtedness of women. *Journal of International Development*, 1–16. doi:10.1002/jid.3633

Bédécarrats F., Angora R.W., and Lapenu C., (2009). Is Social Performance Profitable? The Relationship between Social and Financial Performance in Microfinance. *Feature Articles, MicroBanking Bulletin, 19.*

Beecher, J. A. (2001). Privatization, Monopoly, and Structured Competition in the Water Industry: Is there a role for regulation? *Environmental consequences of privatising water services in Germany*, 327-339.

Benni, N. (2021). *Digital finance and inclusion in the time of Covid-19: Lessons, experiences and proposals*. Food & Agriculture Org.

Berger, A. N. (2006). Potential competitive effects of Basel II on banks in SME credit markets in the United States. *Journal of Financial Services Research*, *29*(1), 5–36. doi:10.100710693-005-5106-3

Bernards, N. (2019). Fintech and Financial Inclusion. In T. M. Shaw, L. C. Mahrenbach, R. Modi, & X. Yi-chong (Eds.), *The Palgrave Handbook of Contemporary International Political Economy* (pp. 317–329). Palgrave Macmillan. doi:10.1057/978-1-137-45443-0_20

Bhatt, N., & Tang, S. Y. (2001). Delivering Microfinance in Developing Countries: Controversies and Policy Perspective. *Policy Studies Journal: the Journal of the Policy Studies Organization, 29*(2), 319–333. doi:10.1111/j.1541-0072.2001.tb02095.x

Bhide, A. (1996). The questions every entrepreneur must answer. *Harvard Business Review, 74*(6), 120.

Bianchi, A. (1993). Who's most likely to go it alone? *Inc., 15*(5), 58.

Bibars, I. (2019). *Transforming Society ~ How micro-credit helped women in Egypt have a choice*. Retrieved October 29, 2019, from http://www.transformingsociety.co.uk/2019/07/02/how-micro-credit-helped-women-in-egypt-have-a-choice/

Bika, Z., Subalova, M., & Locke, C. (2022). Microfinance and small business development in a transitional economy: Insights from borrowers' relations with microfinance organisations in Kazakhstan. *The Journal of Development Studies, 58*(1), 183–203. doi:10.1080/00220388.2021.1956472

Bindu, A., & Aanchal, S. (2013). A comprehensive literature on impacts of microfinance. *Online International Interdisciplinary Research Journal: An International Multidisciplinary Journal, 3*(5), 346–358.

Bisht, N. S., Trusson, C., Siwale, J., & Ravishankar, M. N. (2021). Enhanced job satisfaction under tighter technological control: The paradoxical outcomes of digitalisation. *New Technology, Work and Employment*, ntwe.12222. doi:10.1111/ntwe.12222

Bjerner, J., Theodorsson, E., Hovig, E., & Kallner, A. (2009). Non-parametric estimation of reference intervals in small non-Gaussian sample sets. *Accreditation and Quality Assurance, 14*(4), 185–192. doi:10.100700769-009-0490-2

Boata, A., Gerdes, K., & Risk, D. C. (2019). *European regulatory changes will make banks less willing to lend to SMEs*. Euler Hermes Global.

Boateng, A.A., 2015. An examination of challenges and prospects of microfinance institutions in Ghana. *Journal of economics and sustainable development, 6*(4), pp.52-60.

Boateng, G. O., Boateng, A. A., & Bampoe, H. S. (2015). Microfinance and poverty reduction in Ghana: Evidence from policy beneficiaries. *Review of Business & Finance Studies, 6*(1), 99–108.

Boiral, O., Brotherton, M. C., Rivaud, L., & Guillaumie, L. (2021). Organizations' management of the COVID-19 pandemic: A scoping review of business articles. *Sustainability, 13*(7), 3993. doi:10.3390u13073993

Bouazza, A. B., Ardjouman, D., & Abada, O. (2015). Establishing the factors affecting the growth of small and medium-sized enterprises in Algeria. *American International Journal of Social Science*, *4*(2), 101–115.

Boussetta, A. (2022). Microfinance, Poverty and Education. *Comparative Economic Studies*, *64*(1), 86–108. doi:10.105741294-021-00145-4

Brickell, K., Picchioni, F., Natarajan, N., Guermond, V., Parsons, L., Zanello, G., & Bateman, M. (2020). Compounding crises of social reproduction: Microfinance, over-indebtedness and the COVID-19 pandemic. *World Development*, *136*, 105087. doi:10.1016/j.worlddev.2020.105087 PMID:32834384

Brown, R. (2007). Promoting entrepreneurship in arts education. *Entrepreneurship in the creative industries: an international perspective*, 126-141

Brown, J. D., Earle, J. S., & Lup, D. (2005). What makes small firms grow? Finance, human capital, technical assistance, and the business environment in Romania. *Economic Development and Cultural Change*, *54*(1), 33–70. doi:10.1086/431264

Bryman, A. (2004). Social Research Methods (2nd Ed), Oxford University Press.

Bryman, A., & Bell, E. (2007). *Business Research Methods* (2nd ed.). Oxford University Press.

Cai, S., Park, A., & Wang, S. 2020. Microfinance can raise incomes: evidence from a randomized control trial in China. *HKUST Business School Research Paper*, (2020-006).

Carver, C. S. (2012). *Self-awareness*. Academic Press.

CGAP. (2006). *Performance Indicators for Microinsurance Practitioners*. Consultative Group to Assist the Poorest (CGAP) Working Group on Microinsurance Workshop Report, Luxembourg.

Chemin, M. (2008). The benefits and costs of microfinance: Evidence from Bangladesh. *The Journal of Development Studies*, *44*(4), 463–484. doi:10.1080/00220380701846735

Chen, R., & Divanbeigi, R. (2019). *Can Regulation Promote Financial Inclusion?* World Bank Policy Research Working Paper, No. 8711.

Chen, M. F., & Tung, P. J. (2014). Developing an extended theory of planned behavior model to predict consumers' intention to visit green hotels. *International Journal of Hospitality Management*, *36*, 221–230. doi:10.1016/j.ijhm.2013.09.006

Chen, Z., & Jin, M. (2017). Financial inclusion in China: Use of credit. *Journal of Family and Economic Issues*, *38*(4), 528–540. doi:10.100710834-017-9531-x

Cheston, S., & Reed, L. (1999). Measuring Transformation: Assessing and Improving the Impact of Microcredit. *Journal of Microfinance*, *1*(1), 20–43.

Chhorn, D. (2021). Microfinance illusion, poverty and welfare in Cambodia. *Journal of the Asia Pacific Economy*, *26*(4), 694–719. doi:10.1080/13547860.2020.1826074

Chikalipah, S. (2017). Institutional Environment and Microfinance Performance in Sub-Saharan Africa. *African Development Review*, *29*(1), 16–27. doi:10.1111/1467-8268.12235

Chitimira, H., & Ncube, M. (2020). Legislative and Other Selected Challenges Affecting Financial Inclusion for the Poor and Low-Income Earners in South Africa. *Journal of African Law*, *64*(3), 337–355. doi:10.1017/S0021855320000182

Chit, M. M. (2019). Financial information credibility, legal environment, and SMEs' access to finance. *International Journal of the Economics of Business*, *26*(3), 329–354. doi:10.1080/13571516.2019.1645379

Chomen, D. A. (2021). The role of microfinance institutions on poverty reduction in Ethiopia: The case of Oromia Credit and Saving Share Company at Welmera district. *Future Business Journal*, *7*(1), 1–10. doi:10.118643093-021-00082-9

Chowdhury, M. S., Ahmmed, F., & Hossain, I. (2020). Methodological dilemma in microfinance research: Applicability of a qualitative case study design. *Qualitative Report*, *25*(2), 271–290. doi:10.46743/2160-3715/2020.3962

Chowk, B. (2020). Microfinance as an instrument for economic and social benefits to women : Andréa parent centre for microfinance Nepal centre for microfinance Nepal. *Knowledge Services for Institutions Serving the Poor*.

Christen, R. P. (2001). Commercialisation and Mission Drift: The Transformation of Microfinance in Latin America. Consultative Group to Assist the Poor (CGAP), *Occasional Paper No 5*. Washington, D.C.

Čihák, M., Mare, D. S., & Melecky, M. (2021). Financial Inclusion and Stability: Review of Theoretical and Empirical Links. *The World Bank Research Observer*, *36*(2), 197–233. doi:10.1093/wbro/lkaa006

Cooke, E. F., & Amuakwa-Mensah, F. (2022). Microfinance loans, women's economic empowerment, and poverty: A case study of Baobab Microfinance Company. *Journal of Development Effectiveness*, *14*(1), 34–55. doi:10.1080/19439342.2021.1953568

Copestake, J. (2007). Mainstreaming Microfinance: Social Performance Management or Mission Drift? *World Development*, *35*(10), 1721–1738. doi:10.1016/j.worlddev.2007.06.004

Copestake, J. (2007b). Mission Drift-Understand It. Avoid It. Perspectives. *ESR Review*, *9*(2), 21–25.

Crépon, B., Devoto, F., Duflo, E., & Parienté, W. (2011). *Impact of microcredit in rural areas of Morocco: Evidence from a Randomized Evaluation*. MIT Working Paper.

Crépon, B., Devoto, F., Duflo, E., & Pariente, W. (2014), *Estimating the impact of microcredit on those who take it up: Evidence from a randomized experiment in Morocco*. Working Paper, MIT.

Cull, R., Demirguc-Kunt, A., & Morduch, J. (2009). Microfinance Trade-offs: Regulation, Competition and Financing. *The Handbook of Microfinance, world Scientific Publishing*. https://www.worldscibooks.com/economics/7645.html

Czura, K., Englmaier, F., Ho, H., & Spantig, L. (2022). Microfinance loan officers before and during Covid-19: Evidence from India. *World Development*, *152*, 105812. doi:10.1016/j.worlddev.2022.105812 PMID:35035030

Daher, L., & Le Saout, E. (2013). Microfinance and Financial Performance. *Strategic Change*, *22*(1-2), 31–45. doi:10.1002/jsc.1920

Dandapat, A., & Das, P. (2022). Role of Microfinance to Promote the Growth of Unorganized Manufacturing Enterprises in India: An Analysis. In Microfinance to Combat Global Recession and Social Exclusion (pp. 131-146). Palgrave Macmillan.

Darko, F. 2015. Microfinance and Poverty Reduction: The Case Study of Selected Institutions in the Greater Accra Region of Ghana. In Microfinance and the Millennium Development Goals: Achievements and Strategies for Post 2015 (p. 1).

David, K. B., Aborode, A. T., Olaoye, D. Q., Enang, N. V., Oriyomi, A. K., & Yunusa, I. (2021). Increased risk of death triggered by domestic violence, hunger, suicide, exhausted health system during COVID-19 pandemic: Why, how and solutions. *Frontiers in Sociology*, *6*, 648395. doi:10.3389/fsoc.2021.648395 PMID:34169112

Davidsson, P., Achtenhagen, L., & Naldi, L. (2010). *Small firm growth*. Now Publishers Inc. doi:10.1561/0300000029

De Aghion, B. A., Armendáriz, B., & Morduch, J. (2007). *The economics of microfinance*. Academic Press.

De Koker, L., & Jentzsch, N. (2013). Financial inclusion and financial integrity: Aligned incentives? *World Development*, *44*, 267–280. doi:10.1016/j.worlddev.2012.11.002

Debnath, D., Rahman, M., Acharjee, D. C., Latif, W. U., & Wang, L. (2019). Empowering women through microcredit in Bangladesh: An empirical study. *International Journal of Financial Studies*, *7*(3), 37. doi:10.3390/ijfs7030037

Decker, M., Schiefer, G., & Bulander, R. (2006, August). Specific challenges for small and medium-sized enterprises (SME) in M-business. In *Proceedings of the International Conference on E-Business (ICE-B 2006)* (pp. 169-174). INSTICC Press.

Deininger, K., & Liu, Y. (2013). Evaluating program impacts on mature self-help groups in India. *The World Bank Economic Review*, *27*(2), 272–296. doi:10.1093/wber/lhs028

Dhungana, B. R. (2021). Impact of micro-finance on women : A case of Lekhnath municipality of Nepal impact of micro-finance on women : A case of Lekhnath municipality of Nepal. *The Lumbini Journal of Business and Economics*, *3*(2), 76–84.

Dhungana, B. R., Singh, J. K., Acharya, D., Gautam, S., & Paudyal, P. (2016). Perceived usefulness of a microfinance intervention on health awareness and practices in Nepal. *Frontiers in Public Health, 3*(1), 1–7. doi:10.3389/fpubh.2015.00289 PMID:26835443

Doern, R. (2009). Investigating barriers to SME growth and development in transition environments: A critique and suggestions for developing the methodology. *International Small Business Journal, 27*(3), 275–305. doi:10.1177/0266242609102275

Doh, S., & Kim, B. (2014). Government support for SME innovations in the regional industries: The case of government financial support program in South Korea. *Research Policy, 43*(9), 1557–1569. doi:10.1016/j.respol.2014.05.001

Drolet, J. (2011). Women, micro credit and empowerment in cairo, Egypt. *International Social Work, 54*(5), 629–645. doi:10.1177/0020872810382681

Duong, H. A., & Nghiem, H. S. (2014). Effects of microfinance on poverty reduction in Vietnam: A pseudo-panel data analysis. *Journal of Accounting. Finance and Economics, 4*(2), 58–67.

Dutta, A., & Fischer, H. W. (2021). The local governance of COVID-19: Disease prevention and social security in rural India. *World Development, 138*, 105234. doi:10.1016/j.worlddev.2020.105234 PMID:33106724

Duvendack, M., & Palmer-Jones, R. (2012). High noon for microfinance impact evaluations: Re-investigating the evidence from Bangladesh. *The Journal of Development Studies, 48*(12), 1864–1880. doi:10.1080/00220388.2011.646989

Duvendack, M., Palmer-Jones, R., Copestake, J. G., Hooper, L., Loke, Y., & Rao, N. (2011). What is the evidence of the impact of microfinance on the well-being of poor people? *Systematic Reviews*.

Duvendack, M., Palmer-Jones, R., & Vaessen, J. (2014). Meta-analysis of the impact of microcredit on women's control over household decisions: Methodological issues and substantive findings. *Journal of Development Effectiveness, 6*(2), 73–96. doi:10.1080/19439342.2014.903289

Dzansi, D. Y., & Atiase, V. Y. (2014). Reflecting on micro finance in poverty reduction. *Mediterranean Journal of Social Sciences, 5*(21), 345. doi:10.5901/mjss.2014.v5n21p345

Ebomuche, N. C., Ihugba, O. A. & Bankong, B., 2014. The impact of Nigeria microfinance banks on poverty reduction: Imo State experience. *International Letters of Social and Humanistic Sciences, (05),* pp. 92-113.

Effendi, I., Murad, M., Rafiki, A., & Lubis, M. M. (2020). The application of the theory of reasoned action on services of Islamic rural banks in Indonesia. *Journal of Islamic Marketing, 12*(5), 951–976. doi:10.1108/JIMA-02-2020-0051

Egypt Today. (2017). *MSMEDA provides LE 215M to micro, small projects in 2017*. Retrieved November 7, 2019, from https://www.egypttoday.com/Article/3/38247/MSMEDA-provides-LE-215Mto-micro-small-projects-in-2017

Elantary, S., & Ezzat, M. (2020). *Increasing Rural Women Financial Inclusion*. Retrieved from https://nwrcegypt.org/دليل-الشمول-المالى-وزيادة-فرص-العمل-لل/

Elena, M., Chavez, E., Kramer, R., Rangel, A. C., Garcia, E. M., & Santillan, A. G. (2015). Empirical evidence on locus of control among owner and manager and its relation to success firms. *Journal of Emerging Trends in Economics and Management Science*, *6*(3), 177–184.

Elgar, F. J., Stefaniak, A., & Wohl, M. J. (2020). The trouble with trust: Time-series analysis of social capital, income inequality, and COVID-19 deaths in 84 countries. *Social Science & Medicine*, *263*, 113365. doi:10.1016/j.socscimed.2020.113365 PMID:32981770

Elhadary, Y. A. E. and Samat, N., 2012. Political economy and urban poverty in the developing countries: Lessons learned from Sudan and Malaysia. *Journal of geography and Geology, 4*(1), 212.

El-Nasharty, H. (2022). The Role of Microfinance in Poverty Reduction, Countries Experiences by Regions 2000-2018. *International Journal of Social Sciences and Economic Review*, *4*(1), 01–09. doi:10.36923/ijsser.v4i1.101

Elsafi, M. H., Ahmed, E. M., & Ramanathan, S. (2020). The impact of microfinance programs on monetary poverty reduction. *World Journal of Entrepreneurship, Management and Sustainable Development*, *16*(1), 30–43. doi:10.1108/WJEMSD-05-2019-0036

Elzahi Saaid Ali, A. (2022). The Regulatory and Supervisory Frameworks of Microfinance from Islamic Perspective: The Case of Sudan. In Empowering the Poor through Financial and Social Inclusion in Africa (pp. 73-86). Palgrave Macmillan.

Epstein, M. J., & Manzoni, J. F. (2006). Performance Measurement and Management Control: Improving Organisations and Society. Studies in Managerial and Financial Accounting, 16. JAI Press (Elsevier).

Eric, A., Stephen, N. Y., Augustine, O. M., & Zakaria, A. (2022). The Role of Rural Banks in Micro Financing in Ghana. *Journal of Finance and Accounting*, *13*(8), 32–54.

Ewusie, E. A., Annim, S. K., & Brafu-Insaidoo, W. (2021). The density of microfinance institutions and multiple borrowing in Ghana: Are rural borrowers vulnerable? *Journal of International Development*, *33*(8), 1217–1237. doi:10.1002/jid.3551

Ezeanyeji, C.I., Usifoh, K.S., Obi, C.O. and Ejefobihi, U.F. (2020). Microfinancing, poverty alleviation and Nigeria's economic growth: the nexus. *European Journal of Economic and Financial Research.*

Farag, N. M. (2011). *Microfinance and Poverty Alleviation A Case Study of Al-Darb Al-Ahmar District in Cairo*. The American University in Cairo.

Fofana, N., Antonides, G., Niehof, A., & van Ophem, J. (2015). How microfinance empowers women in Côte d'Ivoire. *Review of Economics of the Household, 13*(4), 1023–1041. doi:10.100711150-015-9280-2

Forster, S., Lahaye, E., & Mckee, K. (2009). *Implementing the Client Protection Principles A Technical Guide for Investors*. Academic Press.

Gabbiadini, A., Baldissarri, C., Durante, F., Valtorta, R. R., De Rosa, M., & Gallucci, M. (2021). Corrigendum: Together Apart: The Mitigating Role of Digital Communication Technologies on Negative Affect during the Covid-19 Outbreak in Italy. *Frontiers in Psychology*, *12*, 701130. doi:10.3389/fpsyg.2021.701130 PMID:34122291

Gakpo, M. D. Y., Wujangi, M., Kwakye, M., & Asante, V. G. (2021). The impact of microfinancing on poverty alleviation and small businesses in ghana. *The International Journal of Social Sciences and Humanity Studies*, *13*(1), 1–28.

Gakpo, M. D. Y., Wujangi, M., Kwakye, M., & Asante, V. G. (2021). THE IMPACT OF Microfinancing on poverty alleviation and small businesses in Ghana. *The International Journal of Social Sciences and Humanity Studies*, *13*(1), 1–28.

Ganle, J. K., Afriyie, K., & Segbefia, A. Y. (2015). Microcredit: Empowerment and disempowerment of rural women in Ghana. *World Development*, *66*, 335–345. doi:10.1016/j.worlddev.2014.08.027

Gaskin, C. J., & Happell, B. (2014). On exploratory factor analysis: A review of recent evidence, an assessment of current practice, and recommendations for future use. *International Journal of Nursing Studies*, *51*(3), 511–521. doi:10.1016/j.ijnurstu.2013.10.005 PMID:24183474

Gathergood, J. (2012). Self-control, financial literacy and consumer over-indebtedness. *Journal of Economic Psychology*, *33*(3), 590–602. doi:10.1016/j.joep.2011.11.006

Ghosh, S., & Vinod, D. (2017). What constrains financial inclusion for women? Evidence from Indian micro data. *World Development*, *92*, 60–81. doi:10.1016/j.worlddev.2016.11.011

Goodman, P. (2006). Microfinance Investment Funds: Objectives, Players, Potential. Chapter 2 of Matthaus-Maier, I. and Pischke, J.D., (2006) (1 Ed.). In Microfinance Investment Funds. Leveraging Private Capital for Economic Growth and Poverty Reduction. Springer-Verlag Berlin Heidelberg: KfW.

Goto, M., & Negash, F. A. (2016). The Effect of Micro Finance Institutions in Growth and Development Small Business. *經濟學研究*, *66*(2), 67-90.

Gott, G. (2022). Microcredit and the Financial Frontiers of Racial Neoliberalism. *Journal of Law and Political Economy*, *2*(2). Advance online publication. doi:10.5070/LP62258228

Guérin, I., Morvant-Roux, S., & Villarreal, M. (2014). *Microfinance, Debt and Over-Indebtedness. Juggling with Money*. Routledge.

Gutiérrez-Nieto, B., Serrano-Cinca, C., & de la Cuesta González, M. (2017). A multivariate study of over-indebtedness' causes and consequences. *International Journal of Consumer Studies*, *41*(2), 188–198. doi:10.1111/ijcs.12324

Hadidi, H. E., & Kirby, D. A. (2015). Universities and innovation in a factor-driven economy: The Egyptian case. *Industry and Higher Education*, *29*(2), 151–160. doi:10.5367/ihe.2015.0248

Hagan, L. H. (2018). *The impact of Microfinance Institutions on Poverty reduction among entrepreneurs in Ghana. A case study in the Ga South Municipal Assembly* [Master's thesis, OsloMet–Oslo Metropolitan University].

Hagan, L. H. 2018. *The impact of Microfinance Institutions on Poverty reduction among entrepreneurs in Ghana. A case study in the Ga South Municipal Assembly* [Master's thesis, OsloMet–Oslo Metropolitan University].

Hagenaars, A. J. (2014). The perception of poverty, s.l.: Elsevier.

Haider S.H., Asad M., Fatima M., and Ul Abidin R.Z., (2017). Microfinance and Performance of Micro and Small Enterprises; Does Training Have An Impact. *Journal of Entrepreneurship and Business Innovation*, *4*(**1**)

Hair, J. F., Gabriel, M., & Patel, V. (2014). AMOS covariance-based structural equation modeling (CB-SEM): Guidelines on its application as a marketing research tool. *Brazilian Journal of Marketing*, *13*(2).

Hamid, A. L. I., & Nisser, I. (2017). Microfinance and Women's Empowerment in Egypt. *International Journal of Business and Economic Affairs*, *2*(1). Advance online publication. doi:10.24088/ijbea-2017-21007

Hartarska, V., Nadolnyak, D., & McAdams, T. (2013). Microfinance and microenterprises' financing constraints in Eastern Europe and Central Asia. In *Microfinance in developing countries* (pp. 22–35). Palgrave Macmillan. doi:10.1057/9781137301925_2

Hasan, N., Singh, A.K., Agarwal, M.K. and Kushwaha, B.P. (2022). Evaluating the role of microfinance institutions in enhancing the livelihood of urban poor. *Journal of Economic and Administrative Sciences*.

Hatta, Z. A., & Ali, I. (2013). Poverty reduction policies in Malaysia: Trends, strategies and challenges. *Asian Culture and History*, *5*(2), 48. doi:10.5539/ach.v5n2p48

Heacock, L., Weissbrot, J., Raad, R., Campbell, N., Friedman, K. P., Ponzo, F., & Chandarana, H. (2015). PET/MRI for the evaluation of patients with lymphoma: Initial observations. *AJR. American Journal of Roentgenology*, *204*(4), 842–848. doi:10.2214/AJR.14.13181 PMID:25794075

Hermes, N., & Lensink, R. 2021. Microfinance and development. Contemporary issues in development finance, pp.51-73.

Hermes, N., & Hudon, M. (2018). Determinants of the Performance of Microfinance Institutions: A Systematic Review. *Journal of Economic Surveys*, *32*(5), 1483–1513. doi:10.1111/joes.12290

Hoa, N. T. (2019). How large is Vietnam's informal economy? *Economic Affairs*, *39*(1), 81–100. doi:10.1111/ecaf.12328

Hockerts, K. (2017). Determinants of social entrepreneurial intentions. *Entrepreneurship Theory and Practice*, *41*(1), 105–130. doi:10.1111/etap.12171

Hossain, M. (2021). The effect of the Covid-19 on sharing economy activities. *Journal of Cleaner Production*, *280*, 124782. doi:10.1016/j.jclepro.2020.124782 PMID:33106734

Hossain, M. K. (2012). Assessment of social impact of Microfinance Operations: A study on BRAC. *Interdisciplinary Journal of Research in Business ISSN*, *2046*, 7141.

Hughes, D., Charles, J., Dawoud, D., Edwards, R. T., Holmes, E., Jones, C., Parham, P., Plumpton, C., Ridyard, C., Lloyd-Williams, H., Wood, E., & Yeo, S. T. (2016). Conducting economic evaluations alongside randomised trials: Current methodological issues and novel approaches. *PharmacoEconomics*, *34*(5), 447–461. doi:10.100740273-015-0371-y PMID:26753558

Hummel, K., & Schlick, C. (2016). The relationship between sustainability performance and sustainability disclosure – Reconciling voluntary disclosure theory and legitimacy theory. *Journal of Accounting and Public Policy*, *35*(5), 455–476. doi:10.1016/j.jaccpubpol.2016.06.001

Hussaini, U., & Chibuzo, I. C. (2018). The effects of financial inclusion on poverty reduction: The moderating effects of microfinance. *International Journal of Multidisciplinary Research and Development*, *5*(12), 188–198.

Hussain, J., Mahmood, S., & Scott, J. (2019). Gender, microcredit and poverty alleviation in a developing country: The case of women entrepreneurs in Pakistan. *Journal of International Development*, *31*(3), 247–270. doi:10.1002/jid.3403

IFC. (2010). *Scaling-Up SME Access to Financial Services in the Developing World*. Financial Inclusion Experts Group.

Imai, K. S., & Azam, M. S. (2012). Does microfinance reduce poverty in Bangladesh? New evidence from household panel data. *The Journal of Development Studies*, *48*(5), 633–653. doi:10.1080/00220388.2012.661853

Imai, K. S., Gaiha, R., Thapa, G., & Annim, S. K. (2012). Microfinance and poverty—A macro perspective. *World Development*, *40*(8), 1675–1689. doi:10.1016/j.worlddev.2012.04.013

Isaga, N. (2018). The relationship of personality to cognitive characteristics and SME performance in Tanzania. *Journal of Small Business and Enterprise Development*, *25*(4), 667–686. doi:10.1108/JSBED-02-2017-0067

Isaia, E. (2005). *Microcredit in Morocco: The Zakoura Foundation's Experience*. University of Turin.

Islam, T. (2012). *Microcredit and poverty alleviation*. Ashgate Publishing, Ltd.

Jain, S. (2022). Impact of Covid-19 on Financial Performance of Micro-Financing Institutions in India. *Journal of Management & Entrepreneurship, 267.*

James, M. and Jane, N. (2018). Role of Microfinance Institutions on the Promotion of Women Entrepreneurship in Uganda. *Available at SSRN 3176583.*

Jamil, M. I. M., & Almunawar, M. N. (2021). Importance of Digital Literacy and Hindrance Brought About by Digital Divide. In *Encyclopedia of Information Science and Technology* (5th ed., pp. 1683–1698). IGI Global. doi:10.4018/978-1-7998-3479-3.ch116

Janssens, W., Pradhan, M., de Groot, R., Sidze, E., Donfouet, H. P. P., & Abajobir, A. (2021). The short-term economic effects of COVID-19 on low-income households in rural Kenya: An analysis using weekly financial household data. *World Development*, *138*, 105280. doi:10.1016/j.worlddev.2020.105280

Jenkins, H. and Batinge, B.K., 2018. Microcredit and the Socio-cultural Obstacles to Women's Empowerment in Northern Territories of Ghana. *Kadin/Woman 2000, 19*(2).

Jha, A., Ranjan, S., Pradhan, P. K., & Jha, T. (2011). Challenges of setting up psychiatric services in Nepal: Lessons from the first year of Janakpur Project. *Asian Journal of Psychiatry*, *4*(4), 297–299. doi:10.1016/j.ajp.2011.10.004 PMID:23051166

Jorfi, S., Nor, K. M., & Najjar, L. (2011). Assessing the impact of IT connectivity and IT capability on IT-business strategic alignment: An empirical study. *Computer and Information Science*, *4*(3), 76. doi:10.5539/cis.v4n3p76

Kaberia, S. K., & Muathe, S. M. (2022). Economic Empowerment of the Poor: Myths and Facts about Microfinance Institutions in Africa. *International Journal of Social Science and Education Research Studies*, *2*(6), 179–186.

Kandil, M. (2018). Investigating determinants of youth's intentions of seeking microcredit in the post-conflict era. *The Electronic Library, 34*(1), 1–5.

Kanyugi, I. N. (2011). *The impact of micro-finance credit on the financial performance of SMEs in Kenya* [Doctoral dissertation].

Kar, A. K., & Bali Swain, R. (2018). Competition, Performance and Portfolio Quality in Microfinance Markets. *European Journal of Development Research*, *30*(5), 842–870. doi:10.105741287-018-0135-6

Karibo, F. B. (2022). *Determinants Of Financial And Operational Sustainability: Empirical Evidence from Microfinance Institutions (MFIS) in Ethiopia* (Doctoral dissertation).

Karlan, D. & Goldberg, N. (2007). Impact evaluation for microfinance: Review of methodological issues. *World Bank, Poverty Reduction and Economic Management, Thematic Group on Poverty Analysis, Monitoring and Impact Evaluation.*

Karmakar, K. G. (1999). *Rural credit and self-help groups: Micro-finance needs and concepts in India*. Sage Publications India Pvt Ltd.

Karmakar, K. G. (Ed.). (2008). *Microfinance in India*. SAGE Publications India.

Karn, S. K. (2018). Challenges and opportunities of microfinance in Nepal. *International Journal of Social Sciences and Management*, *5*(3), 72–75. doi:10.3126/ijssm.v5i3.20612

Kasser, T. (2009). Psychological need satisfaction, personal well-being, and ecological sustainability. *Ecopsychology, 1*(4), 175–180. doi:10.1089/eco.2009.0025

Kayastha, R. (2013). Current issues of microfinance in Nepal. *Yokohama Journal of Social Sciences, 18*(3), 71–83.

Keskġn, H., Ġentürk, C., Sungur, O., & Kġrġġ, H. M. (2010, June). The importance of SMEs in developing economies. In *2nd International Symposium on Sustainable Development* (pp. 183-192). Academic Press.

Ketchen, D. J. Jr, Ireland, R. D., & Webb, J. W. (2014). Toward a Research Agenda for the Informal Economy: A Survey of the Strategic Entrepreneurship Journal's Editorial Board. *Strategic Entrepreneurship Journal, 8*(1), 95–100. doi:10.1002ej.1175

Khan, A. A., Khan, S. U., Fahad, S., Ali, M. A., Khan, A., & Luo, J. (2021). Microfinance and poverty reduction: New evidence from Pakistan. *International Journal of Finance & Economics, 26*(3), 4723–4733. doi:10.1002/ijfe.2038

Khandker, S. (1998). *Fighting poverty with microcredit: experience in Bangladesh.* Retrieved from https://www.cabdirect.org/cabdirect/abstract/19991800156

Khandker, S. R., & Samad, H. A. (2014). Microfinance growth and poverty reduction in Bangladesh: What does the longitudinal data say? *Bangladesh Development Studies, 37*(1 & 2), 127–157.

Khan, M. M. H. (2000). *Rural poverty in developing countries: Issues and policies.* International Monetary Fund.

Khan, M., & Bedi, A. S. (2022). Returns to Interest-free Microcredit: Evidence from a Randomised Experiment in Pakistan. *Journal of Development Effectiveness, 14*(2), 93–107. doi:10.1080/19439342.2021.1964578

Khanna, T., & Palepu, K. (1999). *Emerging market business groups, foreign investors, and corporate governance.* Academic Press.

Khatibi, F. S., & Indira, M. (2011). Empowerment of women through self help groups and environmental management: Experiences of NGOs in Karnataka State, India. *Journal of Human Ecology (Delhi, India), 34*(1), 29–40. doi:10.1080/09709274.2011.11906366

Khoshnodifar, Z., Ghonji, M., Mazloumzadeh, S. M., & Abdollahi, V. (2016). Effect of communication channels on success rate of entrepreneurial SMEs in the agricultural sector (a case study). *Journal of the Saudi Society of Agricultural Sciences, 15*(1), 83–90. doi:10.1016/j.jssas.2014.04.001

Khursheed, A., Khan, A. A., & Mustafa, F. (2021). Women's social empowerment and microfinance: A brief review of literature. *Journal of International Women's Studies, 22*(5), 249–265.

Kiers, J., Seinhorst, J., Zwanenburg, M., & Stek, K. (2022). Which Strategies and Corresponding Competences Are Needed to Improve Supply Chain Resilience: A COVID-19 Based Review. *Logistics, 6*(1), 12. doi:10.3390/logistics6010012

Kiesel, K., & Noth, F. (2016). When Debt spells Sin: Does Religiosity guard against Over-Indebtedness? In *Annual Conference 2016 (Augsburg): Demographic Change* (No. 145774). Verein für Socialpolitik/German Economic Association.

Kiran, E. (2020). Prominent Issues About the Social Impacts of Covid 19. *Gaziantep University Journal of Social Sciences, 19*, 752-766.

Kitamura, Y., Karkour, S., Ichisugi, Y., & Itsubo, N. (2020). Evaluation of the economic, environmental, and social impacts of the COVID-19 pandemic on the japanese tourism industry. *Sustainability, 12*(24), 10302. doi:10.3390u122410302

Kizza, J., & Samali, N. (2022). Microfinance risk management, social mission and financial performance during the Covid-19 pandemic in Uganda. *American Journal of Finance, 7*(2), 13–22. doi:10.47672/ajf.1017

Koltay, T. (2011). The media and the literacies: Media literacy, information literacy, digital literacy. *Media Culture & Society, 33*(2), 211–221. doi:10.1177/0163443710393382

Kondo, T., Orbeta, A. Jr, Dingcong, C., & Infantado, C. (2008). Impact of microfinance on rural households in the Philippines. *IDS Bulletin, 39*(1), 51–70. doi:10.1111/j.1759-5436.2008.tb00432.x

Kozubíková, L., Čepel, M., & Zlámalová, M. (2018). *Attitude toward innovativeness based on personality traits in the SME sector. Czech Republic case study.* Management & Marketing-Challenges for the Knowledge Society. doi:10.2478/mmcks-2018-0013

Krasniqi, B. A. (2007). Barriers to entrepreneurship and SME growth in transition: The case of Kosova. *Journal of Developmental Entrepreneurship, 12*(01), 71–94. doi:10.1142/S1084946707000563

Kredel, H., & Weispfenning, V. (1988). Computing dimension and independent sets for polynomial ideals. *Journal of Symbolic Computation, 6*(2-3), 231–247. doi:10.1016/S0747-7171(88)80045-2

Kristof, N. D. (2009). The role of microfinance. *New York Times.*

Ksoll, C., Lilleør, H., Lønborg, J., & Rasmussen, O. (2016). Impact of Village Savings and Loan Associations: Evidence from a cluster randomized trial. *Journal of Development Economics, 120*, 70–85. doi:10.1016/j.jdeveco.2015.12.003

Kulkarni, L., & Ghosh, A. (2021). Gender disparity in the digitalization of financial services: Challenges and promises for women's financial inclusion in India. *Gender, Technology and Development, 25*(2), 233–250. doi:10.1080/09718524.2021.1911022

Kumari, J. A. P. (2021). The impact of the dimensions of microfinance on poverty reduction : Confirmatory factor analysis (CFA) via individual measurement models. *International Journal of Postharvest Technology and Innovation, 8*(2), 112–121.

Kumari, P. (2020). Theoretical Analysis of Microfinance on Poverty Alleviation. *Journal of Economic Info, 7*(3), 221–236. doi:10.31580/jei.v7i3.1709

Kumar, P., Sahu, S. K., & Kumar, R. (2021). An Analysis of Role of Microfinance Institutions In Inclusive Growth. *Kuwait Chapter of the Arabian Journal of Business and Management Review, 10*(4), 161–167. doi:10.12816/0059989

Kumar, S., & Das, S. (2019). An extended model of theory of planned behaviour: Entrepreneurial intention, regional institutional infrastructure and perceived gender discrimination in India. *Journal of Entrepreneurship in Emerging Economies, 11*(3), 369–391. doi:10.1108/JEEE-09-2018-0089

Kurter, O., & Husseini, İ. A. (2021). Evaluation of Strategic Management Issues Related To The Microfinance Industry And Small And Medium Enterprises In Afghanistan. *Uluslararası Finansal Ekonomi ve Bankacılık Uygulamaları Dergisi, 2*(2), 34–67.

Kwak, S., & Lee, J. (2014). *Financial Inclusion and Microfinance: On the Cases of ODA and Analysis of the Poverty Reduction Effect.* World Economic Update, 14-13.

Lacalle-Calderon, M., Perez-Trujillo, M., & Neira, I. (2018). Does microfinance reduce poverty among the poorest? A macro quantile regression approach. *The Developing Economies, 56*(1), 51–65. doi:10.1111/deve.12159

Lamont, L. M. (1972). What entrepreneurs learn from experience. *Journal of Small Business Management, 10*, 36.

Lam, S. S., Zhang, W., Ang, A. X., & Jacob, G. H. (2019). Reciprocity Between Financial and Social Performance in Microfinance Institutions. *Public Performance & Management Review, 43*(1), 206–231. doi:10.1080/15309576.2019.1604386

Lam, T. Y., & Maguire, D. A. (2012). Structural equation modeling: Theory and applications in forest management. *International Journal of Forestry Research.* doi:10.1155/2012/263953

Lapenu, C. (2007). *Recent Advances on Agricultural Finance: Supply and Strategies. A Review of Literature and Experience*. Paper for the International Conference "What Can Microfinance Contribute to Agriculture in Developing Countries?

Lee, K. H. (2009). Why and how to adopt green management into business organizations? The case study of Korean SMEs in manufacturing industry. *Management Decision, 47*(7), 1101–1121. doi:10.1108/00251740910978322

Lester, D. L., & Tran, T. T. (2008). Information technology capabilities: Suggestions for SME growth. *Journal of Behavioral and Applied Management, 10*(1), 72–88. doi:10.21818/001c.17169

Levy, M., & Powell, P. (2003). Exploring SME internet adoption: Towards a contingent model. *Electronic Markets, 13*(2), 173–181. doi:10.1080/1019678032000067163

Leyer, M., Heckl, D., & Moorman, J. (2015). Process Performance Measurement. In: vom Brocke J., and Rosemann., (2015). Hanbook on Business Process Management. 2nd (Ed). International Handbooks on Information Systems. Berlin, Heidelberg: Springer: 227-241. doi:10.1007/978-3-642-45103-4_9

Li Jr, F. F., & Fu, K. (2009). *Factors Influencing the Growth of Small and Medium Sized Firms in Different Growth Stages-A Study of Four Chinese SMEs*. Academic Press.

Lieberson, S., & O'Connor, J. F. (1972). Leadership and organizational performance: A study of large corporations. *American Sociological Review, 37*(2), 117–130. doi:10.2307/2094020 PMID:5020209

Llewellyn, D. T. (2021). *Introduction: financial inclusion-an overview of key issues*. Inclusive Financial Development.

Lloyd-Jones, T., & Rakodi, C. (2014). *Urban livelihoods: A people-centred approach to reducing poverty*. s.l.:Routledge. doi:10.4324/9781849773805

LockeS. (2004). ICT adoption and SME growth in New Zealand. Available at SSRN 3284905.

López, T., & Winkler, A. (2019). Does financial inclusion mitigate credit boom-bust cycles? *Journal of Financial Stability*, *43*, 116–129. doi:10.1016/j.jfs.2019.06.001

Lumpkin, G. T., & Dess, G. G. (1996). Clarifying the entrepreneurial orientation construct and linking it to performance. *Academy of Management Review*, *21*(1), 135–172. doi:10.2307/258632

Mader, P. (2017). How Much Voice for Borrowers? Restricted Feedback and Recursivity in Microfinance. *Global Policy*, *8*(4), 540–552. doi:10.1111/1758-5899.12474

Mader, P. (2018). Contesting financial inclusion. *Development and Change*, *49*(2), 461–483. doi:10.1111/dech.12368

Madhavi, B. H., & Wickramarachchi, R. (2022, September). Strategic Decision Making for a Resilient Supply Chain during a Pandemic. In *2022 International Research Conference on Smart Computing and Systems Engineering (SCSE)* (Vol. 5, pp. 303-308). IEEE. 10.1109/SCSE56529.2022.9905209

Madonda, A.E., Nyangarika, A. and Nombo, N. (2020). Impact of Youth Microfinance Asset's Ownership in Masasi Districts Council Mtwara Region. *IJARIIE-ISSN(O)-2395-4396, 6*(5), 1345-1353.

Mahmoud Ali, I. A., & Ghoneim, H. (2019). The effect of microfinance on income inequality: Perspective of developing countries. *Journal of Economics and Management*, *35*(1), 40–62. doi:10.22367/jem.2019.35.03

Makri, E., Spiliotopoulos, D., Vassilakis, C., & Margaris, D. (2020). Human behaviour in multimodal interaction: Main effects of civic action and interpersonal and problem-solving skills. *Journal of Ambient Intelligence and Humanized Computing*, *11*(12), 5991–6006. doi:10.100712652-020-01846-x

Malhotra, M. 2018. Role of Microfinance in Financial Inclusion in India. In Microfinance and Its Impact on Entrepreneurial Development, Sustainability, and Inclusive Growth (pp. 322-343). IGI Global. doi:10.4018/978-1-5225-5213-0.ch018

Mandal, K. C. 2013, May. Concept and Types of Women Empowerment. In *International Forum of Teaching & Studies, 9*(2).

Mani, M. (2016). Financial inclusion in South Asia—Relative standing, challenges and initiatives. *South Asian Survey, 23*(2), 158–179. doi:10.1177/0971523118783353

Mansori, S., Safari, M., & Mohd Ismail, Z. M. (2020). An analysis of the religious, social factors and income's influence on the decision making in Islamic microfinance schemes. *Journal of Islamic Accounting and Business Research, 11*(2), 361–376. doi:10.1108/JIABR-03-2016-0035

Manzano-León, A., Camacho-Lazarraga, P., Guerrero-Puerta, M. A., Guerrero-Puerta, L., Alias, A., Aguilar-Parra, J. M., & Trigueros, R. (2021). Development and validation of a questionnaire on motivation for cooperative playful learning strategies. *International Journal of Environmental Research and Public Health, 18*(3), 960. doi:10.3390/ijerph18030960 PMID:33499224

Martin, F., & Smith, R. (2010). What is it that entrepreneurs learn from experience? *Industry and Higher Education, 24*(6), 505–512. doi:10.5367/ihe.2010.0016

Masanyiwa, Z. S., Chusi, T. N., & Haji, A. U. (2022). Determinants for Sustainability of Microfinance Institutions in North "A" District in Zanzibar. *Open Journal of Business and Management, 10*(4), 1583–1600. doi:10.4236/ojbm.2022.104083

Maulana, H., Razak, D. A., & Adeyemi, A. A. (2018). Factors influencing behaviour to participate in Islamic microfinance. *International Journal of Islamic and Middle Eastern Finance and Management, 11*(1), 109–130. doi:10.1108/IMEFM-05-2017-0134

Mazumder, M. S. U. (2022). The effects of microfinance programs on recipients' livelihoods in rural Bangladesh. *European Journal of Development Research, 34*(3), 1383–1418. doi:10.105741287-021-00425-w

McClelland, D. (1961). *The achieving society. Van Nostrand.* doi:10.1037/14359-000

Mearns, R. (1999). *Access to land in rural India: policy issues and options* (Vol. 2123). World Bank Publications. doi:10.1596/1813-9450-2123

Meenu, S. A. (2012). Microfinance interventions and customer perceptions: a study of rural poor in Punjab. *Decision, 39*(1).

Meilani, Y. F., Sihombing, S. O., & Kusuma, B. H. (2018). Roles of Microfinance Institutions for Sustainability of Micro Entrepreneurs in Indonesia. *International Journal of Social Science and Humanities Research, 6*(1), 576–583.

Mersland, R., & Strøm, R. O. (2007). Performance and Corporate Governance in Microfinance Institutions. Munich Personal RePEc Archive (MPRA), Paper No. 3887, posted 7/11/2007. http: mpra.ub.uni-muenchen.de/3887/

Mersland, R., & Strøm, R. Ø. (2010). Microfinance Mission Drift? *World Development, 38*(1), 28–36. doi:10.1016/j.worlddev.2009.05.006

Mersland, R., & Strøm, R. Ø. (2014). Measuring microfinance performance. In *Microfinance Institutions* (pp. 12–30). Palgrave Macmillan. doi:10.1057/9781137399663_2

MFIN. (2022). *Building an Inclusive India.* https://mfinindia.org/assets/upload_image/publications/AnnualReports/AR%202021-22%20-%20Web.pdf

Mia, M. A., Dalla Pellegrina, L., Van Damme, P., & Wijesiri, M. (2019). Financial inclusion, deepening and efficiency in microfinance programs: Evidence from Bangladesh. *European Journal of Development Research*, *31*(4), 809–835. doi:10.105741287-018-0188-6

Milana, C., & Ashta, A. (2012). Developing microfinance: A survey of the literature. *Strategic Change*, *21*(7-8), 299–330. doi:10.1002/jsc.1911

Milana, C., & Ashta, A. (2020). Microfinance and financial inclusion: Challenges and opportunities. *Strategic Change*, *29*(3), 257–266. doi:10.1002/jsc.2339

Miled, K. B. H., Younsi, M., & Landolsi, M. (2022). Does microfinance program innovation reduce income inequality? Cross-country and panel data analysis. *Journal of Innovation and Entrepreneurship*, *11*(1), 1–15. doi:10.118613731-022-00195-7 PMID:35036286

Moen, Ø., Heggeseth, A. G., & Lome, O. (2016). The positive effect of motivation and international orientation on SME growth. *Journal of Small Business Management*, *54*(2), 659–678. doi:10.1111/jsbm.12163

Mohd Shariff, M. N., Peou, C., & Ali, J. (2010). Moderating effect of government policy on entrepreneurship and growth performance of small-medium enterprises in Cambodia. *International Journal of Business and Management Science*, *3*(1), 57–72.

Moorthy, M. K., Tan, A., Choo, C., Wei, C. S., Ping, J. T. Y., & Leong, T. K. (2012). A study on factors affecting the performance of SMEs in Malaysia. *International Journal of Academic Research in Business & Social Sciences*, *2*(4), 224.

Morduch, J. (1999). The Microfinance Promise. *Journal of Economic Literature*, *37*(4), 1569–1614. doi:10.1257/jel.37.4.1569

Morduch, J. (2000). The Microfinance Schism. *World Development*, *28*(4), 617–629. doi:10.1016/S0305-750X(99)00151-5

Morduch, J. (2005). Smart Subsidies for Sustainable Microfinance, Finance for the Poor. *ADB Quarterly Newsletter of the Focal Point for Microfinance*, *6*, 1–7.

Moss, T. W., Neubaum, D., & Meyskens, M. (2015). The Effect of Virtuous Entrepreneurial Orientations on Microfinance Lending and Repayment: A Signalling Theory Perspective. *Entrepreneurship Theory and Practice*, *39*(1), 27–52. doi:10.1111/etap.12110

Moussa, M. (2007). *Regulation and Supervision of Microfinance in Egypt*. Retrieved from https://www.arabic.microfinancegateway.org/sites/default/files/mfg-en-paper-regulation-and-supervision-of-microfinance-in-egypt-2007_0.pdf

Mudaliar, A. and Mathur, A., 2015. Women empowerment through microfinance. *International journal of Arts, humanities, and management studies, 1*(2), 58-65.

Mueller, J. T., McConnell, K., Burow, P. B., Pofahl, K., Merdjanoff, A. A., & Farrell, J. (2021). Impacts of the COVID-19 pandemic on rural America. *Proceedings of the National Academy of Sciences of the United States of America, 118*(1), 2019378118. doi:10.1073/pnas.2019378118 PMID:33328335

Mugori, W. M. (2012). *The effects of access to micro-finance on the financial performance of small and medium enterprises owned by youths in Nairobi Kenya* [Doctoral dissertation]. University of Nairobi.

Muiruri, P. M. (2014). *The Role of Micro-Finance Institutions to the Growth of Micro and Small Enterprises (MSE) in Thika. Empirical Review of NonFinancial Factors.*

Mujtaba, B. G., Javed, M., & Nguyen, L. D. (2013). Management skills of Pakistanis: a comparison of technical, human and conceptual differences. *Advances in Management and Applied Economics, 3*(3), 129.

Mujtaba, B. G., & Kaifi, B. A. (2011). Management skills of Afghan respondents: A comparison of technical, human and conceptual differences based on gender. *Journal of International Business and Cultural Studies, 4*, 1.

Mukherjee, R. (1957). *The dynamics of a rural society*. Popular Prakashan. doi:10.1515/9783112582305

Muriu, P. W. (2020). The Impact of Microfinance Programs: A Review of Data and Methodological Dilemma. *Journal of Economics and Sustainable Development, 11*(22), 100–109.

Mushtaq, R., & Bruneau, C. (2019). Microfinance, financial inclusion and ICT: Implications for poverty and inequality. *Technology in Society, 59*, 101154. doi:10.1016/j.techsoc.2019.101154

Mustapha, M. B., Yusuf, B. I., & Abdullahi, A. N. (2019). Micro-financing and rural poverty reduction: A case of Rima microfinance bank in Goronyo Local Government Area, Sokoto state, Nigeria. *Journal of Development and Agricultural Economics, 11*(10), 256–264. doi:10.5897/JDAE2018.0974

Nair, A. (2005). *Sustainability of microfinance self help groups in India: would federating help?* (Vol. 3516). World Bank Publications. doi:10.1596/1813-9450-3516

Nasr, S. (2006). *Access to Finance and Economic Growth in Egypt*. The World Bank. Retrieved from http://siteresources.worldbank.org/INTEGYPT/Resources/Access_to_Finance.pdf

Natarajan, N., Brickell, K., Guermond, V., Lawreniuk, S., & Parsons, L. (2021). Challenging the financial inclusion-decent work nexus: Evidence from Cambodia's over-indebted internal migrants. *Global Public Policy and Governance*, *1*(3), 361–381. doi:10.100743508-021-00026-7

Nawaz, A. (2010). *Performance of Microfinance: The Role of Subsidies. Working Paper No.* Centre Emile Bernheim (CEB), Brussels Solvay Business School of Economics, Business and Management, Université Libre de Bruxelles (ULB), Belgium. doi:10/008.

Nawaz, S. (2010). Microfinance and poverty reduction: Evidence from a village study in Bangladesh. *Journal of Asian and African Studies*, *45*(6), 670–683. doi:10.1177/0021909610383812 PMID:21174878

Neef, R. (2002). Aspects of the informal economy in a transforming country: The case of Romania. *International Journal of Urban and Regional Research*, *26*(2), 299–322. doi:10.1111/1468-2427.00381

Neff, L. M. (2020). Hidden hunger: Food insecurity in the age of coronavirus. *The American Journal of Clinical Nutrition*, *112*(5), 1160–1161. doi:10.1093/ajcn/nqaa279 PMID:33095254

Negley, K., & Yunus, M. (2011). Sacrificing Microcredit for Megaprofits. *NYTimes*. Retrieved November 3, 2019, from https://www.nytimes.com/2011/01/15/opinion/15yunus.html?_r=1

Ngugi, J., & Bwisa, H. (2013). Factors influencing growth of group owned small and medium enterprises: A case of one village one product enterprises. *International Journal of Education and Research*, *1*(8), 1–14.

Ngumo, K. O. S., Collins, K. W., & David, S. H. (2020). *Determinants of financial performance of microfinance banks in Kenya*. arXiv preprint arXiv:2010.12569.

Niaz, M.U. and Iqbal, M., 2019. Effect of microfinance on women empowerment: A case study of Pakistan. *SSRN 3419834*.

Niaz, M. U., & Iqbal, M. (2019). Effect of microfinance on women empowerment: A case study of Pakistan. *Paradigms*, *13*(1), 52–59.

Nichter, S., & Goldmark, L. (2009). Small firm growth in developing countries. *World Development*, *37*(9), 1453–1464. doi:10.1016/j.worlddev.2009.01.013

Nitzl, C., & Chin, W. W. (2017). The case of partial least squares (PLS) path modeling in managerial accounting research. *Journal of Management Control*, *28*(2), 137–156. doi:10.100700187-017-0249-6

Njagi, J. N., & Njoka, C. (2021). Microfinance Reforms and Financial Inclusion in Kenya. *International Journal of Current Aspects in Finance. Banking and Accounting*, *3*(1), 54–72.

nobelprize.org. (n.d.). *Abhijit Banerjee – Facts – 2019*. Retrieved April 6, 2021, from https://www.nobelprize.org/prizes/economic-sciences/2019/banerjee/facts/

Norman, B. A., Tharmmaphornphilas, W., Needy, K. L., Bidanda, B., & Warner, R. C. (2002). Worker assignment in cellular manufacturing considering technical and human skills. *International Journal of Production Research*, *40*(6), 1479–1492. doi:10.1080/00207540110118082

Ntim, D. O. (2018). Microfinance and poverty reduction: Evidence from market women in the New Juaben Municipality, Ghana. *ADRRI Journal of Arts and Social Sciences*, *15*(6), 12–29.

Nugroho, L., Utami, W., Akbar, T., & Arafah, W. (2017). The challenges of microfinance institutions in empowering micro and small entrepreneur to implementating green activity. *International Journal of Energy Economics and Policy*, *7*(3), 66–73.

O'Sullivan, D., Rahamathulla, M., & Pawar, M. (2020). The impact and implications of COVID-19: An Australian perspective. *The International Journal of Community and Social Development*, *2*(2), 134–151. doi:10.1177/2516602620937922

Odoom, D., Fosu, K. O., Ankomah, K., & Amofa, M. B. (2019). Exploring the Contributions of Microfinance Institutions to the Ghanaian Economy: A Study at Takoradi. *Journal of Economics and Sustainable Development*, *10*(1), 77–90.

OECD/ERIA. (2018). *SME Policy Index: ASEAN 2018: Boosting Competitiveness and Inclusive Growth*. OECD Publishing. Retrieved from https://asean.org/wp-content/ uploads/2018/08/Report-ASEAN-SME-Policy-Index-2018.pdf

Okibo, B. W., & Makanga, N. (2014). Effects of micro finance institutions on poverty reduction in Kenya. *International Journal of Current Research and Academic Review*, *2*(2), 76–95.

Olawale, F., & Garwe, D. (2010). Obstacles to the growth of new SMEs in South Africa: A principal component analysis approach. *African Journal of Business Management*, *4*(5), 729–738.

Olivares-Polanco, F. (2005). Commercialising Microfinance and Deepening Outreach? Empirical Evidence from Latin America. *Journal of Microfinance*, *7*(2), 47–69.

Olu, O. J. O. (2009, November). Impact of microfinance on entrepreneurial development: The case of Nigeria. In The international conference on economics and administration, faculty of administration and business (pp. 536-545). Academic Press.

Omar, M. A., & Inaba, K. (2020). Does financial inclusion reduce poverty and income inequality in developing countries? A panel data analysis. *Journal of Economic Structures*, *9*(1), 1–25. doi:10.118640008-020-00214-4

Omondi, R.I. and Jagongo, A., 2018. Microfinance services and financial performance of small and medium enterprises of youth SMEs in Kisumu County, Kenya. *International academic journal of economics and finance, 3*(1), 24-43.

Oni, E., Imam Paiko, I., & Koholga, O. (2012). *Assessment of the contribution of micro finance institutions (MFIs) to sustainable growth of small and medium scale enterprises (SMEs) in Nigeria*. Academic Press.

Onuka, I. O., & Oroboghae, O. R. (2022). The Impact of the Covid-19 Pandemic on Microfinance Banks Customers in Nigeria. *Journal of Asian Business Strategy*, *12*(1), 35–48. doi:10.55493/5006.v12i1.4598

Oronce, C. I. A., Scannell, C. A., Kawachi, I., &Tsugawa, Y. (2020). Association between state-level income inequality and COVID-19 cases and mortality in the USA. *Journal of General Internal Medicine, 35*(9), 2791-2793.

Osiyevskyy, O., Hayes, L., Krueger, N. F., & Madill, C. (2013). *Planning to Grow? Exploring the Effect of Business Planning on the Growth of Small and Medium Enterprises (SMEs).* Social Science Research Network. https://papers.ssrn.com/abstract=2392921

Osmani, S. (2015). The Impact of Microcredit on Rural Labour Market in Bangladesh. *Institute of Microfinance (InM), 37.*

Ouédraogo, I. M. (2017). Governance, corruption, and the informal economy. *Modern Economy*, *8*(02), 256–271. doi:10.4236/me.2017.82018

Ozili, P. K. (2018). Impact of digital finance on financial inclusion and stability. *Borsa Istanbul Review*, *18*(4), 329–340. doi:10.1016/j.bir.2017.12.003

Ozili, P. K. (2020). Theories of financial inclusion. In *Uncertainty and challenges in contemporary economic behaviour*. Emerald Publishing Limited. doi:10.1108/978-1-80043-095-220201008

Ozili, P. K. (2021). Financial inclusion research around the world: A review. *The Forum for Social Economics*, *50*(4), 457–479. doi:10.1080/07360932.2020.1715238

Ozili, P. K. (2021b). Financial inclusion: a strong critique. In *New Challenges for Future Sustainability and Wellbeing* (pp. 1–16). Emerald Publishing Limited. doi:10.1108/978-1-80043-968-920211002

Ozili, P. K. (2022a). Can central bank digital currency increase financial inclusion? Arguments for and against. In *Big Data Analytics in the Insurance Market* (pp. 241–249). Emerald Publishing Limited. doi:10.1108/978-1-80262-637-720221013

Ozili, P. K. (2022b). Digital financial inclusion. In *Big Data: A Game Changer for Insurance Industry* (pp. 229–238). Emerald Publishing Limited. doi:10.1108/978-1-80262-605-620221015

Ozili, P. K. (2022c). Fault lines in financial inclusion. perspectives on global development and technology. *Perspectives on Global Development*, *21*(3), 188–201. doi:10.1163/15691497-12341624

Oz-Yalaman, G. (2019). Financial inclusion and tax revenue. *Central Bank Review*, *19*(3), 107–113. doi:10.1016/j.cbrev.2019.08.004

Panda, S., & Majumder, A. (2013). A review of rural development programmes in India. *International Journal of Research in Sociology and Social Anthropology*, *1*(2), 37–40.

Pant, I., & Baroudi, B. (2008). Project management education: The human skills imperative. *International Journal of Project Management*, *26*(2), 124–128. doi:10.1016/j.ijproman.2007.05.010

Pasanen, M. (2003). *In search of factors affecting SME performance: The case of Eastern Finland.* Kuopion Yliopisto.

Pathak, H. P., & Gyawali, M. (2012). Role of microfinance in employment generation: A case study of Microfinance Program of Paschimanchal Grameen Bikash Bank. *Journal of Nepalese Business Studies*, *7*(1), 31–38. doi:10.3126/jnbs.v7i1.6401

Patra, R. K., Reddy, K. S. C., Reddy, K. M., & Reddy, T. N. K. (2022). A Study on the Scope of E-Commerce Industry in Covid 19 Situation: A Review of Literature on Indian Incorporations. *Journal of Positive School Psychology*, *6*(3), 9258–9261.

Pawlak, K., & Matul, M. (2004). Realising Mission Objectives. A Promising Approach to Measuring the Social Performance of Microfinance Institutions. *Journal of Microfinance*, *6*(2), 1–25.

Pedrini, M., & Ferri, L. M. (2016). Doing Well by Returning to the Origin. Mission Drift, Outreach and Financial Performance of Microfinance Institutions. *Voluntas*, *27*(6), 2576–2594. doi:10.100711266-016-9707-2

Pekmezovic, A., & Walker, G. (2016). The global significance of crowdfunding: Solving the SME funding problem and democratizing access to capital. *Wm. & Mary Bus. L. Rev.*, *7*, 347.

Peterson, T. O., & Van Fleet, D. D. (2004). The ongoing legacy of RL Katz: An updated typology of management skills. *Management Decision*, *42*(10), 1297–1308. doi:10.1108/00251740410568980

Pomi, S. S. (2019). Impact of microcredit on rural poverty alleviation in the context of Bangladesh. *International Journal of Economics and Finance*, *11*(6), 1–70. doi:10.5539/ijef.v11n6p70

Popescu, L., Iancu, A., Avram, M., Avram, D., & Popescu, V. (2020). The role of managerial skills in the sustainable development of SMEs in Mehedinti County, Romania. *Sustainability*, *12*(3), 1119. doi:10.3390u12031119

Possner, A., Bruns, S., & Musshoff, O. (2021). A Cambodian smallholder farmer's choice between microfinance institutes and informal commercial moneylenders: The role of risk attitude. *Agricultural Finance Review*. doi:10.1108/AFR-07-2020-0105

Prakash, B. B. (2018). Impact Assessment of Microfinance in India: Survey, Issues and Challenges. *Society of Economics and Development, 14*(4), pp.734-742.

Prathap, B. N., Subrahmanya, K. C., & Harisha, B. S. (2018). Microfinance Delivery–Challenges and Remedies. *International Journal of Management Studies*, *3*(9), 138. doi:10.18843/ijms/v5i3(9)/17

Prawoto, N., Priyo Purnomo, E., & Az Zahra, A. (2020). *The impacts of Covid-19 pandemic on socio-economic mobility in Indonesia*. Academic Press.

Rahimnia, F., & Hassanzadeh, J. F. (2013). The impact of website content dimension and e-trust on e-marketing effectiveness: The case of Iranian commercial saffron corporations. *Information & Management, 50*(5), 240–247. doi:10.1016/j.im.2013.04.003

Rahman, A., Rahman, M. T., & Belas, J. (2017). Determinants of SME finance: evidence from three central European countries. *Review of Economic Perspectives.*

Rajadhyaksha, N. (2019). *Opinion | The microfinance mess.* Retrieved April 20, 2021, from https://www.livemint.com/opinion/columns/opinion-the-microfinance-mess-11575825705818.html

Rajbanshi, R. H. M. W. B., Huang, M., & Wydick, B. (2015). Measuring microfinance: Assessing the conflict between practitioners and researchers with evidence from Nepal. *World Development, 68*, 30–47. doi:10.1016/j.worlddev.2014.11.011

Rameshkumar, N. (2022). Impact of Covid-19 among Micro, Medium and Small Enterprises–A Case Study in Coimbatore District. *International Journal of Multidisciplinary Educational Research, 11*(3), 92–97.

Rawhouser, H., Cummings, M., & Newbert, S. L. (2019). Social impact measurement: Current approaches and future directions for social entrepreneurship research. *Entrepreneurship Theory and Practice, 43*(1), 82–115. doi:10.1177/1042258717727718

Reddy, K. R., & Reddy, C. S. (2012). *Self help groups in India. A study on quality and sustainability.* Enable Publication.

Restrepo-Echavarria, P. (2014). Macroeconomic volatility: The role of the informal economy. *European Economic Review, 70*, 454–469. doi:10.1016/j.euroecorev.2014.06.012

Reyes, L.A.D. and Fattori, G., 2019. Microfinance as a means for women empowerment in the Colombian post conflict scenario: Transformational development or a tool for better managing poverty?. *Peace Human Rights Governance, 3*(1).

Rhyne, E. (1998). The Yin and Yang of Microfinance: Reaching the Poor and Sustainability. *MicroBanking Bulletin, 2*, 6–9.

Rijkers, B., Arouri, H., Freund, C., & Nucifora, A. (2014). Which firms create the most jobs in developing countries? Evidence from Tunisia. *Labour Economics, 31*, 84–102. doi:10.1016/j.labeco.2014.10.003

Rizzo, T. L., & Columna, L. (2020). Theory of planned behavior. Routledge Handbook of Adapted Physical Education, 326–346. doi:10.4324/9780429052675-25

Rocco, T. S., & Plakhotnik, M. S. (2009). Literature reviews, conceptual frameworks, and theoretical frameworks: Terms, functions, and distinctions. *Human Resource Development Review, 8*(1), 120–130. doi:10.1177/1534484309332617

Rogaly, B., Castillo, A., & Serrano, M. R. (2004). Building assets to reduce vulnerability: Microfinance provision by a rural working people's union in Mexico. *Development in Practice*, *14*(3), 381–395. doi:10.1080/0961452042000191213

Romijn, H., & Albu, M. (2001). *Explaining innovativeness in small high-technology firms in the United Kingdom.* Eindhoven Centre for Innovation Studies, The Netherlands Working Paper.

Roodman, D. (2012). *Due diligence: An impertinent inquiry into microfinance.* Retrieved from https://books.google.com/books?hl=en&lr=&id=CxGnCoLkt4QC&oi=fnd&pg=PR1&dq=roodman+2012&ots=NTVMDHicF-&sig=MLil7-sDtXEZ0yObnV1sdst_7Xw

Roodman, D., & Morduch, J. (2014). The impact of microcredit on the poor in Bangladesh: Revisiting the evidence. *The Journal of Development Studies*, *50*(4), 583–604. doi:10.1080/00220388.2013.858122

Ropega, J. (2011). The reasons and symptoms of failure in SME. *International Advances in Economic Research*, *17*(4), 476–483. doi:10.100711294-011-9316-1

Roy, S., & Mohanty, R. P. (2020). Microfinance models in improving'quality of life': Empirical analysis on Indian perspective. *International Journal of Business Innovation and Research*, *21*(1), 23–55. doi:10.1504/IJBIR.2020.104031

Rui, G. U., & Nie, F. Y. (2021). Does empowering women benefit poverty reduction? Evidence from a multi-component program in the Inner Mongolia Autonomous Region of China. *Journal of Integrative Agriculture*, *20*(4), 1092–1106. doi:10.1016/S2095-3119(20)63436-0

Runsinarith, P. (2014). The impacts of microcredit on poverty reduction: Evidence from Cambodian rural villages. *The Philippine Review of Economics*, *51*(2), 121–150.

Saccone, D. (2021). Can the Covid19 pandemic affect the achievement of the 'Zero Hunger' goal? Some preliminary reflections. *The European Journal of Health Economics*, *22*(7), 1025–1038. doi:10.100710198-021-01311-2 PMID:33934264

Sahu, T. N., Agarwala, V., & Maity, S. (2021). Effectiveness of microcredit in employment generation and livelihood transformation of tribal women entrepreneurs: Evidence from PMMY. *Journal of Small Business and Entrepreneurship*, 1–22. doi:10.1080/08276331.2021.1928847

Sainz-Fernandez, I., Torre-Olmo, B., López-Gutiérrez, C., & Sanfilippo-Azofra, S. (2015). Crisis in microfinance institutions: Identifying problems. *Journal of International Development*, *27*(7), 1058–1073. doi:10.1002/jid.3129

Sakuhuni, R. C. (2014). Causes, Benefits and Costs Of Informal Economy: Evidence From Zimbabwe. *Researchjournali's Journal of Commerce*, *2*(4), 1–9.

Saleh, A. S., & Ndubisi, N. O. (2006). *SME development in Malaysia: Domestic and global challenges*. Academic Press.

Salgotra, A. K., Kandari, P., & Bahuguna, U. (2021). Does access to finance eradicate poverty? A case study of Mudra beneficiaries. *The Journal of Asian Finance, Economics, and Business*, *8*(1), 637–646.

Salia, S. (2015). *The impact of microfinance on microenterprise development in Ghana* [Doctoral dissertation, Birmingham City University].

Salia, S., Hussain, J., Tingbani, I. and Kolade, O., 2018. Is women empowerment a zero sum game? Unintended consequences of microfinance for women's empowerment in Ghana. *International Journal of Entrepreneurial Behavior & Research.*

Salia, P. J., & Mbwambo, J. S. (2014). Does microcredit make any difference on borrowers' businesses? Evidences from a survey of women owned microenterprises in Tanzania. *International Journal of Social Sciences and Entrepreneurship*, *1*(9), 431–444.

Salifu, I. (2020). The Influence of Geographical Coverage on the Microfinance Sustainability and Outreach in Northern Ghana. *International Journal of Economics and Finance*, *12*(2), 1–82.

Salovey, P., & Grewal, D. (2005). The science of emotional intelligence. *Current Directions in Psychological Science*, *14*(6), 281–285. doi:10.1111/j.0963-7214.2005.00381.x

Sanabel. (2010). *Country Profile (Egypt)*. Retrieved from http://www.sanabelnetwork.org/SanabelFiles/Publications/TransparencyPublications/Sanabel_Profile_Egypt_Eng.pdf

Sanderson, A., Mutandwa, L., & Le Roux, P. (2018). A review of determinants of financial inclusion. *International Journal of Economics and Financial Issues*, *8*(3), 1–8.

Santoso, D. B., Gan, C., Revindo, M. D., & Massie, N. W. G. (2020). The impact of microfinance on Indonesian rural households' welfare. *Agricultural Finance Review*, *80*(4), 491–506. doi:10.1108/AFR-11-2018-0098

Sarkis, J. (2020). Supply chain sustainability: Learning from the COVID-19 pandemic. *International Journal of Operations & Production Management*, *41*(1), 63–73. doi:10.1108/IJOPM-08-2020-0568

Saunders, M., Lewis, P., & Thornhill, A. (2012). *Research Methods for Business Students* (6th ed.). Pearson.

Sawada, Y., & Sumulong, L. (2021). Macroeconomic impact of Covid-19 in developing. *Asia.*

Schicks, J. (2012). *The Over-Indebtedness of Microfinance Customers-An Analysis from the Customer Protection Perspective* [Dissertation].

Setboonsarng, S. and Parpiev, Z. (2010). *Microfinance and the Millennium Development Goals in Pakistan: Impact Assessment Using Propensity Score Matching,* s.l.: eSocialSciences.

Shafique, O. and Siddique, N. (2020). The impact of microcredit financing on poverty alleviation and women empowerment: an empirical study on akhuwat islamic microfinance. *PalArch's Journal of Archaeology of Egypt/Egyptology, 17*(8), 548-562.

Shah, A. M. (2012). *The structure of Indian society: Then and now*. Routledge India. doi:10.4324/9780203085370

Shahed, K. S., Azeem, A., Ali, S. M., & Moktadir, M. (2021). A supply chain disruption risk mitigation model to manage COVID-19 pandemic risk. *Environmental Science and Pollution Research International*, 1–16. doi:10.100711356-020-12289-4 PMID:33400113

Shah, S. F. H., Nazir, T., Zaman, K., & Shabir, M. (2013). Factors Affecting the Growth of Enterprises: A Survey of the Literature from the Perspective of Small- and Medium-Sized Enterprises. *Journal of Enterprise Transformation, 3*(2), 53–75. doi:10.1080/19488289.2011.650282

Shambare, R., & Rugimbana, R. (2012). Financial literacy among the educated: An exploratory study of selected university students in South Africa. *Thunderbird International Business Review, 54*(4), 581–590. doi:10.1002/tie.21485

Shanmugan, K., & Baria, B. (2019). Major Themes and Concerns of Impact Analysis in the Indian Microfinance sector: Analytical Views. *International Journal of Research in Social Sciences, 9*(1), 668–682.

Sharizan, S., Redzuan, N. H., & Rosman, R. (2021). Issues and challenges of financial inclusion among low-income earners in rural areas of Malaysia. *Turkish Journal of Economics, 8*(Special Issue), 277–299. doi:10.26414/A2376

Sharu, H., & Guyo, W. (2015). Factors influencing growth of youth owned small and medium enterprises in Nairobi County, Kenya. *International Journal of Scientific Research, 4*(4), 973–987.

Shepherd, D., & Wiklund, J. (2009). Are we comparing apples with apples or apples with oranges? Appropriateness of knowledge accumulation across growth studies. *Entrepreneurship Theory and Practice, 33*(1), 105–123. doi:10.1111/j.1540-6520.2008.00282.x

Shihadeh, F. H., Hannon, A. M., Guan, J., Ul Haq, I., & Wang, X. (2018). Does financial inclusion improve the banks' performance? Evidence from Jordan. In Global Tensions in Financial Markets (Research in Finance, Vol. 34). Emerald Publishing Limited.

Shrestha, S., Parajuli, S., & Paudel, U. R. (2019). Communication in banking sector: A systematic review. *Quest Journal of Management and Social Sciences, 1*(2), 272–284. doi:10.3126/qjmss.v1i2.27445

Sierra, J., Muriel-Patino, V., & Rodriguez-Lopez, F. (2020). The Quest for the Evaluation of Microfinance Social Performance. *Revista Iberoamericana de Estudios de Desarrollo, 9*(2), 54–108. doi:10.26754/ojs_ried/ijds.351

Simanowitz, A. (2003). Microfinance, Poverty and Social Performance: Overview. *IDS Bulletin, 34*(4), 1–9. doi:10.1111/j.1759-5436.2003.tb00085.x

Simkhada, N. R. (2013). Problems and prospects of the cooperative sector in Nepal for promoting financial inclusion. *Enterprise Development & Microfinance*, *24*(2), 146–159. doi:10.3362/1755-1986.2013.014

Singer, M. B., & Cohn, B. S. (Eds.). (1968). *Structure and change in Indian society* (Vol. 47). Transaction Publishers.

Singh, D. R., Sunuwar, D. R., Shah, S. K., Sah, L. K., Karki, K., & Sah, R. K. (2021). Food insecurity during Covid-19 pandemic: A genuine concern for people from disadvantaged community and low-income families in Province 2 of Nepal. *PLoS One*, *16*(7), e0254954. doi:10.1371/journal.pone.0254954 PMID:34288965

Singh, P. K., & Chudasama, H. (2020). Evaluating poverty alleviation strategies in a developing country. *PLoS One*, *15*(1), e0227176. doi:10.1371/journal.pone.0227176 PMID:31929549

Singh, P., Brown, D. M., Chelekis, J., Apostolidis, C., & Dey, B. L. (2022). Sustainability in the beer and pub industry during the Covid-19 period: An emerging new normal. *Journal of Business Research*, *141*, 656–672. doi:10.1016/j.jbusres.2021.11.066 PMID:36540607

Singh, R. K., Garg, S. K., & Deshmukh, S. G. (2008). Strategy development by SMEs for competitiveness: A review. *Benchmarking*, *15*(5), 525–547. doi:10.1108/14635770810903132

Singh, S., Chamola, P., Kumar, V., Verma, P., & Makkar, N. (2022). Explaining the revival strategies of Indian MSMEs to mitigate the effects of Covid-19 outbreak. *Benchmarking*.

Sinha, F. (2006). *Social Rating and Social Performance Reporting in Microfinance. Towards a Common Framework. EDA*. Ltd, Argidius Foundation and the SEEP Network.

Skenderi, N., Islami, X., & Mulolli, E. (2017). The Impact of Informal Economy in the Development of SMEs-Evidence from Kosovo (2008-2012). *International Journal of Management, Accounting and Economics*, *4*(5), 2383–2126.

Smart. (n.d.). *Campaign Mission & Goals - The Smart Campaign - Keeping Clients First in Financial Inclusion.* Retrieved May 13, 2019, from https://www.smartcampaign.org/about/campaign-mission-a-goals

Smit, S., & Musango, J. K. (2015). Towards connecting green economy with informal economy in South Africa: A review and way forward. *Ecological Economics*, *116*, 154–159. doi:10.1016/j.ecolecon.2015.04.022

Sombultawee, K., Lenuwat, P., Aleenajitpong, N., & Boon-itt, S. (2022). COVID-19 and Supply Chain Management: A Review with Bibliometric. *Sustainability*, *14*(6), 3538. doi:10.3390u14063538

Sridhar, R., Sachithanandam, V., Mageswaran, T., Purvaja, R., Ramesh, R., Senthil Vel, A., & Thirunavukkarasu, E. (2016). A Political, Economic, Social, Technological, Legal and Environmental (PESTLE) approach for assessment of coastal zone management practice in India. *International Review of Public Administration*, *21*(3), 216–232. doi:10.1080/12294659.2016.1237091

St-Jean, E., Julien, P. A., & Audet, J. (2008). Factors associated with growth changes in" gazelles. *Journal of Enterprising Culture, 16*(02), 161–188. doi:10.1142/S0218495808000089

Suguna, B. (2006). *Empowerment of rural women through self-help groups.* Discovery Publishing House.

Taha, S. G. A. (2012). *The effectiveness of microcredit programmes on alleviating poverty and empowering women* [Unpublished thesis].

Tahmasebi, A., & Askaribezayeh, F. (2021). Microfinance and social capital formation- a social network analysis approach. *Socio-Economic Planning Sciences, 76*(8), 100978. doi:10.1016/j.seps.2020.100978

Tajaddini, R., Mujtaba, B. G., & Bandenezhad, M. (2010). Management skills of Iranians: A comparison of technical, human and conceptual differences based on gender, age and longevity in management ranks. *Labour and Management in Development, 10.*

Tan, H. (2009). *Evaluating SME support programs in Chile using panel firm data.* World Bank Policy Research Working Paper, (5082).

Tan, W. C., & Tay, R. S. (1995). Factors contributing to the growth of SMEs: The Singapore case. *Journal of Enterprising Culture, 3*(02), 197–210. doi:10.1142/S0218495895000106

Tarozzi, A., Desai, J. and Johnson, K. (2013). On the impact of microcredit: Evidence from a randomized intervention in rural Ethiopia. AEA.

Tasos, S., Amjad, M. I., Awan, M. S., & Waqas, M. (2020). Poverty Alleviation and Microfinance for the Economy of Pakistan: A Case Study of Khushhali Bank in Sargodha. *Economies, 8*(3), 63. doi:10.3390/economies8030063

Tehulu, T. A. (2022). Capital adjustment process and credit growth of microfinance institutions: Evidence from Sub-Saharan Africa. *Cogent Economics & Finance, 10*(1), 2111791. doi:10.1080/23322039.2022.2111791

Thangamani, S., & Muthuselvi, S. (2013). A study on women empowerment through self-help groups with special reference to Mettupalayam Taluk in Coimbatore District. *Journal of Business and Management, 8*(6), 17–24.

The Hindu. (2022). *Microfinance lenders should not charge usurious rates of interest, RBI says in revised norms for the sector.* Available at: https://www.thehindu.com/news/national/microfinance-lenders-should-not-charge-usurious-rates-of-interest-rbi-says-in-rev
ised-norms-for-the-sector/article65224515.ece

The SEEP Network. (2005). *Measuring Performance of Microfinance Institutions: A Framework for Reporting, Analysing and Monitoring.* The SEEP Network and Alternative Credit Technologies, LLC.

Thomas, J. R., & Kumar, J. (2021). Microfinance Sector and the Supportive Role of Regulator in its Transformation: A Case Study from India. In Financial Inclusion in Emerging Markets (pp. 219-235). Palgrave Macmillan. doi:10.1007/978-981-16-2652-4_11

Thompson Agyapong, G., Mmieh, F., & Mordi, C. (2018). Factors influencing the growth of SMEs: The case of Ghana. *Thunderbird International Business Review*, *60*(4), 549–563. doi:10.1002/tie.21945

Timmons, J. A., & Spinelli, S. (1994). *New venture creation: Entrepreneurship for the 21st century*. Irwin Homewood.

Timotius, E., Sunardi, O., Soenandi, I. A., Ginting, M., & Sabini, B. (2022). Supply chain disruption in time of crisis: a case of the Indonesian retail sector. *Journal of International Logistics and Trade*.

Toindepi, J. (2016). Investigating a best practice model of microfinance for poverty alleviation conceptual note. *International Journal of Social Economics*, *43*(4), 346–362. doi:10.1108/IJSE-05-2014-0091

Townsend, P. (2014). *International Analysis Poverty*. s.l.:Routledge. doi:10.4324/9781315835099

Trang, T. K. (2016). Key success factors of SME entrepreneurs: Empirical study in Vietnam. *International Journal of Business and Management*, *11*(1), 136.

Tucker, M., Jubb, C., & Yap, C. J. (2019). The theory of planned behaviour and student banking in Australia. *International Journal of Bank Marketing*, *38*(1), 113–137. doi:10.1108/IJBM-11-2018-0324

Tulchin, D. (2003). Microfinance's Double Bottom Line. Measuring Social Return for the Microfinance Industry. Social Enterprise Associates (www.socialenterprise.NET) .

Turner, J. A., Klein, B. W., & Stein, N. P. (2016). Financial Illiteracy Meets Conflicted Advice: The Case of Thrift Savings Plan Rollovers. *The Journal of Retirement*, *3*(4), 47–65. doi:10.3905/jor.2016.3.4.047

Uddin, M. A., Jamil, S. A., & Khan, K. (2022). Indian MSMEs amidst the Covid-19 Pandemic: Firm Characteristics and Access to Finance. *Academic Journal of Interdisciplinary Studies*, *11*(3), 71–71. doi:10.36941/ajis-2022-0069

Ufua, D. E., Olujobi, O. J., Tahir, H., Al-Faryan, M. A. S., Matthew, O. A., & Osabuohien, E. (2022). Lean Entrepreneurship and SME Practice in a Post Covid-19 Pandemic Era: A Conceptual Discourse from Nigeria. *Global Journal of Flexible Systems Management*, 1-14.

Ullah, K., Saboor, A., & Ahmad, I. (2020). Effects of Microfinance on Mountain Poverty and Living Standards: An Empirical Investigation from Central Karakorum National Park Region of Gilgit Baltistan, Pakistan. *NUML International Journal of Business & Management*, *15*(1), 30–49.

Uluwaduge, P., & Senathiraja, R. (2019). Micro Finance Institutions Through Entrepreneurship. *Sri Lankan Experience the Lens of Social.*, *05*(1), 49–71.

Ussif, R. (2020). Microfinance institutions challenges in poverty and unemployment reduction in Ghana. *International Journal of Engineering and Information Systems*, *4*(7), 114–123.

Vampa, D. (2021). Covid-19 and territorial policy dynamics in Western Europe: Comparing France, Spain, Italy, Germany, and the United Kingdom. *Publius*, *51*(4), 601–626. doi:10.1093/publius/pjab017

Van Rooyen, C., Stewart, R., & de Wet, T. (2012). The impact of microfinance in sub-Saharan Africa: A systematic review of the evidence. *World Development*, *40*(11), 2249–2262. doi:10.1016/j.worlddev.2012.03.012

Varghese, G., & Viswanathan, L. (2018). Financial inclusion: Opportunities, issues and challenges. *Theoretical Economics Letters*, *8*(11), 1935–1942. doi:10.4236/tel.2018.811126

Varghese, T. (2011). Women empowerment in Oman: A study based on Women Empowerment Index. *Far East Journal of Psychology and Business*, *2*(2), 37–53.

Varpio, L., Paradis, E., Uijtdehaage, S., & Young, M. (2020). The distinctions between theory, theoretical framework, and conceptual framework. *Academic Medicine*, *76*(6), 989–994. doi:10.1097/ACM.0000000000003075 PMID:31725464

Vixathep, S. (2014). Entrepreneurship, government policy and performance of SMEs in Laos (No. 28). Graduate School of International Cooperation Studies, Kobe University.

Waly, G. (2010). *Microfinance in Egypt: An Overview*. Retrieved October 29, 2019, from https://www.fra.gov.eg/content/efsa2_ar/pool_extra_efsa/UG18915UG18916.pdf

Wang, H., Dill, S. E., Zhou, H., Ma, Y., Xue, H., Sylvia, S., Smith, K., Boswell, M., Medina, A., Loyalka, P., Abby, C., Friesen, D., Rose, N., Guo, Y., & Rozelle, S. (2021). Health, economic, and social implications of COVID-19 for China's rural population. *Agricultural Economics*, *52*(3), 495–504. doi:10.1111/agec.12630 PMID:34149132

Wang, Y. (2016). What are the biggest obstacles to growth of SMEs in developing countries?–An empirical evidence from an enterprise survey. *Borsa Istanbul Review*, *16*(3), 167–176. doi:10.1016/j.bir.2016.06.001

Welter, F., Smallbone, D., Slonimski, A., Linchevskaya, O., Pobol, A., & Slonimska, M. (2012). Enterprising families in a hostile environment for entrepreneurship (No. 2012-1). Jönköping International Business School.

Wijewardena, H., Nanayakkara, G., & De Zoysa, A. (2008). The owner/manager's mentality and the financial performance of SMEs. *Journal of Small Business and Enterprise Development*, *15*(1), 150–161. doi:10.1108/14626000810850892

Wilburn, K., & Wilburn, R. (2014). The Double Bottom Line: Profit and Social Benefit. *Business Horizons*, *57*(1), 11–20. doi:10.1016/j.bushor.2013.10.001

William, G. B. I. (2011). Understanding the marketing strategies of microfinance institutions within the Accra metropolis of Ghana: Case of selected institutions. *African Journal of Marketing Management*, *3*(2), 45–55.

Woller, G. (2005). *Proposal for a Social Performance Measurement Framework in Microfinance: The Six Aspects of Outreach. MicroREPORT No. 26*. USAID.

Woller, G. (2007). Trade-Offs between Social and Financial Performance. Perspectives. *ESR Review*, *9*(2), 14–19.

Wondirad H.A., (2020). Competition and Microfinance Institutions Performance: Evidence from India. *International Journal of Corporate Social Responsibility*, *5* (6).

Wondirad, H. A. (2020). The impacts of mobile insurance and microfinance institutions (MFIs) in Kenya. *Journal of Banking and Financial Technology*, *4*(1), 95–110. doi:10.100742786-020-00021-2

Wong, K., & Richards, D. (2014). Commercialization and Microfinance Interest Rates: Usury or Just Prices? *Journal of Markets & Morality*, *17*(2), 381–404.

World Bank. (2018). *Women Economic Empowerment Study*. Author.

Yaron, J., Benjamin, M. P., & Piprek, G. L. (1997). *Rural finance: Issues, design, and best practices* (Vol. 14). World Bank.

Yeboah, T., Antoh, E. F., & Kumi, E. (2022). Strategic responses of microfinance institutions to the Coronavirus disease (Covid-19) crisis in Ghana. *Development in Practice*, *32*(1), 112–127. doi:10.1080/09614524.2021.1991890

Yunus, M. (2011). *Sacrificing Microcredit for Megaprofits*. Academic Press.

Yusufu, O. S., Suleiman, O., & Saliu, H. T. (2020). Effect of micro finance bank on the growth of Small and Medium Enterprises in Nigeria. *KIU Interdisciplinary Journal of Humanities and Social Sciences*, *1*(2), 127–142.

Zafarullah, H., & Nawaz, F. (2019). *Pathways to women's empowerment in Bangladesh: Employment and microfinance as interventions*. Asian Education and Development Studies.

Zeb, N., Jalal, R. N. U. D., Fayyaz, U. E., & Zaheer, M. A. (2021). Micro Finance and Economic Development: The Role of Microfinance Institutions Outreach in Pakistan. *The Journal of Asian Finance. Economics and Business*, *8*(5), 117–126.

Zeller, M., Lapenu, C., & Greeley, M. (2003). Measuring Social Performance of Micro-finance Institutions: A Proposal. *Social Performance Indicators Initiative (SPI) Final Report,* Submitted to Argidius Foundation and Consultative Group to Assist the Poorest (CGAP).

Zheng, C., & Zhang, J. (2021). The impact of COVID-19 on the efficiency of microfinance institutions. *International Review of Economics & Finance*, *71*, 407–423. doi:10.1016/j.iref.2020.09.016

Zhiri, D. D. (2017). Impact of micro-finance services on performance of small and medium scale enterprises (SMEs) In Zaria metropolis. *International Journal of Scientific Research in Social Sciences & Management Studies*, *2*(1), 49–65.

Zhou, H., Wit, G. D., A, H. Z., & B, G. D. W. (2009). *EIM Research Reports reference number*. https://www.un.org/en/development/desa/population/publications/pdf/popfacts/popfacts_2010-6.pdf

About the Contributors

Yahaya Alhassan is a Principal Lecturer in Finance and Strategic Management at the University of Sunderland in London. He is also the Head of Academic Operations. He holds a PhD in Business Management from Anglia Ruskin University and MBA in Finance from the University of Sunderland. He is also a Senior Fellow of the Higher Education Academy (HEA). He has over 20 years' teaching and management experience developed during roles in the higher education sector and the consultancy industry.

Uzoechi Nwagbara is a Professor of Management, The ICT University; Visiting Lecturer University of Sunderland in London & The University of Law; Visiting Scholar University of Worcester, University of the West of Scotland, Cardiff Metropolitan University & University of Wales Trinity Saint David, UK.

* * *

Mamudu Abunga Akudugu holds a PhD in Livelihoods (International and Rural Development) from the University of Reading, United Kingdom; Master of Philosophy (M.Phil.) in Agricultural Economics from the University of Ghana, Ghana; and Bachelor of Science (B.Sc.) in Agriculture Technology from the University for Development Studies, Tamale – Ghana. Dr. Akudugu is currently a Senior Research Fellow at the Institute for Interdisciplinary Research and Consultancy Services (IIRaCS) of the University for Development Studies (UDS). He is the Deputy Director of the Institute. Mamudu has several years of experience in conducting interdisciplinary research, largely employing mixed methods (qualitative and quantitative approaches) in his research activities. He has served as a Consultant to many national and international institutions including the Food and Agriculture Organisation of the United Nations (UN). Dr. Akudugu is an Executive Member of the Ghana Association of Agricultural Economists (GAAE), a Member of the African Association of Agricultural Economists (AAAE) and other professional bodies. He has over 30 peer-reviewed publications including the book entitled, *Understanding Research and Research Paradigms* and *Supply Chain Management in African Agriculture. Innovative Approaches to Commodity Value Chains* published by Palgrave Macmillan.

Margaret Atosina Akuriba is a senior lecturer of Agribusiness Management and Finance at the University for Development Studies, Tamale, Ghana. She holds a PhD in Development Economics from Wageningen University, The Netherlands; Master of Philosophy (M.Phil.) in Agribusiness Management from the University of Ghana, Ghana; and Bachelor of Science (B.Sc.) in Agriculture Technology from the University for Development Studies, Ghana. Over the past 14 years, Margaret has taught a number of undergraduate courses including, Introduction to Agribusiness; Microfinance Practice; Land Tenure and Agricultural Law; Business Laws and Regulations; and Introduction to Computing and Programming. She has also supervised/co-supervised a number of undergraduate and graduate theses in UDS. Her main areas of research include irrigation governance, food security, agricultural technology adoption, and approaches to strengthening agribusiness value chains for rural development. She has over the years collaborated on several research projects funded by World Bank, GEF, UNEP, AVRDC, FAO and IWMI among others, with local and international partners. She currently has over 10 research publications in peer reviewed journals and have presented several findings at national and international conferences and workshops. Margaret is an ardent learner and strives to contribute in diverse ways to solving societal problems through research, teaching, and community outreach.

Abdul-Razak Alhassan is a Senior Lecturer in Strategy and International Business at the Department of Strategy and International Business, University of Surrey. Prior to joining the university, he was previously a Senior Lecturer and Programme Director of the MSc Management Suite Programme at Birmingham City University and Course Director, MSc International Business, Coventry University. He is an international business, development and management academic and consultant with expertise in organisational growth and development; business strategy and growth; Business Ethics and Corporate Political Activity; strategic leadership and organisational transformation; corporate governance among others. He has over 10 years experience managing projects at senior levels both in academia and business working in countries including the UK, Malaysia, Ghana, Tanzania and India. Razak is an active researcher and a Senior Fellow of the UK Higher Education Academy (SFHEA). He has previously studied at the University of Manchester, University of Westminster and the University for Development Studies (UDS, Ghana). He holds a PhD in Development Policy and Management (University of Manchester); an MA in International Development Management (University of Westminster); and a BSc in Agricultural Technology majoring in Economics and Extension Education (UDS, Ghana).

Shymaa Allam has 15 years of proven experience in Social Development and Financial Inclusion in Egypt and the Arab countries. In addition to her hands-on experience, she also demonstrates excellent research skills. Her achievements include developing the Microfinance Mapping Study in Egypt In 2007, and 2008, and assisting in drafting Microfinance law for private sector companies, under the supervision of General Authority of Investment- GAFI, through comparatives studies and research of different legal frameworks of different countries and coordinating study visits for GAFI representatives to Cambodia in 2008, while she was the policy development specialist at the USAID funded activity on Micro-Enterprise Finance (EMF). Also, she managed to expand the operations of Micro-credit program while she worked as an operation manager at NGO-MFI in Cairo, till she moved to Sanabel, the Microfinance Network for Arab countries, and managed the Citi Micro-entrepreneurs Award, and the annual regional conferences for two consecutive years. After having her Master's degree in Sustainable International Development from Heller School for Social Policy and Management in 2014, Boston USA, Ms. Allam returned back to Cairo to join the first Microfinance regulatory team in Egypt and contributed to the development of the regulations on NGOs and especially the client protection manual. After 4 years of successful journey as a regulator, Ms. Allam returned to Boston and started her PhD in Global Inclusion and Social Development at the University of Massachusetts, to explore the Financial Inclusion efforts and poverty alleviation schemes both in theory and on-ground practice.

Manpreet Arora is a Senior Assistant Professor of Management in the School of Commerce and Management Studies, Central University of Himachal Pradesh Dharamshala, India. With around twenty one years of teaching experience she has varied interest areas. A Gold medalist at undergraduate and distinction holder at postgraduate level, she obtained her Ph.d in International Trade from Himachal Pradesh University, Shimla, India. She is an M Phil also from the same university. She is a throughout merit holder with meritorious ranks in 10th and 12th also. Her areas of research interest include Accounting and Finance, Strategic Management, Entrepreneurship, Qualitative Research, Case Study Development, Communication Skills and Microfinance. She has been guiding research at the doctoral level and has worked in the area of Microfinance. As an active seminarian, she has attended more than hundred seminars/ conferences, and has visited several universities and colleges to deliver invited talks on Finance, Strategic Management, Qualitative Research, Business Communication, Interpersonal skills, Entrepreneurship and Skill Development. She is a motivational speaker and conducts workshops on communication and motivation. Having published more than 25 papers in various journals of national and international repute (including SCOPUS, WOS and Category Journals), she has also worked as content developer of MHRD 'e-PG Pathshala' Project and OER's for IGNOU. She has written forty plus book chapters in national as well as international books/handbooks/volumes. Some of them are published with prestigious publishers like Routledge, CABI, Apple Academic Press, IGI Global, Taylor and Francis and latest with Springer Nature etc. With four edited books in her credit she is a persistent researcher in the fields of commerce and management. She is an active social worker also and is working towards the protecting the rights of women.

Mahesh B. N. is presently working at Surana College, Peenya. He has a wide range of Expertise in the Finance and Accounting field. He has 12 years of experience in the teaching accounting and taxation subjects, and has presented various papers at the national and international conferences.

Devid Basyal holds PhD from Department of Public Policy and Administration, Incheon National University, South Korea. He has gained MPhil/MA in Economics from TU, Nepal, and MBA from University of Gloucestershire, UK. Dr. Basyal has has more than 12 years of teaching experience at Graduate and Undergraduate level. He has published some peer-reviewed journal articles about Public Policy, Business management, E-government. His area of research interest is Economics, E-government, Public Policy, Business Management.

Sabina Bohaju is a management student who is studying MBA at Quest International College and undergraduate in finance major. She is currently working as Research Associate in research management cell at Quest International College. To enhance more learning and to develop the skills in research, she is focusing on it. Her interest on research is in the field of digital platform.

Chandan Chavadi is the Dean & Professor of the Presidency Business School, Presidency College, Bengaluru. A PhD from Karnatak University, Dharwad, and an MBA (Mktg.) He holds a primary degree in B.E. (E&C). He has two years of corporate experience before his moving to academics. He has been in academics for the last 21 years. He has 32 papers & 2 book reviews to his credit, published in reputed journals and magazines such as ABDC-C journals, Web of Science, Scopus, UGC Care list and other indexed journals. Under Google scholar indices, he has total citations of 90, h-index of 6 & i10-index of 4. His paper has been accepted for publication in the IIM –A Vikalpa. Five of his research papers were recently published in the IIM Kozhikode Society And Management Review journal, IIM-Shillong Journal of Management Science, Business Perspective & Research journal of K J Somaiya Institute of Management, the MDI journal “Vision”, and IIM-Lucknow journal “Metamorphosis”. He is the recipient of Labdhi Bhandari Best Paper Award for the 7th IIM-A International Marketing Conference held on 11th to 13th Jan 2017. He is a recognized PhD Guide in Management for Bangalore City University.

Niranjan Devkota, currently working as a research associate at National Planning Commission, is an economist with the special focus on cross border activities and climate change related issues focusing adaptation. He has over 15 years of experience in the field of economics related research with varietal dynamics. His recent research focuses ranges from development economics especially in cross-border activities and agriculture. He received his PhD degree from Tribhuvan University Nepal. He has experience in impact analysis and model building. He has worked in terms to prepare strategic and implementation plans of several economic issues as a research associates. He has received high level training and capacity building workshop on international co-operation, natural resource management and trade related activities from several international agencies like SANDEE (ICIMOD), NDRC (China), Hi-Aware (ICIMOD), SANEM (Bangladesh) and from esteemed organizations and universities (online mode). He has command over STATA and basic knowledge of R.

Krishna Dhakal is an MBA graduate from Quest International College. He is currently working as a research associate in Quest Research Management Cell. He has published articles in different journals and attended different national and international conferences. He has brief knowledge on SPSS, AMOS, Kobo Toolbox, Arc GIS and basic knowledge of STATA.

Shivaprasad G. is currently working as an Associate Professor at CMS Business School, Jain University. He has earned Ph.d, MBA, M.Com., MFM., PGDFM., DIFRS., FDP from IIM, M.Phil and B.Com. Dr.Prasad is an author of Financial Management, Fundamentals of Accounting and Chief Ministers of Karnataka textbooks. He has presented and published many papers in both National and International Conferences & Journals. He has published 9 research articles in ABDC indexed journal. He has conducted several MDPs, FDPs and Workshops for corporate and educational institutions. Dr. Prasad, Editor of Empirical Economic Letter, Reviewer for International Journal of Corporate Finance and Accounting - IGI Global, headquartered in Hershey, Pennsylvania (USA) and Editorial Board Member for Amity Journal of Finance, International Journal of Transformations in Business Management and International Journal of Research in Social Sciences & Humanities. He is a life member of Indian Society for Technical Education (ISTE), Indian Commerce Association (ICA) and Indian Accounting Association (IAA). Recently he has been awarded as 'Best Teacher of the year' from TMT at Chamber of Commerce, Hubli.

Hua Jin is a Lecturer in Operations Management at the University of Sunderland in London. She holds a PhD in Management Science and MSc International Banking & Financial Studies from University of Southampton. She is also Associate Fellow of the Higher Education Academy (HEA). She has over 5 years teaching and management experience.

Purnima Lawaju is a management student who did bachelor in BBA at Quest International College and is currently continuing masters (MBA) in the same college. She wants to be a researcher, currently working as a research assistant in Quest Research Management Cell at Quest International College.

Mohammad Izzuddin Mohammed Jamil is currently a PhD Candidate at Universiti Brunei Darussalam, conducting researches in the field of Business Management and Entrepreneurship. He received his Bachelor's Degree in Business Administration at Coventry University, United Kingdom, and Master's Degree in Management at Universiti Brunei Darussalam. He has also studied other courses including Software Engineering and Programming, Multimedia and Graphic Design. At Universiti Islam Sultan Sharif Ali, he studied Intermediate Level Arabic Language, Tadabbur Al-Quran programme and Pengurusan Jenazah Mazhab Syafi'i course. His industry experiences started when he first became a salesman and distributor, and has since worked in various industries including becoming a Tutor/Teacher, App Developer, Graphic Designer and Business Executive Officer. He is teaching in various academic branches in Entrepreneurship, Business Management, Financial and Management Accounting, Macroeconomics and Microeconomics, Commerce, and Information and Communication Technology. He has also been involved in academic research for several years, and his research areas include Entrepreneurship, Growth and MSMEs.

Satheesh Pandian Murugan is presently working as Assistant Professor in the Department of Economics and Centre for Research in Economics, Arumugam Pillai Seethai Ammal College, Tiruppattur, Sivaganga (Dt), Tamil Nadu, India. He is having Nine years of teaching experience along with the M.A., M.Phil., Ph.D., qualifications. He has earned his Ph.D from the Madurai Kamarajar University. He has published more than 10 research papers in his credit both in National and International level. His areas of research interests are Agricultural and Industrial Economics.

Geoff Paul is the Assistant Director (Academic) for the University of Sunderland in London. He is responsible for the development of academic staff. This includes areas such as teaching and learning standards, innovation in practice and quality management. Through the development of research and enterprise initiatives, he ensures students receive the highest quality academic experience available. He also oversees the development of innovative market-facing academic programmes, serving both industry and the commercial sector. Geoff became a Senior Fellow of Advance HE (formally the Higher Education Academy) in August 2020.

Samuel Salia has held various academic roles both within the UK and abroad (for over 9 years) before joining De Montfort University as Senior Lecturer in Accounting and Finance in July 2019. He holds PhD in Finance from Birmingham City University, as well as MSc Financial and Legal Management from University of West London. He has also worked as a Management Consultant at the Management Development and Productivity Institute, under the Ghana Ministry of Employment and Labour Relations. He has supervised PhDs in the area of finance.

Swati Singh is an Assistant Professor in the Department of Management, Maharaja Agrasen University, Baddi, Himachal Pradesh. She holds her Ph.D in the area of Microfinance from Central University of Himachal Pradesh. She has presented research papers in many national and international conferences. She also has publications in conference proceedings and indexed journals.

Sahadeb Upretee earned a PhD in Mathematics (Specializations: Actuarial Science; Statistics) from the University of Wisconsin Milwaukee, USA. Dr. Upretee is an assistant professor at the Department of Mathematics, Central Washington University, Ellensburg, WA. He teaches undergraduate courses in Mathematics, Statistics, and Actuarial Science. His research interest includes Data Science, Applied Statistics, Actuarial Science, Loss Data Analytics, Financial Economics, Structural Equations Modeling, Business Analytics, Model Uncertainty, Risk Measures, and Math Education. He collaborates with faculty members and researchers across different countries for scholarly activities.

Sriram V. P. is currently working as a Professor of Acharya Bangalore B School (ABBS), Bengaluru, Karnataka, India. His breadth of experience includes 11 years of Academic Teaching Experience in University Level and 4 years of Industry Experience. In addition to that, he had completed International Certification on SAP Business One and worked as a Senior Functional Consultant in various projects of India. His Area of Expertise includes Retail Management; Consumer Behaviour; Services Marketing; Sales and Marketing Management. He had participated and published research articles in both National and International Conferences of Reputed Organizations in India and Overseas. He had acted as Reviewer cum Scientific Committee Member for several IEEE International Conferences and also he's been currently acting as a senior reviewer in many of reputed national and International Journals. Recently He was honored by the Central Programme Committee of NPTEL (Supported by MHRD) along with Indian Institute of Madras (IIT) by issuing the certificate of Appreciation for being as the mentor for Consumer Behaviour and Human Resource Management.

Index

G

I

J

L

M

N

O

P

www.ingramcontent.com/pod-product-compliance
Lightning Source LLC
LaVergne TN
LVHW061538290926
849162LV00004B/838